Fundamentals of Teaching with Audiovisual Technology

SECOND EDITION

Carlton W. H. Erickson
The University of Connecticut, Storrs

David H. Curl
Western Michigan University, Kalamazoo

The Macmillan Company *New York*
Collier-Macmillan Limited *London*

THE MACMILLAN COMPANY
866 Third Avenue, New York, New York 10022

COLLIER-MACMILLAN CANADA, LTD., Toronto, Ontario

LIBRARY OF CONGRESS CATALOG CARD NUMBER: 76-170871

Printing: 1 2 3 4 5 6 7 8   Year: 2 3 4 5 6 7 8

PREFACE

TO TEACHERS AND LIBRARIANS:

We hope this book will help you to make creative use of instructional media in your own classroom or media center. Your students will gain the most benefit from the books they read and from audiovisual technology if these media are made available when the students are interested in the subject and ready to learn. Although some of our examples depict media in use to enhance teacher presentations, you may detect the authors' bias toward self-directing, learner-centered education.

TO INSTRUCTORS OF COLLEGE COURSES AND IN-SERVICE WORKSHOPS:

This text contains case studies and questions to stimulate individual thought and group interaction. Emphasis is placed upon innovative methods of teaching based on meaningful objectives.

Because we involve students in active problem-solving experiences in our own undergraduate and graduate courses, we have designed this book to make it easier to organize classes in this way. Discussion questions and problem-solving activities are prominent in picture captions and appear at the end of each chapter. Many problems can be used as a basis for discussion; others demand a wide range of professional activity including actual experience in evaluating, selecting, producing, and teaching with media. We recommend small-group seminars and microteaching as opportunities for trying out techniques and demonstrating media competencies. The self-instructional laboratory has proven to be an ideal environment for acquiring skills of basic media production and operation of audiovisual equipment.

We urge you to involve your students in the ordered sequence of responses included as a part of each of the nine case studies of media utilization presented in Chapter 6. We suggest also that you call for creative project work by individuals and groups.

In a one-credit required undergraduate course, for example, each student submitted an outline plan for

v

using a motion picture, a similar plan for using a film-strip, two brief self-instructional units for use of visuals with audio tape and guide sheets, and evaluation reports on various media. Production activities included overhead projection transparencies of various types, basic graphics processes, 2 × 2-inch slide production, and a short videotaped "lesson" using student-produced visuals. Graduate students in a three-credit course produced twice this amount of work and it was judged according to higher standards of quality and completeness.

Instructors who encourage students to do more than write papers and answer examination questions must find ways to interact directly and individually with students. Cassette tapes can be employed instead of written papers for some assignments, the instructor recording his comments and suggestions directly onto the student's cassette. Other projects may be evaluated by students themselves according to known criteria. Perhaps a media course does not have to meet on a regularly scheduled basis. Certain class periods might be reserved for whole-group presentations, with the balance of the time allotted to seminar, self-instructional laboratory, and independent work in consultation with the instructor.

So many people helped us to compile this book that we cannot name them all. But we are especially grateful to our students and to our colleagues and professional associates who helped generate and test ideas, and to teachers, administrators, authors, publishers, manufacturers, distributors, media producers, and professional organizations for suggestions, quotations, and illustrations.

Whenever possible, we have credited sources of tangible contributions in footnotes and picture captions. Some of the material in this book has been rewritten and adapted from *Administering Instructional Media Programs* by Carlton W. H. Erickson (The Macmillan Company, 1968) and from articles written by David H. Curl for the magazines *Training in Business and Industry, Educate, Meetings and Conventions,* and *Photo Methods for Industry,* copyright 1967, 1968, 1969, 1970, and 1971 by The Gellert Publishing Corporation.

We are indebted to C. William Stonebarger for permission to include extensive excerpts from his provocative manuscript, *Finding a Way to Be a Human.* Finally, we acknowledge the many helpful suggestions made by Vernon S. Gerlach of Arizona State University, Bruce Waldman of Jersey City State College, and James William Armstrong of Western Michigan University.

The University of Connecticut   C. W. H. E.

Western Michigan University   D. H. C.

CONTENTS

Fundamentals of Teaching with Audiovisual Technology

1

The Teacher and Technology

Teaching for the Twenty-first Century

We adults are teaching *in* the decade of the 1970s, but we ought not to be teaching merely *for* the 1970s (or, heaven help us, for the bygone world of the 1930s, 40s, 50s, or 60s in which we grew up). We should be teaching for a time in which *we* will be the conservative old men and women. We should be teaching for the time when today's children will be making decisions about science and agriculture; about art, love, life and death, and world peace.

With or without adult help, young people race headlong toward the twenty-first century; the century in which they must live and find meaning in life. Today's youth is acutely aware of the world's problems and feels frustrated and restless because he sees so little being done to eliminate fear, waste, greed, and poverty. Questioning, doubting, challenging, he is unwilling to accept the dogma of the past in a tumultuous world fragmented by selfishness and hostility. Youth is eager for action—experimenting with life itself; sharing experiences with others—through instant communication, but at the same time battling intense drives and agonizing conflicts within himself. Space travel, electronic communication, and study of behavioral science have aroused the lust of youth for a revolution of the mind, of the spirit, and of social values. Keenly aware, acutely sensitive, dissatisfied with hypocrisy, youth substitutes impatience for intolerance. He cries out in anger and indignation as mindlessness and greed pollute the air he breathes, the water he drinks, the food he eats, and destroy the beauty of the Earth he loves. Moved to action, sometimes to irrational violence, by the injustice of racial discrimination and the futility of war, youth stands helpless and frustrated as adults strangle creative thought and unthinkingly pollute the minds of children with myth and prejudice. Bored with the pleasures of affluence, sex, alcohol, and drugs, youth worries about whether it is too late to save the world he is inheriting.

1

Figure 1–1. Drugs, crime, vandalism—three of the Big Issues facing youth today. In what ways can films and other media bring these problems into focus? Can media stimulate awareness and self-scrutiny without preaching or indoctrinating? (From Your Amazing Mind [LEFT], from A Nation of Spoilers [BELOW], courtesy Alfred Higgins Productions)

Computers change youth's name into a number; sometimes he feels that his identity has been reduced to a punched card. He turns from his parents' blind faith in established institutions toward fear for his own future and doubt for the very existence of his own children. Today's youth thinks long thoughts. Few adults can answer the questions he asks.

Figure 1–2. Do people sometimes form opinions on a basis of prejudice, rather than fact? Films can involve people emotionally in problems of society; when given the added credibility of being seen on television, films can have enormous impact upon attitudes. How would you reply to the charge that all *films are biased?* Under what conditions can "biased" materials stimulate independent, critical thinking? (From *J. T.* [ABOVE]; *and* Pull The House Down [BELOW], *courtesy of Carousel Films)*

More than a million high school students will leave school this year without graduating, mostly because they simply see no reason to stay. More than half a million freshmen will quit college this year for the same reason. Are these ex-students drop-outs from a system that is too difficult and too sophisticated, or are they *push-outs* from a system that does not give them a chance to succeed on their own terms?

Norman Greenberg tells the story of the attendance teacher (truant officer) who approaches a recent drop-out who is idly dangling his fishing line over the railing of a bridge near the school.

"You should be in school," asserts the adult.
"Why?" asks the boy.
"To learn things, of course," replies the teacher.
"Why?" asks the boy.
"So you can make a lot of money."
"Why?"
"So you can take life easy," explains the teacher patiently.
"But," exclaims the drop-out, "that's what I'm doing now!"

What is the purpose of going to school or college anyway? Why do schools and colleges exist? Does the educational establishment exist primarily for the teachers or for the students?

Robert Gerletti[1] describes James Finn's apt analogy between educational focus on teacher or learner and the rival historical Ptolemaic and Copernican theories of the nature of the solar system.

[1] Robert C. Gerletti, "What is a Media Center?", *Audiovisual Instruction,* **14** (September 1969), 22.

Figure 1–3. According to Ptolemaic Theory, the sun and planets revolved about the earth, which was the center of the solar system. By analogy, the teacher has been viewed as the center of the school system. (Courtesy Robert C. Gerletti and the Association for Educational Communications & Technology)

Figure 1–4. In Copernican Theory, the earth revolves around the sun, which is a small star in the universe. By analogy, the student is the center, around which the teacher and other members of the school "solar" system revolve. (Courtesy Robert C. Gerletti and the Association for Educational Communications & Technology)

In the teacher-centered school, the adult teacher is the source of all information and authority and the textbook is a duly appointed substitute teacher. Many beginning teachers start out lecturing to their classes because it seems sensible to do so—they seem to have all the information and the students have none. Few teachers have the talent to give an effective lecture, so most lectures deal with things students could learn more efficiently and effectively for themselves if they knew how and where

Figure 1–5. Need a dividing line be drawn between "learning" and "play"? Is there necessarily a difference between play and simulation? How realistic and structured must play become before it can be called gaming or simulation? (Courtesy Coronet Instructional Films)

The Teacher and Technology

to look. A student raises his hand to ask a question. The question is irrelevant. The class laughs. One student rolls a pencil back and forth on the top of his desk. Others yawn and doodle in the margins of their textbooks. Students soon learn that school is boring and meaningless.

In a teacher-centered school, anyone with a good memory can get good grades. It isn't necessary to question the morality of the atomic bomb, only to be able to write on a test that it was first dropped August 6, 1945 on Hiroshima, Japan. You get an A in English if you can read the correct stanza in a poem when the teacher calls on you to recite, and if you can remember what she said yesterday to explain what the poet meant.

Children now in elementary school may still be in the labor force in the year 2030. But who can say which skills learned today will still be useful in the twenty-first century? The educated man or woman is not merely well informed, or skilled enough to earn a living, but must also be adaptable to continuing changes in technology, politics, economics, and morality. The truly educated person lives a sensitive and creative life, constantly learning, and in turn educating others with whom he comes in contact. The student-centered school, because it is concerned primarily with the hummaness of each learner, tends to produce educated graduates who have *learned how to learn*—thinking adults who really can change aspects of their world, not just accept things as handed to them by those who went before.

The traditional "bucket" theory that knowledge and virtue can be transmitted literally from a teacher's mind to the consciousness of a pupil is as obsolete as the slate, the hickory stick, and the dunce cap. Modern teachers are discovering that it is less satisfying to lecture and to maintain discipline and much more satisfying to watch young people discover things about the world and about themselves. Professionally, rather than being a dispenser of facts and retriever of information, the teacher finds it much more challenging, satisfying, interesting, and productive to be the *creator* and *manager* of a stimulating learning environment.

Everyone must be a lifetime learner and lifetime communicator in today's changing world, especially those who would dare to teach or lead others. Modern learning theory no longer focuses on the teacher, nor on the textbook, nor on units of subject matter or administrative credits, but upon each human learner and his personal needs and goals. The key is how these personal needs and abilities fit individuals to lead satisfying and productive lives. *Relevancy* is the concept underlying educational change in the 1970s. "What's in it for me—how

Figure 1–6. The traditional "bucket" theory of instruction.

will this help me to improve my world?" demands every student; and students immediately turn off or rebel if no meaningful answer is forthcoming. And so it happens with most aware people, jealous of precious leisure time and new-found personal freedom of choice.

Teaching as Communication

I know you believe you understand what you think I said, but I am not sure you realize that what you heard is not what I meant.

Figure 1–7. Communication can occur only when people share common meanings and experiences.

The teaching-learning process is a process of communication between individuals—but only if people share

I LOVE FISH

SO DO I!

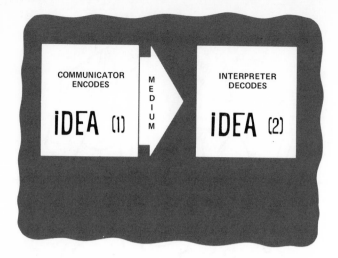

Figure 1–8.

common meanings and experiences can communication occur.

Meanings are in people, not in things. *Messages* can be transmitted between people; but ideas, concepts, or knowledge can not. To be communicated, thoughts must first be changed (encoded) into some form of verbal or visual symbol or *stimulus*. This symbolic message may then be transmitted through some channel or *medium*. Someone else must notice the message and interpret (decode) it according to his previous experience. Obviously, no communication has taken place unless the person perceiving the message has also understood it. The receiver must show the sender of the message that he understands, either by doing something appropriate or by sending back another message (feedback) indicating that he understood, *partially* understood, or *misunderstood* what the original communicator had in mind.

Seldom does a message travel unchanged from the

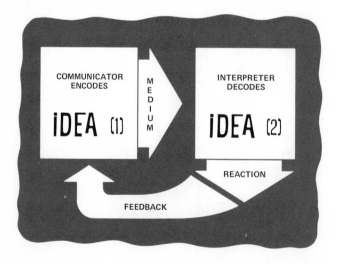

Figure 1–9.

Figure 1–10. Individualized Learning Center, Hagerman High School. Is this room a library? An audiovisual center? A study hall? On the shelves are stored about 12,000 instructional items (6,000 of which are books), all keyed to a computerized resource catalog, organized by author, title, and subject; it is updated every six months. Each class has a copy of the catalog and every student knows how to find materials and use the equipment in this Learning Center. (Courtesy Joint School District #233, Hagerman, Idaho. Photo by S. Z. Thayer)

mind of the sender to the mind of a receiver. The receiver can only draw inferences from what he perceives (and feels). If glare obscures a diagram on the chalkboard, or if an explanation contains many unfamiliar words, or if a TV image is broken up because of poor adjustment of the set, or if lettering is too small on a projected transparency, this interference, or "noise" limits the amount of the message that can get through. Teachers have extra problems as communicators, because they have to be sure that timely, worthwhile, and helpful messages reach every student, regardless of the kind or amount of interference present in the classroom or learning environment. But if students do not understand or accept messages offered by the teacher, who is at fault—the students or the teacher? Who needs motivating?

Although *visual aids* have been around for a long time, only recently has technology developed to the point that what we now refer to as *instructional media* can be used in many flexible, individually challenging ways, called *instructional systems.* The teacher is one key component of an instructional system. Each student is a system component, too, as are the media or tools of instructional communication. Instructional systems will be discussed further in Chapter 3.

Classroom use of the earliest technological materials was called *visual education.* Advancing technology changed this in a few years to *audiovisual education.* The most fortunate teachers, then and now, had and have at their fingertips the resources of school-building, school-system, and regional service centers known by various names. Audiovisual Center, Instructional Media

Center (IMC), Curriculum Materials Center, Instructional Communications Center, Learning Resources Center, Regional Enrichment Center are just a few of the titles various school systems have applied to the organizations which have been established to help teachers make best use of modern methods, materials, and equipment.

Millions of dollars in local and federal funds were spent beginning in the late 1950s in order to provide resources for teachers to use. But educators soon began to realize that merely having money to buy things did not ensure that students would learn any better. They began to look at the way in which schools were organized, the various roles and responsibilities of professional, technical, and clerical employees, and how best all of these expensive resources could be organized and scheduled to ensure the most effective education for each student and the greatest returns from taxpayers' dollars. Some school systems experimented with mass instruction via television. Others tried making available to teachers and pupils all kinds of media in each classroom. The most innovative teachers and administrators began to restructure the school day and the curriculum and to discard some traditional patterns of teacher duties and student grouping and scheduling in favor of non-graded schools, modular scheduling, team teaching, flexible grouping, and individually prescribed independent study. Technological

Figure 1–11. Is a teacher doing her job when she is not presenting information to a class or leading a discussion? Is she still a "teacher" when she is a diagnostician, counselor, evaluator, resource person, clerk, programmer, and media technician? Can a good teacher be all of these things to all students? Which of these functions ought to be performed by librarians and other classifications of professional and technical personnel? (Courtesy of EDL/McGraw-Hill, Huntington, New York)

media were used instead of teachers to dispense information when media could do the dispensing more efficiently. Some teachers then found, much to their satisfaction, that for the first time they were really able to observe the learning process and to deal with the uniquely personal needs, interests, abilities, and difficulties of each student. It is never easy to adopt new technology and to adapt to new roles. Good teachers know that you don't "just show" media to learners any more than a textbook is "just read." Using technology in creative and stimulating ways sometimes is much harder than simply assigning a textbook and giving daily lectures.

This book is not devoted to helping prospective teachers to teach as they were taught, or even as they may have been taught to teach, but to help them to discover ways in which they can become better communicators and more effective expeditors of learning. And so we set forth the main topic of this chapter in a question: What is the need for technology in instruction; how does audiovisual technology help each teacher to communicate more effectively and change learner behavior? The answer will be found in an analysis of the roles that technological media can play in helping teachers find greater success. Prior to answering the question, however, let us eliminate some of the confusion about terminology

Figure 1–12. Where is the teacher? What is she doing? Can teachers be replaced by tape recorders, projectors, or computers? (Photo by 3M/Wollensak)

in this rapidly growing field, in which the meanings of many terms are not agreed upon by everyone.

Years ago educators changed *visual* to *audio-visual* education and then removed the hyphen. *Aids* were called *materials*, sometimes *multi-sensory materials*, or *teaching tools. Instructional materials* and *curriculum materials* seemed too inclusive and did not reflect recent technology. Hence educators now often refer to *educational communications technology, audiovisual media, learning resources, instructional* or *educational media*, or *new educational media* to describe the field. Terminology has not been standardized, and professionals may refer to any of these terms and others to mean the same thing. We use several of the terms synonymously in this book, but we abhor use of the expression *aids. Aids* is an obsolete term long associated with the idea of making the learning "pill" more palatable. We now recognize that other terminology is needed to imply the expanded roles of media in the teaching-learning process. *Media*, concisely and generically defined, are: *Printed and audiovisual forms of communication and their accompanying technology.*[2] What is *technology*? Dictionary definitions of this term include: "technical means for improving human productivity"; or "the use of machines to eliminate manual labor." Hence, *audiovisual technology* employs

Eliminating Confusion About Terminology

[2] *Standards for School Media Programs* (Chicago: American Library Association; and Washington, D.C.: National Education Association, 1969), p. *xv*.

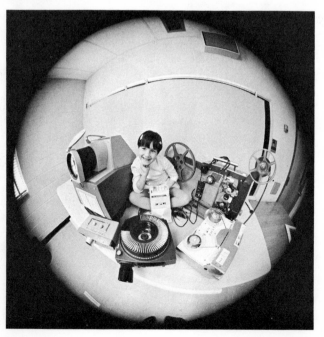

Figure 1–13. Today's teachers have at their disposal a wide array of media and materials—hardware and software. What roles may these media play in the process of learning? In what ways are teachers responsible for wise and effective use of media? Is there a distinction between effectiveness and efficiency in the use of media? (Courtesy The National Education Association. Photo by Joe Di Dio)

Figure 1-14. Microforms are increasingly important sources of documentary information. What are some advantages of doing research from original sources rather than solely from textbooks and encyclopedias? (Courtesy The National Education Association. Photo by Esther Bubley)

technical means for efficient storage and presentation of information and visual and auditory experiences. The meanings of other specific terms we use need to be clarified, and we explain first a widely used and commonly accepted expression.

Audiovisual Media

To be defined, this term must be separated into two parts, namely, *materials* and *equipment*. *Audiovisual Materials* is the term commonly used to refer to those instructional materials that may be used to convey meaning without complete dependence on verbal symbols or language. Thus, according to the definition, a textbook or reference book does not fall within the *audiovisual* grouping of instructional materials, but a text illustration does. Some audiovisual activities, like taking a field trip, dramatizing an event, or demonstrating a procedure are in the nature of processes and experiences. Some, like

Figure 1-15. Books, also, are educational media. Librarians sometimes are surprised to discover that students' enthusiasm for books seems to rise in proportion to their use of audiovisual materials. Can you explain why this might happen? (Courtesy The National Education Association. Photo by Ben Spiegel)

The Teacher and Technology

a motion picture or a filmstrip, require the use of equipment to release their latent value. Still others, like an exhibit or a study print, need little or no equipment. Some materials such as maps and globes have been in use for decades; others, such as overhead transparencies, 2×2-inch slides, tape cassettes, television, computers, and functional combinations of these media are relatively new. Tape and disc audio recordings belong in this category, even though they certainly are more audio than visual. The term *audiovisual materials* is not fully satisfactory because it designates in common usage both processes and material things.

Software and Hardware

The publishing industry has adopted the term *software* to describe tangible stimulus items, in contrast to *hardware* which designates equipment and related electronic and mechanical components. A tape recorder (hardware) is used to produce the audio portion of an instructional unit. The recorded program on the tape is software. A 35mm camera (hardware) helps a teacher assemble material for subsequent presentation in the form of slides (software). One of the uses of the opaque projector is to help a teacher enlarge material so everyone in the class can see it. It is obvious that projectors, tape recorders, TV receivers, and computers are hardware. Likewise, bulletin boards, exhibit cases, feltboards, and chalkboards are not stimulus materials or software but means of displaying materials, hence, also hardware. While the line of separation between materials and equipment is not always distinct, equipment or devices should be recognized as the means for producing or presenting message or stimulus materials.

But what is the relationship between *audiovisual materials*, which are *software*, and programmed learning sequences, workbooks, and textbooks which also by definition are *software*? Specifically, audiovisual materials may serve as rich resources of illustration and sensory experience for the verbal frames of a programmed sequence or for the paragraphs, sentences, and study questions in a book. Various media and other experiences frequently overlap and support or strengthen one another. Teachers may prescribe certain media to stimulate interest; others to communicate basic facts; still others to clear up misconceptions and deepen understanding.

There is no longer any need to argue over whether the librarian or the audiovisual coordinator has physical custody of a given item of software. The broad *media center* concept encompasses both print and non-print forms of instructional media. Tradition, coupled with inflexible systems of storage and retrieval, is the only barrier to complete, functional unification of media services. In this book it is hardly necessary to be frus-

Figure 1–16. Will this girl remember her experience with the giant tortoise? What attitudes might be inferred from the picture of the girl holding the goat? Explain how different learning objectives could be achieved through seeing animals and hearing their sounds; handling and petting animals; feeding and caring for animals; raising and breeding animals; examining preserved specimens of animals; viewing films of animals in their natural habitats; seeing still pictures or drawings of animals; discussing animals; listening to a teacher tell about animals. (From Things to Do When You Visit the Zoo *[LEFT], courtesy Journal Films, Inc.; and* The Kibbutz *[RIGHT], courtesy Consulate General of Israel and Perennial Education, Inc.)*

trated about the assignment of responsibility for classification and control of software and hardware. Instead, we need to recognize fully that it is the teacher who will take responsibility for helping students to achieve valid learning objectives through a combination of roles and duties involving selection of all kinds of appropriate media and arranging for their most effective use.

Now we are ready to return to the major question of this chapter, namely, How does audiovisual technology help the teacher? Audiovisual technology refers to the systematic use of a particular category of instructional materials. We say that these materials, or media may play seven basic roles in helping teachers to arrange more effective environments for learning. This help from media, however, is not automatic. This help accrues to those teachers who are competent and creative, and who have at their disposal reasonably effective local resources and services.

Roles Played by Audiovisual Technology

In the following pages we assert that audiovisual materials, which comprise this aspect of technology, may perform some superhuman tasks for the teacher. We must caution the reader to note, however, that each of the materials does not necessarily play each of the roles. On the other hand, some of the materials or media may actually function in more than one role at the same time or at different times, or different media may be selected

to perform different roles simultaneously, as the examples will show.

The discussion in this chapter presents a simplified overview that points out the vital need for audiovisual media in the teaching-learning process. Each successive chapter develops in detail the nature of the teacher decisions required to unleash the potential impact of media.

Every teacher's job would be easier if students came to school possessed with the optimum amount of real experience that would facilitate learning. You may ask what kinds of experience? Shall we list some quickly? Would it make a difference in teaching methods? Would accomplishment be greater in our classes if students had had experiences in lunar orbit, experiences in artistic creativity, experiences in visiting far-off lands, experiences in sailing great clipper ships? Experiences of being in historic places and being near to great personalities of history? How much real experience is actually necessary before learners can comprehend what they read and what is presented and verbally explained to them? How much experience with real things and situations is needed before pupils can proceed to profit from abstractions? Reading a book and memorizing a series of conditions, or a list of causes, may not be rich enough in meaning. Pupils need actual and realistic, although frequently vicarious, experiences to build insight that will serve as

Figure 1–17. Some films provide a convincing sense of reality—a feeling of "being there." Paying a 20-minute film visit to a Malayan jungle may engender a feeling of acquaintanceship with the people shown in these pictures. Why might this be important in a given course or subject? (From Nomads of the Jungle, *courtesy United World Films, Inc.)*

ROLE NUMBER ONE: EXTEND HUMAN EXPERIENCE

Figure 1-18. Dramatic, action-filled motion pictures can bring to life events and personalities from history and literature. Can such films function under roles 1, 2, and 3? Under what conditions might some of the other roles apply? (From The Crusades: Saints and Sinners [TOP], *and* Galileo: The Challenge of Reason [MIDDLE], *courtesy Learning Corporation of America; and* Macbeth [BOTTOM], *courtesy Encyclopaedia Britannica Educational Corporation)*

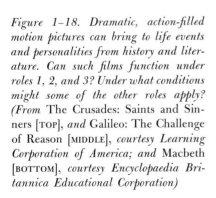

The Teacher and Technology

Figure 1–19. Field trips provide students with useful experiences in the study of real things and real places. Informal family field trips are worthwhile and often take children to places beyond the reach of school-sponsored trips, although field trips taken during school hours should normally be considered as formal instructional activities. Here students visit the Stephen Fitch House, one of 40 exhibit buildings at Old Sturbridge Village, Sturbridge, Mass. (Courtesy Old Sturbridge Village)

a basis for forming new relationships from unfamiliar verbal materials.

Therefore we state the first and most basic role as follows: *Audiovisual technology provides the teacher with a means for extending his students' horizon of experience.* By this role we seek to provide a counter-part of firsthand experience. A student may sit in a simulator and, under realistic stimuli from film sources, practice responding to highway conditions and to other drivers with amazingly realistic effects, just as astronauts simulate the experience of a space mission down to the last detail. A teacher may "take" his class by means of an appropriate motion picture to a remote jungle, or to an arctic glacier to "meet" the people who live there and to observe places and things. Some media may thus serve as a "magic carpet" for providing needed experiences, however vicarious, but experiences perhaps extremely close to reality in observational value. Motion pictures, television, and carefully prepared slide-tape sequences would be particularly valuable in this role.

Such "real" experiences may be planned and utilized in many teaching situations—as part of a presentation, as a means of introducing a new teaching unit, and, within an independent study context, as a means of seeking "firsthand" information for solving a problem. Such "real" experiences may actually last half an hour or only a few minutes. Thus through film one may be seated in the United States Senate on January 21, 1861 and listen as Jefferson Davis delivers his awesome speech of secession; or walk, on July 21, 1969, with Neil Armstrong and the first astronauts to explore the surface of the moon. In proper context, vicarious experiences can be intensely realistic. And who can doubt that memorable experiences frequently alter the course of our lives? Technology serves teachers by providing simulated experiences for pupils almost upon call. Who can predict the vividness of computer-based electronically simulated environments of the future?

ROLE NUMBER TWO: PROVIDE MEANINGFUL INFORMATION

The second role of media is stated as follows: *Audiovisual technology helps the teacher provide his students with meaningful sources of information.* Museum specialists refer to real things, or realia, as *primary visual sources.* Teachers in this complex age should be able to guide learners to the vast reservoir of realia as well as to graphic and pictorial material. This is in no way a statement that books and documentary materials are of less value today because of technological developments. The opposite is true. The task confronting education is now greater. We have not only to teach more subject matter, but we have also broadened the scope of our goals. Learners need to be prepared for experiences, need to obtain directions for performing procedures, need to obtain facts about situations and vivid descriptions of the application of principles. Hence we turn to additional resources—television, films, diagrams, charts, globes, and maps, to slides and transparencies, to models and to real things—to enhance clarity of communication and to increase speed of comprehension.

Audiovisual technology is able to provide learners with easily understood information in various forms. The eye of the camera makes reality manageable for the learner. The lens can be a time-machine or a telescope; a magnet

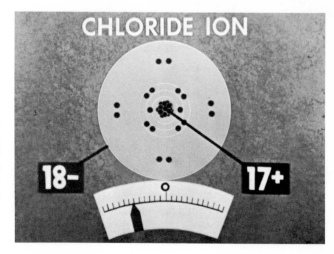

Figure 1–20. Motion pictures may diagrammatically show the unobservable. Animation techniques bring charts and diagrams to life to clarify concepts which otherwise could only be described (imagine explaining the structure of a chloride ion without visuals!) (From Chlorine: A Representative Halogen, *courtesy Sutherland Educational Films, Inc.)*

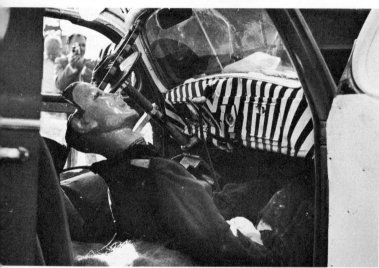

Figure 1–21. The content and continuity of events, processes, and conditions portrayed in motion picture films provide rich sources of information. These pictures show, starting at the top, an optical demonstration of changes in the mass of bodies traveling at very high speed, the normally unobservable action of a steel ball falling into a bowl of milk, the effect of forces acting on a dummy of a human body during an automobile collision, and a striking close-up view of a housefly grounded because of an impaired gyroscope that usually vibrates at 10,000 times a second. All these scenes are from the motion picture, Mystery of Time. *(Courtesy Moody Institute of Science)*

Figure 1–22. What have these boys learned from the experience of assembling the skeleton of a fetal pig? Will the finished product be a valuable learning device for other students? (Courtesy The National Education Association. Photo by Ben Spiegel)

or a microscope. Only through visual media may we see what happens to a driver's body when his car is in collision; or observe the internal workings of a jet aircraft engine. Reading a book can stimulate readers to imagine what things may have looked like in the past. Pictures can show everyone the same visual information from which each observer may draw highly personal inferences and conclusions.

Technology in this second role may free teachers from the repetitive and burdensome task of giving information, allowing them more time for creative work with students. In schools where combinations of printed and audiovisual media are available to present needed facts and principles, teachers must be sure that students use the resources in school libraries or media centers, laboratories, and in their community environments as the basis for solving real, meaningful problems. Information not put to functional use is easily forgotten. Problem-solving activity calls for teacher guidance. Audiovisual technology may well prove

Figure 1–23. Students share vicarious experiences through media. Pictures can show everyone the same visual information, but each viewer may draw different and highly personal inferences and conclusions from what he sees. How can teachers find out how students react to media? How can reaction be turned into motivation and commitment? (Courtesy of EDL/McGraw-Hill, Huntington, New York)

to be the means for providing extra hours for vital face-to-face interaction between teachers and learners.

This role is the best known and most widely used (and abused) by teachers. There is nothing wrong with creating interest in pupils, even if interest is rather narrowly conceived in terms of one's own subject-matter specialty. The important thing is what happens after the interest is aroused. Teachers fail too often to follow up effectively on the interest-compelling power of dynamic media such as films. Role Number Three is stated as follows: *Audiovisual technology provides the teacher with interest-compelling springboards which can launch students into a wide variety of learning activities.*

Interest is not an end in itself. Gaining attention is not the same as building motivation. Teachers must be concerned with understandings, abilities, attitudes, and appreciations that relate to behavioral objectives, but we must motivate learners to set up worthwhile purposes of their own. We need to seek better, more lifelike, realistic, functional, and significant problem-solving activities for students if we wish to stimulate bona fide, long-lasting *interest.* Audiovisual media can develop an awareness of problems, open up possibilities for exploration, present meaningful preliminary information, and thus open up avenues to new activity.

Teachers should be aware of other possibilities for developing readiness to learn. Other fascinating uses for audiovisual technology will be described in this book;

ROLE NUMBER THREE: STIMULATE INTEREST

Figure 1–24. Can learning be taking place here? Must students always be seated in neat rows of chairs, in study carrels, or at library tables? Will students necessarily get into trouble if they are allowed to move from place to place in the classroom, the school building, or out into the community? (Courtesy The National Education Association. Photo by Esther Bubley)

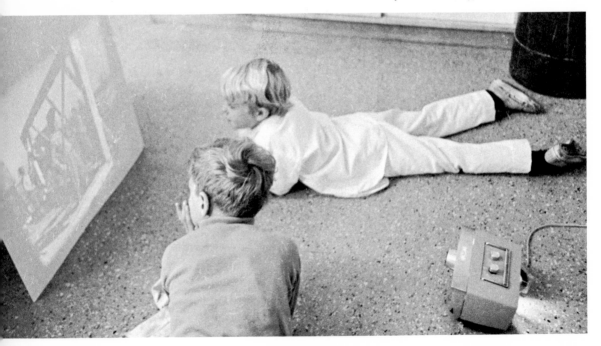

Figure 1–25. These children are building birds' nests. What value might there be in doing things that wild creatures do? If you were their teacher, would you encourage such messy activity in the classroom? (Photo by David H. Curl)

a stimulating film experience, for example, in direct relation to a problem already set up and accepted by a group or by an individual student. A field trip, taken not on the indefinite basis of starting a new unit of work, but taken instead in response to a significant project for which student groups need specific information, is another example. In this case the students' visit is the means for interviewing people, making observations, taking pictures, then returning to school to assemble the material for a presentation. Success breeds success. When students are satisfied by (and reinforced for) successful completion of an assignment calling for observation, research, and creative communication, they are more likely to develop such skills to a degree needed by functioning adults. Media may be appropriately used at all stages of the learning process but may be especially valuable in the "springboard" role.

Figure 1–26. "Last year, I spent a lot of time doing research on insects," said the biology teacher, "and I wound up lecturing on the subject for two weeks. The students listened, but didn't learn much. So, this year, they did the research and taught each other—I listened." (Courtesy Joint School District #233, Hagerman, Idaho. Photo by S. Z. Thayer)

When teaching by the conventional presentation method, the instructor himself is the center of attention and the primary source of information. Audiovisual media may be used, but mainly as "supplements"—to illustrate, to clarify, to focus attention, or to show otherwise inaccessible material.

But, when properly programmed, media alone can teach. And students can learn a great deal alone, working with media at their own pace. Role Number Four may be stated as follows: *Audiovisual technology multiplies teacher efficiency by providing tutorial stimuli and response guidance for individual students and small groups.*

An electronic learning laboratory provides guided, individualized instruction. In such laboratories, students participate actively throughout each lesson. They receive prompt confirmation or correction of each response they make. Ideally, the material is programmed so that each learner may adjust to his own rate of learning—repeating or skipping portions of the program as needed and desired.

The so-called teaching machines are self-instructional devices for presenting programs; but without good programs, or software, teaching machines and other hardware are useless. Programmed textbooks and teacher-prepared

ROLE NUMBER FOUR: GUIDE STUDENT RESPONSE

Figure 1–27. Learning German by audio-tutorial. Which of the seven roles of Audiovisual Technology are probably being applied here? Which role(s) can be played by the audio tape? Which role(s) by the workbook or student manual? What should be the roles and responsibilities of the teacher? (Courtesy Joint School District #233, Hagerman, Idaho. Photo by S. Z. Thayer)

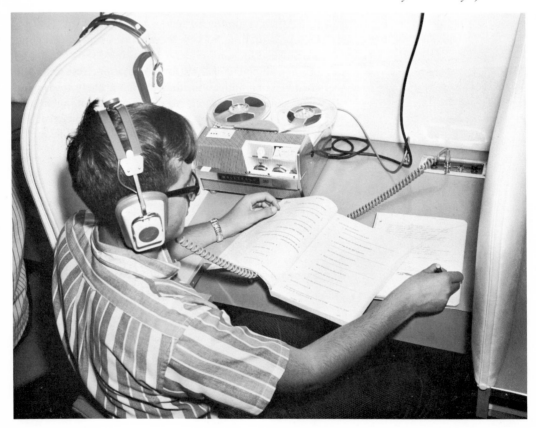

Figure 1–28. Multiplying teacher efficiency. Teachers are free to concentrate their attention on students who need help, when individuals or groups of students are actively engaged with self-instructional programs. To what extent can media provide information and drill that would otherwise be given directly by the teacher to the entire class? Can a tape recorder be a "private tutor?" (Photo by 3M/Wollensak)

worksheets have often proved to be a highly convenient way of presenting materials for independent study, particulary verbal material such as technical vocabulary. A programmed text or workbook often forms the nucleus of an individualized audiovisual-tutorial learning system employing tape recordings, slides, filmstrips, short motion pictures, models, or other media.

Figure 1–29. When a course is organized so that learners obtain much of their information through media in an individually prescribed self-instructional environment, what are the responsibilities of the teacher? Of the student? (Courtesy Lansing Community College)

Figure 1-30. Telephone Teaching can benefit students who, for health or other reasons, cannot attend school in the regular way. A special telephone hook-up allows this boy to be in contact with his class and even to ask questions. If there are enough students needing special help, a teacher can be assigned a "telephone class" of individuals with whom she is in contact only by telephone. (Courtesy AT&T)

Figure 1-31. Telewriting makes it possible for a distant teacher or resource person to supplement a telephone lecture (Tele-Lecture) or discussion with handwritten notes or drawings transmitted by telephone lines and projected onto a screen. (Courtesy AT&T)

Teachers face great difficulties each day in making information available to students as they work toward meeting their learning objectives. Students even in medium-sized classes cannot see demonstrations, small models, and objects, such as a skull, or small pictures. How, for example, might a teacher show a small printed diagram to the entire class? Or reveal the vein structure in a leaf, or the unique weave in a fabric sample, or show a political cartoon from the morning newspaper? How can teachers avoid spending time each year redoing complicated chalkboard drawings? Suppose different kinds of information and directions are needed by individual students or small groups within the class simultaneously. How can the teacher be several places at the same time? These are all communication problems. Audiovisual media can help the imaginative teacher solve them all. Hence we state Role Number Five as follows: *Audiovisual technology helps the teacher to overcome physical difficulties of presenting subject matter.*

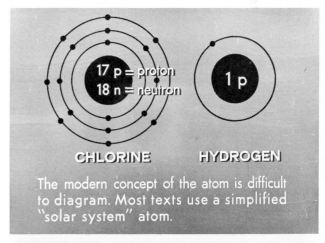

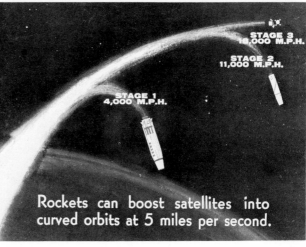

Figure 1–32. Filmstrips are sources of valuable pictorial and diagrammatic material. Meaningful student problems are ideal bases for filmstrip use; however, filmstrips are also an excellent means for introducing a unit of study. (From Chemistry for Today *and* Space and Space Travel *Series, courtesy SVE Division, Singer Education and Training Products)*

The Teacher and Technology

Figure 1–33. How many students have seen elephants in their natural habitat? Is a natural history museum diorama a suitable substitute? Are motion pictures or slides? (From Animals of the Indian Jungle, *courtesy Encyclopaedia Britannica Educational Corporation)*

Now let us review the situations described in the preceding paragraph and show specific applications of audiovisual technology.

1. Use films, television, slide-tape presentations, and so forth as an alternative to a lecture for presentation of information. Use audiovisual-tutorial programmed sequences when individual, self-paced learning is appropriate.
2. Buy, borrow, or produce 2×2-inch color slides showing steps in a process to be demonstrated, closeups of small objects such as leaves or bones, or copies of graphic materials or small illustrations.
3. Use an opaque projector to show printed diagrams, cartoons, or illustrations, or flat objects such as laminated leaves or samples of cloth.
4. Make a transparency from a cartoon or drawing in a few seconds on a thermographic copier and show it to the class by using an overhead projector.
5. Draw "chalkboard" diagrams once, on transparency masters, then project transparencies made from these masters on the overhead projector, thus saving time wasted in redrawing them each year.
6. Record questions, problems, exercises, and background information on different subjects or at different levels of difficulty on tape for use by individuals or small groups with cassette playback units. While some students are interacting with the recorded material, you will be free to work intensively with others.

These are just a few examples of how audiovisual technology can overcome physical difficulties of presenting subject matter. And do not overlook the advantages of cooperating with other teachers. Most types of locally produced slides, transparencies, tapes, and printed hand-out materials are easily duplicated and shared.

Figure 1–34. *What values are there in small-group activities such as collecting and identifying insects? In what ways might these youngsters use media to help them with their project? How can their teacher be most helpful? (From* Insects: How We Recognize Them, *courtesy Coronet Instructional Films)*

Figure 1–35. *The overhead projector is especially good for presenting student reports. Can you describe some advantages of using it instead of the chalkboard or other media for this purpose? (Courtesy The National Education Association. Photo by Esther Bubley)*

Figure 1–36. Youngsters like the challenge of planning, constructing, and operating post offices, stores, and banks. The dramatic activity involved broadens the scope of objectives to which such a project contributes. (Photo by Harry H. Haworth, Altadena, Calif.)

Students learn more and like it better if they are engaged in significant and appealing activities. Active participation maintains interest and increases learning, whether students are working at meaningful individual activities or cooperating with others in group or class projects. Students can learn more than subject matter. Of course, the student who prepares a written report of his investigations receives practice in writing, but usually his work is seen and reacted to only by the teacher.

ROLE NUMBER SIX: STIMULATE PROBLEM SOLVING

Figure 1–37. Problems and assignments may be large enough in scope to be worked on by all members of a class group, or they may be undertaken as projects for various purposes by individuals or smaller groups. The electric map shown was, in this case, a service project by two pupils for use by the whole class. (Photo by Harry H. Haworth, Altadena, Calif.)

Figure 1–38. Can media "turn on" kids? How important are the personality and enthusiasm of the teacher? To what extent are students' attitudes toward both print and non-print media influenced by the attitudes of adults? (Courtesy Hudson Photographic Industries, Inc. [ABOVE]. *Photo by David H. Curl* [BELOW].)

Admittedly, an oral report to the class helps to develop poise and confidence. But students who do all the necessary planning, research, and creative and technical work to actually make a movie or produce a slide/tape presentation or photo report have a unique communication opportunity. Role Six, then, states that: *Audiovisual technology offers rich opportunities for students to develop communication skills while actively engaged in solving meaningful problems.*

This role of audiovisual technology helps the teacher by opening up a vast new world of challenging assignments and problem-solving opportunities. A ninth-grade civics teacher, for example, might work together with her group in planning and producing a set of color slides with taped commentary on bicycle safety to be presented

Figure 1–39. Is gaining attention the same as building motivation? How can teachers select and use media to arouse long-lasting interest—to stimulate students to find out more about a topic? (Courtesy SVE Division, Singer Education and Training Products)

to third-, fourth-, and fifth-grade classes. Would the young producers be likely to learn anything themselves? Acquire information? Modify or strengthen attitudes? Develop new interests and skills? Could high school science students produce a series of audiovisual presentations for elementary grades on such diverse topics as good diet, littering and pollution, prevention of colds, and so on? Or on other levels—on the topics of good citizenship, effective study habits, historic places in the community? Older elementary and secondary school students could tackle community problems for public showing. Why not a presentation on the need for off-street parking downtown? Or on how school tax dollars are spent? Or—even more relevant in an urban school—interracial understanding?

If the equipment is available, 8mm and 16mm motion pictures are possible media for student production, and so are slide sets, filmstrips, tapes for radio or television use, or exhibits for school display cases, store windows, or building lobbies. If we consider the entire gamut of the audiovisual technology field, we see the practically limitless possibilities for making models and exhibits, writing and producing plays and programs, constructing model stores, factories, offices and communities, and making murals, charts, diagrams, maps and globes as communicative materials. Students feel important when given responsibility for producing significant media. They are surrounded by media everywhere in the real world. Successful experiments with audiovisual media help students learn to survive in the midst of communication competition.

ROLE NUMBER SEVEN: PROVIDE DIAGNOSTIC AND REMEDIAL TOOLS

As instruction becomes more individualized, teachers are better able to observe and to analyze the learning process. Teachers soon discover that every student needs special help of some kind. The use of media can shift the teacher from a presentational role toward that of diagnostician, counselor, and tutor. Role Number Seven may be stated as follows: *Audiovisual technology provides the teacher with tools to carry out diagnostic testing, research, and remedial work.*

Uncovering and correcting weaknesses in student performance is a common teaching task in many fields from physical education to mathematics. Teachers, working with specialists, can help to discover faulty hearing, eyesight, and speech as well as to increase visual span for speedier reading and increased comprehension. In a sense, the electronic learning laboratory with its listen, respond, and compare modes is an automatic device that leads learners to recognize their own difficulties and to proceed with remedial work as needed. This is also true of other forms of programmed instruction. Examples are

Figure 1-40. Developing communications skills. These students have done the research and photography for their presentation, and now their teacher helps them with the technical details of synchronizing recorded narration. To what extent should teachers become involved with such projects? While the teacher is working with these two students, what are the other members of the class doing? (Photo by 3M/Wollensak)

The Teacher and Technology

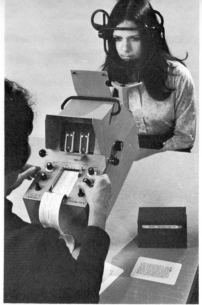

Figure 1–41. Tools for diagnostic testing, research, and remedial work. Teachers must be alert to identify students whose reading and language skills lag behind because of perceptual and physical handicaps. Trained specialists diagnose causes and prescribe exercises for correction of such problems on a group or individual basis. (Courtesy of EDL/ McGraw-Hill, Huntington, New York)

endless. A camera may photograph eye movements, speech gestures, and facial expression; an audiometer may indicate levels of hearing sensitivity; optical devices test for visual defects; a tachistoscope (slide or filmstrip projector with a shutter attachment) may help to remedy short-visual-span trouble as a cause of reading difficulties; and motion pictures and videotape may serve in analyzing defective coordination or physical weaknesses under game or other practical situations in which instructors wish to develop remedial programs. Still picture sequences or slides may aid in the analysis of perceptual limitations and help to develop skills of observation and logical reasoning.

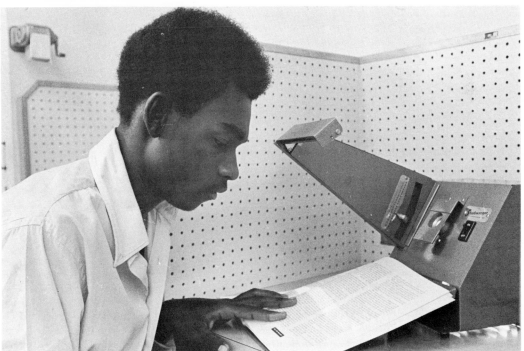

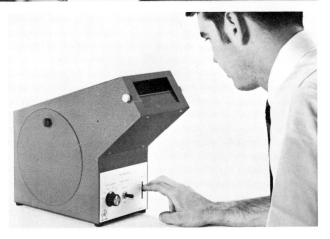

Figure 1–42. Media devices are employed by individual students to improve reading speed, comprehension, and vocabulary. The Language Master [TOP] uses cards striped with magnetic tape, allowing the user to see and hear a word or phrase simultaneously. A reading pacer [MIDDLE] draws the reader's eyes along at a predetermined rate, while the tachistoscope [BOTTOM] sharpens perception and widens visual span through very brief exposure to syllables, words, or phrases. (Courtesy The National Education Association, photos by Esther Bubley [TOP, MIDDLE]; and courtesy Lafayette Instrument Company [BOTTOM]).

What I hear I forget.
What I see I remember.
What I do I know.

—ANCIENT PROVERB

**Audiovisual Technology
in the Learning Process**

Students deserve good communication efforts by their teachers. Students want various media available and used, not only because media are interesting and seem to make school time pass more quickly, but because students are accustomed to the reality and immediacy of television and films in their everyday lives. Teachers who emphasize effective communication seek to give adequate explanations, seek to understand and anticipate the difficulties of students, seek to understand how they think and feel, and seek to provide the necessary real and vicarious experiences for solving problems, building new ideas, insights, and abilities, and for carrying on other meaningful learning tasks. When teachers develop penetrating insights into the breadth and variety of instructional objectives, when they better their understanding of the difficulties of effective communication, and when they come to feel a real concern for individual student achievement they will recognize more clearly the need for the help offered by audiovisual technology.

In this section we do not propose to enter on a detailed and comprehensive analysis of learning theory. Even if such a unified system had been discovered, agreed upon, and established, it would be far too complex to describe in a text of this kind. However, let us identify the kinds of learner activity and reaction that many psychologists agree take place and then point out the contributions of audiovisual technology to the intensely subjective process of learning.

As a point of departure, let us consider a condensed and excerpted view of the learning process as described by one psychologist, and then show how an instructional motion picture can facilitate desirable learner activity within that proposed model.

Lee J. Cronbach describes seven elements in behavior and asserts, "These seven elements . . . express in miniature a theory of behavior, and we shall also use them as the base for a theory of learning. Learning is shown by change in behavior, that is, by new interpretations and altered responses." These seven elements, as stated by Cronbach, will serve as an approach to an overall view of the learning process.

1. SITUATION. *The situation consists of all the objects, persons, and symbols in the learner's environment.* Experience in one situation prepares a person to respond to similar situations in the future. Curriculum planning is, in essence,

the selection of situations (Tasks, lessons, questions, objects) to which the pupil should learn to respond, and the arrangement of them in the best sequence.

2. PERSONAL CHARACTERISTICS. *Under this heading we include all the abilities and all the typical responses that the person brings to the situation.* "Abilities" include such physical qualities and skills as strength, reach, and ability to swim, and intellectual attainments such as ability to hold a long sentence in mind after one hearing. . . . The phrase "typical responses" . . . refers to what the person usually does. . . . These abilities and typical responses indicate how the pupil is likely to interpret and respond to a situation arranged by the teacher. Certain characteristics are needed if the pupil is to profit from the experience; we refer to this as the *readiness* required for the activity. If the pupil does not have the abilities and typical responses suited to the activity proposed, some other task must be found for which he does have readiness.

3. GOAL. *The goal of the learner is some consequence (i.e., state of affairs) that he wishes to attain.* His desire may be for an object, a certain response from another person, or some internal feeling. The goal is defined by an opportunity or a threat he perceives in the situation. The person has many goals at the same time, and usually sees any immediate goal (such as completing an assigned task) as related to a whole series of future goals (earning a respectable grade in the course, finishing school, and succeeding in a career). Since goals direct effort, the teacher's problem of motivation is essentially one of arranging situations in which the learner will see goals he wants to attain.

4. INTERPRETATION. *Interpretation is a process of directing attention to parts of the situation, relating observations to past experiences, and predicting what can be expected to happen if various actions are taken.* Interpretation may be conscious and deliberate, but a person makes many interpretations without putting them into words or giving them his full attention. The interpretation suggests what action to try. . . .

5. ACTION. *The person's actions include movements and statements: they are observable responses.* A person chooses whatever action he expects to give him the greatest satisfaction. . . .

   If the learner is in doubt about his interpretation in a strange situation, he acts tentatively. We speak of his act as a *provisional try*. Then he is especially likely to look at the consequences of his act and to learn from them. This questioning, experimental attitude is one of the traits that sets apart the creative person, and the one who continues his learning long after he leaves school.

6. CONSEQUENCE: CONFIRMATION OR CONTRADICTION. *Some events that follow the action are regarded by the learner as consequences of it.* Consequences include the direct effort of the action, such as getting the basketball through the hoop, and less direct accompaniments, such as the popularity attained by a good player. If the consequences are those he predicted, the learner's interpretation is con-

firmed. Then he is likely to make a similar interpretation on another occasion. For the teacher, one of the important problems is to help the learner observe consequences accurately, and sometimes to arrange pleasant consequences so that correct interpretations and actions will be reinforced.

If the consequences are not what the person expected, his interpretation is contradicted and he does not reach his goal. He learns not to make this interpretation in the future.

7. REACTION TO THWARTING: ADAPTIVE OR NONADAPTIVE. *Thwarting occurs when the person fails to attain a goal.* If his first try is not confirmed, he may make a new interpretation and change his action. Through such *adaptive behavior,* he will usually hit on some action that brings him closer to the goal. At the same time, his goal may also be modified as he changes his idea of what he can attain.

The learner may instead respond nonadaptively, stubbornly repeating the same unsuccessful act, giving up entirely, or acting erratically and thoughtlessly. To distinguish between adaptive and nonadaptive behavior is difficult, because giving up, for example, is sometimes sensible. [3]

Now, by using a specific plan to utilize a motion picture in the classroom as an example, we shall point out relationships to the seven aspects of learning just described, emphasizing the facilitation of pupil action.

THE EXAMPLE. *A ninth-grade teacher of mathematics has set up and introduced a problem for her class in a unit on making graphs.* [4] *The main problem is to construct a corridor display to show graphically the results of the school's Junior Red Cross Drive. According to the teacher's plan, the students viewed the motion picture,* The Language of Graphs *after they had accepted and discussed their problem.* (The film portrayed the activities of a high school group concerned about a communication problem of increasing the circulation of their school newspaper). The students then went to work, planning their action as individuals and as a group or team of workers.

Relationship of the Film to Seven Aspects of Learning

We now point out some of the ways that the motion picture experience may have a formative influence as the learner acquires understanding, ability, attitude, and appreciation, which constitute the desired changes in his

[3] From *Educational Psychology* Second Edition by Lee J. Cronbach, copyright, 1954, © 1962, 1963 by Harcourt, Brace & World, Inc. and reprinted with their permission.

[4] Based on a film-utilization plan prepared by Marilyn Neri, teacher at Farmington High School, Unionville, Conn. The film, *The Language of Graphs* is a Coronet Instructional Films production.

behavior. As you examine the following statements you should refer again to each of the seven aspects of learning previously quoted: *situation, personal characteristics, goal, interpretation, action, consequence,* and *reaction to thwarting.* Do not view the seven elements as separate and distinct steps; they are interrelated and interwoven, but are separated here purely for discussion purposes.

Situation Aspect   The motion picture became a part of the situation that included problems, books, and all classroom arrangements. The assignment or problem became an obstacle, and students viewing the film in this framework of reference had a realistic experience because the film was about another group of students in a similar situation. As they watched the action they received suggestions (stimuli, cues) for directing their own constructional procedures later. As students make responses during their viewing in terms of questions and directions introduced before the film showing they may know at once if they are correct, and hence may receive reinforcement from supporting action in the film story. The film experience would very likely appear to be meaningful to the students because of their needed understanding and skill. They may recognize the need for other sources of information and direction such as text and reference books. In this film students saw specific examples of how graphs can portray information, and they probably eventually generalized about graphs as effective tools of communication. As a result of the film experience, the students knew their own situation better and were thus able to choose or suggest a wise course of action. It is also very likely that they recognized and defined new personal needs.

Personal Characteristics Aspect   Certainly this class of mathematics students, with all of the wide diversity among its members, was together in its *readiness* for action and focused on the problem to be solved by the group by concentrating on the film experience with its realistic source of information. It is likely that the film experience intensified or reinforced the readiness of students to attack their problems and to study their texts for additional facts and directions principally because of increased insight developed by watching others solve similar problems. Naturally, the work of the students was carried on in the light of their own differences, strengths, and weaknesses.

Goal Aspect   The students' goal in this case, was to complete the basic problem. Watching the film was an important step, that is, a means of getting needed information from the film (as guided by the teacher). Other goals as well doubtlessly operated in this situation. The importance of motivation in each pupil must be recognized. In this situation, students were motivated primarily by a problem that they had accepted before use of the film. The motion picture helped the students to become more aware of the nature of the main problem or objective, thus intensifying motivation through reinforcement.

As the students observed and reacted to the action in the film they probably identified themselves with the decisions and actions of the film actors. The experience helped them to interpret and define their own graphic communication problem. Some students were stimulated, in the process of interpreting the film, to suggest a plan of action for the group, and to conceive of several possible individual contributions of effort. Thus the film experience facilitated the process of interpretation, and, under the guidance of the teacher, they responded with ideas for action, for the group and for themselves.

Interpretation Aspect

The action suggested as a first attempt is of course met by consequences—confirming or contradicting. Students in the group suggested plans for study and construction. A display design took shape, and work groups were organized. The necessary work demanded text study, discussion, extensive practice, cooperation, and teamwork, and development of skills to collect and arrange data, to make computations, and to construct graphs. Throughout such activity student actions are being affected by group criticisms. It is during this process that insight and ability, attitudes, and appreciations are being shaped. Films, books, models, charts, the teacher, and classmates thus contribute to new responses as a result of experience—vicarious experience in the film, and real experience in solving the functional lifelike problem. Such successful action is intended to prepare students for increasingly more complex problem-solving behavior.

Action Aspect

In this particular aspect of a group project there is a series of consequences to which pupils react. Some of their ideas are accepted by the group (with reinforcing effects), and others may be refused, hopefully leading to new and better responses. Some of the students' unexpressed ideas may have been strengthened during their observation of the film. Actually, the film, through its concrete imagery and interesting and realistic action, probably served the students well by facilitating a high rate of correct choices. Much individual study and work was called for following the film, and needed insights and skills were acquired as the project proceeded toward completion. Hence the students constantly had to face the consequences of their individual actions as well as the action undertaken by the group, until termination of the project.

Consequences Aspect

Students who were forced to modify their actions and to make new trials to gain success may have been guided by their impressions of film content. Under strong moti-

Reaction to Thwarting Aspect

vation and under guidance of the teacher and help from classmates, those students who did not master the techniques were led to engage in more practice as the solution of the problem neared completion. Study sheet guides and homework assignments were suggested and made available. Thus, desirable, adaptive behavior was reinforced. (But unfortunately, by the same process, under certain circumstances, it is also possible for nonadaptive behavior to be reinforced.)

This group problem-solving example has been greatly simplified and condensed to emphasize the points of relationship to each of Cronbach's seven aspects of learning. As has already been pointed out, a number of different audiovisual media may frequently be used by a teacher, each medium making its own systematic and planned contribution at different stages of activity in the class. Also, many other examples of the use of audiovisual media might have been given. In Chapter 6 there are nine case studies of technological media used in classrooms; each of these examples may be analyzed according to Cronbach's seven aspects of learning, or they may be examined in the light of other conceptualizations of the learning process.

Before we depart from this particular orientation to the learning process, we should call your attention to the way motion pictures and other experiences may influence the acquisition of concepts, generalizations, abilities, and attitudes.

New insights arise when old experiences are related to new experiences. Insights are of personal origin, and the process of putting together a group of specific and meaningful experiences into a generalization is a thrilling, personal discovery. But the reverse of this inductive process is also frequently necessary for rich understanding. The learner may find it necessary to reconstruct his generalization by identifying and assembling the elements of the personal experiences and observations that made his generalization possible. Teachers must understand that the process of generalization applies to the synthesis of values, the drawing of conclusions, the growth of values, and to the development of skills.

If we review our analysis of the learning process, we note the following vital aspects of classroom action that have a bearing on the development of generalizations, abilities, attitudes, and appreciations:

1. The students worked on a problem that had meaning for them. They were highly motivated. The film experience was related to the arrangement of conditions for learning. Such a functional problem-solving situation is likely to be conducive to formation of concepts and subsequent generalizations.

2. Students worked individually as they planned and constructed graphs; they also worked in groups, planning and constructing displays. Hence solution of the problem called for complex activity, resulting in the drawing of conclusions, the building of insights into graphic processes, and the development of communication skills.

3. The film about people like themselves engaged in a similar problem activity must have seemed highly realistic and thus strongly motivating in its effect on continued activity.

4. Opportunities were provided to link conclusions from past experiences with new ideas under the stimulus of the group and individual activity. This process also has a marked influence on development of concepts and generalizations.

5. The film supplied information on how to make graphs, showed high-quality graphs as standards for class achievement, stimulated the desire to consult their textbooks and other reference sources, aided students in setting up specific personal goals, and stimulated them to work toward achieving those standards. All these influences would foster the development of ability and attitude as well as concepts and generalizations.

6. The span of work on skill-building activity plus the planning activity by the group and the possible satisfaction by successful display completion probably provided opportunity for extensive feedback, or knowledge of results. It provided the students with an opportunity for creative interaction in a varied experience that involved visual imagery, language activity, and motor and emotional activity.

In situations possessing such elements of action under strong motivation, where perhaps both successes and failures are made possible, where group and individual pressures are operating, and where desirable value systems are in evidence, students may be led to reorganize experience through language into meaningful generalizations.

This book focuses on teacher decisions about the use of media. The study and close observation of the learning process needs to be a part of every teacher's lifelong professional endeavor, requiring study of educational psychology far beyond the scope of this book. The fundamentals stressed in the following pages possess rich potential for effective teacher planning and action. We offer a pattern for teacher creativity in incorporating audiovisual media in arranging the conditions for learning.

Problems and Activities

1. List specific instructional media with which you have already had experience in your college classes, or in classes that you have taught.

2. Think back over some of your own experiences as a student in high school and college. List three motion pictures that were used in class by your instructors, describing the subject and the situation. Study the Basic Roles of Media described in Chapter 1, then answer the following questions:
   (a) Identify the specific instructional roles played by the films listed.
   (b) Explain whether you think any of the films were shown for reasons other than those stated in Roles One through Seven.

3. List the "noise" factors that may be present to inhibit classroom communication. Mention as many ways as you can to reduce or compensate for such "noise."

4. Analyze the following communication situations in terms of sender (communicator), receiver (interpreter), medium, and message (idea):
   (a) You approach the door in a supermarket and it opens automatically.
   (b) A boy in your class wears his hair exceptionally long.

5. From a communication viewpoint, analyze the behavior of:
   (a) The teacher who has trouble maintaining discipline in the classroom.
   (b) The student who refuses to do homework.

6. Explain what is meant by the statement: "Words and pictures have no meaning in themselves."

7. Discuss the criticisms of American education leveled by writers such as Silberman, Holt, and Postman & Weingartner. Describe ways in which media can be used to overcome certain of their objections.

8. Describe ways in which print media (text and reference books, periodicals and pamphlets, and microforms) can fulfill some of the Roles of Media. Compare the effectiveness of print and nonprint (audiovisual) media in fulfilling each of the seven roles listed.

9. Compare Cronbach's analysis of the learning process as quoted here with the theories of learning described by Skinner, Travers, and Gagné in the Selected References at the end of the chapter and in more recent works. Which point of view seems most appropriate and accurate to you? Can you say that there is one true theory of learning upon which to base your own teaching-strategy decisions?

10. Refer to the captions under Figures 1–1 and 1–2. Prepare a dialog in which the questions of indoctrination, bias, and propaganda in media are raised and replied to. Present your dialog as a forum or a panel discussion.

11. Analyze and compare the daily activities of teachers under "traditional" and under "open" or "individualized" patterns of classroom management. Differentiate between Roles of Media under differing forms of organization.

12. Describe how, in ways other than name alone, an "Educational Resources Center" or "Media Center" might be expected to differ from a "library."

13. Refer to the caption under Figure 1–16. Explain how different instructional objectives might be achieved through the experiences listed.

14. Describe an incident of communication failure in which confusion resulted from misunderstanding of words or visuals.

15. Examine the communication model (diagram) shown in Figures 1–8 and 1–9. Does this diagram depict the communication process to your satisfaction? If not, explain why not, and prepare your own communication model.

16. Respond to the following statement: "Teachers should always use audiovisual media because research has shown that people learn 10 per cent of what they *read*, 20 per cent of what they *hear*, 30 per cent of what they *see*, and 50 per cent of what they *see and hear*."

17. Following the example given in employing the film, *The Language of Graphs*, prepare a plan for the use of a different film (suggestion: *Democracy: Your Voice Can Be Heard*—Coronet Instructional Films) in which the action depicted in the film is intended to stimulate similar activity on the part of your own class. Show how your plan is either based on the Cronbach principles listed, or derives from a different analysis of the learning process.

Selected References

Audiovisual Resources for Teaching Instructional Technology. Area of Instructional Technology, Syracuse University, Syracuse, N.Y. 13210, 1971, 164 pp. Annotated listing of materials extracted from various catalogues and publications.

Berfunkle (16mm film, 9 min) Portafilms, 4180 Dixie Hwy., Drayton Plains, Mich. 48020, 1967. Demonstrates through animated cartoon treatment how words can have different meanings for different people.

BROWN, JAMES W., RICHARD B. LEWIS, and FRED F. HARCLEROAD. *AV Instruction: Materials and Methods*, 3rd ed. McGraw-Hill Book Co., 1221 Avenue of the Americas, New York, N.Y. 10020, 1969, 621 pp. An encyclopedic reference source widely used as an audiovisual textbook. Convenient reference section. Laboratory manual and teacher's guide are available.

DALE, EDGAR. *Audiovisual Methods in Teaching*, 3rd ed. The Dryden Press, Holt, Rinehart and Winston, Inc., 383

Madison Ave., New York, N.Y. 10017, 1969, 720 pp. Extremely well-written basic text on media for classroom teachers.

Educational Technology Publications Catalog. Educational Technology Publications, Inc., 140 Sylvan Avenue, Englewood Cliffs, N.J. 07632, revised periodically. Lists materials covering the broad spectrum of technology, many of which are compilations of articles appearing in *Educational Technology* magazine.

GAGNÉ, ROBERT M. *The Conditions of Learning,* 2nd ed. Holt, Rinehart and Winston, Inc., 383 Madison Ave., New York, N.Y. 10017, 1969. Outlines a theory of learning with implications for the design and utilization of audiovisual media.

GARDNER, JOHN W. *Self-Renewal.* Harper and Row Publishers, Inc., Keystone Industrial Park, Scranton, Pa. 18512, 1963, 142 pp. Philosophical examination of the responsibility of individuals and organizations for innovation.

HANEY, JOHN B., and ELDON J. ULLMER. *Educational Media and the Teacher.* William C. Brown Co., Publishers, 135 South Locust St., Dubuque, Iowa 52001, 1970, 130 pp. Concise introductory survey of the media field with emphasis on classroom utilization.

HOLT, JOHN, *What Do I Do Monday?,* E. P. Dutton & Co., Inc., 201 Park Avenue South, New York, N.Y. 10003, 1970, 318 pp. In a gentle, but articulate voice, Holt calls for imagination and perception on the part of adults to free children from stultifying, boring aspects of traditional schooling. This book, like others by the same author, is filled with ideas for projects, activities, and environments for stimulating awareness and spontaneity.

KOHL, HERBERT R., *The Open Classroom.* The New York Review, 250 West 57th St., New York, N.Y. 10019, 1969, 116 pp. Observations and advice for teachers who want to create an "open environment" in their classrooms. Urges teachers to initiate change and make use of the surprising amount of freedom they actually have.

LEONARD, GEORGE B., *Education and Ecstasy.* Dell Publishing Co., Inc., 750 Third Ave., New York, N.Y. 10017, 1968, 239 pp. Enthusiastic forecast of the kind of new education that could allow every child, every person to delight in learning.

More Than Words (16mm film, 15 min) Henry Strauss Co., 31 West 53rd St., New York, N.Y. 10019, 1961. Deals directly with communication between people—how to get better understanding and acceptance from others and how to be a better communicator.

NEA Catalog, Publications and Audiovisual Materials. National Education Association, 1201 16th St., N.W., Washington, D.C. 20036, revised annually. Current listing of books, periodicals, and audiovisual materials produced by NEA affiliates, including the Association for Educational Communications and Technology (AECT).

POSTMAN, NEIL, and CHARLES WEINGARTNER. *Teaching as a Subversive Activity.* Delacorte Press, 750 Third Ave.,

New York, N.Y. 10017, 1969, 219 pp. Attacks the methods of the Educational Establishment and appeals to teachers to act as change agents, helping students learn how to learn.

————. *The Soft Revolution.* Dell Publishing Co., Inc., 750 Third Avenue, New York, N.Y. 10017, 1971, 183 pp. In a decidedly straightforward and irreverent manner, the authors urge their readers to take specific kinds of nonviolent action to "overthrow" obsolete and irrelevant portions of the Educational Establishment.

Searching Eye, The (16mm film 18 min) Pyramid Film Productions, P.O. Box 1048, Santa Monica, Calif. 90406, 1969. Seeing is the tool through which a small boy discovers the world. The film shows what he sees and what he cannot see: the world that is yet to be discovered by him.

SILBERMAN, CHARLES E. *Crisis in the Classroom.* Random House, Inc., Westminster, Md. 21157, 1970, 553 pp. Incisive criticism of American public schools with some suggestions for dramatic improvement—based on the English primary schools—and the more liberal education of American teachers.

SKINNER, B. F. *The Technology of Teaching.* Appleton-Century-Crofts, Division of Meredith Corp., 440 Park Avenue South, New York, N.Y. 10016, 1968, 271 pp. A behavioral psychologist's view of the learning process from the standpoint of contingency reinforcement or operant conditioning as contrasted to aversive control.

STOTLER, DONALD W. *The Self-Learning Society.* Northwest Library Service, Inc., P. O. Box 25112, Portland, Oregon 97225, 1970, 133 pp. Presents an imaginative view of life and learning in the future. Emphasizing the importance of a free flow of dialogue among all people, the author stresses the advantages of establishing a system of community learning centers for people of all ages and all interests.

THOMPSON, JAMES J. *Instructional Communication.* American Book Company, 55 Fifth Avenue, New York, N.Y. 10003, 1969, 234 pp. Introductory survey of technological media viewed within a framework of communications theory.

TRAVERS, ROBERT M. W. *Man's Information System.* Chandler Publishing Company, Intext, Scranton, Pa. 18515, 1970, 175 pp. Analysis of research in perception, learning, information theory, and neurophysiology with implications for the design and application of audiovisual media.

Visual Fable, A (filmstrip with record, 18 min) AECT Publications Sales Section, 1201 16th St., N.W., Washington, D.C., 20036, 1968. Shows how visual literacy develops from birth, through school experiences, into adulthood. Suggests that formal education should play a leading role in helping youngsters learn to perceive and respond to their visual world.

WITTICH, WALTER A. and CHARLES F. SCHULLER. *Audiovisual Materials, Their Nature and Use,* 4th ed. Harper & Row, Inc., Keystone Industrial Park, Scranton, Pa. 18512, 1967, 554 pp. Basic text for teachers emphasizing principles for thoughtful selection and effective utilization of audiovisual materials for instruction.

2
Media and Instructional Objectives

Our responsibility is not discharged by the announcement of virtuous ends.

—John F. Kennedy

Getting an education is like traveling—if you don't have a destination in mind and a map to guide you, you may end up no place in particular—and wondering how you got there!

Side-trips from a planned itinerary frequently are rewarding and interesting. Aimless excursions around the countryside sometimes lead to discovery and excitement, but in school they lead more often to frustration and boredom. Teachers who describe course objectives in terms such as: *"Appreciating* music," *"really understanding* the sacrifices made by our patriotic forebears," *"knowing* how to solve quadratic equations," *"believing* in equality of opportunity," *"enjoying* photography," *"having faith* in democracy," probably don't know where the students are going. The saddest part is that neither will the students.

Broadly stated goals have some value in philosophical discussion, but such generalizations have little value to teachers as they plan, organize, and direct students' practical day-to-day learning activities. On the other hand, valid, *behavioral* objectives help students by letting them know what is expected of them. Behavioral objectives help teachers by offering a performance blue-print and a consistent evaluation checklist. Once student performance objectives are established, it is much easier for teachers to decide what kinds of problem-solving activities will be most appropriate and which media will be the best sources of information for solving these problems. Without specific objectives, teachers tend to proceed according to whim and expediency. Without meaningful objectives students often perform grudgingly or poorly. What, then, are some basic characteristics of useful instructional objectives? There are two schools of thought—the cognitive and the behavioral. As we use these terms, *cognitive* pertains to knowledge and awareness of information, principles, and attitudes; *behavioral* refers to a student's actual ability *to use* what he *knows.*

47

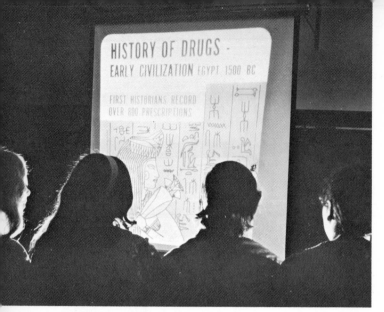

Figure 2–1. Visual media can focus the attention of viewers and provide a common point of reference for members of a group. What must a teacher do to ensure the most effective learning from visuals? (Courtesy International Education and Training, Inc.)

Specifying Useful Objectives

The Cognitive Approach

Educators often describe educational objectives in terms that have been widely used by writers in the fields of curriculum development and educational psychology, by the late William H. Burton[1] for example, namely, *understandings, abilities, attitudes,* and *appreciations.*[2] Objectives, or *teaching purposes* stated in these terms generally describe desired mental activities, but, except for the *abilities* category, seldom include specifications of observable behavior or state expected levels of performance. Lack of specific performance measures not only can create misinterpretation, but can result in inconsistent or unreasonable expectations on the part of teacher, learner, or both. Another danger of cognitive classification alone is that readers of such objectives receive the erroneous impression that each type of objective is to be taught and achieved separately. The exact opposite is true. All are interwoven and enmeshed in a complex of mental action. The development of any given physical performance by a learner calls for understanding of facts and concepts, development and modification of physical and cognitive skills, changes in mental set, a commitment to action, and a tendency to choose or to discriminate among certain things, processes, and behaviors.

When a valid set of purposes has been formulated for a course, a unit of work, or a portion of a unit, it is much easier to make decisions about methods, procedures, and media. In the absence of purposes, when

[1] William H. Burton, *Guidance of Learning Activities* (3d. ed.). New York: Appleton-Century-Crofts, Inc., 1962, pp. 348–353.

[2] The term *cognitive* as used in this chapter includes mental activities involving awareness and judgment, therefore applying to attitudes and appreciations. Other writers, however, have classified understandings and abilities within what has been called *the cognitive domain*, and attitudes and appreciations under *the affective domain*.

Figure 2-2. How would you "grade" this visual report on human anatomy? While crude by adult standards, was making this three-dimensional chart a meaningful learning experience for the boys who produced it? Would others in the class have learned as much if an oral or written report had been presented? (Courtesy The National Education Association. Photo by Ben Spiegel)

teachers have a film or an activity they wish to employ, they should ask themselves, *What might be accomplished by showing this film?* Or, *What will my students do if I lead them through a given problem-solving activity?* At this point the teacher must either move a step beyond the *purpose* concept and check the validity of his thinking or admit that he wants merely to *entertain* his students, or *enrich* the previous material, as so many say, or use the materials with the vague hope that somebody will

Figure 2-3. How important is it to "know the answers?" Does "knowing the answers" depend on who is asking the questions? How much should students themselves be involved in deciding about the kinds of questions they will be expected to answer? Instead of demanding facts, should teachers sometimes ask, "How do you feel about ____?" or "What would you do, if ____?" (Courtesy AT&T)

Media and Instructional Objectives

Figure 2–4. Can a film such as Life in a Cubic Foot of Soil *stimulate students to design and conduct their own experiments? What kinds of advance planning and follow-up supervision should be performed by the teacher to ensure that students receive the most value from this type of film? (Courtesy Coronet Instructional Films)*

learn something of value. Many teachers believe that audiovisual technology will help them teach "the book" better, as it undoubtedly will. But now we have to ask why is "the book" being taught?

The following list of characteristics of cognitive objectives (teaching purposes) is presented as a basis for study and discussion. It will be helpful to teachers in bridging the gulf between broad, philosophical goals and clearly defined behavioral objectives.

UNDERSTANDINGS:

1. Are the generalizations, beliefs, conclusions, insights, ideas, concepts, definitions, principles, statements of fact (when related to broader concepts and abilities), and directions for procedure that we want our students to develop, learn, know, acquire, draw, or comprehend.
2. Should be expanded enough in structure to convey clear meaning. (For instance, state why a process is important.)
3. Should be stated by the teacher in language likely to be used by students in their responses to situations involving the concepts.
4. Should grow from student problem-solving experiences.
5. Should be declarative in nature, and the statements should be preceded by the words *Understanding that*, as a safeguard against inconsistency and incompleteness.

ABILITIES:

1. Are the kinds of performance students are to produce in any given course or unit of work; in general, to be carried on in life after the course is finished.

Characteristics of Teaching Purposes

Abilities may be learned directly or may be an incidental product of class action.

2. May be stated briefly but should be accompanied by qualifications of degree of desired efficiency. Statements of purpose are more easily understood when each item contains only one ability. Therefore two or three abilities should not be combined.

3. May be stated in considerable breadth and then broken down into subsidiary abilities.

4. Must be thought of as growing from, not identical with, the specific learning activities.

5. Should be preceded by the words *Ability to*, as a safeguard against inconsistency. To reduce redundancy, extra phrases such as "To develop in students the" should be avoided. Abilities are frequently stated as *Ability to know, Ability to learn,* and so on. Such expressions refer to learning capacity and are incorrectly stated as abilities.

ATTITUDES:

1. Are statements describing relatively stable mental sets, stable patterns of conduct, pervasive action at home, play, and work.

2. Should be kept brief, one word if possible. It may help to characterize descriptive terms by an ending of *ness*, like cooperative*ness* and considerate*ness*. Some descriptive terms for well-known attitudes like inquiry and patience do not lend themselves to the *ness* ending. In these cases precede the word or words by *Desire to* or *Willingness to*, otherwise let it remain *attitude of patience*, for example.

3. Should be so stated that pervasive application is obvious.

Figure 2–5. Students learn cooperation by cooperating. What kinds of joint activities are facilitated by media? In what tangible ways are teachers able to observe or measure changes in attitudes and appreciations? (Courtesy of EDL/McGraw-Hill, Huntington, New York)

Media and Instructional Objectives

4. Should be stated one at a time in the list for maximum emphasis.
5. Precede descriptive terms by *Attitude of,* as a safeguard against inconsistency.

APPRECIATIONS:

1. Are the things, processes, actions, and characteristics that it would be desirable for students to like and choose.
2. Should be listed one at a time for maximum clarity.
3. Should not include such expressions as *value of, contributions of, importance of, need of,* or *role of.* Such statements, if spelled out, are understandings, hence should be included where they belong. Apply the test of *choice.* An individual may understand or comprehend *facts* about the *role of* air transportation in our economy, but he does not *choose* the role. Either he likes and will choose air travel as a process or he does not like to fly and will not choose to travel in that way.
4. Should be stated briefly and specifically, allowing for an implied alternative choice, such as *good craftsmanship* (as chosen against *poor workmanship*).
5. Should be preceded by *Appreciation of,* as a safeguard against inconsistency.

Examples of Purposes

After examining the criteria for stating purposes, we turn to an edited statement of purposes made by a teacher[3] in connection with the showing of the film, *Pioneers of the Plains,*[4] part of a teaching unit on the *Westward Movement.* In this case the film was used as a "magic carpet," that is, a realistic trip into the early West accompanying some pioneers. Showing of the film was intended to be a springboard for a unit of work. The teacher mimeographed a trip guide as a readiness device for the students and had made plans for discussion and work on significant problem activity for a number of class periods after the film showing in order to accomplish the purposes stated.

This statement is offered for purposes of evaluation. How well do the purposes in each category meet the criteria? The statement follows:

EXAMPLE 1

UNDERSTANDING THAT:

1. A pioneer is one of the first to explore the unknown, to prepare the way for others.
2. The pioneer and the spirit of the pioneer have been a vital force throughout the history of mankind. Columbus,

[3] Shirley M. Titus, West Hartford, Connecticut Schools. By permission.
[4] Encyclopaedia Britannica Educational Corporation.

Figure 2–6. These still pictures from the film, Pioneers of the Plains, *reveal the nature of its potential to afford pupils the opportunity to make observations. (© Encyclopaedia Britannica Films, Inc.)*

Pasteur, the crew of the Nautilus, and the astronauts are examples of pioneers.

3. The pioneer has made an invaluable contribution to the growth and development of the United States by settling new territories, meeting the challenge of a new environment, and transmitting this knowledge to those who followed him.

4. The pioneer gave new zest to the spirit of democracy in the United States.

5. There were many dangers and hardships confronting the pioneer. He struggled against nature, other men, and his own personal weaknesses.

6. Geography and climate are important in determining the social and economic life of people. In the Plains region, one cannot earn his living by being a fisherman. The loneliness of the Plains made one appreciate his neighbors.

7. The sod hut was usually the first kind of home that a pioneer family of the plains had.

Media and Instructional Objectives

8. The seasons of the year are often important in determining the activities of man.
9. Many of the problems encountered by the pioneer are the same kinds of problems that people of all periods of history have met.
10. Men venture into the unknown for many reasons, including a desire for wealth, a desire for fame, a desire for freedom, a desire to spread religion, and a desire to seek adventure.

ABILITY TO:

1. Cooperate with others to achieve a common goal
2. Use the research method
3. Communicate ideas effectively.

ATTITUDE OF:

1. Desire to explore the unknown
2. Helpfulness
3. Perseverance
4. Criticalness.

APPRECIATION OF:

1. Courageous acts
2. Cooperation with others
3. Original thinking
4. Challenging problems
5. Good planning.

In analyzing the set of purposes in Example 1, you are urged to answer the following questions or make the suggested judgments:
1. How should the understandings in the list be taught to the learner? Memorized as such? Concluded after observation and based on data? Concluded as a result of problem-solving activity?
2. Identify in the list a definition and a broad generalization.
3. Are the statements sufficiently long to be clear in meaning? Are they stated in language pupils would use themselves in writing or answering an examination question or making a report?
4. Expand understanding number 4. Also expand number 7. Make the meaning clear.
5. What kinds of practice are implied in the stated abilities?
6. How would challenging and interesting problems help to develop some of the attitudes and appreciations?
7. Are the attitudes pervasive enough?
8. Are the appreciations specific? Which appreciation does not describe a behavior? Should a pupil *like and choose* problem-solving activity?

9. What vital facts, if any, have been omitted from the list of understandings?
10. Jot down a few acceptable additions to each category in the statement of purposes being sure to judge them in the light of the stated criteria.
11. Are you aware that this set of purposes was a part of a larger set of objectives for the whole teaching unit on the *Westward Movement*? Are not the purposes stated here those that the film and its related activities would help to accomplish?

Now let us turn to another statement of teaching purposes by a physical education teacher[5] which provides an opportunity for study of understandings that are directly related to a series of abilities, where the abilities would be developed through both physical and mental activity. In this instance, the teacher was planning the use of the film *Volleyball Techniques for Girls*.[6] After introductory activity and screening, the class was to engage in practice and developmental activity, and then be organized into teams for a "ladder" tournament and an intramural program. Her statement follows.

EXAMPLE 2

UNDERSTANDING THAT:
1. Volleyball is a team sport and is best played through cooperation and teamwork with other team members.
2. Good playing can only be achieved through the practice and utilization of basic skills.
3. To keep from holding the ball, only the fingertips should be used.
4. A vigorous arm extension and snapping of the wrist are necessary to give the ball proper direction.
5. The best way to gain control of a poor pass is to do a set-up to yourself.
6. The best defense for a spike is a block or underhand volley.
7. Players should watch the ball at all times and be in a good position to receive a pass.
8. The volleyball service is very important, as only the serving team can score points.
9. To perform a spike, the spiker must be able to leap high enough so that her hand is above the ball.

ABILITY TO:
Participate effectively in a game of volleyball, specifically to:
1. Serve
2. Pass accurately
3. Perform a spike
4. Work with other team members
5. Play own position.

[5] Janet L. Arnold, Willimantic, Connecticut Schools. By permission.
[6] Coronet Instructional Films.

Figure 2–7. Pictures revealing the nature of content in the film, Volleyball for Girls, *indicate the power of motion pictures to give directions for action, and, through stimulation of appropriate pupil responses, to contribute to development of desirable attitudes and appreciations. (Courtesy McGraw-Hill Films)*

ATTITUDE OF:

1. Cooperativeness
2. Alertness
3. Criticalness
4. Perseverance.

APPRECIATION OF:

1. Good timing sense
2. Good body control
3. Good sportsmanship
4. Vigorous physical activity.

Again as before, evaluate the specific statements in the preceding list to find out if they are stated in consistent form and satisfy the criteria, by answering the following questions or carrying out the suggested operations:

1. Check the Characteristics of Teaching Purposes section on page 50, item 1, under Understandings, and determine the nature of the understandings listed in Example 2. That is, how are the understandings related to the abilities?
2. Why are the attitudes and appreciations in this list appropriate?
3. Explain why the attitude of *perseverance* is valid for both fields of student activity, in the list for *Example 1* as well as in the list for *Example 2.*

Fundamentals of Teaching with Audiovisual Technology

Figure 2–8. This scene is from the film, Baby Animals. *What kinds of mental action in response to film content like this lead pupils to develop the behavior goals identified by the teacher? (Courtesy McGraw-Hill Films)*

4. Do you know anyone who lacks good body control? Good sportsmanship? Who abhors vigorous physical activity?
5. What do you believe the tournament and intramural participation organized by the teacher have to do with the purposes as stated?
6. Write out at least one of your own teaching purposes of each type, real or hypothetical, for your own teaching field, and check them against the list of Characteristics of Teaching Purposes.
7. Should not purposes like those stated by the teacher have been already formulated in the *Course of Study* for the physical education program? If they had been, would teacher planning be easier?

In Example 3 we shall see the efforts of a primary grade teacher[7] to identify valid teaching purposes. In this instance the teacher used the film *Baby Animals.*[8] Preceding the screening she discussed the children's past experiences with animals, and raised a series of questions to guide observation of the film. Afterward she set up a pet-care check list in a bulletin-board display, organized a cat and kittens in-class observation project that led to a language chart reading activity. Her statement of teaching purposes follows.

EXAMPLE 3

UNDERSTANDING THAT:

1. Some very young animals are different from their parents in appearance.
2. Many baby animals are helpless and require the care and training of their parents.

[7] Elizabeth G. Banks, Groton, Connecticut Schools. By permission.
[8] McGraw-Hill Book Company, Text-Film Department, New York, N.Y.

a. Some animals teach their young to swim, fly, climb, and so forth.

b. Some animals teach their young to be cautious, and protect them from danger.

c. Some animals teach their young to find food.

3. Food requirements vary for young animals.

a. Some animals eat food similar to that of their parents.

b. Some young animals require milk.

4. Different kinds of animals carry on different kinds of activity.

5. Different kinds of animals require different types of care.

ABILITY TO:

1. Read
2. Make simple generalizations
3. Keep simple but accurate records
4. Care for young animals.

ATTITUDE OF:

1. Kindness
2. Patience
3. Responsibility
4. Reliability and alertness in making observations.

APPRECIATION OF:

1. The loving care that animals give their young
2. Well-cared for pets.

Now again as in Examples 1 and 2 of statements of purpose, answer the following questions or make the suggested observations:

1. Note the completeness of the second and third understandings in the list, and the insights called for by items 1, 4, and 5.

2. What further conditions or qualifications are needed to clarify Ability 1 (Ability to read)?

3. What activity, pointed out in the introductory remarks immediately preceding the statement of purposes, was designed to develop Abilities 3 and 4?

4. How might this teacher have used this science unit in her reading ability development program?

5. Is it perhaps a technical error to double attitudes in item 4?

6. Is it entirely correct to refer to the *loving* care that animals give their young in the first appreciation in the list?

7. Suggest at least one new purpose of your own for this or any other teaching topic unit. Check yourself against the criteria.

8. Could teachers work together to prepare *curriculum guides?* Could sets of purposes and objectives be exchanged, and evaluated cooperatively?

The Behavioral Approach to Stating Instructional Objectives

Teaching purposes using words such as "understanding," "comprehension," "attitude," and "appreciation" point to noble aims, to be sure. But teaching purposes stated only in this form do not allow us to evaluate how well the student actually does learn, because the statement of purpose does not describe anything that is directly *observable* or *measurable*.

It is not enough for the teacher to believe that a student has achieved a certain aim. The emphasis must be on what the student can actually do. "Ability to . . ." is a good beginning, but when such a statement of purpose describes the expected *criterion performance* it becomes a measurable behavioral objective. For example, which of the following two statements is expressed in terms of observable student performance?

A. Ability to pronounce vowel sounds correctly.
B. Given a list of twenty common English words containing from one to three vowels each, the student will pronounce at least 18 of the words correctly.

Statement B is a behavioral objective because it tells what the student must do, describes the conditions under which he must demonstrate competency, and states the degree of perfection required. Let us examine three more pairs of statements, each pair containing both a cognitive teaching purpose and a behavioral objective covering the same basic idea, but providing an observable basis for evaluation. First, an "understanding":

C. Understanding that the number of members of the House of Representatives from each state is based upon population.
D. Given a population density map of the United States, the student will rank all fifty states in descending

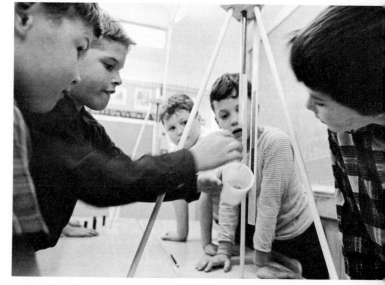

Figure 2–9. What are these boys learning by performing their own experiment? What would they learn if the teacher did the experiment and showed them the results? How does one state behavioral objectives for an experience such as this? What understandings, abilities, attitudes, and appreciations are being developed? (Courtesy The National Education Association. Photo by Ben Spiegel)

Media and Instructional Objectives

order, without error, according to the number of members of the House of Representatives from each state.

Notice that statement D not only describes the student activity required to demonstrate understanding of the concept of apportionment according to population, but also gives the student a chance to visualize U.S. population distribution through use of a map.

How can "attitude" be measured? Try these:

E. Attitude of cooperativeness.

F. Given an assignment to solve a measurement problem jointly with another student, the child will cooperate quietly and harmoniously with the other student to plan, then to accurately carry out the assigned task.

Because there is no way to see inside a student's brain, we can only deduce the existence of a certain mental set or predisposition by watching how he behaves in a prearranged situation. Although some subjective judgment is necessary on the part of the teacher (how do you measure "quietness" and "harmony"?), still statement F does give us something concrete to observe and compare.

"Appreciations" are nearly impossible to change into behavioral objectives unless you remember that *choice* or *discrimination* must always be involved. Consider these two statements:

G. Appreciation of good craftsmanship.

H. Given two wooden cabinets, one of good commercial furniture quality and the other of rough, amateur construction, the student will orally compare the two cabinets on the following points: beauty and functionality of design, choice of materials, accuracy of measurement, squareness, neatness, strength of joints, fit of doors and hinges, and quality of finish.

Statement H tells both teacher and student what is expected, so no one need be surprised when grading time comes around.

Perhaps you think that rigid, behavioral objectives stifle creativity. Not at all. Performance criteria don't have to be rigid unless they are interpreted that way by a teacher. The wise and clever teacher will always build-in ways for imaginative students to vary or expand any stated limits. In teaching poetry, for example, a teacher's goals may be stated as the following instructional purposes:

A. Understanding that haiku is a form of Japanese poetry consisting of three rhymeless lines of five, seven and five syllables, respectively, for a total of 17 syllables.

B. Ability to write an original haiku from an observed experience.

C. Attitude of creativeness (and so on)

Figure 2–10. The student worksheet is the heart of most self-instructional programs. But who determines the responses that are to be called for? Is the worksheet a drill? Is it a test? How useful would a list of behavioral objectives be as a guide for developing an instructional program or for evaluating commercial materials? (Photo by 3M/Wollensak)

D. Appreciation of imaginative use of words (and so on) Or the same teacher might specify his instructional objectives in a somewhat different manner: [9]

Purpose (or goal)

To engage students in a formal poetic exercise that will encourage brevity, relevance, and the use of words in fresh, new ways.

Criterion Performance (or objective)

Given any item of experience (music, literature, film, an observed event, a recollection), the student will make a personal response in the form of a haiku (17 syllables, 5–7–5, in three lines) of his own creation.

How would a teacher test for achievement of this objective? One interesting possibility is to present the student with a literal English translation of some Japanese haiku and ask him to write his own haiku based upon whatever this translation suggests to him.

Sample Test Situation

Here is the literal English translation of a Japanese haiku: Caged bird/butterflies envy/eye-expression.

Look at the words carefully. Then write a haiku of your own, capturing whatever meaning the literal translation suggests to you.

[9] Adapted from Thorwald Esbensen, *Working with Individualized Instruction* (Palo Alto: Fearon Publishers), 1968, p. 10. (*Note:* Fearon Publishers are now known as Fearon Publishers/Lear Siegler, Inc., Belmont, Calif.)

If you are wondering just what a student might do with this problem, here is what one ninth grade girl came up with:

> The caged yellow bird
> envies the spring butterflies'
> remorseless freedom.

Are behavioral objectives harder to write than general, cognitive, goals or teaching purposes? Of course. They are much harder to prepare because the writer has to *think!* The writer of behavioral objectives must put himself in the place of the learner. The learner wants to know where he is going and how he is going to know that he has arrived. How many teachers are able to *empathize* with the aims, aspirations, and frustrations of their students? Mastering the discipline of writing good behavioral objectives is a giant step along the road toward becoming an effective teacher. You will know you have come a long way down this hard road when you are able to resist the temptation to use audiovisual media as technological tinsel when such attractive toys are not closely tied to meaningful behavioral objectives. We don't want you to make this kind of mistake. The rest of this book is devoted to helping you plan for the most effective use of audiovisual technology.

Problems and Activities

1. Specify a subject area and grade level. List at least three *teaching purposes* of each category: understandings, abilities, attitudes, and appreciations, according to the Characteristics of Teaching Purposes in Chapter 2.

2. Convert your list of teaching purposes to *behavioral objectives*. Include conditions and performance criteria as demonstrated by the examples in Chapter 2.

3. Explain the difference between the terms, *outcomes, goals, purposes*, and *objectives* as used in education. Is it correct to use these terms interchangeably, as if their meanings were the same?

4. Differentiate between the *cognitive* and *affective* domains of instructional objectives as defined by Bloom and Krathwohl, et al, in the *Taxonomy of Educational Objectives, Handbooks I and II*. Compare this approach to the teaching purposes (cognitive) and behavioral objectives distinction made in Chapter 2 of this book.

5. Expand the concept of behavioral objectives to include *identifying, naming, describing, ordering*, and *constructing*, as suggested by Gerlach and Ely in *Teaching and Media, a Systematic Approach*. Compare this approach to the examples of teaching purposes and behavioral objectives included in Chapter 2 of this book.

6. Go through Mager's short programmed text, *Preparing Instructional Objectives*. Compare (or contrast) Mager's approach to the statement of objectives with other authors' approaches.

7. Respond to the following statement: "Behavioral objectives are de-humanizing. They pertain only to mechanical-type skills. Behavioral objectives stifle creativity because they imply to the student that there can be only one correct answer."

Selected References

Behavioral Objectives: A Guide for Individualizing Learning, Westinghouse Learning Corporation, 100 Park Ave., New York, N.Y. 10017, 1971. A four-volume set containing more than 4,000 objectives developed by a team of teachers involved in the development of Project PLAN, an extensive experiment in individualizing instruction.

BLOOM, B. S., M. D. ENGLEHART, E. H. FURST, W. H. HILL, and D. R. KRATHWOHL, (eds.) *Taxonomy of Educational Objectives, Handbook I: Cognitive Domain*. David McKay Co., Inc., 750 Third Ave., New York, N.Y. 10017, 1956. Describes a hierarchy of instructional goals applicable to the cognitive domain (understandings and abilities), providing definitions and sample test items for each level of the proposed hierarchy.

GRONLUND, NORMAN E., *Stating Behavioral Objectives for Classroom Instruction*. The Macmillan Co., 866 Third Ave., New York, N.Y. 10022, 1970, 58 pp. Emphasizes the distinction between *general* objectives (broad purposes or goals) and *specific* objectives which include measurable criteria of performance. Ties in conveniently with the Bloom and Krathwohl taxonomies.

Instructional Objectives Exchange Catalog. The Instructional Objectives Exchange, Box 24095, Los Angeles, Calif. 90024, revised periodically. Listing of tested objectives in many subject areas which have been obtained from various sources.

KRATHWOHL, D. R., B. S. BLOOM, and B. B. MASIA, *Taxonomy of Educational Objectives, Handbook II: Affective Domain*. David McKay Co., Inc., 750 Third Ave., New York, N.Y. 10017, 1956. Describes a hierarchy of educational goals applicable to the affective domain (attitudes and appreciations), providing definitions and sample test items for each level of the proposed hierarchy.

MAGER, ROBERT F., *Developing Attitude Toward Learning*. Fearon Publishers/Lear Siegler, Inc., 6 Davis Drive, Belmont, Calif. 94002, 1968, 104 pp. Shows how to send students away from instruction with at least as favorable an attitude toward the subject matter as they had when they started.

————. *Preparing Instructional Objectives*. Fearon Publishers/Lear Siegler, Inc., 6 Davis Drive, Belmont, Calif. 94002, 1962, 60 pp. This little programmed book makes it easy to understand why behavioral objectives are necessary and helps teachers to state objectives more clearly.

————, and KENNETH M. BEACH, JR. *Developing Vocational Instruction*. Fearon Publishers/Lear Siegler, Inc., 6 Davis Drive, Belmont, Calif. 94002, 1967, 83 pp. Identifies four functions of the teacher-manager: planning, organizing, leading, and controlling. Describes a systematic plan for organizing instruction of any kind, not only vocational.

————, and PETER PIPE. *Analyzing Performance Problems*. Fearon Publishers/Lear Siegler, Inc., 6 Davis Drive, Belmont, Calif. 94002, 1970, 112 pp. Aimed at industry, but equally applicable to education, this book suggests ways to identify and attack "performance" problems that arise because someone isn't doing what he is supposed to be doing or what you would like him to be doing.

MCASHAN, H. H. *Writing Behavioral Objectives*. Harper & Row, Publishers, Keystone Industrial Park, Scranton, Pa. 18512, 1970, 116 pp. Concise guide to the techniques of writing performance objectives for instruction.

POPHAM, W. JAMES, and EVA L. BAKER, *Establishing Instructional Goals*. Prentice-Hall, Inc., Englewood Cliffs, N.J. 07631, 1970, 130 pp. A programmed book which introduces behavioral objectives as one component of a four-step instructional system model.

3
A Systematic Approach to Media

Most organizations have a structure that was designed to solve problems that no longer exist.

—JOHN W. GARDNER

Even when we realize that audiovisual technology makes available a wide range of instructional choices at the curriculum planning level, we tend to shoehorn media, as Robert Heinich has suggested, into traditional patterns of organization. Heinich deplores the fact that "the implications of the shift in technological focus from classroom to curriculum planning—from tactics to strategy—are not at all well accepted, particularly as they affect roles of personnel, instructional management rearrangements, budgetary considerations, and research requirements."[1]

Teachers and administrators are still accustomed to making all media decisions in terms of presentational requirements of the classroom teacher. Curriculum revision frequently goes up to the point of specifying student behavioral objectives and then stops, without wrestling with these essential objectives or considering strategies for helping students reach them or evaluation instruments to measure their success. Instead, curriculum revision should follow *the systems approach*, an operational planning concept borrowed from the engineering sciences.

Defining a System In the first definition offered by *Webster's Seventh New Collegiate Dictionary*, a system is "a regularly interacting or independent group of items forming a unified whole." Therefore, an *audiovisual communication system* could be considered as an integrated collection of media and materials designed to get a definite message (with predicted results) across to an identified audience under specified conditions. *Webster's* also defines a system as "an organized or established procedure."

The employment of technology in any field eventually requires the systems approach to make it work efficiently. Charles F. Hoban and John K. Galbraith both have

[1] Robert Heinich, "What Is Instructional Technology?", *Audiovisual Instruction*, **13** (March 1968) 221.

Figure 3–1. Tapes, slides, and printed worksheets are the basic instructional resources for an audiovisual-tutorial course in Physical Geography. Educators developing a new course of this type logically would follow a version of the systematic approach described in this chapter. (Photo by David H. Curl)

something to say about the relationship between technology and the systems concept. Educational researcher Hoban speaks:

Technology is *not* just machines and men. It is a complex, integrated organization of men and machines, of ideas, of procedures, and of management. The introduction of this complex organization generates many systematic problems that can be and have been ignored or generally neglected in theory, research and practice in education. [2]

Economist Galbraith extends the definition:

Technology means the systematic application of scientific or other organized knowledge to practical tasks. Its most important consequence, at least for purposes of economics, is in forcing the division and subdivision of any such task into its component parts. Thus, and only thus, can organized knowledge be brought to bear on performance. [3]

Briefly, then, the systems approach is a *systematic attempt* to coordinate all aspects of a problem toward specific objectives. In education this means planned, organized use of all available learning resources, including audiovisual media, to achieve desirable learning objectives by the most efficient means practicable. The systems approach means focusing first upon the learner and the performance required of him and then, and only then, making decisions about course content, learning experiences, and the most effective media and instructional tactics.

[2] Charles F. Hoban, "From Theory to Policy Decisions," *AV Communication Review* **13** (Summer 1965), 124.
[3] John Kenneth Galbraith, *The New Industrial State* (Boston: Houghton Mifflin Company 1967), p. 12.

Figure 3–2. An instructional system *is in operation in this Botany laboratory at Purdue University. A key component of the system is the senior professor, Dr. S. N. Postlethwait (in photo at right). He, or an assistant, is available at all times for consultation with students both individually and in small seminars. Besides the instructor/programmer, what other system components can be identified? (Reprinted by permission of Audio-Tutorial Systems, Division of Burgess Publishing Company, Minneapolis, Minnesota)*

The learner always comes first. Even though we use words such as *technology, objectives, resources,* and *efficiency* in discussing media, we are *not,* as some people are quick to assume, trying to program the lives of individual students. What thoughtful educators are attempting to systematize and regulate are facts and facilities, artifacts and apparatus, specimens and situations. What the systems approach does for education is not to confine or control the student so much as to make it possible for him to explore man's knowledge more quickly and to discover, with somewhat less frustration and anxiety, what his own place might be in the general scheme of the universe. Buckminster Fuller, one of the most creative men of our time—designer-architect-scientist-philosopher—has written:

It is possible to design environments within which the child will be neither frustrated nor hurt, yet free to develop spontaneously and fully without trespassing on others. I have learned to undertake reform of the environment and not to try to reform

Figure 3–3. Most instructional systems are like icebergs—the manifestations meeting the eyes and ears of the learner are merely the surface. The learner himself is one key component of the system, but behind the screen and beneath the surface are the specialists and technicians who designed and produced the software and hardware, the planners and organizers whose efforts preceeded the physical work, and the concerned teacher who prescribes, monitors, and evaluates both the progress of each learner and the effectiveness of the instructional system itself. (Courtesy The National Education Association. Photo by Esther Bubley)

Man. *If we design the environment properly,* it will permit child and man to develop safely and to behave logically. [4]

In this same vein, Robert Gagné defines an educational system as "that arrangement of people and conditions which is needed to bring about the changes in the human individual, attributable to the process of learning, which transform him from a dependent child to a productive adult member of society." [5]

The systems concept obsoletes the once-familiar view of media as instructional "aids." There is no doubt that media alone can teach, when thoughtfully programmed and when presented to students in an environment of inquiry conducive to learning. Employed in this way, audiovisual media and devices may be considered as components of a larger instructional system, of which the learner himself is the key component. The teacher is another. Previous knowledge and experience which the learner already possesses will either help or hinder his learning. Other system components with which the learner will interact in mastering his new tasks are the programmers—people who prepared the instructional unit—and others on the teaching team: technicians, group leaders, counselors, subject-matter specialists, and fellow students. The "voice on the tape" or the "face on the film" is simply the programmer himself communicating or interacting with the learner through media. Such a person can be a teacher in as real a sense as a teacher who is physically present in the classroom.

Complex learning systems are composed of a series of distinct subsystems, each designed to guide learners through a sequence of learning experiences toward spe-

[4] R. Buckminster Fuller, "What I Have Learned," *Saturday Review* **XLIX** (November 12, 1966), 70.

[5] Robert M. Gagné, *The Conditions of Learning* (New York: Holt, Rinehart, and Winston, 1965), p. 240.

Figure 3–4. The learner himself is the key component of an instructional system. His teacher is another. Other system components with which each learner will interact, directly or indirectly, are people—programmers, subject experts, counselors, technicians, other students—as well as software, hardware, and facilities.

cific educational objectives. For example, a subsystem planned so that a student will learn to perform a certain chemical-testing procedure might consist of general coaching presented through headphones from a cassette tape recording, a visual demonstration from a single-concept film loop, samples of the actual chemicals and

Figure 3–5. A specially modified cassette tape recorder and a remote-control slide projector are linked with a "responder" device which re-starts the tape/slide program when the student presses the correct answer button, as well as providing a punched-card record of the student's responses. Would the contents of this carrel be termed an instructional system? A sub-system? (Courtesy Howe Folding Furniture, Inc.)

testing equipment for the learner's use, and a spiral-bound flipbook containing diagrams, analysis data, and space for the student to enter and compute the results obtained through his own experiments carried out in the Learning Center.

> The greatest problem of communication is the illusion that it has been achieved.
>
> —Joe Coffman

Learning is evidenced by some kind of behavioral change resulting from meaningful experience or from effective communication. But all too often teachers and other communicators *assume* that immediate or latent behavioral change will occur simply because they have broadcast The Message. Effective communication for any purpose requires careful planning and thoughtful selection of system components. We must start at the beginning, with the planning.

Planning a media presentation is much like writing a speech. One eloquent public speaker, former Vice-President Hubert Humphrey, says the necessary components to building a good speech are "a full understanding of the facts of the subject, thorough understanding of the particular audience, and a deep belief in what you are saying." Assuming knowledge of the subject and confidence about message content and objectives, an understanding of the audience begins by asking the old, familiar newspaperman's questions: "Who? What? Why? When? Where? and How?"

Whom is the message intended to reach? Who are the students in your class? What makes them tick? What

Systematic Communication

Figure 3–6. Audiovisual technology makes possible vital and realistic experiences like this driving simulator. In view of the relationship of automobiles to our economy, what contribution to the lives of present and future generations of people could result from intensive experience in off-the-road driving? Is this Aetna Drivotrainer an example of the multi-media approach in teaching? Is it an example of an instructional system? What system components can you identify? Traffic conditions and emergency situations are presented through motion pictures; as students react to the filmed stimuli by steering, braking, shifting, and accelerating, the evaluation unit records their responses and supplies the instructor with a print-out. Why should students be given immediate knowledge of the appropriateness of their own responses? (Courtesy Aetna Life Insurance Company)

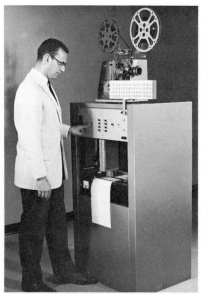

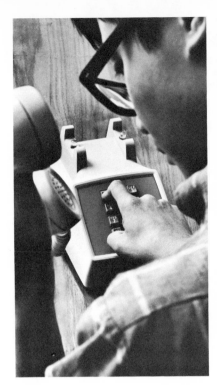

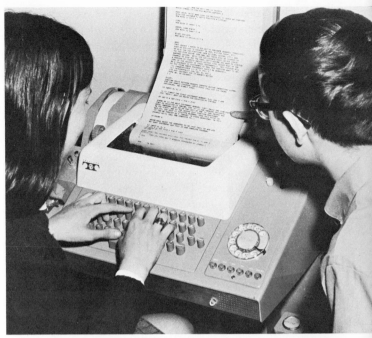

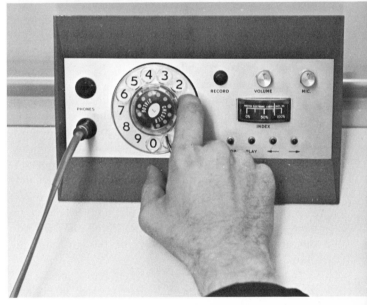

Figure 3–7. Access to information components of instructional systems may be by telephone-type dial or touch-tone panel, by computer terminal, or by such simple expedients as viewers, cassette playbacks, and printed materials. (Courtesy AT&T [ABOVE, LEFT & RIGHT]; and Western Michigan University [RIGHT])

turns them on? What do they have in common? How do they differ in sex, maturation, cultural background, economic level, and social status? What are their prevailing habits, attitudes and prejudices, drives, anxieties, and aspirations? How well developed are their perceptual skills? Have they experienced the subject matter in question? Will they understand the words and symbols, the jargon, the vocabulary, the language of your presentation?

What are learners in your group supposed to do, think or feel, after perceiving your message? Unless your audience is changed afterward in some way, you have failed as a communicator. Do you want students to visibly change their behavior, to change the method used in performing a task? To change the way they think about school, the subject matter, the community, their teacher, or one another? Do you hope they will change the way they feel about themselves and resolve insecurity about their own ability to discover, to learn, and to succeed? Will students be expected to demonstrate a new skill? To put together related bits of knowledge and experience to form new conclusions? To search for new information? To make a decision? To solve a real problem?

Why should students take time to watch, read, or listen to your message? What's in it for them? Their bodies may be captive in the classroom or study carrel, but what about their minds? Can you assume that each student in your class will know why he should pay attention? Does everyone realize how "important" your message is? Will everyone attach the same meaning and importance to your message as you do?

When will your message be received? During scheduled class time? On the students' own time? Is the time of day important—morning, after lunch, late afternoon, evening? Does this material belong at the beginning of a new unit of study or should it be a concluding activity? Or does it make any difference?

Where is the message going to be received? In a classroom? In the auditorium? In the library? In the lab or shop? At home? Will learners be alone, or will they be with peers, siblings, teachers, or parents? How much time is likely to be available? Will there be unique characteristics and distractions in the learning environment? What will the students be doing immediately before your presentation and what will follow?

Now that you have three planning elements in mind—subject, audience, and belief in the message—you can give some thought, finally, to the medium, the "how."

How can your message be gotten across most effectively? First of all, are you limited by lack of budget? Exactly how much money can you spend on this particular project? Will your choice of media be limited by financial considerations or by lack of time? By a shortage of commercial resources or equipment? By a lack of professional or technical help? What kinds of software can you expect to produce yourself or have produced locally? How can you measure success? What will be your criteria for evaluation?

Finally, after all this exhaustive thinking, the teacher-with-a-message is ready to start selecting system components—with a better-than-average chance for success in the great competition for students' attention, acceptance, and participation.

A System for Designing a System

Planning is the secret of systematizing or recombining ideas. Planning a system is simpler than it seems. It is helpful to begin by drawing a map—called a *flow diagram*—of the desired behavior or activity. Figure 3-8 compares two simplified flow diagrams depicting a possible relationship between students, media, and a teacher, in which students do some of their learning/interacting face-to-face with the teacher and some in direct *interface* with media. In a more extended example, Figure 3-9 shows in detail the path followed by a student in a self-instructional laboratory learning to operate a piece of audiovisual equipment. For examples of flow diagrams actually used by students as a part of an independently structured, self-directed science course, see Case Studies on "The Universe" and "The Moon" in Chapter 7 (Figures 7-12 and 7-24).

A flow diagram should indicate all major components of the system or learning process and show the paths and alternatives that may be followed by the learner as he proceeds through each step of the process. His interaction with human, media software, and hardware com-

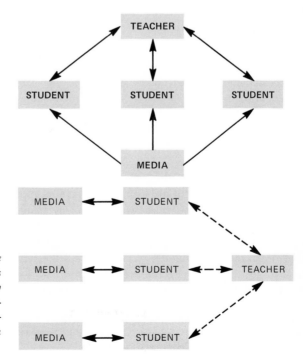

Figure 3–8. What assumptions are made in these diagrams about the relative roles of students, teachers, and media? How might these roles be changed if interaction arrows were added between students, and, in the top diagram, from students back to media?

A Systematic Approach to Media

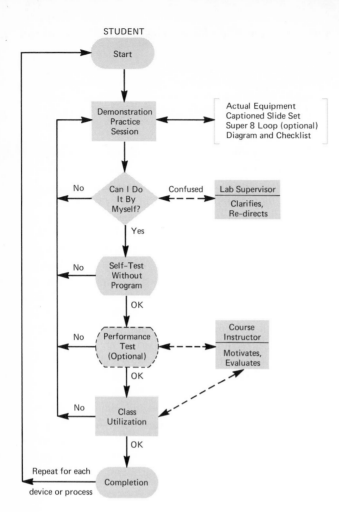

STUDENT

Figure 3–9. Flow diagram for self-instructional audiovisual equipment operation laboratory. Note opportunities for evaluation (feedback) by the student himself and by others.

ponents is shown, as are his points of decision and evaluation. A flow diagram is an abstract graphic model of a process. Such a model makes it easier to visualize the system at the planning or design stage, while changes may still be made easily with eraser and pencil.

An attempt by several media specialists to visualize the *process of instructional system-development* resulted in the models shown in Figure 3-10[6]. Notice that development proceeds in an unending cycle of design, construction, and evaluation, insuring that the system is kept in a constant state of modernization and improvement.

The systems-development "constellation" could be thought of as existing and operating within a "galaxy" of educational theory, principles, and research (Fig. 3-10 bottom, p. 75). Starting with the *subject or task analysis* component, each segment of the system represents an

[6] Adapted from the ideas of A. Abedor, D. Hessler, K. Dickie, J. Armstrong, A. Watson, M. Fenton, C. Krenek, P. Vaughan, J. McKittrick, J. Saper, and other media specialists.

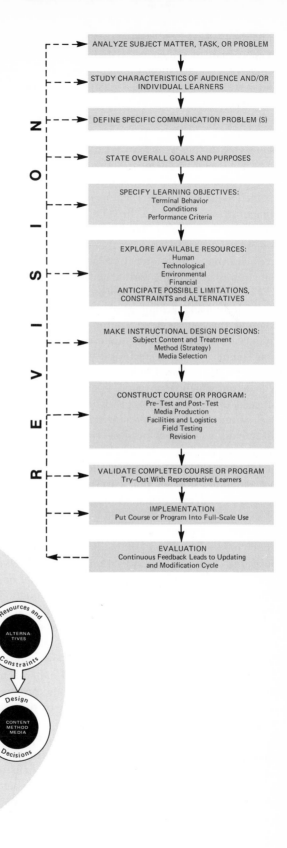

Figure 3–10. [RIGHT] *Flow diagram depicting a systematic process for development of a course, unit, instructional program, or presentation;* [BELOW] *The systems development process could be thought of as a "constellation" of analyses and activities existing and operating within a "galaxy" of educational theory, principles, and research.*

A Systematic Approach to Media

individual microcosm of parameters, decisions, and activities, each of which is related to the whole system through the "gravitational force" of continuing feedback and evaluation. Let us follow this process from its logical beginning.

Suppose you wish to develop a new course or instructional unit according to the systems concept. You would begin with a survey and analysis of the subject matter, task, or general problem, isolating at this stage the significant topics or skills to be dealt with, identifying the characteristics of potential learners, and defining specific communication problems. Broad statements of goals and instructional purposes would be the outcome of the subject-matter and learner analyses, with specific objectives, learning conditions, terminal behavior, and performance criteria being formulated next.

The logical following step would be an inventory of available human, technological, and financial resources; combine this with a consideration of limitations or constraints likely to be placed upon the project by lack of time, money, facilities, technical assistance, or administrative support. Based upon a realistic picture of the climate in which you could operate, you might then proceed to the actual design of the course or program itself. Course design would include decisions, based on objectives, concerning subject content and treatment, strategy or method to be employed, and, finally, choice of specific media deemed most effective and efficient for programming, storage, and retrieval by the learner of information and experience leading to attainment of the objectives.

Course construction and software production can begin upon completion of content, method, and media strategy decisions. Individual teachers often must themselves follow through on each phase of the instructional development process; but when the services of a production team are available, it is at the course-construction stage that programmers, graphic artists, photographers, and evaluation specialists work hand-in-hand with subject-matter specialists and instructional development coordinators to produce actual modular or packaged units of instruction. During the production process, some revision may be required necessitating brief recycling to the previous stage of design decision.

Field testing and *validation* provide opportunities to try out newly developed instructional units with a representative sampling of students. Early field testing may involve very pragmatic trial-and-error "debugging" methods—the programmer or instructor observing each student carefully as the student works through the program, the observer taking note of every error, hesitation, and question. Probably some students will encounter unforeseen difficulties: the course may be too long or too lean (not enough cues or prompts), student performance scores may be too low, or there may be too broad a range of scores. (Why should a "normal curve" be used as an evaluative scale? Should not the object of instruction be competence for *all* students?)

Implementation is the final step of putting the validated (and revised and re-validated) program or course into full-scale operation, although continuous feedback should be obtained from learners which will lead eventually to a cycle of updating and modification.

Instructional Kits

With increasing frequency, kits or packages of material on diverse topics, ranging from *Adventures With Sound* to *Sex and Family Living*, are appearing. Some are designed especially for so-called "slow learners" or for the "culturally disadvantaged" and combine appealing and easy-to-read paperback books with "discovery" and discussion guides and graphically interesting audiovisual materials on current topics such as *Law and Order, Family Life, Drugs and Other Social Problems,* and *Drag Racing.*

Kits usually contain a variety of systematically related materials which may include motion pictures or film loops; slide sets or filmstrips; disc recordings or cassette tapes; large prints and posters; specimens and models (either assembled or unassembled); apparatus such as meters, scales, and simple instruments; and guide sheets or booklets for teachers and students. Two staff members of the Los Angeles City Schools said the following about instructional kits:

Figure 3–11. Why are "multi-media" instructional kits becoming so popular—is it because they can be produced and marketed in a relatively short time in order to capitalize on current topics of interest? Do such kits often lend themselves well to individualized instruction? (Courtesy McGraw-Hill Book Company)

The enthusiastic acceptance of this type of audiovisual resource in Los Angeles can be attributed to several advantages. A thoughtfully prepared kit offers a variety of useful materials to strengthen and supplement a specific area of study; it is a package of related materials organized to simplify procurement; it provides sequential materials geared directly to curricular need; it offers a collection of ready made lessons for inexperienced teachers and flexible resource materials for experienced inventive teachers. [7]

Good kits really are packaged mini-systems. Beginning teachers usually find that modifying and improving upon an existing instructional kit is less time consuming than developing an entire individualized instructional unit from scratch. Unless you are lucky enough to find commercial materials that meet exactly the objectives of your students, the rule should be "*Adapt,* don't *adopt!*" The fact that commercial media kits may be available never relieves a teacher from the responsibility for specifying meaningful objectives first, before deciding to use a certain kit or any other components of any instructional

Figure 3–12. This instructional kit on Mexico contains filmstrips, recordings, study prints, posters, pamphlets, objects, models, artifacts, and reference guides. Should this kit be kept in the classroom or in the resource center? How can teachers and librarians arrange for students to have maximum access to these materials? (Courtesy International Communications Foundation)

[7] Patsy Seely and Gene White, "The Audiovisual Kit," *Audiovisual Instruction* **6:** 9 (November, 1961), 440.

system. It may seem expedient to build a unit around whatever media are available, but resist this temptation. It is the lazy way out. And most of the students will realize what you have done.

Edgar Dale reminds us, "Some educators discuss instructional technology as though there were a real choice as to whether we should introduce it in schools and colleges. There is no such choice. It is already there in greater or lesser degree. Our only choice is whether we use educational technology wisely and purposefully or whether we use it reluctantly, ineptly, purposelessly." [8]

All audiovisual media require conscious, planned, *systematic* effort for maximum impact. Although media may present information and experiences to students whether or not the teacher is physically present, media left on the shelf do not teach. Creative, aware, sensitive human beings must arrange for interaction between learners and media in optimum settings, whether the teacher employs traditional and comfortable presentation methods, or dares to experiment with more complex and innovative approaches to media systems described in this and subsequent chapters.

Problems and Activities

1. List the components of an instructional system that you might design for the subject matter and grade level that you teach or expect to teach.

2. Examine Figure 3–9. Draw a flow diagram showing the paths to be followed by a learner interacting with the instructional system you have outlined in Problem 1.

3. Examine Figures 3–8a and 3–8b. What assumptions are made in these diagrams about the relative roles of students, teachers, and media? Explain how these roles might be changed if interaction arrows were added in Figure 3–8a from students back to media.

4. Play the game of I D (Instructional Development) with some other members of the class. Discuss parallels between the game, which is based on the system model shown in Figures 3–10a and 3–10b, and the actual process of preparing for a unit of instruction using media.

5. Examine several multi-media instructional kits. Select a kit that you feel would be effective as a self-contained unit. State behavioral objectives and prepare a system model (schematic or flow-diagram) based upon use of this kit as a subsystem or "mini-system".

Selected References

Designing Effective Instruction (set of 12 filmstrips with tapes and guides), (General Programmed Teaching, P. O. Box 402,

[8] Edgar Dale, *Audiovisual Methods in Teaching* 3d ed. (New York: Holt, Rinehart and Winston, 1969), p. 612.

Palo Alto, Calif. 94302, 1969. Intended to be used as a complete workshop or course, these materials cover behavioral objectives, criterion tests, content analysis, and validation of instructional materials.

Effective Visual Presentations (2 × 2-inch slides with tape and 16mm film clip, 35 min) Eastman Kodak Company, Rochester, N.Y. 14650, 1970. Describes methods for audience analysis and planning, production, and presentation of visualized material. Stresses that a good visualized presentation is not merely a speech with visuals added, but rather a completely developed communication package with pictures and narration working together for maximum audience impact.

GERLACH, VERNON S. and DONALD P. ELY. *Teaching and Media: A Systematic Approach.* Prentice-Hall, Inc., Englewood Cliffs, N.J. 07632, 1971, 395 pp. Rigorous approach to specification of instructional objectives and development of instructional materials for different teaching strategies and learning environments. "Media Facts" are dealt with in a concluding chapter.

KEMP, JERROLD E. *Instructional Design—A Plan for Unit and Course Development.* Fearon Publishers/Lear Siegler, Inc., 6 Davis Drive, Belmont, Calif. 94002, 1971, 130 pp. Offers a plan that can be employed by a single teacher or a team to develop or revise a curriculum or a course of study. Gives examples of how to proceed based on the author's schematic model of the instructional development process.

4
Nonprojected Visual Media

Every child should have mud pies, grasshoppers, waterbugs, tadpoles, frogs, mud turtles, elderberries, wild strawberries, acorns, chestnuts, trees to climb, brooks to wade in, water-lilies, woodchucks, bats, bees, butterflies, various animals to pet, hayfields, pine cones, rocks to roll, sand, snakes, huckle-berries and hornets; and any child who has been deprived of these has been deprived of the best part of his education.

—Luther Burbank

We have seen that communication is a two-way process. The teacher, as communicator, must change ideas into messages that can be seen or heard or sensed by each student in his own characteristic way. These messages must be passed on as stimuli by some tangible method or medium to the learner, who must show that he received the message and indicate by his actions how much he understood. This chapter describes various kinds of nonprojected media and offers specific suggestions for their use. There are as many novel and intriguing ways for applying media to instruction as there are creative teachers. But do not be tempted to use media for their own sake. Technology is not a crutch. If what you are presenting is not worth teaching, all the glamorous audio-visual methods in the world will not make school worth your students' time—or your own. Never forget that you are teaching *students*—not just *subject matter!*

Books and Printed Materials

The textbook is the educational medium known best to all of us, but books were not always so popular. Socrates refused to acknowledge the written word and refused to learn to read. The first textbooks were "visual aids" supplementing oral instruction. Everyone who learned to read could receive the same instruction. When printing was invented, certain philosophers of that time warned that the printing press was an instrument of the Devil— that man's mind and memory would shrivel from disuse if knowledge were to be preserved on paper. Despite these warnings, teachers have for centuries revered the printed page, forcing pupils to memorize and recite material without meaning in the name of "preserving our cultural heritage and disciplining the mind." No, the Devil's work lay not in the invention of print, but in

Figure 4–1. Classical and contemporary literature is more accessible to students in the form of paperbook books. Paperbacks are less costly; they can be carried and read anywhere. Is there logic to the analogy that "cassette tapes and super-8 films are the "paperbacks" of audiovisual media?" (Courtesy of EDL/McGraw-Hill, Huntington, New York)

misguided regard for verbalism by those to whom the printed word became an end in itself, instead of a means for clearer communication.

Not all educators fell into the verbal trap. In 1658, John Comenius (1592–1670) prepared the first school picture book. He wanted more pictures, but photography was not to be invented for another 200 years. Johann Pestalozzi (1746–1827) said, "Realities come first in learning." He wanted active learner participation. Friedrich Froebel (1782–1852) held that "All education should be pleasurable. . . . In education there should be no break between thought and action." Horace Mann (1796–1849) predicted "Some simple apparatus employing the eye, more than the ear will be found. . . . Real instruction will replace the mere hearing of lessons." John Dewey (1859–1952) asked for "definite, vivid, growing images," asserting that education would be infinitely easier and better "if nine tenths of the energy . . . directed toward making the child learn certain things were spent in seeing to it that the child was forming proper images." Surely these prophetic men foresaw the future world of audiovisual media!

But back to the books. Written language, perhaps, was man's greatest invention. Books are superbly compact, economical, and practical devices for storing and retrieving information. You can skim a book. You can make notes in the margins (if you own the book!). You can easily put a book down, mark your place, and pick it up again later—or go back and review what you read. Local duplication of printed instructional materials is a simple and familiar daily task in every school equipped with a spirit duplicator, mimeograph machine, or small offset press. Books of all kinds can be extremely valuable instructional media. So can pamphlets and microforms. But students ought to have as easy access to other media as to books.

Words and pictures usually complement one another, together clarifying abstract concepts far better than either medium alone. Well-written words may stimulate a reader's imagination in a wonderful way. But, on the other hand, seeing a good film may awaken a student's interest to the point that he will be eager to read the book! Not surprisingly, increased circulation of both fiction and nonfiction books has been reported by librarians in schools in which nonprint media are readily accessible to both teachers and students.

Most criticism of textbooks is aimed at their frequently poor design and improper use. Some texts, unfortunately, are not exciting to read. They are inadequately or irrelevantly illustrated, and they are rigidly organized sequentially or topically, lending themselves too easily to assignment and memorization of details without understanding. According to Edgar Dale, "The textbook skims over the surface of many ideas . . . it covers the ground but does not *uncover* it." [1] The textbook often tells the reader

[1] Edgar Dale, *Audiovisual Methods in Teaching*, 3d ed. (New York: Holt, Rinehart and Winston, Inc.), 1969, p. 668.

Figure 4–2. Programmed textbooks are vastly different from conventional textbooks in the manner of presenting information and in the kind of control they exercise over the responses of the learner. Programmed textbooks are in a sense a kind of teaching machine without hardware. (Courtesy Board of Education, Westport, Conn., and George E. Ingham)

much more about a subject than he wants to know. Textbooks lend themselves to lock-step teaching methods. Teachers assume that most of the content of the course is included in the book and that all students can read and understand it at the same rate. Textbooks usually give the answers before the student asks the questions. That is why they seem so dull. Because of the unimaginative way they are assigned and read, textbooks often fail to stimulate inquiry, discovery, and

CORONET LEARNING PROGRAMS
Latitude and Longitude

programmed by Learning Incorporated for Coronet Instructional Films

Figure 4–3. Programmed learning sequences may be short or long; they may employ several media components, or they may be contained in a single printed booklet. Programs can represent an entire unit or portion of a course, or merely a subsidiary concept or process within a unit. Programmed books such as this Coronet Learning Program *on the topic of* Latitude and Longitude *may be worked on during scheduled independent study times or assigned as supplementary homework. (Courtesy Coronet Instructional Films)*

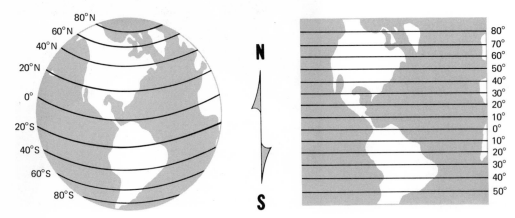

Fundamentals of Teaching with Audiovisual Technology

problem solving. Because the process of publication takes so long, textbooks frequently are out of date.

William Stonebarger urges that learning be arranged in *bite-size* increments:[2]

> If you want a child to eat a lot, give him very small portions. Then he will ask for seconds and maybe thirds, and proudly. If you heap his plate with food the first time, he will take a long look and it will seem too impossible. He will eat only a very little and feel defeated.
>
> So with information. Textbooks are too big . . . full of undigested and undigestible matter so far as the child is concerned, enough to make him sick (and defeated).
>
> Solution? Go with short books, booklets, articles, programs, films, tapes, whatever—but keep them short and one at a time. Then, who knows, he may ask for seconds.

The authors hope this textbook will not be our readers' only source of inspiration and information about media. We hope instructors assigning this book will also make available a wide array of timely, relevant, and practical audiovisual tools with which to involve young teachers in this fascinating field.

[2] C. William Stonebarger, *Finding a Way to be a Human* (Unpublished manuscript), 1970.

Figure 4–4. What can children learn from manipulating real objects and materials and from constructing models and mock-ups from real components? In what ways can media help learners to find and to solve real problems? What is meant by problem-based *use of media? (See examples in Chapters 2, 6, and 7). (Photo by David H. Curl)*

Nonprojected Visual Media

Everywhere in our environment real things become sources of content and serve as stimulators for learning when they are studied, handled, tasted, and manipulated. The real things we speak of may include such diverse objects as an Indian arrowhead, a fragment of moon rock, the Constitution of the United States, a pig fetus, a live salamander, or the president of the Board of Education. We therefore readily identify as instructional materials all kinds of specimens, both animate and inanimate—equipment, buildings and construction sites; every business concern and government agency; every bee and bird's nest; every stream, tree, rock, and mountain; every ship, plane and spacecraft; every plant and animal; every fossil and every bone.

We must learn to select and use these real things in unique ways. Teachers should provide chances for pupils to have intimate contact with some of the objects brought in for study; for example, breaking a crystal of Galena or Calcite, or holding for a guarded instant a piece of dry ice. Some real things, of course, are so valuable or so fragile that they must be viewed under glass or locked in display cases. But detailed observation should be conducted at close range whenever possible. The field trip is a practical way of arranging for an entire class to observe real things, but because of travel and time limitations, such objects are often brought to school for prolonged study. In classrooms we put some items in exhibit cases; others we suspend by wire or arrange on tables and shelves for students to hold, feel, and examine. Some real things are experimented with and apparatus

Figure 4–5. Does actual, hands-on participation increase the learning from field trips? Is it sometimes possible for teachers to arrange for real or very realistic field trip experiences for their students? Can teachers allow individual students or committees to arrange for out-of-school participation in worthwhile activities which interest them? (Courtesy Coronet Instructional Films)

Figure 4–6. Is a museum exhibit sometimes a better learning resource than "the real thing?" Some teachers and school administrators consider field trips a waste of time and money. What must a teacher do to ensure that students learn more from a field trip to the museum than the locations of rest rooms, soft-drink coolers, and souvenir counters? (Courtesy The National Education Association. Photo by Joe Di Dio)

used to demonstrate their properties. Students discover still more about the real things they see and touch, by reading about them in text and reference books, by viewing films and filmstrips, and by interviewing experts. By questioning and directing, teachers can help students draw significant conclusions about such objects.

The use of real things as a basis for observation in the classroom makes possible an accuracy of impression and concept that other materials cannot match. But the limitations in their use are obvious. First, it is difficult to arrange for simultaneous observation by everyone, especially when small objects are to be handled or experimented with. Second, most things students would like to study cannot actually be brought into the classroom, nor are teachers usually permitted to reorganize classroom schedules extensively enough to permit a great deal of out-of-school activity.

Field Trips   Field trips certainly provide the most realistic means for studying real things and real processes and for meeting real people in their actual environments, but field trips require careful planning. Teachers and students should have specific objectives in mind, each stop or activity on the trip providing opportunity to gather data for a significant problem agreed upon by everyone. A strong problem base is important because the nature of the problem should dictate certain kinds of advance planning, determine the nature of observation, inquiry, and documentation activities students should carry out during the trip, and then provide a basis for follow-through activ-

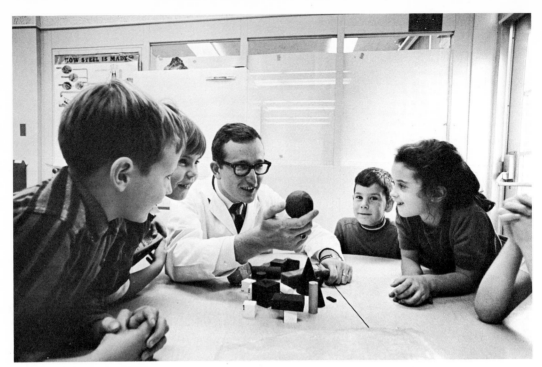

Figure 4–7. By manipulating miniature models, students learn to generalize concepts of shape and form within larger real-world objects. Should teachers merely show and describe such objects? How can students demonstrate understanding of geometric concepts? (Courtesy The National Education Association. Photo by Ben Spiegel)

Specific Teaching Practices

ity after the trip is over. Those teachers who are naive enough to herd students onto buses and start off on a *lark* are advised to carry an extra supply of aspirin and tranquilizers. But an expertly organized and carefully arranged field trip that is based on a relevant problem to be solved is very likely to be an extremely rewarding experience for the students and for their teacher.

The following suggestions are offered to help you arrange for a worthwhile field trip:

1. Set up with the students a vital problem, either constructional or investigative in nature, and then plan the trip as a means of obtaining information for solving the problem. Analyze the problem with the students and guide them in getting needed facts by actual on-the-spot observation.

2. Involve students in all aspects of planning for the trip. Make advance arrangements for travel and appointments, food and lodging, financing, clothing needs, cameras and film, portable tape recorders, and so forth.

3. Use school buses or public transportation whenever possible. Some schools permit private cars to be driven on field trips, but be sure to clear this in writing and find out about liability insurance.

4. Inquire about local precedents and regulations governing field trips and find out who is responsible in case of an accident. If in doubt about policies,

obtain a written letter of authorization from the board of education through your principal.

5. Ask parents to sign permission slips as a matter of information and good school-home relations. Such permissions do not release the school or an individual teacher from liability, however, in event of carelessness or negligence.

Models and Mock-ups

Although it is valuable to observe real things in their actual environments, the difficulties for formal study are often insurmountable. It is then that teachers turn to representations of real things by obtaining or making models and mock-ups of them. Mock-ups are differentiated from models by their usually larger size and by their moving and operating parts; for example, a full-size replica of a lunar landing module into which children can climb and manipulate controls, or a wooden cut-away model showing the working parts of an electric motor. Apparatus setups used at all levels, especially in science, are often the counterparts of natural objects or of industrial machinery and components.

In a somewhat extended meaning a model post office, store, or bank may be organized and operated in a classroom; pupils may themselves become "models" of people

Figure 4–8. Someday these two boys may become real astronauts; meanwhile this experience gives them some of the feelings of orbiting the earth. The spacecraft mock-up in which they are "riding" has some attributes of a mission simulator—while the nose of the mock-up rocks up and down, its young passengers hear a countdown and then see, on a screen before them, a film of the earth 100 miles below. How does a mock-up differ from a model? How realistic must a simulator be? What kinds of simulated experiences might be provided in a school? (Courtesy NASA)

Nonprojected Visual Media

Figure 4–9. Models often are good substitutes for reality. But how should they be used? Are there times when it might be appropriate for a teacher to hold a model up in front of the class and describe it? How can opportunities for guided study of models be organized? (Courtesy La Mesa-Spring Valley School District, La Mesa, Calif.)

in dramatic portrayals or they may use dolls or puppets as they engage in role-playing situations or re-enact historic events. Students at all grade levels can make models as absorbing learning activities, ranging from a snap-together plastic spacecraft to a complex mathematical or molecular structure. Biology teachers use not only preserved specimens as examples of real things but also life-size models or enlarged, take-apart anatomical models. Well-developed media resource centers and public museums provide professionally made exhibits and dioramas, many of which are portable so that they may be loaned to teachers and students. Students who build their own models and displays develop pride in craftsmanship and can learn much more than facts about the subject matter.

Models offer a kind of short cut or substitute for the

Figure 4–10. Models may be made by students as significant learning activities; see Role Number Six, Chapter 1. How much information is needed before accurate models can be constructed or created? (Photo by Harry H. Haworth, Altadena, Calif.)

Figure 4-11. Are puppets considered audiovisual media? Is it important that students participate in a puppet play? How might the teacher arrange for involvement by the entire group? (Courtesy American Guidance Service, Inc.)

study of real things, and sometimes models can be even more effective than reality. Aside from the fact that students cannot always actually visit a glacial valley, or travel by chariot to the Roman Forum, models may clearly show the most important and memorable features. Indeed, photographs of the Earth taken from space, together with relief maps and globes may be far more effective in developing concepts of physical geography

Figure 4-12. The use of models may become a part of other learning activities, as, for example, the project globe in this classroom situation. A globe may, of course, be considered as a model of the Earth. (Courtesy A. J. Nystrom & Co.)

Nonprojected Visual Media

Figure 4–13. Maps and globes are among the most familiar reference and research tools. Under what conditions should students be encouraged to work together with such resources? Cooperation is necessary when students are working as a committee, but what if students are pursuing related topics according to individual contracts or study plans? (Courtesy The National Education Association. Photo by Ben Spiegel)

than an actual trip around the world. Models and mock-ups can be rich sources of experience for students, but not unless teachers arrange for them to be seen, used, and constructed as meaningful problem-solving activities.

Teachers need to judge the amount and kind of direct experience with real things that is needed before abstract concepts and symbols can be comprehended and retained. Another way of saying this is that teachers must never forget that untrained eyes, ears, and memories cannot fill in the missing information that adults assume "every-one knows." Although models and apparatus may be far more effective in promoting understanding than words alone, teachers need to recognize and overcome certain problems and pitfalls inherent in their use.

The following ideas will help students to receive the most value from experiences with models:

Specific Teaching Practices

1. Clarify misconceptions that may occur because of in-consistent scale, color, and shape of various models.
2. Make arrangements so that models may be clearly seen and identified. Use large labels where necessary.
3. Ask students to predict happenings or changes that are to take place. This heightens attention, observa-tion, inference, and response.
4. Arrange models and apparatus with suitable labels and work-sheets with questions for observation by individual students. Make assignments that call for problem solving based on what is observed.
5. Remember when giving demonstrations that students may see right- and left-hand positions as reversed. This may confuse the students. Whenever hand

positions are important, demonstrate processes and operations from a subjective position (over-the-shoulder view) and be sure to point out the importance of hand positions and movements.

6. Ask students to explain differences between models and apparatus and the real things they represent. When real objects are observed, check accuracy of students' concepts about the real-life setting for the objects.

7. Pre-plan demonstrations using models, objects, and apparatus. List the items needed and outline the procedure beforehand. Rehearse the experiment or demonstration and try to anticipate any difficulties students may have in observing or understanding.

8. Outline the main points of a procedure for the students. Use slides, charts, or closed circuit television to show close-up views of complex processes.

9. Stimulate students to ask questions immediately and share their inferences and conclusions with one another.

Simulation and Games

Simulation means realistic imitation. To young children, a model "store" made from an empty refrigerator carton can be the scene of some very realistic role-playing. The large cardboard carton is, to them, a *simulated* store. In buying and selling "merchandise," they are participating in *social simulation* of real-world roles and situations. A more advanced form of simulation occurs in certain types of driver training simulators in which each student

Figure 4–14. An episode from CON-FRONTATION, a human relations training unit simulation game for teachers and administrators in a multi-ethnic high school. Developed by the Far West Laboratory for Educational Research and Development. Distributed by the Anti-Defamation League of B'nai B'rith. How realistic can simulated experiences be? Will students viewing short, filmed incidents react as though they had actually been present? What inferences or conclusions might be drawn by students? What kinds of follow-up activities are essential for behavioral or attitudinal change? (Courtesy Anti-Defamation League of B'nai B'rith)

Nonprojected Visual Media

sits behind the wheel of a realistic automobile driver's seat mock-up and reacts by turning the wheel or stepping on the brakes as he views motion pictures of traffic incidents and potential emergencies. Other very sophisticated simulation experiences help pilots and astronauts learn to fly. Robert Gagné describes an aircraft flight simulator in the following passage:

Seated in a covered cockpit, the operator of such a device carries out nearly all of the activities required in a real airplane. He makes preflight checks, starts the engines, goes through a typical take-off procedure, flies a prescribed mission, contends on the way with various weather and emergency conditions, and carries out the activities involved in landing. During all this time, he observes instruments and operates controls which simulate those of the real airplane with a high degree of precision; even the movement of the cockpit and the noise of the engines may be simulated in a highly realistic manner. [3]

Astronauts train for space exploration in simulators that reproduce all aspects of a real mission, including the feel of weightlessness and the anxiety of emergency procedures. Medical students practice anaesthesia on a computer-controlled robot that looks, feels, and reacts like a real patient undergoing surgery. Even though many simulators are fantastically expensive, they can reduce training time in critical skills from years or months, in some cases, to a matter of days or hours.

[3] Robert Glaser (ed.), *Training Research and Education* (Pittsburgh: University of Pittsburgh Press, 1962), pp. 223–224.

Figure 4–15. A simulated school bus on the stage of the school auditorium. Do the participants seem to be enjoying this experience? Is the audience enjoying it? What kinds of learning may be taking place? In what ways might a good-natured dramatization such as this one be more effective than a lecture or panel discussion on the topic of school bus behavior and safety? (From the film School Bus Safety: With Strings Attached. Courtesy Journal Films, Inc.)*

Figure 4–16. A bargaining session in NAPOLI, a game about national politics, developed by Western Behavioral Sciences Institute and published by Simile II, LaJolla, Calif. Although the billions of dollars at stake are imaginary money, the issues are genuine. Students make real plans, decisions, compromises, and must defend their points of view. As in real politics, successful participants must think before acting and they must become good listeners and persuasive communicators. (Courtesy Simile II)

Of what use is simulation in everyday classroom work? Contrived, vicarious experiences actually can help teachers improve learning through each of the seven roles of audiovisual technology outlined in Chapter 1. Perhaps the most obvious uses for simulation are in *extending human experience* (Role One) and *stimulating interest* (Role Two—the "springboard" role).

Organized social simulation is called *gaming.* An educational game is actually a model of a real process or situation. In a historical game, for example, the basic data would be factual, and the roles based upon real biographical material, but players would be free to "be themselves" as they play their roles, placing their own personalities in historical context and perhaps altering somewhat the true course of events and outcomes as they are recorded in history books. Barbara Bock describes such a game:

Empire is a game for junior high school history students that simulates the mercantile conflict between England and the American colonies just before the American Revolution. Students take the roles of New England merchants, London merchants, Southern planters, colonial farmers, West Indian planters, European merchants, and the Royal Navy. They exchange the commodities of the period which are produced by the various colony teams and consumed by other teams. The Navigation Acts are more and more strongly enforced by the British Navy, arousing the colonists' ire and forcing them to conspire for increased smuggling activities. This gradually leads to a great sense of alienation between the players who are the American colonists and the players who are the London merchants. [4]

[4] Barbara Bock, "Games as Teaching Tools," *Educate* 1 (September 1968), 28.

Figure 4–17. Are boys ever as interested as girls in playing "dolls" or playing "family?" Are kits available that depict other than white, middle-class families? Could such materials be created by students? What values might derive from "family" and "community" games centered around ethnic and minority cultures? (Courtesy Westinghouse Learning Corporation)

Strategic games of reality challenge the cleverest students because there is no single "right" outcome or any one best strategy. The bright player's intuition and insight are frequently rewarded. Good educational games emphasize thinking and planning instead of memorization.

Learners who are slow in grasping concepts through print understand games and often develop self-confidence through role-playing. Students are motivated to read the little reading material that is required. Boys declared functionally illiterate managed to communicate by written notes in a game situation that called for that form of communication between players. [5]

Simulation and educational games are models of reality. They can be intensely vivid and absorbing experiences for students and should be considered as such by teachers.

Specific Teaching Practices

1. Involve students in preplanning for the activity. Students should choose their own roles in games and exchange roles and points of view as frequently as possible.
2. Provide resources for essential background material. Students must have access to facts upon which to base decisions they will make.
3. Allow enough time. Many games require several class periods to complete.
4. Set aside space so that game materials may be left intact between sessions.
5. Give students enough follow-up time to discuss thoroughly their reactions to the game and draw parallels between their own decisions and game outcomes and those of the "real world."

[5] Ibid., 30.

Graphic Symbols

Models and simulations usually are made to be as realistic as possible; but maps, graphs, cartoons, diagrams, and charts are intentional abstractions of reality. Students need to learn how to perceive visual, or graphic symbols in terms of the real things and ideas they represent.

Teachers sometimes falsely assume that students understand symbols because they may have experienced the real thing. Some symbols look like the reality they are supposed to represent. International road signs are a good example. Nearly everyone can interpret them because these simplified pictures are easily recognizable to those who might be unable to read words describing the road conditions, objects, or services depicted. On the other hand, students may not have had enough experience to figure out the meanings of certain arbitrary lines, colors, and symbols that appear on maps, charts, and graphs. Both teachers and students can sharpen their communication skills through the challenge of devising and preparing their own graphic materials. Such activity can be as much a thrill as creating a "secret" code or learning to speak a foreign language.

Excellent maps, charts, and diagrams are available from commercial sources, but they tend to be costly, too small, and often contain too much detail for classroom use. Individuals and small groups may use such materials for reference, or teachers and students can prepare further abstractions—simplified versions which may be projected with opaque, overhead, or slide projectors or duplicated and inserted into reports and notebooks.

Figure 4–18. Whatever his native language, nearly everyone understands most international road signs because they look like what they represent. Are symbols used on maps, charts, and graphs always as easily recognized and understood?

OPENING BRIDGE	DANGEROUS HILL	ROAD NARROWS	TRAFFIC CIRCLE	DIRECTION TO FOLLOW	NO LEFT (RIGHT) TURN
MEN WORKING	SLIPPERY ROAD	PEDESTRIAN CROSSING	STOP AT INTERSECTION	COMPULSORY CYCLE PATH	TELEPHONE
WATCH OUT FOR CHILDREN	BEWARE OF ANIMALS	INTERSECTION WITH SIDE ROAD	NO OVERTAKING	FILLING STATION	MECHANICAL HELP

Nonprojected Visual Media

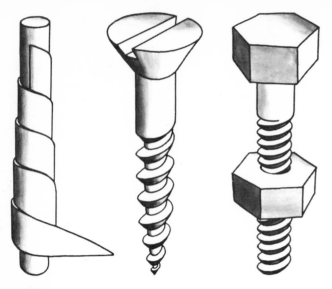

Figure 4–19. The significant details of this diagram of a screw as an inclined plane may be observed from a distance of 30 feet. It is 11 by 14 inches in size and is from a set of study prints titled Simple Machines. *(Courtesy Encyclopedia Brittanica Educational Corp.)*

One annoying problem that must be borne in mind continually when using charts and diagrams in a conventional class setting is that details and lettering may be too small to be visible to students at their seats. Teachers must either point to and read certain portions ("I know you can't see this, but . . . ") or else change the format of the material or arrange for it to be viewed individually or in small groups. Another problem that requires special teacher action is the need to bridge the gap between diagrammatic symbols and the reality they are supposed to represent. Teachers should question students about

Figure 4–20. Commercially made charts depict various phases of complex processes in great detail. Should such charts be used by a teacher to illustrate a lecture? Does it matter how large the class is? How could charts be used effectively by individual students? (Courtesy Denoyer-Geppert)

Figure 4–21. Can maps and charts be references for individual research? How can they be employed effectively in reporting the results of research? How may a teacher determine whether students understand the graphic symbols used on maps and charts? (Courtesy The National Education Association. Photo by Joe Di Dio)

Figure 4–22. The ACTIONMAP® is big enough for children to climb around on. They can paint on time zones and other information, pace off distances to scale, and locate actual samples of produce and natural resources. How might such a gigantic map help to clarify concepts of geography? How might students go about creating such a map of their own local area? (Courtesy Denoyer-Geppert)

their experience levels and understanding, and find out whatever misconceptions may exist.

Projection tracing is an easy way to make a large chart or diagram from a small illustration. Simply project the image of the illustration with an opaque projector onto a large sheet of paper or posterboard taped to the chalkboard or wall. The outline may then be traced with a pencil or marker (or with chalk directly onto the chalkboard).

Teachers should consider remaking diagrams and charts in simplified slide or transparency form for more effective use and for easier storage and handling.

Bulletin Boards and Exhibits

Some teachers ignore vacant or cluttered bulletin boards and empty display cases. Others take a personal interest in beautifying the school building and spend hours putting up seasonal decorations or topical materials. Wise

Figure 4–23. Making these paper-mache animals and this mural become challenging problems. What should pupils learn? How to make a model or use a brush? These would only be incidental outcomes. What information do they need to find? Note the research that is called for in answering the questions about Boats in the Harbor? What conditions for learning do teachers need to arrange? How to organize pupil study activity? What motion pictures, filmstrips, and books need to be shown to facilitate work on these problems? What materials need to be set out, then cleaned and put away? (Courtesy La Mesa Spring Valley School District, La Mesa, Calif.)

Figure 4–24. Who should prepare classroom displays and exhibits: Teachers? Students? Teachers and students together? What should be the purpose of classroom displays and exhibits: To inform? To motivate? To impress? To decorate? How important is it to employ principles of good design and color and eye-catching lettering? How does one learn how to create an effective display? (C....... T.. ....)

(Photo by Joe Di Dio)

teachers let students do the work. When students are actively pursuing independent and group problem-solving activities they naturally need space to display the results of their research.

Sometimes, teachers organize major unit activities around the joint pupil-teacher planning and construction of an extensive exhibit, perhaps even for display in a downtown building or other public place outside the school. Although esthetics can be very important, teachers should not lose sight of definite learning purposes and objectives when designing "inside" displays for direct instructional purposes in the classroom. When the teacher alone constructs a display for presentation to students in class, however, teachers must not get carried away with the idea of decorating the classroom. Esthetics are important, but such directly instructional bulletin board or display presentations can be more functional in appearance so long as they meet definite informational or motivational purposes.

Specific Teaching Practices

Bulletin boards and exhibits require the same kind of purposeful planning and legibility considerations described for other media. In addition, displays intended for public viewing should catch the eye the way good advertisements do. The following points will help:

1. Invent a dynamic, verb-first directive headline, such as:

> Think Conservation!
> Put Yourself in the Picture.
> Help Stamp Out Litterbugs!
> Prevent Fire!
> Match These Names and Faces.

Figure 4–25. Are these bulletin board displays eye-catching and involving? Would they be as dynamic without the verb-first headlines? How important are legibility and design? (Courtesy Thomas A. Koskey, Baited Bulletin Boards, and Fearon Publishers)

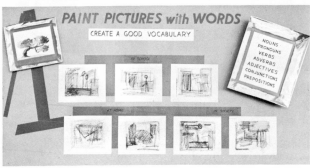

[OPPOSITE] *Figure 4–26. Materials and devices such as these markers, pens, guides, scribers, templates, stencils, and dry-transfer, paste-up, and cutout letters, take the drudgery out of lettering and make it possible for any teacher or student to prepare neat, legible visuals for projection, publication, or display. (Courtesy The University of Connecticut)*

Or else use a question or statement with impact that will catch the eye of the viewer and get him interested in looking at the display, for example:

> Can *You* Do This?
> Fire Prevention is *Your* Business!
> Smokers Cause *Air Pollution*!
> Drugs Are For *Sick* People!
> Have You Thanked a *Green Plant* Today?

Make the headline big and bold and colorful.

2. Use good illustrations. Pictures, objects, diagrams, moving parts, dials, flashing lights should take up where the headline leads, making the viewer curious and holding his interest until he has understood the message.

3. Arrange illustrations dynamically, in an informal, contrasting way. Static, formal balance seldom attracts attention.

4. Use elements of varying sizes to avoid monotony.

5. Use appropriate colors that harmonize for tranquility or clash for contrast; but avoid using too many different colors, or colors that may be confusing or misleading.

6. Involve viewers with a question to answer or a puzzle to solve. People should leave your exhibit with awareness or information that they did not have before. Hopefully, they will also be interested in finding out more, or be resolved to take action about the problem depicted.

Chalkboards and Chartpads

Most teachers still use the chalkboard a great deal. Of course, those who are lucky enough to have an overhead projector permanently in their classrooms will not want to spend hours redrawing complicated diagrams, quotations, lists, and assignments every year, but the chalkboard and a chartpad or flip chart are likely to be used so much that some suggestions are in order.

Specific Teaching Practices

Whether writing with chalk on the chalkboard or with marker or crayon on chart paper, the following tips from experienced presenters should be kept in mind:

Figure 4–27. Pen and guide sets simplify neat lettering. Such pens should be held vertically, and the lines retraced until letters are dense and bold. (From the self-instructional slide program, WRICO/Dry Mount—Making a poster combining WRICO lettering with a picture mounted with a Seal dry mounting press. Courtesy Training Services)

Nonprojected Visual Media

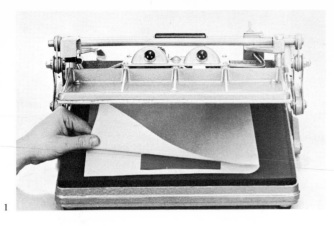

1

Figure 4–28. A dry mounting press can be used for mounting and laminating pictures and for producing picture-lift transparencies with laminating film. The basic picture mounting process consists of the following steps: (1) Pre-heat picture and mounting board to remove excess moisture; (2) use the tip of the tacking iron to adhere a sheet of dry mounting tissue to the back of the picture; (3) trim picture and mounting tissue at the same time; (4) tack the picture to the mount by lightly adhering two diagonally opposite corners of the tissue with the tacking iron; (5) cover picture with plain paper and insert in press for 10–20 seconds at 225°F; (6) remove mounted picture from press and allow it to cool briefly under weight. (From the self-instructional slide program, WRICO/Dry Mount—Making a poster combining WRICO lettering with a picture mounted with a Seal dry mounting press. *Courtesy Training Services*)

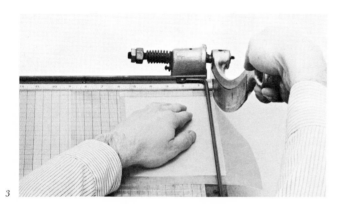

2

3

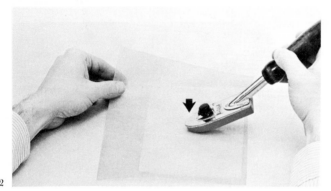

4

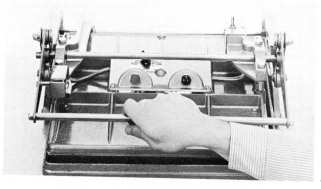

1. Be sure the writing surface is large enough and is placed so that everyone can see it clearly and without glare.
2. Write boldly and legibly. Draw figures clearly. Use different colors for emphasis.
3. Be brief. Stick to key words and phrases.
4. Don't put too much on at once. Add material in logical sequence. Dramatically reveal previously prepared material which you have covered with a sheet of paper, a drape, or a projection screen.
5. Prepare diagrams or drawings (try projection tracing) ahead of time with barely visible lines, then fill them in boldly in front of the class. Don't waste class time drawing complicated diagrams or writing long lists. Prepare these ahead of time.
6. Most newer chalkboards are magnetic. Glue or tape small magnets to strips of thin cardboard on which you have previously lettered words or sentences or drawn diagrams. These cards may then be placed with a flourish onto the chalkboard where they will stay where you put them or you can move them around.
7. Eye contact with students is important. Face the class when you talk. Don't turn your back to the class any more than necessary.

Figure 4-29. Is the overhead projector limited to presentational use by the teacher? How many ways can you think of to use the overhead to better advantage than the chalkboard? For what purposes might the chalkboard be preferable? (Courtesy The National Education Association. Photo by Esther Bubley)

8. Don't stand in front of what you have written.
9. Explain or discuss items as they are needed.
10. If you use a pointer to focus attention, put it down when you are finished. Do not caress the pointer, tap it, point it at people, bend it, or stab the air or floor with it.

Flannelboards

Although flannelboards are used for arithmetic demonstrations and story-telling by nearly every lower elementary teacher, other teachers often overlook the possibilities of this simple device for such sequential presentation of material as advanced as molecular structure and electrical circuitry. A yard or two of outing flannel stretched and taped or stitched over a piece of plywood or building board will provide the basic display panel. Screw eyes or hooks in one edge will allow the board to be hung on the wall or suspended from map hooks above the chalkboard. Some teachers build easels for their flannel boards or simply rest them on the chalk rail.

The rough surface fibers of the flannel board will hold shapes cut from flannel, felt, or styrofoam, or paper cut-outs backed with rough sandpaper. The pieces may easily be moved. Surprisingly heavy real objects can be supported by the tenacious nylon hooks of Velcro material. Commercial Velcro "hook-and-loop" material is available from which excellent display boards can be made. While the "loop" material needed for the background is rather expensive in large pieces, the cost is partially offset by the fact that only tiny squares of "hook" material are needed to support the movable pieces. (One square inch will support up to ten pounds!)

Specific Teaching Practices

Flannelboards and hook-and-loop boards require the same consideration as the chalkboard for all demonstrations as far as visibility is concerned. In addition:

1. Be sure there is enough contrast between figures and background. Dark, neutral, backgrounds are better ~~...~~ purposes, with the movable figures being cut from lighter and brighter material.
2. Put items in place sequentially, with a little showmanship.
3. Involve students in placing items on the board and with questions such as "What should come next?" or "Where does this shape fit?"

Study Prints

Apparently some teachers believe that decorating their classrooms with pictures relieves them from further responsibility. Consequently, it is not uncommon to see pictures mounted all over the walls where they cannot readily be seen by students, or else flamboyantly dis-

Figure 4–30. The educational potential of study prints and other illustrations depends on the nature of the contact between learner and picture. How does a teacher arrange to have students make significant contact with a picture? How can perception be heightened, and judgment, comparison, and inference be encouraged? (Courtesy SVE Division, Singer Education and Training Products)

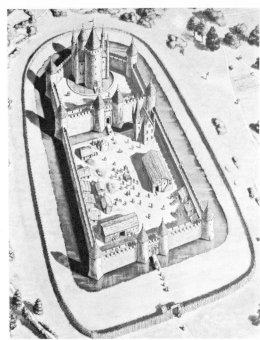

Figure 4–31. Study prints may consist of photographs of actual objects or processes, or they may consist of drawings, sketches, or diagrams. Drawings may achieve maximum relevancy for teacher purposes, and photographs may be more realistic. Study prints provide opportunity for prolonged individual study. The pictures shown are photographs of pictures selected from two sets titled, Middle Ages *and* American Transportation. *Picture arrangements as illustrated, which present sharp contrasts and comparisons, are often very stimulating and revealing. Students may be benefited greatly in their concept-building processes by the concrete images presented. An analysis of picture-reading processes is presented herewith. (Courtesy Informative Classroom Picture Publishers; H. Robert Armstrong, Photography, Philadelphia; and the Smithsonian Institution)*

Fundamentals of Teaching with Audiovisual Technology

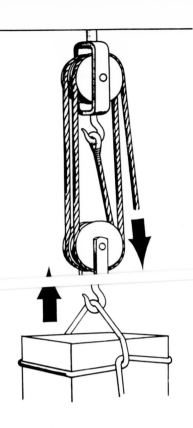

played in places where they could be a constant distraction.

Media resource centers recognize the value of wisely selected and effectively mounted study prints by making sets of significant pictures available to teachers and students. Besides materials from the library or resource center, a comprehensive, up-to-date personal picture file developed from magazine and calendar pictures, photographic enlargements, and other sources can be a creative teacher's most useful asset. Pictures which might become soiled by grubby little fingers ought to be laminated or sprayed with plastic to keep them clean and presentable. Other pictures may be dry-mounted on light poster board as shown in Figure 4–28, for convenience in handling and displaying.

The _____ potential of any illustration depends on active contact between learner and picture. Such effective contacts are too frequently overlooked even by experienced teachers, although perception and reaction form the foundations of visual literacy. How does a teacher arrange to have students make significant contact with a picture? And just what contact is significant? Significant contact with still pictures, as with other instructional materials and devices, calls for perception, observation, recall, comparisons, judgments, inferences, and conclusions which lead to solid generalizations; or a contact that provides the student with a set of illustrated directions for carrying on a specific and worthwhile operation or task. The one guiding principle is to *get action by asking questions.*

Just how can teachers stimulate students to interact actively with pictures? Here are some suggested teaching practices:

Specific Teaching Practices

1. Guide students by asking questions—leading or detailed questions—as the objectives demand. Write questions on the chalkboard or on prepared transparencies or handout sheets.
2. Make sets of study prints available in the classroom or library, and ask groups of students to work on designated questions and report back to the class at a scheduled time.
3. Fasten pictures to a display wall or hang them by card holders or paper clips on a stretched wire at *eye level.* Pictures may be fastened to display surfaces with tape or bulletin board wax, or with staples, thumbtacks, and pins, none of which need pass through the paper if carefully applied.
4. Display pictures in optimum learning sequence with one or more crucial questions typed on sheets hinged to the back of each picture. Pictures may be subse-

Figure 4–32 [ABOVE]. *This diagram is a part of a set of study prints, 11 × 14 inches in size. Sometimes it is an advantage to prepare diagrams without labels, thus permitting a broader range of pupil study activity. Naming the parts, for example, in a testing situation is one example. (© Encyclopaedia Britannica Films, Inc.)*

quently displayed with or without the questions being visible.

It would be naive to assume that simply *looking* at a picture means *learning* from it. Therefore, what kinds of mental activity and what kinds of active learner responses are basic to the effective observation of pictures? In a frequently quoted article Bartlett made the following analysis:

it is clear that several distinct levels of response exist. These stages are (1) naming objects; (2) grasping import; (3) observing details; (4) relating the picture to experience; (5) drawing inferences; (6) adding imaginative elements; and (7) engaging in further activities suggested by the picture. [6]

This analysis clearly reveals how the naming of objects, or differentiation, leads to synthesis, or the putting together of ideas, which leads in turn to further differentiation and synthesis. As the learner's own experience leads him to make inferences from his observations, he integrates ideas, reacts more intensely by using his insights, and perhaps may even define new problems beyond the scope of the picture. Finally, the learner begins to generalize as a natural result of the active processes that have occurred.

To illustrate the process of learning from pictures, we can identify several levels of response to a particular picture and we ourselves can carry out the mental activity suggested. Let us study the picture, *An Ohio River Flatboat* (Figure 4–33) from the set, *Pioneer Days*,[7] and get a cross section of responses tabulated here.

LEVELS OF RESPONSE	EXAMPLES
1. Naming objects in the picture	River, rudder, man, woman, plow, tub, boy, chicken.
2. Grasping importance of the picture	Living on a flatboat or traveling on a flatboat.
3. Observing relevant details	Plow is fastened to boat. A little girl at the stern with the cow. The woman is cooking.
4. Connecting the picture to our experience	Have we been in rowboats, motor boats, in canoes, in cabin cruisers, in sailboats, on ocean liners? Have we been on a river with the current? Against the current?

[6] Mary M. Bartlett, "Early Stages of Picture Reading," *Teaching with Pictures* (Grand Rapids, Mich.: Informative Classroom Picture Publishers), p. 10.

[7] Published by Informative Classroom Picture Publishers, Grand Rapids, Mich.

[OPPOSITE] *Figure 4–33. This picture of* Life on a Flatboat *is from the set* Pioneer Days. *This drawing focuses attention on relevant details. The implied action gives this picture a potential for pupil experiencing. Study this picture in connection with the exercise in using various levels of mental activity. (Courtesy Informative Classroom Picture Publishers)*

Mental Activity in the Study of Pictures

[OPPOSITE] *Figure 4–34. Study prints may be used effectively by individual students and in class groupings. How important is it for students, especially young children, to identify themselves with the content of media they use? Will they learn more? How might interest and attitude be affected? (From* Black ABC's *series, courtesy SVE Division, Singer Education and Training Products)*

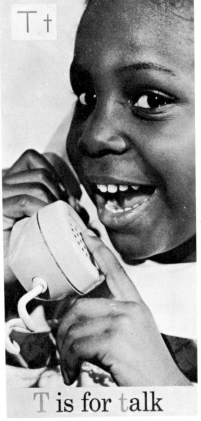

T is for talk

5. Making inferences

This flatboat is never going back. This is a family and the family is moving to a new home. (Can we infer temperature, season of the year, weather, sound, odor of cooking, movement?)

6. Adding imaginative elements to picture content

Where is this family going? What might the mother be cooking? Why might these people be moving to a new home?

7. Engaging in extended-study activities

Investigate the following: Which rivers did flatboatmen travel on in pioneer days? What direction did this travel take (that is, on a particular river)? Make a mural based on map study. About how long is this flatboat? When the boat arrives what might the lumber be used for? Analyze the characteristics of successful pioneers and visualize them in a series of posters that apply to life today.

We can be quite sure that unless students engage in vigorous mental activity with pictures, they will be likely to engage in only a superficial perusal, leading to the mistaken idea that they have in fact studied a picture and have no need to examine it further.

Guidance and direction of learners' perception and response are keys to helping students get the most from pictures and from their entire visual environment. Teachers should be certain that students meet objectives by setting problems, projects, and questions calling for observation, collection of data, development of insights, and practice of communication skills in reporting findings, conclusions, and generalizations.

Although excellent sets of study prints and other non-projected visual media are readily available from school libraries and resource centers, these valuable materials represent only an introduction to the array of projected and electronic media which we will examine in Chapter 5.

Problems and Activities

1. Briefly summarize several different ways in which textbooks were used by the instructors in previous courses you have taken. Would you have used them differently if you had been the instructor?

2. Explain how programmed books differ from ordinary texts. Describe how you would evaluate programmed materials for use in your classes.

3. Describe several problems that you might assign to or develop with your students that would demand field study of real things. Be imaginative. Seek lifelike activities. Must students always do these assignments as a class or on an organized field trip?

4. Define and differentiate between the terms, *model, mock-up,* and *simulation.*

5. Devise an instructional game that could be played by your students, or obtain a suitable commercially produced game. Specify behavioral objectives and point out how students could achieve these objectives by playing the game.

6. Describe several methods for mounting and preserving pictures, charts, and clippings. Explain how they can be stored and retrieved for use.

7. Laminate a chart, diagram, leaves, or other visuals as directed by your instructor. (Both sides should be laminated unless the visual is mounted on heavy stock.)

8. Build your own picture or "clip-art" file. Make a list of sources for illustrations in your teaching field.

9. Submit several neatly mounted, or mounted and laminated pictures, charts, or maps as directed by your instructor.

10. Demonstrate your ability to letter neatly using one or more of the methods specified by your instructor.

11. Make a list of ten dynamic (verb first) headings for displays in your subject area.

12. Prepare a scale layout plan for a bulletin board display. Include a description of the intended audience and purpose for the display, the location, sketches or reproductions of the illustrations to be used, choice of colors, and wording of captions and headings.

13. Design and construct an animated display, working model, or mock-up. Describe it.

14. Discuss the following statement: "Improper or thoughtless use of color in preparing instructional materials can lead to confusion and development of false conceptions by students, particularly those who may be colorblind."

15. Prepare a brief micro-teaching "lesson" to be videotaped, in which you present a concept using chalkboard, chartpad, or flannelboard. Prepare a second one in which you lead students in examining a picture for different levels of detail and meaning. Evaluate playbacks of these sessions first by yourself, if possible; then, with your instructor.

Selected References

Better Bulletin Boards (16mm film, 11 min) Audio-Visual Center, Indiana University, Bloomington, Ind. 47401, 1956. Shows many examples of bulletin-board planning and effective display methods. Emphasizes instructional values in appropriateness, format, design, and placement.

Bulletin Boards: An Effective Teaching Device (16mm film, 11 min) BFA Educational Media, 2211 Michigan Ave., Santa Monica, Calif. 90404, 1956. Gives suggestions for the organization of creatively designed bulletin boards. A teacher and her pupils discuss and plan a bulletin board. Different surfaces and mounting methods are shown.

CALDER, CLARENCE R., JR., and ELEANOR M. ANTAN. *Techniques and Activities to Stimulate Verbal Learning.* The Macmillan Company, 866 Third Ave., New York, N.Y. 10022, 1970, 326 pp. Rationale, techniques, and ideas for hundreds of construction, display, and craft projects, primarily for elementary grades.

Chalk & Chalkboards (16mm film, 15 min) BFA Educational Media, 2211 Michigan Ave., Santa Monica, Calif. 90404, 1959. Discusses the physical properties of chalk and chalkboards, showing what chalkboards are made of and demonstrating how they should be cared for. Shows many techniques of chalkboard utilization to improve presentations at all grade levels.

Chalkboard Utilization (16mm film, 15 min) McGraw-Hill Films, 1221 Avenue of the Americas, New York, N.Y. 10020, 1954. Demonstrates the many ways a chalkboard can be used more effectively in teaching. Explains various methods for transferring drawings to the chalkboard.

Dry Mounting of Instructional Materials (seven 16mm films, 5–7 min) University of Iowa, Audiovisual Center, Iowa City, Iowa 52240, 1965–69. This series includes the following titles: *Display and Use, Basic Techniques, Cloth Backing, Laminating and Lifting, Special Techniques, Using Ideas,* and *Creative Application.*

Electric Boards (16mm film, 6 min) University of Iowa, Audiovisual Center, Iowa City, Iowa 52240, 1965. Introduces various types of electric instructional display boards, shows their construction, and suggests a variety of uses for these simple but effective teaching devices.

Flannel Boards and How to Use Them (16mm film, 15 min) BFA Educational Media, 2211 Michigan Ave., Santa Monica, Calif. 90404, 1958. Explains what flannelboards are, how they are made, and how they can be used in presenting subject matter and stimulating interaction.

Globes: An Introduction (16mm film, 10 min) Audio-Visual Center, Indiana University, Bloomington, Ind. 47401, 1964. Pictures the globe as a model of the earth and points out the representative shape and color of land and water areas. Identifies the continents and compares their sizes and locations. Explains the poles and scales of latitude and compares various types of globes.

How Does a Picture Mean? (filmstrip with guide) AECT Publications Sales, 1201 16th St., NW, Washington, D.C. 20036, 1968. Discusses elements of meaning in a photograph, and how these elements are composed for the purpose of intentional communication. Includes sets of pictures illustrating visual-verbal parallels.

How to Make and Use a Diorama (16mm film, 20 min) McGraw-Hill Films, 1221 Avenue of the Americas, New York, N.Y. 10020, 1956. Discusses the use of dioramas in instruction at various grade levels. Shows teachers and students making dioramas and describes each step in the process in detail.

KOSKEY, THOMAS A. *Baited Bulletin Boards.* Fearon Publishers/Lear Siegler, Inc., 6 Davis Drive, Belmont, Calif. 94002, 1954, 32 pp. Contains drawings and photographs of actual displays which may be adapted for use on many different levels and in various subject matter fields. Suggests materials to use. This booklet is one of a series on bulletin boards available from the same publisher.

Lettering Instructional Materials (16mm film, 20 min) Audio-Visual Center, Indiana University, Bloomington, Ind. 47401, 1955. Shows easy-to-use lettering equipment for signs, posters, displays, and materials for projection. Techniques shown include rubber stamps, cutouts, stencils, pens and guides, mechanical lettering systems, and methods of projection and photographic reproduction.

Magic of The Flannel Board (16mm film, 12 min) Association

Films, Inc., 600 Madison Ave., New York, N.Y. 10022, 1964. Shows ways creative cutout visuals may be used to stimulate student curiosity and motivation, to drill students in mathematics and reading, and to introduce abstract ideas and difficult concepts.

Making Sense Visually (filmstrip with guide) AECT Publications Sales, 1201 16th St., NW, Washington, D.C. 20036, 1968. An introduction to some of the basic ideas and vocabulary of visual communication, including such concepts as "body language" and "object language." Gives examples of creative communication opportunities in real life.

Maps: An Introduction (16mm film, 12 min) Audio-Visual Center, Indiana University, Bloomington, Ind. 47401, 1964. Describes how maps are made by picturing a class constructing a map from a model of the community. Shows use of a legend and how a scale is derived in order that distance may be measured on the map. Illustrates relationships between county, state, and U.S. maps and a world globe.

MORLAN, JOHN E. *Preparation of Inexpensive Teaching Materials*. Science Research Associates, Inc., 259 East Erie Street, Chicago, Ill. 60611, 1963, 103 pp. Instructions for preparing a wide variety of materials and devices for instruction, display, and dramatization.

Photo Story Discovery Sets (5 sets of still pictures, 3 1/2 × 3 1/2 in, with guides, AECT Publications Sales, 1201 16th St., NW, Washington, D.C. 20036, 1967. Working with the pictures to discover story sequences, students of all ages learn fundamental skills in visual literacy.

Poster Making: Design and Technique (16mm film, 10 min) BFA Educational Media, 2211 Michigan Ave., Santa Monica, Calif. 90404, 1953. Stresses principles of layout, lettering, optical spacing, color contrast, and painting.

WALTZ, SONDRA KAY. *Handbook of Instructional Devices for Intermediate Social Studies*. Teachers Publishing Corp., Darien, Conn. 06820, 1967, 62 pp. Besides maps, displays, and other devices, this booklet suggests several activities that could serve well as "problem bases" for use of media at various levels.

WILLIAMS, CATHARINE M. *Learning from Pictures*, 2nd ed. Publications Sales, National Education Association, 1201 16th St., NW, Washington, D.C. 20036, 166 p., 1968. Suggestions for effective use of study and display prints at all grade levels in most subject areas, plus a detailed listing of sources.

WRICO/Dry Mount (2 × 2-in captioned slide set, 27 frames) Training Services, 8885 West F Ave., Kalamazoo, Mich. 49009, 1968. Step-by-step instructions for making a poster combining WRICO lettering with a picture mounted with the use of a Seal dry-mounting press.

ZUCKERMAN, DAVID W., and ROBERT E. HORN. *The Guide to Simulation Games for Education and Training*. Information Resources, Inc., 1675 Massachusetts Ave., Cambridge, Mass. 02138, revised periodically. Descriptions and sources of games and simulation materials, with reference section.

5
Projected and Electronic Media

In one of the most famous and fateful incidents in the Bible, the Lord summoned Moses to the top of Mount Sinai. There he appeared to Moses in the form of a fiery cloud, and there—to the appropriate accompaniment of thunder and lightning—he presented Moses with the Ten Commandments. That, so far as I know, is the earliest recorded use of audiovisual techniques for mass education.
—HAROLD HOWE II, former U.S. Commissioner of Education, addressing the National Audio-Visual Association.

Marshall McLuhan would describe the above illustration by asserting that *the medium was the message.* What is the message your students will receive when you show them a film or play a recording in class? Besides the actual content of the media, will you be telling the students, in effect, "I-am-the-teacher-and-you-must-sit-still-and-be-quiet-and-pay-attention-because-I-am-going-to-show-you-something-I-think-you-ought-to-know!'"? Or will your students interpret your message as: "I have noticed that you are very interested in finding out more about this problem. See whether this material will help." (Or, "This material will answer your questions in the following specific ways: . . .").

Creative utilization is the key to getting an hour's worth of learning from an hour of teaching with the projected and electronic media described in this chapter.

Motion Pictures   Motion pictures can provide intensely realistic experiences. More than any other medium, films can extend human perception by revealing the remote, the inaccessible, the invisible, or the inaudible, or by enabling viewers vicariously to re-live the historic past. Each learner can have a front row seat at a surgical operation, peer with the same well-focused eye into the mysterious world of micro-organisms, or analyze the rapid functioning of complex machinery. But teachers must never overlook the fact that many of their students may not yet have had enough experience to interpret what they see in a fast-moving film. Teachers must help fill in the perceptions missed by untrained eyes, ears, and memories.

Good films constantly are being released which have

Figure 5–1. Is it worthwhile for American children to discover that a Japanese boy wears blue jeans and loves to fly a kite? What other learnings can occur from observing events in the lives of other people? How can teachers sharpen students' perception, awareness, and understanding? (From Boy of Japan: Ito and His Kite, *courtesy Coronet Instructional Films)*

been produced for specific achievement levels and for definite concepts and instructional objectives. Skill-building films that give directions for action, films that show processes, define problems, and show people at work, and films that show continuities otherwise unobservable may play significant teaching and learning roles.

Film experiences should be chosen with full awareness of their possible relationships to the teaching-learning process; but in this respect films are not different from other media. Above all, teachers must realize that films differ widely in their internal characteristics. Some are intensely real in dialogue and in pictorial and dramatic treatment; others are devoid of the "action" that characterizes the medium; some are not photographically realistic, but utilize abstract, diagrammatic animation techniques to portray reality; other films simply are illustrated lectures—straightforward presentations by chart, diagram, photograph and voice of a given segment of knowledge, as a paragraph or chapter in a textbook. A few stimulating and creative films may have worthwhile application for learners of *all* ages and backgrounds, but teachers should beware of such claims by film producers and distributors. Most good films are designed for a specified audience, and teachers should always preview such materials to be sure they are appropriate.

The motion picture is indeed a complex medium, unique in that it combines three components of portrayal, namely, motion, sound, and realistic images in black and

Figure 5–2. People cease to be strangers and cultures seem no longer foreign when we begin to find out about them for ourselves. Why are motion pictures so suitable for stimulating interest and influencing attitudes as well as conveying factual information? (From Japan: Miracle in Asia, Japan: Harvesting the Land and the Sea, *and* Japanese Boy: The Story of Taro. *Courtesy Encyclopaedia Britannica Educational Corporation)*

white or color. When these elements for effective communication are skillfully blended by a competent and creative producer, viewers may respond emotionally much as though they were experiencing a real situation instead of its representation.

The range of realistic experiences through the motion picture medium is greatly increased by specialized photography. For example, erosion and silting may be portrayed by photographing rapid changes caused by water acting upon a miniature model of a river delta. Animation techniques constitute another striking contribution of the film medium to teaching. Generally, unobservable action may be skillfully portrayed diagrammatically. Still another feature of the film is the potentially valuable process of altering the time reference of an action sequence. Thus processes occuring too rapidly, or objects moving too swiftly, such as a bullet in flight, may be photographed by slow-motion or high-speed techniques. Time-lapse photography, on the other hand, can speed up such

Figure 5–3. Animated cartoon treatment is often used in films to simplify and clarify concepts. But who ever heard of an elephant on a teeter-totter? Although the situation seems preposterous, will young children be likely to understand and remember this illustration? Do you think children will be able to deduce the principle of leverage from this teeter-totter analogy? (From the film Let's Look at Levers, *courtesy Journal Films, Inc.)*

Projected and Electronic Media

slowly occurring processes as growth of a plant toward a source of light, or the approach of a thunderstorm.

Fortunately, a growing body of research is available to guide teachers in their efforts to understand and use motion pictures. Hoban and Van Ormer, after painstaking work in collecting and analyzing findings of film researchers from 1918 to 1950, formulated ten principles that indicate the nature of the influence of motion pic-

Figure 5–4. Animation techniques allow improbable situations and unfamiliar relationships to be portrayed clearly on film. Might there be occasions in which abstract or generalized animation treatment might be more effective than realistic, live action? (From [A] The Animal Movie and [B] Dance Squared, courtesy National Film Board of Canada, and [C] Why We Have Laws, courtesy Learning Corporation of America)

tures. More recent research by others tends to support Hoban and Van Ormer, so their principles and a brief excerpted explanation of each are quoted here, in simplified form; however, the reader will be quick to recognize relationships to professional concepts in educational psychology and curriculum development. These film principles relate closely to the basic principles of media utilization stated and analyzed in Chapters 6 and 9. The Hoban-Van Ormer principles of film influence follow:

1. *Principle of Reinforcement.* Films have greatest influence when their content reinforces and extends previous knowledge, attitudes, and motivations of the audience. They have least influence when previous knowledge is inadequate, and when their content is antagonistic or contrary to the existing attitudes and motivation of the audience.
2. *Principle of Specificity.* The influence of a motion picture is more specific than general. We cannot expect an audience to have a broad general attitude, a general motivation, a general increase in knowledge, or a general improvement in perceptual-motor skills after seeing a single film, espe-

Figure 5–5. What effect might "famous" cartoon characters and fictional heros have on learning from films? Can historical events be made more memorable, such as in these episodes from Uncle Sam Magoo? *(Courtesy United Productions of America, Inc.)*

Projected and Electronic Media

cially when these objectives are not treated directly in the film.

3. *Principle of Relevance.* The influence of a motion picture is greater when the content of the film is directly relevant to the audience reaction that it is intended to influence.

4. *Principle of Audience Variability.* Reactions to a motion picture vary with most or all of the following factors: film literacy, abstract intelligence, formal education, age, sex, previous experience with the subject, and prejudice or predisposition toward the subject.

5. *Principle of Visual Primacy.* The influence of a motion picture is primarily in the strength of the visual presentation, and secondarily in the narration or commentary. It is relatively unaffected by "slickness" of production as long as meaning is clear.

6. *Principle of Pictorial Context.* An audience responds selectively to motion pictures, reacting to those things which it finds familiar and significant in the pictorial context in which the action takes place.

7. *Principle of Subjectivity.* Individuals respond to a motion picture most efficiently when the pictorial content is subjective for them.

8. *Principle of Rate of Development.* Rate of content and sequence development influences the instructional impact of a motion picture on its audience.

9. *Principle of Instructional Variables.* Established instructional techniques, properly built into the film or applied by the instructor, substantially increase the instructional effectiveness of a film.

10. *Principle of Instructor Leadership.* The leadership qualities of the instructor affect the efficiency with which his class will learn from the film or filmstrip.[1]

[1] Charles F. Hoban, Jr., and Edward B. Van Ormer, *Instructional Film Research, 1918–1950* (Rapid Mass Learning), pp. 9–2 to 9–8. Sponsored jointly by the Departments of the Army and the Navy, December 1951. Distributed by U.S. Department of Commerce, Office of Technical Services, Washington, D.C.

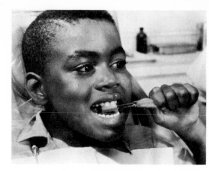

Figure 5–6. What kinds of subjects lend themselves to repetitive motion picture film loops: Athletic skills? Operation of tools and equipment? Mathematical computation? Handwriting? Art techniques? Try naming some more. (From a film loop: Brushing Your Teeth, *courtesy SVE Division, Singer Education and Training Products)*

Figure 5–7. Besides handwriting practice, what other applications can you think of for continuous loop movies? What equipment and skills are needed to produce such films locally? (Reprinted by permission of Technicolor, Inc.)

Fundamentals of Teaching with Audiovisual Technology

Figure 5–8. The physical education teacher or coach has good use for a motion picture projector (or video recorder) that shows normal or slow-motion, forward or backward. In what other subjects could such flexibility be an advantage? (Courtesy Eastman Kodak Company)

The versatile film medium lends itself to instructional use in both large and small groups, and for individual study the compact, super 8 format is especially effective. The sound problem is solved by having viewers wear headphones in rooms in which other activities are going on. Also, films and film clips are widely used in television programming. Film, especially in the less expensive super 8 format, may serve as the hub of learning activity in another way, when motion pictures are produced as a joint endeavor by students and teachers as a major class project, or by a selected group of students working on their own. Of course this unique learner activity demands additional equipment such as a super 8 camera with zoom lens and automatic exposure control, tripod, lights, film viewer and splicer, together with enough money to pay for film and processing. (See Chapter 8 for hints on filming.)

Figure 5–9. This super 8 motion picture projector uses a reel-type rather than a continuous loop film cartridge, allowing fast rewind to the beginning of the film. Under what conditions would the reel-type cartridge be desirable? (Courtesy Eastman Kodak Company)

Projected and Electronic Media

Teachers who use 16mm films frequently will find the following facts useful. (*a*) There are 40 separate frames or individual pictures in every foot of 16mm motion picture film. (*b*) The image is in a gelatin-based emulsion which is coated on the *dull* side of the film. (*c*) Standard sound speed, or the rate of film travel past the projector aperture, is 24 frames per second. (*d*) The running time of a 400-foot reel of 16mm film is approximately 11 minutes; hence, a reel with 800 feet of film requires 22 minutes to run off at sound speed, a 1200-foot length of film therefore requires about 33 minutes, and so on. (*e*) Standard speed for 16mm silent film (very rare nowadays) is 16 frames per second; hence, the running time is more than 15 minutes per 400-foot reel. (*f*) Most projectors still have a silent/sound speed switch, and when a sound film is accidentally projected at silent speed the sound becomes too slow and too low in pitch.

A motion picture may be made available in the form of a complete film production running up to half an hour or longer, or it may be a single-concept segment (film clip) running a few seconds or a few minutes. The short *film clip* is universally used in television news broadcasts and instructional TV programming. Because no projector threading is required, single-concept films in super 8 cartridges are very popular for teacher demonstrations and for self-instructional use by individual students. Teachers should learn to use films systematically as an integral part of the instructional process, for films frequently are the most appropriate and most evocative media available.

Not enough is yet known about the specific influence of films upon attitudes, but researchers in the armed forces, industry, and education have learned how to use films to present facts, concepts, skills and procedures more efficiently. Summarized simply, their advice for presenting instructional films to groups of students runs something like this:

Specific Teaching Practices

1. *Choose an appropriate film.* Select each film on the basis of clearly defined objectives, even if these objectives relate more to esthetic or attitudinal values than to specific behavior.
2. *Preview the film.* Be familiar with both content and treatment of the content before using any film. Note what is included and what is left out. Pay special attention to technical terms and to implied background knowledge that may be unfamiliar to your students.
3. *Plan the lesson.* Write down pertinent questions and problems for discussion both before and after the film. List new vocabulary and introductory material. Include other appropriate materials and references.

4. *Motivate the students.* Be sure they know what they can expect to learn from the film and why this knowledge or skill will help them perform a task or solve a meaningful problem. Explain how the students will be expected to demonstrate what they have learned.

5. *Introduce the film.* Before showing the film, make sure that all students know the key points to look for. Quiz them on terminology and essential background to check their readiness to profit from using the film as a resource.

6. *Discourage note-taking.* Distribute in advance study guides outlining the major points, so that students will not have to risk missing important content while jotting down notes during the film presentation.

7. *Encourage mental practice.* The best way to learn a skill is to practice actively while observing a demonstration. When skills or procedures are to be learned and direct practice is not possible, tell students not to watch passively, but to imagine themselves performing the procedure as it is being shown on the screen, and to summarize facts and concepts in their minds during the course of the presentation.

8. *Eliminate distractions.* Do not try to compete with distractions such as construction equipment outside

Figure 5–10. What conditions must the teacher or teacher-projectionist control in order to obtain the most learning value from instructional motion pictures? How are the suggestions listed in this chapter related to the five utilization principles cited in Chapter 6 and to the specific operational techniques described in Chapter 9? (Courtesy Graflex Division, Singer Education and Training Products)

the building, heating or ventilating noises, glare from windows, and people coming and going. Do not expect learners to be alert in a hot, stuffy room, or to stay awake in a darkened room during a film shown after lunch. Move to another room if necessary, or reschedule the film. Students will not learn if they cannot see the picture, and they will daydream if they cannot hear the sound.

9. *Stay with the projector.* Keep the volume at the proper level and adjust the tone control to compensate for room acoustics. Keep the picture framed and in focus. Stay alert for loss of loop and know how to restore film loops without film damage or needless interruption. Have a spare projection lamp ready, and be prepared to change it without delay.

10. *Stop for review.* If the film is very long, stop at appropriate points for discussion and review of key points. If only part of the film is really relevant, show only that part and ignore the rest. Or, if your school owns the print and you have permission, cut the film into single-concept segments, splice on leader, and discard the outdated or inappropriate footage.

11. *Repeat significant sequences.* If the film itself does not reinforce by repetition, do so yourself, either during the showing or immediately afterward. Try turning off the sound track occasionally, asking students to narrate or describe the action being shown.

12. *Discuss the film.* Discuss principles and applications of the subject matter immediately, especially if the students must transfer their learning to dissimilar situations—for example, when apparatus or procedures they will use differ from those shown in the film.

13. *Show the film a second time.* Often, students will learn more if they can see the film again, either immediately after discussing it or at the start of the next class period. If class time is not available for a second showing, make it convenient for individuals to review the film on their own time.

14. *Test learners' performance.* If the film presents a procedure to be learned, testing should demonstrate the skills involved, either with actual apparatus and materials or in a realistic simulation. Verbal tests seldom are valid measures of procedural skills.

15. *Give immediate feedback.* After problem solving and testing, prompt confirmation of the right responses and correction of wrong or inappropriate responses is satisfying to most students and helps to prevent the learning of incorrect habit patterns.

Remember that films are resources; they are seldom complete teaching units in themselves. Their value is like that of all instructional media; it will depend on how well you use them. In presenting slide sets, filmstrips, and televised lessons, remember to consider these same procedures as they relate to the five principles enunciated in Chapter 6, and to specific operational techniques in Chapter 9.

Television and Videotape

The ubiquitous tube is a part of life in the last half of the twentieth century. The TV set is no longer a glamorous "magic box"—it has become an everyday household appliance. TV plays many roles: babysitter, companion, entertainer, and instructor. Most American children spend more hours watching television than they will ever spend in school. But where does learning occur? According to Marshall McLuhan:

Today in our cities,
most learning occurs outside the classroom.
The sheer quantity of information conveyed
by press-mags-film-TV-radio
far exceeds
the quantity of information conveyed by
school instruction & texts.
This challenge has destroyed
the monopoly of the book as a teaching aid
& cracked the very walls of the classroom,
so suddenly,
we're confused, baffled.[2]

When McLuhan said, "The Medium is the Message" he meant that the form of the presentation may overshadow the content; that merely being seen on TV may give people or places or ideas prominence and credibility far out of proportion to their true significance. Jay Chidsey discussed this phenomenon:

The Heisenberg Principle, in atomic physics . . . proposes that on the small particle level, processes cannot be observed because the intrusion of any instrumentality of observation (protons, electrons) so interferes with the phenomenon being observed as to fundamentally change the process itself; that such intrusion raises the system to a new energy level or degrades it to a more chaotic one. The television camera, whose energy derives from its connection to perhaps 200 million television sets, represents such an intrusion into a process. No event, from a grand tour of the President to your Aunt Minnie's ice cream social, can take place as it *would* have in the absence of the snouted red-eyed intruder, with the camera going.

Not only does the presence of the camera put the participants in the process "on stage" in their own consciousness, but even its hidden presence creates, once the film or direct-feed hits

[2] Gerald E. Stearn (ed.), *McLuhan: Hot & Cool* (New York: The Dial Press, 1967), p. 120.

Figure 5–11. *Fresh approaches to the teaching of basic material such as letters of the alphabet, numbers, and reasoning skills were pioneered on the* Sesame Street *TV series intended for preschoolers. Success of* Sesame Street *was due in large part to frank and honest use of television as a medium, rather than attempting merely to show materials on TV which were designed for other purposes. Animated cartoon stories, presented in advertising commercial form, sell the letters (such as the letter D, upper left in the picture below) and numbers (upper right) instead of detergents and corn flakes. Puppets such as Kermit the Frog, here (lower right) delivering a short, humorous lecture on the letter W, are also used. Reasoning skills are taught in a variety of ways including the regular antics of Buddy and Jim, two classic comedians who wrestle with problems in a way calculated to boost a child's own sense of logic. (Courtesy Children's Television Workshop)*

Fundamentals of Teaching with Audiovisual Technology

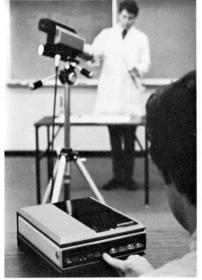

the home screen, an importance for the event registered which raises it to a new energy level; TV coverage *makes* the event, by virtue of its having been covered, super-real—larger than life by hundreds of percent.

Ordinary people become as gods, ninety-feet tall, potent, overwhelming. And there *is no cure!* Whatever it turns its attention to, the intruder transforms to godlikeness in power and significance . . . .

Television *cannot* present the trivial. By *being presented* even trivia becomes of enormous importance.[3]

The medium *is* the message. Can this effect be attributed to novelty and can we expect it soon to wear off? Many people still believe everything they read in the newspapers, and revere, literally, the contents of hardcover books. To what extent has the credibility of print media diminished in three hundred years?

But the media of the electronic age bring awareness and enlightenment, as well as perplexing problems. The media stimulate criticism of themselves. The so-called "mass media" of commercial TV and film have, as McLuhan suggests, pushed written English toward the spontaneity and freedom of the spoken idiom. At the same time, the media have made us intensely aware that words often cannot communicate true feelings as effectively as facial expression, tone of voice, and bodily gesture. McLuhan again:

[3] Jay Chidsey, "TV and Trivia and the Heisenberg Principle," quoted in *ERIC Newsletter,* December 1969, 4.

[ABOVE] *Figure 5–12. Portable video cartridge recorder and camera system permits simplified recording of demonstrations and events for immediate or delayed playback. Could students operate such equipment? Under what conditions might students of different ages benefit from analyzing their own performance on TV? (Courtesy Ampex Corporation)*

[RIGHT] *Figure 5–13. The video cassette or videorecord makes TV broadcasts or films available conveniently without scheduling. A single unit plays back both color picture and sound through a conventional television set. With such extreme flexibility, is a large-group classroom setting necessarily the most effective environment? Is the video cassette or videorecord really a new medium, or does it merely provide a much more convenient format for viewing? (Courtesy CBS Electronic Video Recording)*

Projected and Electronic Media

If these "mass media"
should serve only
to weaken or corrupt
previously achieved levels of
verbal & pictorial culture,
it won't be because
there's anything inherently wrong with them.
It will be because we've failed
to master them as new languages in time
to assimilate them to
our total cultural heritage.

Today these new media
threaten, instead of merely reinforce,
the procedures of (the) traditional classroom.
It's customary to answer this threat
with denunciations of
the unfortunate character & effect
of movies and TV,
just as the comicbook
was feared & scorned & rejected
from the classroom.
Its good & bad features
in form & content,
when carefully set beside
other kinds of art & narrative,
could have become a major
asset to the teacher.

Where student interest is already
intensely focused
is the natural point
at which to be
in the elucidation of
other problems & interests.
The educational task
is not only
to provide

Figure 5–14. Micro-teaching before a TV camera. Videotape recording allows student teachers to playback and critique their own work. How does it feel to see yourself teach on TV? Would it be most beneficial to view your own tapes with classmates, with an instructor or counselor, or by yourself? To what uses could a basic closed-circuit television outfit (TV camera, videotape recorder, and playback monitor) be put in a secondary school? In an elementary school? (Photo by James McKittrick, Kalamazoo College)

Figure 5–15. Instant replay: Coach and performer review the athlete's routine seconds after its completion. The two are watching a sidehorse routine taped at a University of Washington meet. Washington competed with the University of Illinois via video tape. Both teams sent video tapes of their performances to an impartial panel of judges. (Courtesy Ampex Corporation)

*basic tools
of perception,
but to develop
judgment & discrimination
with ordinary social experience.*

It's misleading to suppose
there's any basic difference between
education & entertainment.

This distinction merely relieves people
of the responsibility of
looking into the matter.

It's like setting up a distinction between
didactic & lyric poetry
on the ground that one
teaches, the other pleases.

However, it's always been true
that whatever pleases
teaches more effectively.[4]

[4] Stearn, op. cit., pp. 122–123.

Figure 5–16. Students participate in a game-simulation project conducted by the San Jose, California, Unified School District. The program employs videotape recording to increase student skills in English and mathematics. (Courtesy Ampex Corporation)

Projected and Electronic Media

A

B

C

D

Fundamentals of Teaching with Audiovisual Technology

Figure 5–17. Through documentaries and special programs, the mass media often deal frankly and realistically with the moral and environmental questions of modern man. Youth do care—upon graduation from high school they will become voting members of society. Should not classroom film experiences be as provocative as those viewed so casually on home TV screens? What kinds of real or simulated problem-solving activities might provide a basis for use of some of these films? ([A] PREJUDICE—Willie Catches On, *courtesy National Film Board of Canada;* [B] DROPPING OUT—No Reason To Stay, *courtesy National Film Board of Canada;* [C] SEX AND PREGNANCY—Phoebe, *courtesy National Film Board of Canada,* [D] MINORITIES—Lonnie's Day, *courtesy Coronet Instructional Films;* [E] POLLUTION—Pollution Is a Matter of Choice, *courtesy National Broadcasting Company;* [F] DISSENT—Freedom of Expression: The Feiner Case, *courtesy Encyclopaedia Britannica Educational Corporation;* [G] URBAN CONGESTION—Transportation Around the World, *courtesy Coronet Instructional Films;* [H] DRUG ABUSE, *courtesy International Education and Training, Inc.)*

Projected and Electronic Media

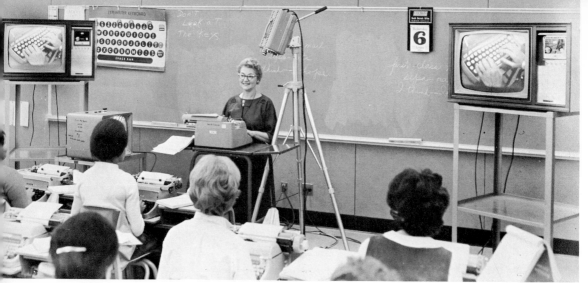

Television is used in schools in four basic ways:

1. A television program of educational value viewed at home. Teacher and students are aware of the program and have planned a significant assignment calling for students to observe, study, and draw conclusions from what they see, as part of ongoing classroom activity. Such TV programs may originate from public educational stations, or they could be sponsored or public service programs on a commercial network or local station.

2. A scheduled television program, specifically intended for school use, viewed by an organized group in the classroom. Such programs generally are produced by a state educational TV network or by a community educational TV station and relate to general areas of the curriculum such as music, art, regional history, or local government; they may be part of a series.

3. A series of scheduled telecasts intended to present the content portion of a particular course and received in designated classrooms. Such programs generally are produced locally in facilities owned and operated by the school system, and distributed to schools in the area on a "closed-circuit" basis by cable or microwave.

4. A television program from any source, recorded on videotape for playback when requested. Playback may be either in a classroom with portable equipment or via a closed-circuit system for either group or individual viewing. Since few individual school buildings are equipped with centralized video facilities, portable video "chains" are likely to be a good solution. A video chain consists of a TV camera with tripod and microphone, a videotape recorder, and a viewing monitor.

Figure 5–18. Television camera and monitors provide a close-up view of this typing teacher's hands as she demonstrates correct fingering technique before this class and several others assembled in other rooms. Note that the teacher is wearing a lavalier microphone around her neck. What are some pros and cons of providing this type of mass demonstration as opposed to using film loops or other self-instructional media in an individualized, self-paced situation? (Courtesy Board of Education, Norwalk, Conn.)

Fundamentals of Teaching with Audiovisual Technology

Each of these four educational television situations demands different teaching practices. In the first case, home viewing, the teacher must keep up to date on telecasting schedules and consider the possible contributions of selected programs to school subjects, activities, and objectives. If students who view telecasts are properly motivated, they should be eager to tell about what they saw on TV and describe how they felt about it. Students' reactions to TV can be a great stimulus to creating and producing their own "shows." How better to become an intelligent critic of the mass media?

In the second case, broadcast educational programming, the teacher presumably has a chance to learn something of the content and format of forthcoming telecasts through published schedules and teachers' guides. Teachers should find out what system-wide agreements exist between school curriculum leaders and the teaching staff. Some school systems may require a certain series of programs to be used as scheduled; other schools allow teachers freedom of choice. Regardless of the program source, there is the same obligation to plan for expert utilization in the light of course objectives as would apply if the TV program were a motion picture, filmstrip, or other packaged medium. Like setting up a projector, preparing for a TV program requires pre-tuning and testing the receiver before class to make sure of clear picture and intelligible sound.

When programming is generated locally, teaching practices usually are agreed upon within the school system. Therefore it is possible to know in advance the roles that will be played by both the television or "on-

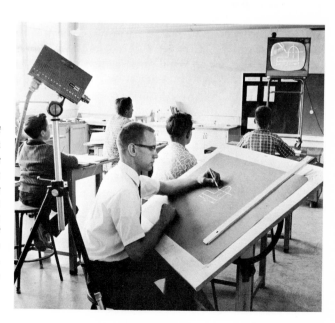

Figure 5–19. Here a basic closed-circuit television chain, consisting of camera and monitor, is being used to display the teacher's own work. Each student gets a close-up over-the-shoulder view of the drawing while it is being rendered. Can you think of other applications for this technique of electronic enlargement? Would an overhead or opaque projector serve the purpose as well as this television equipment? (Courtesy La Mesa-Spring Valley School District, La Mesa, Calif.)

Projected and Electronic Media

camera" teacher and the classroom teacher in making effective use of program content. The locally owned and operated closed-circuit system with videotape recording and playback capability is probably the most efficient and creative way to capitalize on the potential of instructional television. Television equipment is expensive, and technical personnel may be required to operate it; but having local facilities permits more flexible and creative scheduling of large-group, small-group, and even individual viewing. Moreover, teachers who have assisted in planning and even producing TV programs are more likely to use the material enthusiastically and in fresh and innovative ways.

When classroom teachers assume control of related instructional activity as direct follow-up to scheduled telecasts, they must basically carry out the teaching plans of the television teacher. The Anaheim, California City Schools were pioneers in large-scale direct television instruction. An excellent guide for classroom teachers developed for use in the Anaheim project explains the system of teaching practices and sets forth a detailed listing of responsibilities for regular classroom teachers using television, without seriously limiting their authority or freedom. This helpful guide is quoted here in full.[5]

Figure 5–20. Special television presentations may be made "live" by unusually well-qualified studio teachers, or by videotape, to large audiences of students, thus eliminating the necessity for repetitive presentations by classroom teachers. Should entire courses be mass-taught by television? Is it essential to provide opportunities for student feedback—discussion and response? How can the optimum balance between television presentation and other teaching modes be determined? (Courtesy South Carolina ETV Network)

Specific Teaching Practices

---

[5] *Instructional TV Guide*, pp. 16–20, Instructional Television, Anaheim City Schools, Anaheim, Calif. By permission.

Responsibilities of the Classroom Teacher

Physical Climate of the Classroom

Temperature and ventilation

Lighting (best placement of television set)

Tuning of set (check glare on sets from pupils' eye level). The set should be left on until telelessons are completed for the day.

Elimination of distractions

Efficient distribution of materials

Seating arrangements

Orderly movement of groups to and from the classroom, and within the classroom

Definite procedures for such organizational necessities as taking attendance, distribution of papers, leaving the room, sharpening pencils, etc.

Meeting Individual Needs

Provide proper placement of pupils with physical problems.

Be aware of the ability range within the classroom and provide for in the "pre-" and "post-" lesson experiences.

Clarify and adapt assignments to extend and enrich the learning of each individual within the group.

Before the Telelesson

Evaluate learning activities which pupils are developing.

Thoroughly read and study telelesson guide sheets for each lesson. Know the scope and sequence of each unit and how each telelesson is correlated with scope and sequence guide.

Prepare and have available all materials, texts, etc., for pre-telelesson preparation and related teaching activities in advance.

Create a readiness for learning; discuss lesson and its purpose, what pupils may expect, what they will learn. Introduce new vocabulary.

Organize the classroom so that distribution of materials to be used during telelesson is made before the lesson; television sets are turned on and adjusted, drapes pulled, pupils seated properly, and all materials other than those needed during the lesson are out of the way to avoid distraction.

Watch the time and schedule closely so that the pre-lesson activities are presented thoroughly.

Develop a method in the classroom for handling questions asked by the studio teacher.

During the Telelesson

Help pupils who need individual help during a work-type lesson.

Take notes. (Teacher's notes can be used to emphasize main points of the lesson and as a guide for discussion following the lesson.)

List vocabulary for further definition and discussion.

Observe pupil reaction throughout lesson; make notes of any reactions valuable to the studio teacher. Handle behavior problems immediately.

Move about the room to see that pupils understand and are using materials properly.

Give pupils additional directions when necessary during the telelesson.

Become enthusiastic—answer questions asked by the studio teacher during the presentation—if the teacher is enthused and participates, the pupils understand that they are a part of the lesson and should respond to the studio teacher.

Encourage "controlled" overt responses to ideas and questions raised during a lesson. The studio teacher indicates by the way questions and ideas are presented, the type of response that is expected of pupils observing. (He may say, "What famous man, whom we have heard about before, died at the Alamo?" He may say, "Can you *think* of other types of plants that adapt to their environment in a different way?" The first question should be answered audibly by pupils in the classroom with the teacher guiding and encouraging the response. The second question requires a covert response from each pupil which the classroom teacher may wish to bring up after the telecast for further discussion.) Types of response that detract from the intimacy of the studio teacher-pupil relationship should be avoided. (The studio teacher might state, "Let's *think*

Figure 5–21. Audiovisual technology has opened new and challenging roles for teachers with unusual talents. This TV studio teacher has a wide array of media at his command and more time to plan and prepare his presentations than is generally available to classroom teachers. In addition, the studio teacher has available the services of technicians and production specialists to ensure that each presentation is of high quality. (Courtesy South Carolina ETV Network)

about why the pioneers went west." The classroom teacher responds. "Mary, what do you think?" Mary may or may not give a correct response. The teacher in the studio cannot anticipate the timing for an oral response to this type of question and the attention and rapport existing between studio teacher and pupil is divided during the discussion in the classroom.) *Participation is an important factor in learning; it must be developed, encouraged, and controlled by both studio and classroom teacher working together during the telecast.*

After the Telelesson

Check pupils' understanding of concepts presented by the studio teacher. Stress areas of the telelesson that need re-emphasizing.

Re-teach in areas where there is lack of understanding in relation to ability levels.

Check to see that new vocabulary is understood.

Organize class into established groups to summarize lesson and to coordinate and carry out further learning activities.

Use suggested related classroom instruction activities for group work extended over a period of time. Correlate the activities from lesson to lesson so that continuity is established.

Guide discussion according to concepts and understandings which pupils should gain from the telelesson.

Provide experiences to enable the pupils to more fully understand and apply concepts presented.

Provide enrichment activities to meet the special needs and interests of pupils.

Encourage pupil reports of supplementary activities such as experiments, projects, reading reports that grow out of telelessons. Pupil participation is essential to effective education. Participation by using ideas in assignments, projects, discussion and research stimulate active responses so important to good education.

Check pupils' notebooks to assure their maximum value. Folders should be provided for storage of related materials.

Encourage the method of having pupils rise and face the group when speaking.

Guidance, Encouragement, and Assistance to the Studio Teacher

Complete and send to studio teacher telelesson reaction sheets and evaluation reports.

Give constructive criticism at meetings, personal conferences, or by phone—let studio teacher know *what most interests pupils—what teaching techniques "pay off" in learning.*

Give recommendations for future lessons.

Share materials and projects developed by teacher and pupils.

Professional Support

Give support to the television project in contacts with pupils, parents, teachers, and general public.

Give professional support to the efforts of the studio teacher.

Figure 5–22. Is it true that slides and filmstrips are merely a lower-cost substitute for motion pictures? Are there learning situations in which projected still pictures might actually be more effective than movies? (From film Child of the Future; *courtesy National Film Board of Canada)*

Projected Still Pictures

Far from being a "poor man's movie," still pictures offer advantages of their own—they are inexpensive, convenient, relatively easy to produce locally, and they lend themselves to prolonged study or repeated viewing either by groups of students or by individuals. We shall examine specific characteristics of various types of projected still pictures, then list teaching practices which apply generally to all such visuals.

Slides

The first "magic lantern" slide show, (more than three hundred years ago!) amazed the curious with hand-drawn

images thrown on the screen by the flickering flames of a kerosene lantern. The invention of photography in mid-nineteenth century brought realism to the screen. Although larger-format photographic and handmade "lantern" slides are still in use, the invention of Kodachrome film in 1935 popularized miniature cameras and made the familiar 35mm or 2 × 2-inch color slide a world standard. Automatic projectors with remote control of slide advance and focus make slides easy to show. Slides have the advantage of being easily arranged or rearranged in whatever sequence is appropriate for a given audience and topic. Anyone can make 2 × 2-inch slides with a simple camera and there are many commercial sources of professionally photographed slides on subjects such as art, history, nature, and geography. Production of slides is discussed in detail in Chapter 8.

Filmstrips

Filmstrips are sometimes called "slide films" because they are simply a series of small slides photographed in permanent sequence on a strip of 35mm film. Prepared either in color or black and white, filmstrips may include printed captions on each frame or may be designed for use with narration recorded on tape cassette or disc.

Literally thousands of filmstrips are available in nearly every area of subject matter. Filmstrips usually are much less expensive than motion pictures, and they are easily shown, handled, stored, and shipped. Although filmstrip sequences cannot be rearranged like slides, both media have a definite advantage over motion picture films in that the rate of presentation can be completely controlled by the teacher (or by the student in self-instruction). The material may be stopped, reversed, or advanced rapidly to bypass unwanted information. Many self-instructional

[OPPOSITE] *Figure 5–23. Portable viewing units make homework more interesting. Some such devices show filmstrips, slides, or super 8 cartridge films. Audio may be provided by tape cassette and some models may be programmed to advance according to student response. (Courtesy Graflex Division, Singer Education and Training Products)*

Figure 5–24. Captioned filmstrips allow students to respond by reading. Is it a valuable learning experience to require students to take turns reading the captions aloud? Why do some teachers prefer not to show captions? How can you adjust an ordinary filmstrip projector so that captions are not visible? (Courtesy The National Education Association. Photo by Ben Spiegel)

Projected and Electronic Media

A

B

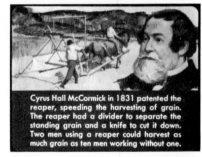

Cyrus Hall McCormick in 1831 patented the reaper, speeding the harvesting of grain. The reaper had a divider to separate the standing grain and a knife to cut it down. Two men using a reaper could harvest as much grain as ten men working without one.

C

A money panic hit America in 1893. A drain on the gold supply was the cause. The stock market crashed and 400 banks closed.

[ABOVE] *Figure 5–25. The captions on these filmstrip frames contain a lot of information. Should the captions be read aloud? What might a teacher do to stimulate students to do further research on each topic? Might the teacher's approach be different if the filmstrips were to be viewed individually, rather than seen by the entire class? (Courtesy United States History Society, Inc.)*

D

[LEFT *and* OPPOSITE] *Figure 5–26. Filmstrips are available on a wide variety of subjects; most are in color, and many*

Fundamentals of Teaching with Audiovisual Technology

have recorded disc or tape cassette sound tracks. Filmstrips, being much less costly to produce and distribute than motion pictures, are more likely to be accessible to teachers and students without advance scheduling. Most media resource centers provide catalogs of filmstrip holdings. (From: [A] The Wonderful World of Plants, [B] Modern Biology: Environment & Survival, [C] Children of The Inner City, [D] This is the Soviet Union, [E] America's Urban Crisis, courtesy SVE Division, Singer Education and Training Products)

E

devices utilize software in filmstrip format, including reading pacers, tachistoscopic projectors, and "teaching machines."

Overhead Transparencies

The overhead projector is a versatile and convenient instructional tool. Many teachers prefer it to the chalkboard. One advantage of the overhead is that transparencies may be shown without darkening the classroom. The big advantage that the overhead gives over the conventional chalkboard, of course, is that you can have materials already prepared and need not turn your back to the group nor take valuable class time for writing. Excellent, colorful transparencies are available at reasonable cost from software publishers, but many teachers make their own visuals, either from commercially printed

Figure 5-27. This art teacher presents basic design concepts by moving bits of transparent colored plastic around on the stage of her overhead projector. With projector and screen in this position, will she need to be careful not to obstruct the view of students who may be seated to her left? Notice that the screen is placed in one corner of the classroom and the lights have been left on. (Courtesy 3M Company)

Projected and Electronic Media

masters or from original drawings which may be made into transparencies using the procedures described in Chapter 8.

Science teachers want students to be able to make accurate observations and to draw conclusions from what they see. The microprojector allows the teacher to show a group of students the same specimens or prepared slides that could otherwise be observed through the microscope by only one student at a time. However, in biology, for example, the use of the microscope by individuals may add glamorous impact to the learning situation and give a feeling of personal discovery. Also, many teachers believe that the ability to operate a microscope is a valid teaching objective even though the biology course is not

Microprojection

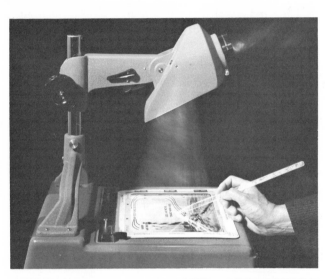

Figure 5–28. A unique feature of the overhead projector is the ease with which complex diagrams can be built up using the overlay technique described in Chapter 8. In this picture the last layer of several has been flipped down into position. Note the three tape hinges on the far side of the transparency as well as the teacher's use of a transparent plastic pointer. (Courtesy Tecnifax Corporation)

[LEFT] *Figure 5–29. Sing-along with the overhead! The transparency that this music teacher is using saves her a lot of chalkboard work and lost time, as well as allowing easy use of color and other illustrations for variety. Does she have to be careful where she stands, however, to avoid blocking any student's view of the screen? (Courtesy 3M Company).*

[OPPOSITE] *Figure 5–31. A microprojector enlarges actual microscope slides for viewing by a small group. How is this different from photographing the specimen with a 35mm camera and then projecting the resulting slide? (Courtesy The National Education Association. Photo by Esther Bubley. Mosquito slide courtesy Central Scientific Company)*

Figure 5–30. The ubiquitous opaque projector will show almost anything thin enough to be inserted against its platen. Despite its limitations, the big advantage of the opaque is, of course, the fact that materials do not have to be photographed or converted into a transparency in order to be projected. (Photo by David H. Curl)

vocational in the same sense as a program for training medical technicians.

Special projectors and attachments are available for showing microscope slides made from stained specimens or even live organisms in a liquid medium. Some science teachers, however, prefer the brighter image from a conventional slide projector and the flexibility of handling and showing 2 × 2-inch slides. Photographic slides of microscopic material may be purchased from commercial sources or made by a teacher or students using a good microscope, a single-lens reflex camera, and an appropriate adapter or mount for connecting the two pieces of equipment.

Opaque Projection

Vastly different from other projectors, the opaque projector contains a mirror which reflects light from the surface of the picture or object being shown through a lens onto an ordinary projection screen. The size of projectable objects, however, is limited to the space between the top of the projection platen and the body of the projector, and the size of pictures or sheets on

Projected and Electronic Media

Figure 5–32. Projection tracing is a very handy way to enlarge maps, diagrams, and pictures for presentation and display. Which projectors can be used for this purpose? This student is drawing on a large sheet of wrapping paper. Can projection tracing be done on a chalkboard? (Courtesy The National Education Association. Photo by Joe Di Dio)

which material may be mounted is limited to approximately ten inches square or a strip ten inches wide.

The scope of materials available is practically limitless when teachers have an opaque projector and a satisfactory room darkening system. An arrowhead, a fern leaf, a swatch ˙of cloth, a page from a manuscript or a student's theme, cancelled checks, postage stamps, coins, crystals, hand-drawn diagrams, snapshots, postcards, and magazine, newspaper, and textbook illustrations are a few of the items that may be projected.

Despite the advantage of being able to show original materials without photographing them or re-drawing them onto transparency film, the opaque projector is relatively bulky and noisy and the image it projects is not nearly as bright as that of most overhead and slide projectors. One of the most popular uses of the opaque is for projection tracing—any image projected onto drawing paper, poster board, or even onto a chalkboard can be traced around in minutes with marker or chalk, leaving a permanent outline image of the desired size.

All projected materials require pre-planning before use. Slides, filmstrips, transparencies, and opaque materials, however, are more under control of the presenter, allowing some special opportunities, but requiring certain precautions:

1. Try setting up equipment so that the projector (except for the opaque) can be operated conveniently from the front of the room. Overheads are designed for this use and many slide and filmstrip projectors can be operated either with short focal length lenses or with remote control cords.

Specific Teaching Practices

Figure 5–33. Using the overhead projector from a seated position gives everyone an unobstructed view of the screen. Notice that cut-out figures on sticks are being laid on the projector stage, the effect being much like a puppet show. (Courtesy The National Education Association. Photo by Esther Bubley)

2. Adjust the screen, if possible, to eliminate the annoying "keystone" effect that occurs when projector and screen are not lined up correctly. Many tripod screens have a "keystone-eliminator bar" allowing the top of the screen to be tilted toward the viewers. The bottom of a roll-down screen often may be pulled backward toward the wall and fastened with a hook to square-up the projected image.

3. Reveal only one item at a time. Overlay techniques can be used on overhead transparencies, or portions of the picture can be masked off until wanted, either on the overhead or the opaque. Slide series may be prepared using a "pop-on" sequence, so that additional material appears as each subsequent slide is brought to the screen.

4. If materials are captioned, try covering the caption. Ask students to react in their own words to what they see.

5. Guide students as they analyze pictures in depth. Carry on dialog with the students, asking them questions such as, "If what you just saw is true, what would you expect to see in the next picture?"

6. Encourage students to create and show their own projected pictures as visual reports.

7. Review picture sequences, asking students how they would go about finding answers to questions raised, but not answered by what they have seen.

Audio Recordings Every student listens to favorite musical groups on radio and records; many have their own tape recorders and cassette tape players. But sometimes people who are

Figure 5–34. Phonograph records and record players are available in almost every school. Under what conditions might it be advantageous for the teacher to play a record to the entire class? When might it be more appropriate for individuals or small groups to listen to a record privately? (Courtesy SVE Division, Singer Education and Training Products)

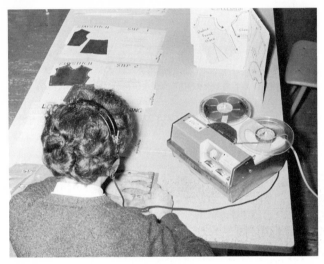

Figure 5–35. This tape recorder is part of a very basic type of instructional system being tried out in home economics. The teacher has prepared descriptive visual panels that provide step-by-step instruction for cutting and fitting patterns. The tape-recorded component guides the student as she goes through the process, giving her tutorial-type comments and anticipating problems she may encounter. If students wear headphones, several self-instructional stations may be in use simultaneously in the same laboratory or workroom. (Courtesy Ithaca City School District, Ithaca, N.Y.)

accustomed to radio and recordings as entertainment media find it hard to think of the same media as resources for learning. Including musical appreciation, there is not a single aspect of the school curriculum in which recordings, primarily in the form of cassette tapes, cannot add new dimensions of versatility to the learning process.

Despite the excellent programming available to schools from a few educational radio stations, scheduling problems and increasing emphasis on individualized, rather than group listening make magnetic tape dominate the field of audio instruction. Even disc recordings frequently are "dubbed" or re-recorded onto cassette tapes for longer life and greater convenience.

There are several different ways of putting the tape recorder to work. The first technique is to play a taped audio program for the class under the guidance of the teacher, in the same manner as a phonograph disc or a motion picture is presented in relation to a student

Figure 5–36. Commercial recordings are widely available and relatively inexpensive. Are disc recordings suitable for individualized instruction? Can young children be trusted to use them without damage? (Courtesy The National Education Association. Photo by Esther Bubley)

problem, as an introduction to a topic or unit, as a part of a lecture or an explanation, or as a vicarious travel experience to a foreign country. Recorded piano accompanyment for a music lesson, a tape-recorded interview, and a dramatization of a play are a few examples.

The second technique is to use a recorded tape as an extension of the teacher's presence and guidance, that is, employ a tape recorder to play back an instructional tape made by the teacher for one group while the teacher is at work in another area. Hosts of possibilities for both large and small groups, for team or conventional teaching situations, present themselves. Such taped content may call for written or spoken responses by the students, may refer students to pictures or diagrams in textbooks, or to filmstrip frames and slides in individual viewing devices. Some of the technological developments for carrying on such activities have become quite complex, and such operations are frequently carried on in specially equipped rooms. For example, the familiar language laboratories, or more broadly applied, the electronic learning laboratories, make use of the teacher's own voice and guidance in precisely planned exercises, and it should be emphasized that this same procedure may be applied in all teaching fields. Hence it becomes obvious that the language laboratory in broader use should be called an electronic learning laboratory, or audio listening-response center. Thus the tape recorder may be fitted with a special extension cord or wiring channel, or a multiple outlet box may be installed into which sets of headphones may be plugged for individual student listening. More complicated installations involve a master console installation either in the listening room or in an adjacent "studio" from which signals may be fed to student lis-

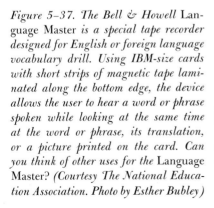

Figure 5–37. The Bell & Howell Language Master is a special tape recorder designed for English or foreign language vocabulary drill. Using IBM-size cards with short strips of magnetic tape laminated along the bottom edge, the device allows the user to hear a word or phrase spoken while looking at the same time at the word or phrase, its translation, or a picture printed on the card. Can you think of other uses for the Language Master? (Courtesy The National Education Association. Photo by Esther Bubley)

Projected and Electronic Media

Figure 5–38. This sophisticated electronic learning laboratory allows students to listen and respond individually to dialog and questions recorded in a foreign language. The teacher can monitor each student's progress by "listening in" on headphones. Can similar functions be accomplished without built-in equipment? If all students are not working on the same lesson (or even the same subject matter), how could the needed flexibility be provided? (Courtesy The National Education Association. Photo by Ben Spiegel)

tening-responding stations either by wireless or conventional circuitry.

The fully equipped electronic learning laboratory is a sophisticated independent learning environment. In such labs, each student participates actively throughout each lesson. He receives prompt confirmation or correction of each response; frequently, the programming is arranged so that he may skip or repeat portions of the program that he does not need or want. Some schools and colleges are installing dial-access learning laboratories in which students merely dial a code number on a telephone dial or touch-tone panel to connect themselves with one of several audiovisual tutorial programs (see Chapter 7).

Figure 5–39. Instead of writing comments on students' themes and term papers, some teachers record suggestions and criticism at length on tapes provided by the students (cassettes are even more convenient than the reel-type shown). Each student listens individually to his own tape and corrects his own paper as guided by the teacher's comments. Might this be a more valuable learning experience than receiving back a paper already marked by the teacher? (Courtesy 3M Company)

Figure 5–40. What are the other members of the class doing while each child takes his turn to record? Is speaking into a microphone before a group a different experience from recording privately? (Courtesy The National Education Association. Photo by Esther Bubley)

A third technique is for either the students or the teacher to use the tape recorder to record project activities. Students may write, rehearse, and record a play or dialog using the classroom as a production studio. They may record classroom discussion or debate, or committee meetings; they may record a rehearsal or performance of the school orchestra or chorus, or conduct interviews with celebrities, community figures, and subject-matter experts. The possibilities are endless for imaginative use of the versatile tape recorder in the school setting.

Specific Teaching Practices

For best use of audio instruction:

1. Organize recorded instructional content around student activities and questions.
2. Include both explanatory and motivational material. Inject occasional music, verse, or humor for change of pace.
3. Use your own voice, no matter how self-conscious you may feel at first. Speak in a rather intimate,

Figure 5–41. Have you tried using a battery-powered cassette tape recorder on location? What can students learn from preparing a taped interview? How can slides or movies be coordinated with recorded voices of local officials, public servants, businessmen, and townspeople? (Courtesy The National Education Association. Photo by Esther Bubley)

Projected and Electronic Media

Figure 5–42. A student presses a key on this viewing device (top picture) to indicate his answer to a question presented to him in a filmstrip. If his answer is correct, he can advance to the next frame. A cassette tape recorder (bottom picture) carries a spoken message and signals turn the recorder and a slide, filmstrip, or motion picture projector on and off. When the student selects the right answer to a multiple-choice question and pushes the appropriate button, the program continues. How do these "responders" differ from ordinary viewers and cassette recorders? Should all learning programs be designed so that the learner must make a correct, overt response before proceeding to the next visual or to the next question? (Courtesy General Electric Research and Development Center)

conversational tone. Don't worry about an occasional minor "goof." Students will appreciate your efforts and be relieved to realize that their teacher is human.

4. Fit individualized listening and responding by students into the overall instructional plan. Decide on methods for checking student progress.

5. Test all equipment to be sure tape speed and volume are correct and that headphones (and microphones in listen-respond systems) are working.

6. Arrange for extra microphones, headphones, extension cords, and plug adapters as needed. Have a few spare components on hand.

Teaching Machines

The term *teaching machines* should not be confused with the projectors, recorders, and other hardware discussed previously. In defining the basic difference A. A. Lumsdaine pointed out:

All of the devices that have been called teaching machines ... present the individual student with programs of questions and answers, problems to be solved, or exercises to be performed. In addition, however, they always provide some type of feedback or correction to the student, so that he is immediately informed of his progress at each step, and is given a basis for correcting his errors.[6]

B. F. Skinner explained how teaching machines could place learners into direct contact with efficiently organized programmed instructional material:

Obviously the machine itself does not teach. It simply brings the student into contact with the person who composed the material it presents. It is a labor-saving device because it can bring one programmer into contact with an indefinite number of students. This may suggest mass production, but the effect on each student is surprisingly like that of a private tutor ... the machine insists that a given point be thoroughly understood, either frame by frame or set by set before the student moves on.[7]

It is quite clear that the programmed learning sequence itself (the software) is the heart of the process and that so-called teaching machines merely present the programs in visual or audiovisual form. Of course, well-organized workbooks, guide sheets, and programmed texts can perform the same function. So can multimillion dollar computer systems.

Teaching machines usually provide some kind of "cheat proof" control function so that students either

[6] A. A. Lumsdaine, "Teaching Machines and Self-Instructional Materials," *Audiovisual Communication Review*, **7**:3 (Summer 1959), 164.

[7] B. F. Skinner, "Teaching Machines," *Scientific American*, **205**:5 (November 1961) 97. Quoted by permission.

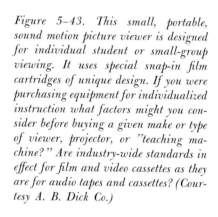

Figure 5–43. This small, portable, sound motion picture viewer is designed for individual student or small-group viewing. It uses special snap-in film cartridges of unique design. If you were purchasing equipment for individualized instruction what factors might you consider before buying a given make or type of viewer, projector, or "teaching machine?" Are industry-wide standards in effect for film and video cassettes as they are for audio tapes and cassettes? (Courtesy A. B. Dick Co.)

cannot see the correct answer until they have entered their own answer in the machine, or so that the mechanism remains locked until the student presses the correct response button. Teaching machine programs generally employ a linear chain of individual frames consisting of carefully interrelated questions, statements, or problems. Linear programming can be quite helpful for learning perceptual-motor skills and for drill purposes such as in spelling, word and object recognition, and literal translation of foreign or scientific vocabulary. However, since there can be only one "right" answer to each question or problem in a linear program, it is open to question whether this format is suitable for subject matter in which it is desirable for students to *ask* questions rather than just *answer* them, because no opportunity is provided for students to devise original solutions to problems.

Another programmed instruction format, called *branching*, can allow considerably more freedom for students to analyze and select from a series of alternatives, if not to create new solutions of their own. Although branching programs require more flexibility than that provided by all but the most sophisticated teaching machine hardware, the branching format lends itself admirably to individualized instructional systems using computers and combinations of media.

Computers can be thought of as enormously complex teaching machines. Scientists tell us that human beings use only a very small portion of the potential storage capacity of their brains; likewise, computers often have been grossly underworked when employed as devices for arithmetic drill and storage of linear program frames and responses.

Computers are being used in some exciting, experimental ways, too, but the future will show the true worth of these expensive electronic investments. Robert W. Sarnoff, president of the Radio Corporation of America (RCA), optimistically projected the educational future of the computer in the present decade:

I believe that before the end of the 1970s, the everyday use of the computer in the American home will become commonplace. Through a home terminal, the household will be linked with a computerized central information utility, providing a multitude of personal, business, and educational services on a time-sharing basis. . . . We must begin to think of it as a device for widespread personal use, comparable ultimately to the telephone.[8]

Computer-Based Instruction

[8] Alvin C. Eurich, "The Role of Independent Study in the 21st Century," *Training in Business and Industry*, **7** (January 1970), 44.

Figure 5–44. *Computer-based instruction allows students to work at their own pace with a variety of programs. Teletypewriters operated by students are linked by telephone lines to a central computer. When the pupil gives a "ready" signal, the teletypewriter prints "Please type your name." Then the computer finds in its "memory" the proper program for the student and types the first question. If the pupil types a correct answer, the computer prints the next question. If the answer is incorrect or delayed, the computer answers "Wrong. Answer is _____," or "Time is up. Answer is _____," whichever is appropriate.*

Other computer terminals permit students to respond either by touching a "light-pen" to the correct answer displayed on a screen, or by speaking aloud. (Courtesy AT&T)

Figure 5–45. *Computer-controlled TV. At Oak Park and River Forest High School, Oak Park, Ill., a computer performs all memory and control functions between audio and video program sources and 75 individual student positions. (Courtesy Ampex Corporation)*

Projected and Electronic Media

Figure 5–46. Electronic response systems enable one teacher to monitor the answers given by everyone in a large class. Using the console, the instructor can ask questions during lectures or have questions presented within a film or tape. Each student replies by pressing a button on his responder, furnishing the instructor with an immediate visual display of both individual student and class composite scores. Using such a system the instructor gets feedback on whether the class is "following" his presentation and students receive immediate confirmation or correction of their responses. Upon what premises about the nature of teaching and learning is such a system based? (Courtesy Link Division, Singer Education and Training Products)

The computer, whether housed physically in the home, in the school, or in some central data-processing center, has tremendous potential for guiding independent learning. A computer can function as the central nervous system of an instructional complex, concentrating the unique power and advantages of each medium at the exact place and instant when needed by each learner. Alvin C. Eurich describes the kind of apparatus future students may use:

Sophisticated learning terminals will be available . . . as commonly as telephones, radios and televisions today. Each terminal will include an instrument with a keyboard that looks like an electric typewriter with a telephone. It will also include a screen for visual display, with sound, of anything from a printed page to a programmed lesson to a motion picture of a Shakespeare play or an amoeba reproducing. The student will be able to dial a number for a lesson, problem, or the information he needs to complete a lesson. The response will be typed (just as airline or hotel reservations are today) or displayed immediately. The student will therefore be able to carry on a continuous dialogue with the computer . . . .[9]

Computers, as all projected and electronic media, will be used most effectively as components of instructional systems. As the cost comes down, nearly everyone will be able to use computers for everything from making routine calculations to composing music. Perhaps the most challenging possibilities, however, lie in simulation. Almost any imaginable situation or environment could be simulated, from nuclear disaster to overpopulation. Even elementary school students could try their hand at solving problems of this magnitude, with computers

[9] Ibid, 45.

[LEFT] *Figure 5–47. Reflections in a computer's eye. This on-board computer, known affectionately by the astronauts as* HAL, *has* TV *cameras through which "he" can see activities in all parts of the nuclear-powered spaceship* Discovery. *Here* HAL *is engaged in a technical conversation with Mission Commander David Bowman (Keir Dullea).* HAL *is in control of nearly every aspect of* Discovery's *mission to explore the planet Jupiter in Stanley Kubrick and Arthur C. Clarke's provocative film,* 2001: A Space Odyssey.

Can computers actually converse with people today? Will they be able to do this in the year 2001? Do the potentialities of computers include the processes of reasoning and interacting with humans? © *1968 by Metro-Goldwyn-Mayer, Inc.*

[BELOW] *Figure 5–48. Brain surgery on a computer. Apparently because of an error made by his human programmer, the computer* HAL *has malfunctioned and, in seeming paranoia, has killed all of the crew of the spaceship* Discovery *except Mission Commander Bowman. Here, in a crucial episode from the film* 2001: A Space Odyssey, *Bowman deactivates certain of the computer's logic circuits in an attempt to save the mission to Jupiter.*

Do computers ever make mistakes? If computers make mistakes, who is to blame? Is it possible that a computer could become mentally ill? © *1968 by Metro-Goldwyn-Mayer, Inc.*

Projected and Electronic Media

supplying data for decision making and information about the probable consequences of each possible solution. How better to learn problem solving then by actually trying to solve some of the major problems of mankind?

1. Make a list of the various media described in Chapters 4 and 5, then regroup them in abbreviated form under the following new headings (a), (b), (c):
   (a) Media that do not depend upon hardware or other equipment for their use.
   (b) Media that students themselves may produce as a significant learning activity.
   (c) Media most appropriate to your own specific teaching field.

2. Explain Marshall McLuhan's enigmatic statement: "The Medium is the Message" and its curious variation, "The Medium is the *Massage*." Give an example that illustrates the meaning of each phrase.

3. Discuss the following statement: "The public mass media dominate our culture—why should children interrupt their education by going to school?"

4. List several different concepts or areas of instruction in your subject area that might best lend themselves to film presentation. Describe how certain specialized motion picture techniques could be used to advantage.

5. List several subjects that could be presented effectively in the form of short "single-concept" or "simple-concept" films.

6. Give examples of the effective use of each of the following motion picture production techniques:
   (a) Slow-motion photography
   (b) Time-lapse photography
   (c) Animation
   (d) Dramatization

7. Prepare a plan or curriculum guide for home viewing of a current commercial or public educational television program or series. State objectives and questions for students and describe follow-up activities that could occur in class.

8. Describe several potential uses of a portable television camera and videotape recorder in your school.

9. List several circumstances in which visuals require prolonged analytical study—projected still pictures being, therefore, more effective than motion pictures.

10. Describe ways in which a teacher can stimulate students to get the most out of viewing filmstrips and slides.

11. Projection-trace a small illustration or diagram to a size large enough for class presentation or display.

12. Locate sources of commercially produced overhead transparencies. Prepare sketches for producing your own transparencies when commercial ones are not available.

13. Write a short script for an instructional tape recording and a portion of an accompanying student work sheet.

14. Prepare a few sample frames from a programmed instructional unit. Use either linear or branching format, but specify objectives of the program in behavioral terms.

15. Visit a computer-based instruction installation. Try out a terminal. Interview the supervisor. Report back to the class on what you see as the possibilities and limitations of computer-based instruction.

Selected References

Better Communications Through Tape. Magnetic Products Division, 3M Company, St. Paul, Minn. 55101, 1968, 30 pp. plus tear-outs. A how-to-do-it guide book for more effective use of tape recorders. Includes detailed checklists for recording classes and meetings, conferences, and special presentations.

Child of The Future, The (16mm film, 58 min) McGraw-Hill Films, 1221 Avenue of the Americas, New York, N.Y. 10020, 1965. Marshall McLuhan presents the thesis that the current generation has the ability to gain full educational benefit from technology through total involvement of the senses. Demonstrates various types of media in use.

Children Learn From Filmstrips (16mm film, 16 min) McGraw-Hill Films, 1221 Avenue of the Americas, New York, N.Y. 10020, 1963. Shows teachers presenting filmstrip content by various ingenious techniques including active student participation. Points out that a filmstrip used with imagination can lead children naturally into learning.

DIAMOND, ROBERT M. (ed.) *A Guide to Instructional Television.* McGraw-Hill Book Co., 1221 Avenue of the Americas, New York, N.Y. 10020, 1964, 304 pp. A collection of case studies and articles on production, distribution, utilization, and evaluation of ITV in schools and colleges.

LEE, THOMAS GRAHAM. *Microform Systems, A Handbook For Educators.* Michigan Audio-Visual Association, 401 South Fourth Street, Ann Arbor, Mich. 48103, 1970, 64 pp. Brief, but informative introduction to microform systems for information retrieval in schools.

Let Them Learn (16mm film, 28 min) Encyclopaedia Britannica Educational Corporation, 425 N. Michigan Ave., Chicago, Ill. 60611, 1969. Examines the characteristics of educational films that make them significant teaching materials. Shows examples of films being used in both planned and spontaneous teaching situations, stressing availability of both materials and equipment to teachers and students.

New Dimensions Through Teaching Films (16mm film, 27 min)

Coronet Instructional Films, 65 East South Water St., Chicago, Ill. 60601, 1965. Emphasizes the educational film as a basic curriculum tool. Uses excerpts from several films to stress the effectiveness of film-utilization programs planned for specific subject areas and grade levels.

Producers Manual. Magnetic Products Division, 3M Company, St. Paul, Minn. 55101, 1968, 43 pp. Concise, illustrated short course in television production intended primarily for users of videotape recording equipment. Glossary and bibliography.

Rhetoric of The Movies (set of six super-8 motion pictures, 3 min each, with guide) AECT Publications Sales, 1201 16th St., N.W. Washington, D.C. 20036, 1968. Demonstrates movie-making techniques based on verbal language parallels. Primarily for teachers of English Language Arts who introduce movies as a medium of communication.

RING, ARTHUR E., and WILLIAM J. SHELLEY. *Learning with the Overhead Projector.* Chandler Publishing Co., 124 Spear St., San Francisco, Calif. 94105, 1969, 126 pp. Collection of specific ideas for creative use of the overhead projector in various subject areas and at different levels.

Sign-On/Sign-Off (16mm film, 23 min) Pennsylvania State University, Film Library, University Park, Pa. 16802, 1968. Examines computer-assisted instruction and the social changes and technological advances that have made the computer an educational tool. Emphasizes the role of the computer in individualizing instruction.

SPEAR, JAMES. *Creating Visuals for TV.* National Education Association Publications Sales, 1201 16th St., N.W., Washington, D.C. 20036, 48 p., 1962. Practical suggestions for improving TV programs through the more effective use of visual materials. Includes many ideas for projected and nonprojected resources and props and describes how to create special effects.

Teachers Guides to Television, Box 564, Lenox Hill Station, New York, N.Y. 10021, semi-annual. Each issue contains selected lesson plans covering nationally televised programs of special educational value. Includes synopses of forthcoming programs and suggestions for activities before and after viewing, along with bibliography and related film list.

Television in Education (16mm film, 28 min) American Telephone & Telegraph Co. Free loan through local Bell System offices, 1962. Visits classrooms in which broadcast and closed circuit television are being used for instruction. Shows studio teachers at work and emphasizes the needed cooperation between curriculum planner, studio teacher, and classroom teacher. Several educators relate their experiences with ETV.

TV in The Classroom (videotape, 28 min) Great Plains National Instructional TV Library, University of Nebraska, Lincoln, Neb. 68508, 1970. Introduces teachers to the unique functions and uses of instructional television. Several other videotapes in this series deal with aspects of production, utilization, and management of ITV.

Unique Contribution, The (16mm film, 29 min) Encyclopaedia Britannica Educational Corporation, 425 N. Michigan Ave., Chicago, Ill. 60611, 1960. Uses several excerpts from educational films employing time-lapse photography, animation, and other motion picture techniques to point out contributions of the film medium in education.

WITHERSPOON, JOHN P. and WILLIAM J. KESSLER. *Instructional Television Facilities: A Planning Guide,* Superintendent of Documents, U.S. Government Printing Office, Washington, D.C. 20402, Catalog No. FS 5.234:34043, 1969, 73 pp. Comprehensive guide for schools contemplating an investment in television equipment and facilities. Tells where to get help.

Worth How Many Words? (16mm film, 8 min) Eastman Kodak Company, Rochester, N.Y. 14650, 1969. Shows unique and useful applications of photography, probing and revealing subject matter in ways no other medium can and demonstrating various filming techniques.

6
The Teacher Uses Media

The things which are taught children are not an education, but the means of education.

RALPH WALDO EMERSON

One standard for judging competence of teachers is the inventiveness of their classroom use of media. Media utilization techniques should arise out of a matrix of principles and actual experience, and should involve original thought instead of merely being a list of recipes absorbed from textbooks or borrowed from colleagues. Burton and Brueckner stressed this point of view:

Techniques are necessary and important—in fact, nothing could take place in any field without ways of doing things. *Principles*—that is, general truths or concepts or accepted tenets—are also necessary. New techniques are constantly being devised which are better ways of carrying out principles and which, furthermore, must be chosen discriminatively to fit given circumstances. Principles are guides that help in selecting techniques. Studies in both industry and education show that workers equipped with the "theory of the thing" are more efficient than those equipped only with sets of techniques which they may not fully understand. . . . The so-called practical teacher is the worst offender, since his level of training and insight is that of the device and not that of intelligent independent invention of techniques based upon principles.[1]

We suggest five utilization principles that may form such a matrix of learnings and thus serve teachers well in making day-to-day decisions about their uses of media. The principles we have formulated demand specific kinds of action on the part of teachers, and the principles obviously are infused with vitality only as teachers come to understand valid principles of teaching and learning.

Principle One—Selection

Teachers should base their selection of media on valid learning objectives and the unique characteristics of learners.

This principle becomes the ability to find and choose appropriate media, from textbooks to field trips, and from

---

[1] William H. Burton and Leo J. Brueckner, *Supervision: A Social Process*, 3d ed., (New York: Appleton-Century-Crofts, 1955), p. 73.

163

models and mock-ups to videotape recordings. This basic ability demands subsidiary abilities to:

1. Identify and write out appropriate teaching purposes and specific performance criteria and conditions in clear and consistent form.
2. Locate suitable media from resource files, catalogs, and sourcebooks.
3. Select specific media to make optimum contributions to the objectives that were formulated.
4. Predict that an identified learning experience will influence students in desirable and specific ways.
5. Relate precisely various kinds of selected media to specific problems as they are being worked on by individuals and groups.
6. Select media for use in new and more efficient ways to involve students in self-instructional processes and/or large-group or team-teaching methods.
7. Select appropriate media to play a variety of instructional roles.
8. Judge the quality and suitability of specific media on the basis of the interests, experiences, maturity, and powers of comprehension of a specific group of learners.
9. Plan and prepare simple, specialized media such as slides, transparencies, instructional tapes, and displays for immediate local use.
10. Plan and assist with production of such complex, specialized media as sound motion pictures, instructional television programs, and programmed instructional packages.
11. Test the selection process by observing the extent

Fundamentals of Teaching with Audiovisual Technology

to which media affected attainment of instructional objectives.

Although many teachers choose instructional materials because they seem to coincide with subject-matter content in a given textbook, this rationale is not always consistent with student-centered learning. Most worthwhile and permanent learning takes place when students and teachers agree on objectives and performance criteria; therefore, selection of media should be based first on the needs and desired achievements of specific learners, whether taken as a group or (more desirably) as individuals. The ideal library/media center provides reference services, browsing and preview facilities, and immediate access to every kind of book, pamphlet, picture, film, tape, transparency, kit, or game available within the building or local school system and information about rental or loan of additional media from other sources.

Characteristics of Learners

The characteristics of individuals are many and complicated within any given group of learners. These variations in cultural environment, past experience, physical, mental and emotional makeup, needs, goals, attitudes, and perceptual "literacy" must influence the teacher in his selection of media and methods. It is vitally important to consider each student's level of maturity and background of experience to predict whether content is too easy or too difficult. Consider how limitations within the materials themselves, such as obsolete clothing and hair styles or unfamiliar life styles, behavior patterns, and language might amuse, confuse, or alienate certain students.

Figure 6–2. Librarians, as well as teachers, are finding their traditional roles and duties changing as school facilities are built and remodeled for extensive use of audiovisual media. Many librarians think of themselves as media specialists *and enjoy the role of resource consultant better than the role of book custodian and silence-maintainer. (Courtesy The National Education Association. Photo by Esther Bubley)*

Young children like to act out adult roles. They love to "try out" what it might feel like to be an astronaut, an astronomer, an ecologist, a teacher, or an actress. Media in the "springboard" role can launch children into ecstasies of exploration and self-discovery. Older youth prefer to grapple with real problems of interpersonal relations and competitive value systems. Politics, economics, sex, and vocational aspirations are concerns of high school students, and wise teachers provide opportunities for students to find and interact with media relevant to such concerns.

Figure 6–3. The three filmstrip frames shown in this group are from the Classification of Plants *and* Prehistoric Life *series. What criteria should teachers use to determine whether filmstrip content is appropriate and significant?* (© Encyclopaedia Britannica Films, Inc.)

Selection Criteria

Both teachers and students need to evaluate media in terms of their potential value in stimulating inquiry or meeting specific objectives. The factor of availability will enter into every final media-use decision; but the following list of general curriculum factors also should be considered as applying to all forms of media:

1. Is the content useful and important *to the learner?*
2. Will it be *interesting* to students?
3. Is there direct relationship to a *specific objective* or problem-solving activity?
4. How will the format and presentation treatment affect the organization and sequence of *learner activities?*
5. Is the material *authentic, typical,* and *up to date?*
6. Have facts and concepts been *checked for accuracy?* Are the producers expert in the subject matter or have they employed competent consultants?
7. Do the content and presentation meet contemporary standards of *good taste?*
8. If controversial, are both sides given *equal emphasis? Should* they be?
9. Is *bias* or *propaganda* evident? If so, how should students deal with it?
10. Is *technical quality* satisfactory? Are images clear? Narration or dialog intelligible? Color, motion, and special effects used authentically and creatively?
11. Do content and structure reveal *careful planning* by the producer?

12. Has the material actually been *validated,* or tested with learners? If so, who performed the evaluation? Under what conditions? What were the characteristics of the students? How successful were the results?

Teachers occasionally will show a film or use other material "just because it's in the building today." Obviously, valid judgments cannot be made about media without examination or previewing. Catalog descriptions alone, producers' brochures, and comments by other teachers may not be very appropriate in helping you select materials to be made available for the specific backgrounds, interests, and objectives of your students. Locating, evaluating, selecting, and obtaining appropriate media resources is a most important part of every teacher's job.

Sources of Media

Teachers who read educational journals, attend professional meetings, and compare notes frequently with media specialists and with colleagues in their own subject

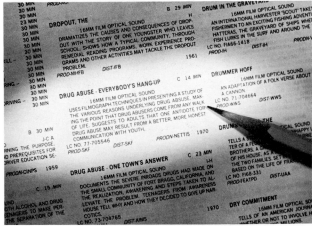

Figure 6–4. Catalogs, both general and specific, are available to help users locate appropriate audiovisual media. Many resource centers supply teachers with catalogs of materials available locally as well as those that may be rented or borrowed from outside sources. Some catalogs are limited to specific kinds of materials such as tapes, filmstrips, or local community resources. What precautions must a wise teacher exercise before using materials ordered on the basis of a catalog description? (Photos by David H. Curl)

The Teacher Uses Media

field are the ones who most frequently find out about and use modern media. Media-center administrators like to receive preview requests and rental and purchase recommendations from such teachers, because they know their requests have been thought out thoroughly and that the materials requested will be put to effective use. The search for media is a continuous one. Besides the reference sources listed at the end of this chapter, most media centers have their own catalogs or card files of locally available materials. Become familiar with all of the resources available to you and consult them often.

The use of media should be preceded by the development of adequate learner readiness for effective participation.

Principle Two: Readiness

This principle becomes the ability to build student readiness. When good teaching-unit problems and student concerns are the basis for using instructional media, readiness plans come easy. However, even though media are tied directly to specific problems and detailed responses, teachers need to take proper action in introducing them.

This basic ability demands subsidiary abilities to:

1. Develop a specific readiness plan of what to do and say.
2. Guide learners in determining individual or group needs for the media selected.
3. Relate specific media to specific problem-solving activities.
4. Employ a variety of methods for building readiness, including the procedure of setting up a class problem before the materials are presented, and including readiness plans in written form.
5. Use a number of sources of information in making readiness decisions, such as specific performance criteria and knowledge of learner characteristics.

Figure 6–5. Must a teacher be present for students to learn from film loops and other media? How does student use of media fit the pattern of utilization principles described in Chapter 6, especially the readiness and follow-up action principles? (Courtesy The National Education Association. Photo by Esther Bubley)

Principle Three: Control   *Physical facilities and conditions for using media should be arranged for by the teacher in a manner that provides for economy of time and optimum learner attention and participation.*

This principle becomes the ability to control equipment and physical facilities. Teachers have to be good organizers and, in addition, have to know when learning conditions are appropriate. Improperly used, media equipment and materials may be damaged and their learning value reduced or destroyed. Special equipment know-how is needed for certain kinds of media activities (see Chapter 9).

This important ability demands subsidiary abilities to:

1. Operate available kinds of audiovisual equipment.
2. Detect improper use or malfunctioning of equipment.
3. Judge the degree of darkness needed for proper viewing of projected images under various learning conditions.
4. Arrange proper placement of screen, seats, speakers, and other apparatus for proper learner attention and participation.
5. Make efficient arrangements for viewing and responding to media presentations and for manipulating or handling models, charts, maps, demonstration materials, and related devices.
6. Plan proper timing for using or presenting audiovisual media within existing school schedules.

Principle Four: Action   *Teachers should guide learners in their response to experiences with media.*

Mutually agreed upon objectives will determine the kinds of follow-up action that learners need to engage in. Seeing a film on a certain topic may logically be followed by some form of problem solving and application, or perhaps language activity or self-analysis.

The basic ability to guide student responses demands subsidiary abilities to:

1. Identify and call for learner activity in direct relationship to teaching purposes and objectives.
2. Formulate and use valid, provocative, and illuminating thought-type questions.
3. Employ good discussion techniques based on known and accepted problems, topics, and issues.
4. Organize student action around imaginative, challenging and unique problem-solving experiences and projects.
5. Prepare worksheets and arrange media sequences calling for specific responses in the light of (a) objectives; (b) a given audiovisual presentation or reading assignment; and (c) a particular instructional environment.
6. Organize and manage individualization and/or

large-group situations in which media are programmed to carry out specific aspects of the instructional process.

7. Organize action of students around the production
of audiovisual materials as significant group and
individual learning activities.

*Teachers should subject both media and their own utili-
zation techniques to continual evaluation.*

Principle Five: Evaluation

This principle becomes the ability to appraise the value
of media and the appropriateness of utilization techniques. No evaluation can be sound unless valid reference
points are known. Such reference points, of course, must
be the performance criteria underlying organized problem-solving activities.

This basic ability demands subsidiary abilities to:

1. Engage in the process of self-criticism, with willingness to modify previous plans of action.
2. Judge the worth of all media in terms of specific
learning objectives, without losing sight of human
values.
3. Scrutinize the procedures used in the light of student
growth.
4. Make use of various sources of data in making judgments of strengths or weaknesses in media and
methods.

The influence of the principles described in this chapter is revealed in the work of teachers who have learned
to think in critical terms about the *why* of media and
in terms of principles-techniques relationships. We need
also to stress the point that these five utilization principles
apply to all kinds of media. When teachers apply them
to any given teaching-learning situation, whether in a
traditional or modern curriculum design, their collection
of related decisions becomes a unique plan for the utilization of a given medium or combination of media.
Sometimes, this collection of decisions is put together
quickly a few minutes before the class meets. Sometimes,
decisions have to be made and altered in a continuous
fashion as learners and groups respond. Sometimes, decisions must be made long in advance, as when an instructional system is being constructed for validation. And
sometimes, decisions are put together only after painstaking study, as when designing a television program
for videotaping and remote retrieval. We now turn to
the focal point of this chapter as we examine several case
studies prepared by individual teachers which show applications with various media for each of the five utilization principles.

We are not suggesting that every teacher write out
a full and complete plan for every film, filmstrip, audio
tape, or slide set to be used in class. What is meant

is that teachers must learn to think, plan, and act in the light of facts, principles, and objectives. It is the application of this planning process with which we are concerned. Please note that while the specification of objectives in these examples has been carried only to the point of stating *teaching purposes*, each of the teachers who prepared the following case studies would be expected to formulate and state *performance criteria and conditions* (as described in Chapter 2) before putting these utilization plans into practice.

In Case Study Number 1 we offer a film utilization plan prepared by an industrial arts teacher.[2] Here, as in most of the case studies to follow, the teacher patterned his thinking according to a prescribed outline plan based on the five utilization principles of *selection, readiness, control, action,* and *evaluation.*

Case Study Number 1   The teacher has singled out the objective of developing in his students the main ability to bore holes with a bit and brace. He has decided to relate his own teaching activity to a pupil purpose, the problem of constructing a coffee table. Each of his students has accepted an extensive project of this magnitude. The teacher then brings together the instructional materials, that is, the audiovisual technology and job sheets, and also the text material on operation of various tools to meet the constructional needs of his pupils. We now turn to an outline of the teacher's plan for using the film.

PLAN FOR USING THE FILM
BORING AND DRILLING TOOLS[3]
(Teacher Decisions)

A. Class Description

Industrial Arts, Woodworking, Ninth Grade. Unit on Home Furnishings.

B. The SELECTION Principle in Action

My main teaching purposes that the film will help me achieve in my pupils:

UNDERSTANDING THAT:

1. A bit will splinter the back-side of a piece of wood if allowed to go all the way through from one side.
2. A bit or drill must be kept at right-angles to the wood being cut to insure a hole that is straight and true.
3. Bit sizes are given in thirty-seconds of an inch.

[2] Carl T. Erickson, Stratford, Connecticut Schools. By permission.
[3] *Boring and Drilling Tools,* McGraw-Hill Films, New York, N.Y.

4. The cutting angle on drills is larger for wood-cutting than for metal cutting.
5. Chips are carried out of the hole by means of drill flutes.
6. A positive starting point is necessary for the accurate placement of the drill or bit.
7. A ratchet-type bit brace allows the individual to bore a hole in places difficult to reach.
8. Screw heads may be placed flush by means of countersinking the hole.
9. A bit cannot be used to enlarge an existing hole.

ABILITY TO:

1. Bore a hole using bit and brace.
2. Adjust a ratchet bit brace to its three positions.
3. Fasten a drill in a hand-power drill.

ATTITUDE OF:

1. Exactness.
2. Industriousness.
3. Willingness to practice skills.
4. Patience.

APPRECIATION OF:

1. Good craftsmanship.
2. Orderly procedure.
3. Accurate layout.
4. Manipulative dexterity.

C. MAIN PROBLEM

To construct a coffee table (identified by teacher and pupils before the film was shown).

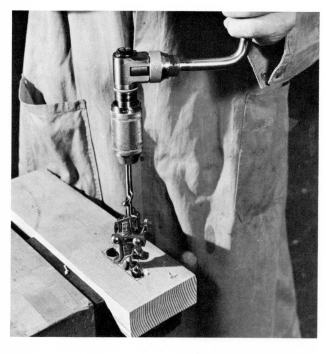

Figure 6–6. The demonstrations of proper use of tools in the film, Boring and Drilling Tools, *may be observed by large groups of students without obstruction by means of close-up motion picture photography. (Courtesy McGraw-Hill Films)*

D. Film Title

Boring and Drilling Tools. Selected as a basic technological material to speed the development of the main objectives in relation to a project to which the pupils attached significance.

1. *High Quality.* The film will provide experiences in some of the basic skills that are included in my purposes. Camera work, especially the close-up shots, clearly shows the entire class many of the intricacies involved in the various operations. Scene sequence provides smooth transition from one activity to another. The vocabulary used is within the level of the students. Terms used throughout the narration are those that should stimulate pupil participation when the film is over.

2. *Unique Characteristics of the Group.* The class will, under normal circumstances, have had two years previous industrial arts experience. It is expected that each pupil will have an understanding and comprehension of many of the related materials seen in the film. Normal physical development of the boys should be such that they will be capable of performing the operations as shown.

E. The READINESS Principle in Action
(Elements of the Readiness Plan.)

1. Having planned to set up the problem before the film is the first and foremost element in my readiness plan. The student is aware that his project must be assembled in order to serve its intended purpose. He has already cut to size the elements, i.e., legs, cross-pieces, table top, etc. To further prepare the students for this film I plan to comment as indicated in the subsequent items:

2. "Now that the parts of your table are cut to size, what will you have to do to assemble them?" (A display of model joints will be exhibited for study to guide their choice.)

3. "Most of the joints and methods of assembly that have been discussed require the use of certain tools and machines. These are, bit, brace, etc." (I shall put the list on the chalkboard.)

4. "We are fortunate in having a very good film to help us solve some of our problems. By means of this film, you will see skilled workers using the same tools, doing the same things that you will do in order to put these pieces of wood together in such a way that your table won't fall down when your folks put that tray full of cookies and doughnuts on it."

5. "Watch carefully the way the bit is kept at right angles to the wood, how the problem of working near a corner is solved, and how the screws are put in flush with the surface of the wood."

F. The CONTROL Principle in Action

I shall make arrangements to insure that the film, projector, and screen will be in the shop at the appointed time. A qualified student projectionist will handle the projector operation. I shall check such items with him as proper focus, cleanliness of the lens, proper tone control and volume settings, amplifier "warm-up" period, and starting signals. As soon as the projectionist is ready to start the film, I shall call the class to the viewing area. Students previously assigned to such duties as pulling the shades, standing by the light switch, and posting a notice on the door informing potential visitors that a film is in progress would then carry out their work. I shall then carry out my introduction of the film and carry out the steps in my readiness plan.

G. The ACTION Principle at Work
(Elements in the plan to elicit student responses.)

1. At the conclusion of the film I plan to conduct a rapid-fire question period according to students' needs, starting off with the following:

(a) "How was the bit checked to see if it was at right angles to the wood being bored?"

(b) "What do you think would happen if the chips were not carried out of the hole by means of the flutes?"

(c) "A number of mechanical principles were involved in such tools as the automatic screw driver, the bit point, the edge of the drill, the ratchet, etc. What are these principles and in what other tools or machines are they found?" (This would be suitable for a production experience such as a display depicting mechanical principles in everyday tools.)

2. After this discussion I plan to suggest a second showing of the film to permit a careful analysis of the steps in the bit and brace drilling processes. I plan to stop after each basic operation and check the steps in the process.

3. I would then emphasize the main problem of proceeding with a project in the light of the film content and ask the following question: "Having seen the processes in the film, how do you think the cross-piece would be fitted to the table legs? The leg to the top? What tool would you use to make the screw holes? Would you countersink the screw on the bottom of the table top? Why?

4. I then plan to set up a practice session before proceeding with the work on the main project.

5. This action plan relates to the main problem because the pupils will construct their project using the tools, machines, and processes that they have viewed in the film.

H. The EVALUATION Principle at Work

I plan to ascertain if the film quality and content are helping me teach more effectively, and determine also if I have employed the best teaching techniques to accompany the film. I plan to make these judgments in the light of my teaching purposes, the previously listed understandings, abilities, attitudes, and appreciations.

This chapter provides opportunities for the reader to develop insight into the ways that the *five basic utilization*

ANALYSIS OF CASE STUDY NUMBER 1

Fundamentals of Teaching with Audiovisual Technology

principles are applied to teaching with audiovisual technology. It has been emphasized repeatedly that fundamental to all creative teaching is the need for valid objectives. In Case Study Number 1 the five principles were applied in the creation of a simple though rather complete design for a given teaching situation, one design among an infinite number that is valuable here because it can be examined by the prospective teacher to derive guidance for his own real and/or hypothetical planning activity.

In carrying out the analysis, the case study itself and the discussion and statement of each of the five principles should be used as basic points of reference. Here we are concerned with mastery of ideas. Therefore in order to derive maximum benefit it is suggested that the reader proceed item by item in the following list to make the responses called for.

Ordered Sequence of Responses

1. According to the order of major items in the teacher's plan, did the purposes come first?
2. In this plan did the selection of the film appear before or after the statement of purposes?
3. Is the film in this instance, then, selected to help achieve this teacher's objectives? Or, was the film chosen first to be shown as an end in itself?
4. In this plan does the *main problem* appear before the film?
5. If the film follows the main problem, it must then contribute in some way to the solution of the problem. What can the motion picture and other materials like the textbook, charts, filmstrips, tapes, and visualized programmed learning sequences contribute? Serve as a visual source of information and direction for procedure? Help establish standards of excellence, that is, standards for achievement? Develop a desire to practice? Provide a favorable viewing position otherwise unavailable for a whole group? How do you think the successful completion of the coffee table after hard work and painstaking practice would help to develop the stated attitudes and appreciations? How should the teacher make sure that needed information was learned? Check sheets? Short quizzes?
6. Formulating purposes and planning effective learning experiences are two prime acts of a good teacher. Now, in the teacher's plan, the construction project is the significant, challenging pupil purpose. The problem-solving activity is vital and central. Check the *teacher's purposes* and then answer the following: How does work on the problem achieve the understandings, abilities, attitudes, and appreciations? How would textbooks and charts help? How would

the motion picture help the teacher? (Check your answers in item 5 again.)

7. Was the film therefore selected in the light of a pupil problem-solving activity? What did the teacher believe about the quality of the film and its fitness for his particular group? What characteristics of the motion picture made it appropriate for achieving the stated objectives?

8. Note that the *readiness principle* is applied by a plan with several elements. What does having a *pupil problem first* have to do with readiness to look at a film? What other specific techniques did the teacher plan to carry out? How does having a problem first make the readiness plan easy to make? Help analyze the needs of pupils? Make it easy to decide what questions to ask? Set up main points to look for in terms of their project operations?

9. There must be a minimum of distraction in handling a film screening. What can you do to become a good organizer? How can students help? Should you hold the screening process to high standards? Check Chapters 5 and 9 for complete information.

10. Note the teacher action plan in this case study, then answer the following questions:
    (a) Why is the action planning made easy by having a problem prior to film showing? [Note G (1) (a) (b) (c).] Is it easy to ask better thought-type questions to guide student thinking? When developing handwork abilities is knowledge important? Judgment?
    (b) Note reference to main problem in G (3), then note the practice session with the tools before application to the project in G (4).

11. Anyone who organizes his work well and has good purposes finds evaluation easy. What basic and simple questions should you ask yourself?

12. Case Study Number 1 indicates original thinking on the part of the teacher. Identify the parts of the teacher's plan that clearly indicate areas for your own potential ingenuity:
    (a) Formulation of understandings, abilities, attitudes, and appreciations? (Improve or add additional items.) Specifying student performance criteria?
    (b) Having a good pupil problem or group problem or a series of thought-type questions and assignments first? Suggest some possibilities in your own field. Do you see that a good learning activity is the medium for learning? Is the problem in the teacher plan one that demands use of the ability that the teacher seeks to teach?

Do teachers have to be creative in their choice of problems for students to solve?

(c) Do teachers have to be creative in devising ways to motivate students? What are some additional readiness-building techniques? How could you use students to help build readiness in the class to view, think, react, take action, and work hard at practice? What creativity is needed in preparing guide sheets before a film or filmstrip, tape or overlay transparency, and slide-set or television program?

(d) Do teachers have to be creative organizers and managers in the efficient handling of classroom arrangements for utilization?

(e) Do teachers have to be ingenious in the guidance of student reaction during or after use of devices and materials? Does good guidance in discussions demand good thought-type questions? Are how-to-do-it guide sheets often helpful? In the preceding plan the main pupil problem was identified first to maximize the readiness of pupils and to serve as a focal center for the learning of skill, understandings, and attitudes. Could not the teacher have decided to show the film first as an introduction, then discuss and practice, and then introduce functional application of the ability to the construction of an important piece of furniture or device for home, school, or another school? Could the information giving and the demonstration aspects for several skills have been presented by means of closed-circuit television to large groups, that is, to several classes combined or to individual class groups in various rooms, with guide sheets for readiness and subsequent action, in a team-teaching situation?

(f) Do teachers need to think clearly when they appraise materials just used? Does the critical scrutiny of one's own previously used techniques (decisions) demand courage and objectivity?

(g) Is the whole process of deciding what to do a creative process? A systematizing process? Focused on and through a set of valid teaching purposes?

(h) Would a good set of teaching objectives, as a part of a teaching unit, make teacher decisions easier?

The pivotal factor in the preceding utilization plan is the place of importance given to the constructional problem. The placement of the problem deliberately before the film deserves emphasis. A great many teachers do not understand this procedure very well and hence do not use it. In the next case study we shall explore the *problem base concept* further.

This case study gives the reader an opportunity to get an overall view as a fifth-grade teacher[4] has planned to use a film, *Panama Canal*,[5] in direct relationship to a project of the class that was encouraged by the teacher in the light of her objectives. Her planning is revealed in the same outline format shown in Case Study Number 1, but only edited excerpts of the complete plan are shown here for the sake of emphasis. We now turn to the teacher's purposes, the project, and the plan for ensuing action and relationships.

Case Study Number 2

PLAN FOR USING THE FILM,
PANAMA CANAL
(Teacher Decisions)

A. CLASS DESCRIPTION

Fifth-grade Social Studies. The topic under immediate study is the Panama Canal Zone.

B. THE SELECTION PRINCIPLE IN ACTION

My main teaching purposes that the film will help me achieve in my pupils:

UNDERSTANDING THAT:

1. The construction of the Panama Canal was a long, difficult, and dangerous project because of the
   (a) High mountainous area.
   (b) Dense jungles.
   (c) Tropical climate.
   (d) Presence of disease-carrying insects.
2. The Panama Canal is a vital link in the world's trade because it connects the Atlantic and Pacific Oceans at a central point.
3. A lock is an enclosure in a canal with gates at each end, used in raising or lowering boats as they pass from one level to another.
4. The Panama Canal is made up of a series of locks.
5. The Panama Canal would not be possible without the system of locks because the land is higher at the center of the isthmus than at the coastlines.
6. The United States owns the Panama Canal Zone, but it lets boats of many countries use the Canal.
7. The Panama Canal is constantly and carefully guarded from destruction because of its importance as a vital waterway for world trade.

---

[4] Cora Kibbe Pelletier, Ledyard, Connecticut, Public Schools. By permission.
[5] *Panama Canal*, Coronet Instructional Films.

Figure 6–7. This view from the film, Panama Canal, indicates why it would be of value in the problem-solving processes of the youngsters. (Courtesy Coronet Instructional Films)

8. Even in this air age, more boats than airplanes are used for transport because water travel is cheaper.
9. The Panama Canal is of vital importance to the United States Navy because it provides the shortest water route for the naval fleets from one coast to the other.

ABILITY TO:

1. Solve problems.
2. Use new sources of information.
3. Keep accurate, detailed records.
4. Generalize from specific facts.

ATTITUDE OF:

1. Cooperativeness.
2. Friendliness.
3. Open-mindedness.
4. Inventiveness.
5. Responsibility.
6. Desire to base opinions on facts.

APPRECIATION OF:

1. Good workmanship.
2. Well-planned action.
3. Good problem-solving techniques.

C. MAIN PROBLEM

Organize and construct a display dealing with the Panama Canal Zone for the Pan-American Day Exhibit (a model of the Canal to be included in the display).

D. FILM TITLE

Panama Canal. Selected in direct relation to the pupils' project but also in relation to the teacher's purposes.

1. *High Quality.* The film, *Panama Canal,* is of high quality because:

   (*a*) The picture images are sharp especially in the important lock scenes.

   (*b*) The sound is clear and natural and the commentary is given at a comfortable rate for our purposes.

   (*c*) The action is at a sufficiently rapid speed to maintain interest.

2. *Unique Characteristics of the Group.* The children have previously studied the continents of North and South America, and the film's content and continuity endow it with a rich potential to serve the needs of this class because of the project to be worked on.

E. THE READINESS PRINCIPLE IN ACTION
(Elements of the Readiness Plan.)

1. Having the problem first sets up a significant basis in the minds of the pupils for using the film.

2. The film will be related to the problem in the following manner:

   "As planned yesterday, we are going to construct a school display for Pan-American Day.

   We have been studying the North and South American countries and it certainly would be unwise for us to end our study of this hemisphere without having taken a close look at one of the most important zones in this hemisphere. This zone is the Panama Canal Zone.

   The Panama Canal is a good example of cooperation between many countries. This cooperation in the Canal Zone can serve as a good problem for our display for Pan-American Day which is coming up soon.

   We are going to see a film today which will help us to understand more about the Panama Canal Zone; the film is called *Panama Canal.*"

3. "Before we view the film, I would like you to:

   (*a*) Skim through the pages of your text to find the meanings of two terms that I have written on the chalkboard.

      (1) Panama Canal Zone.

      (2) Locks.

   (*b*) Find the Panama Canal Zone on the wall map and trace the route of the Canal.

   (*c*) Look at the map in your textbook—trace the route of the Canal—note the land forms on either side of the Canal."

4. "On the back of the sheet of paper that I am handing out to you, write three good questions about the Panama Canal and Zone which you hope the film will answer for you. The answers should also be of good use to you in constructing the display."

5. "Now turn to the front of the sheet and look at the five questions that I have listed there for you to answer with

the help of the film. If you have written a question that is the same as one of mine, cross out my question and use the question that is written in your own words.

These are the questions that we hope the film will answer for us:

(*a*) What hardships and problems had to be overcome before the Panama Canal could be completed?

(*b*) Why did the United States decide to build the Panama Canal? What other countries had tried to build the Panama Canal?

(*c*) Who owns the Panama Canal? Who owns the Panama Canal Zone?

(*d*) How do the locks in the Canal operate? (Note details.)

(*e*) Why is the Panama Canal so important to world trade?"

6. "Now watch the movie closely to answer the questions and to pick out all the important facts and details which you would like to tell others about by means of your display."

F. THE CONTROL PRINCIPLE IN ACTION

As in the Case Study Number 1 this teacher made all necessary arrangements to have projection take place at the right time, dovetailing precisely with the preceding readiness plan.

G. THE ACTION PRINCIPLE AT WORK
(Elements in the plan to elicit pupil responses.)

1. Immediately after the film has been shown, the students will be given a few minutes to answer the questions devised in the Readiness Plan, in a brief, concise form. At the same time noting any further helpful questions or ideas they might have.

2. I expect to start a discussion with my class concerning the main problem: to organize and construct a display dealing with the Panama Canal Zone for the Pan-American Day Exhibit (a model of the Canal to be included in the display). The discussion will be held with the idea in mind that the answers to the questions presented will lead to a plan of action for solving the main problem. I intend to use questions from the question sheet. In addition, these questions will be raised:

(*a*) What information did this film offer us that would be useful in constructing a model of the Panama Canal?

(*b*) What ideas presented in the film will be useful to use in preparing our display for Pan-American Day?

3. Additional questions needed to help analyze the main problem will be raised:

(*a*) How may we gather additional information to aid us in giving a complete and accurate display? (Identify needed information and sources.)

(*b*) How may we assemble the facts, figures, and diagrams to help people understand the importance of the Canal? (Identify basic ideas that should be portrayed and decide on the design.)

(c) What research jobs need to be done? What reports should be prepared, and who should make them?

(d) What work groups do we need to organize?

It is obvious that the teacher is now ready to work with her class in a stimulating and potentially rich learning activity. The film has provided a vital experience, and the class or selected groups will want to see all or parts of the film again as a source of additional information.

Before proceeding with the analysis of the case study and working through the sequence of responses, readers should return to the beginning of this chapter for a review of the explanatory material there. The utilization planning process demands unique decisions in terms of guiding principles.

ANALYSIS OF CASE STUDY NUMBER 2

1. Are the basic elements in the planning of both Case Study Number 1 and Case Study Number 2 the same? Purposes? Main problem before the film is shown? Relationship of the film to *teacher's purposes* and to *pupil purpose* (*problem*)? What is the difference between the teacher's and pupils' purposes?

2. How do the *understandings* arise in the pupils' minds? From a complex of mental activity, viewing, recalling, comparing, selecting, manipulating, agreeing after debate, and memory too? How can these understandings be measured?

3. Would the abilities stated in the list of purposes develop in the pupils as a result of practice and functional work on the display construction? Work on research? Deciding what to include and how to display it?

4. What other unstated abilities would be likely to develop in addition to those stated? How about learning to read better? Express ideas better? Organize information better? (If the teacher had stated that one of her abilities for the students was to construct models from diagrams, would she have been correct? Is not constructing a model a learning activity?)

5. Refer to *Characteristics of Teaching Purposes*, item 4, near the beginning of Chapter 2 under *Abilities*. Take a sharper look at the activity itself. What lifelike performance grows out of making a model? Ability to plan action? Ability to seek and find information? How might the work on the display be likely to develop attitudes of inventiveness, friendliness, responsibility, or perseverance?

6. Do the procedures for pupil action (questions and guidance) reflect the teacher's deliberate attempt to achieve her identified purposes? In other words do

Ordered Sequence of Responses

the stated purposes channel the thinking of the teacher and help her decide what to do and say? Help her guide students in their responses unerringly toward desirable development?

7. Is it clear how books, group work and the film are organized around problem-solving activity? Might not the main problem be, in effect, a topic for the whole teaching unit? A hub for all teaching unit activity?

8. The teacher did not use the film as a "magic carpet" medium. Could she have introduced the film as a journey to the Canal via film? What additional media could be of service? Filmstrips? Recordings? Newspaper pictures? Maps and globes?

9. When the problem is set up before the film, are pupils better oriented for observation and action?

10. Would it not be advisable for teachers to work together to prepare lists of desirable teaching objectives for specific units of work? For courses of study? For curriculum guides?

Case Study Number 3   We now return to a plan for the use of a motion picture[6] created for another high school class. Again the film is being used by the teacher[7] in direct relationship to a problem already accepted by the students. The construction type of project set up with the students is particularly suitable because of the measuring and scaling that would be necessary. The planning by the teacher is shown, as in the previous case studies, in edited, excerpted, outline format.

PLAN FOR USING THE FILM,
THE MATHEMATICIAN AND THE RIVER
(Teacher Decisions)

A. CLASS DESCRIPTION
General Mathematics, tenth grade. Unit: The application of Mathematics to Flood Control.

B. THE SELECTION PRINCIPLE IN ACTION
My main teaching purposes that the film will help me achieve in my pupils:

UNDERSTANDING THAT:

1. By language of mathematics big ideas are compressed into small time and space.

---

[6] *The Mathematician and the River* (Princeton, N.J.: *Horizons of Science Series,* Educational Testing Service.)

[7] William D. Wright. Middle Georgia College, Cochrane, Ga. By permission.

2. Computers solve problems much too big and complicated for a single mathematician to handle by himself.
3. Mathematics is the language of the physical sciences.
4. Mathematics is a language of quantity, not quality, that deals with quantities, forms, and relationships.
5. Mathematics facilitates a complete analysis of any problem situation.
6. Mathematics goes beyond facts to underlying principles.
7. The power of mathematics comes not only from its ability to measure quantity, but from its ability to deal with numbers and abstract symbols.
8. Mathematical equations that are used as models of physical situations are even more compressed than physical scale models that compress time and space.
9. From the proper mathematical equations for the flow of a river that are fed into a computer it is possible for the computer to give the depth of the river at any desired point along it.
10. Mathematics provides a relatively simple way of expressing the forces (e.g. pressure, friction, resistance) and factors (e.g. volume, mass, velocity, momentum, depth, cross section) at work in a river.
11. Mathematical equations are the only way of precisely expressing, analyzing, and applying the principles of the physical universe.

ABILITY TO:

1. Formulate simple physical problems symbolically.
2. Locate sources of information.
3. Interpret graphs and charts.
4. Construct graphs and charts.
5. Compile accurate records and statistics.
6. Evaluate the effect various factors have on one another and on the total physical situation.
7. Draw conclusions from facts.

ATTITUDE OF:

1. Inquisitiveness.
2. Perseverance.
3. Criticalness.
4. Cooperativeness.
5. Responsibility.

APPRECIATION OF:

1. Effective scientific observation and experimentation.
2. Analytical problem solving.
3. Logical procedure.
4. Thorough research.
5. Good organization.
6. Good teamwork.

C. MAIN PROBLEM

Construct a school display showing the many ways in which mathematics can be used in flood control. The display will consist of a scale model of a section of a river, charts, graphs, tables, flat pictures, diagrams, drawings, and maps.

Figure 6–8. These views of a portion of the scale model of the Mississippi river and of the actual river terrain are from the film, The Mathematician and the River. *(Courtesy Educational Testing Service)*

The Teacher Uses Media

D. FILM TITLE

The Mathematician and the River. This film was selected in direct relation to the pupils' problem, but in addition was also selected in direct relation to the teacher's purposes.

1. *High Quality.* This film is a good one because it truly answers a question most students ask, namely, "Of what real practical use is algebra and plane geometry and all that theoretical math?" It shows the relationship between the abstract world of mathematics and the real world of nature and does so with plenty of action in color and with the excitement of many intriguing and thought-provoking questions.

2. *Unique Characteristics of the Group.* Most of the students in the class are interested in weather, nature, and outdoor living. The study of flood control fascinates them. Since all have studied simple algebraic equations and their applications and have had a good course in ninth grade general science, their experience level is of sufficient depth for them to comprehend the film's instruction and to profit from it.

E. THE READINESS PRINCIPLE IN ACTION
(Elements of the Readiness Plan.)

1. The first element of readiness is having the main problem prior to the film since this establishes in the minds of the students a significant basis for viewing the film.

2. The film is related to the main problem as follows:

"As we planned last Friday you are going to construct a school display exhausting in so far as possible the ways in which mathematics can be used in flood control. Already each of you has applied the principle of division of labor by voluntarily joining one of the three committees you decided to set up. (You recall you discussed and suggested as a class how each of the Committees—the Research and Statistics, the Scale Model, and the Graphic Arts—might get started on its part of the project.)

Today we shall view a film which will give you further ideas on how your committee can do its job. As you watch *The Mathematician and the River,* if you are a member of the Research and Statistics Committee, jot down words, such as velocity, volume, mass friction, Louisville Flood, that will guide you in your reading and lead you to facts useful to the other committees in making the display. If you are on the Graphic Arts Committee, jot down ideas for graphs, charts, diagrams, drawings, pictures, photos, and the like. And if you are a member of the Model Committee, you will want to jot down ideas and list kinds of materials that will help you in making your scale model. The Scale Model Committee may wish to see the film several times in order to understand better how to utilize these ideas and materials."

3. Write the following key technical words and phrases on the chalkboard and discuss their meanings before showing the film: friction, mass, velocity, momentum, Newton's

equation for the conservation of mass, Newton's law of conservation of momentum, resistance.

F. The CONTROL Principle in Action

I will arrange to have the film, the projector, the loud-speaker, and the screen in the classroom before the beginning of the class hour in which the film is to be shown and properly placed for optimum viewing and effortless listening, rearranging the seating where necessary. When all the equipment is set up I will check and correct where necessary the following: the speaker connections, the cleanliness of lens and aperture, the sharpness of image of the projector's "field of light" upon the screen, the winding of the film on the reel, the film threading, and the volume and tone. At the end of the readiness period, previously appointed students will pull the window shades and turn off the lights upon a signal from the projectionist.

G. The ACTION Principle at Work
(Elements in the plan to elicit pupil responses.)

1. As soon as the motion picture has been shown I will hold a brief discussion with the entire class, asking what new ideas they got from the film that would be of help to each of the committees in doing its part to construct the display. Three students (one from each committee) will write each new idea on the chalkboard as it is mentioned. In this way each committee pulls ideas and observations not only from member students but also from students on other committees.

2. "Because the film is rather technical you may not feel that you have been able to see in one viewing all the ways it can help your committee in the construction of the display. For this reason we will re-run the film again tomorrow. Immediately following this re-run, you will be tested on the mimeographed questions that I shall now hand out. If there are any answers you cannot recall, you'll be able to get them at this second showing. Also, you can check your answers as you view the film this second time. These questions and their answers will stimulate your thinking and some of them will contribute directly in helping you and your committee to do its job in the display. The questions referred to are as follows:

    (a) When present-day problems are much too big and complicated for an individual mathematician to handle by himself, how are they solved?

    (b) What kind of language is mathematics?

    (c) What is the most direct way in which mathematics can be used in flood control? (HINT: What is the problem that Prof. Eugene Isaacson is working on?)

    (d) What physical factors must be considered when studying the flow of water in rivers?

    (e) Where does mathematics derive its power?

    (f) How can a scale model of a river be used? Which

factors affecting the flow of water in the model are kept constant?

(g) With regard to the principles of the physical universe, of what practical use are mathematical equations?"

3. At the beginning of class the next day we will re-run the film without comment, stopping it whenever this is requested. After the film, a quiz will be given on the assigned questions. To conclude the session I will re-state the main problem to the class, summarize what action has been taken thus far to solve the problem, and recapitulate the new ideas gained from viewing the film. Then I will ask each committee what specifically its next step will be and ask it to devise and submit for approval a brief written specific step-by-step plan of action in outline form. I will then distribute to each group the following list of additional guide questions needed to help analyze the main problem of constructing the display and to provide suggestions for further action on the part of each committee.

Research and Statistics Committee

(a) With respect to the topic "Mathematics in Flood Control," list all potential sources of flat pictures for mounting, of information for obtaining or constructing tables, graphs, charts, diagrams, drawings, and maps, and of subjects suitable for photographing.

(b) From this list obtain whatever materials and information are requested by the Graphic Arts Committee for use in making all parts of the display except the scale model.

(c) What sort of statistical and technical data will you need to compile for use by those who are constructing the scale model? List the names and addresses of those in the Army Corps of Engineers who were responsible for constructing the scale model of the Mississippi system and who could provide helpful suggestions as to how to go about making such a model, and supply answers to technical difficulties encountered by the Model Committee.

(d) What kind of statistical information on rivers and flood control can be obtained from county, state, and national conservation agencies?

Scale Model Committee

(a) How will you go about deciding what river and what section of that river you will model to scale?

(b) What materials will you use in constructing the scale model of a section of a river?

(c) How will you indicate on the scale model what physical factors are at work? What audio-device could you use alongside the model in order to explain to observers of the display how these factors interact and affect one another?

Graphic Arts Committee

(a) Prepare a list of as many titles and captions as possible for potential graphs, charts, diagrams, flat pictures, maps, photos and drawings to be used in the display. How will you indicate how mathematics is involved in each?

(*b*) Prepare a series of rough work sketches of the actual graphs, charts, diagrams, drawings, maps, and mounted photographs and flat pictures you intend to construct and collect for the display.

(*c*) What kinds of drawings and photographs will you make in order to alert the viewers of the display to the contributions mathematics can make in educating the public to the need for flood control and to the practical measures that can be taken to achieve it?

This teacher is apparently now ready to guide members of his class in their attack on a new and challenging problem-solving experience.

ANALYSIS OF CASE STUDY NUMBER 3

The pattern of teacher decisions clearly follows the five principles as set forth at the beginning of this chapter. This case study shows that the teacher was concerned not only with the process to be followed by pupil committees in their own research and construction, but in addition he showed a laudable concern for the subject-matter substance, not wanting it to get lost in the process of the class project. He therefore planned a quiz, as one way to encourage the mastery of some of the basic ideas as presented in the motion picture, which had been already identified in his purposes. We shall now turn to the list of questions and judgments to aid the reader not only in his analysis of Case Study Number 3, but also in his own thinking and planning for his present and future teaching activities.

Ordered Sequence of Responses

1. Compare the statements of teaching purpose in this case study with those preceding. Why do teachers seem to repeat attitudes in different courses at different levels? Are attitudes pervasive or specific in character?

2. Would the list of abilities stated be likely to be developed in the activity of committee processes to plan, figure, and construct? Are pupils likely to learn much of factual information together with the abilities? Should not the teacher guide and encourage students to read widely and to work vigorously? Should the teacher demonstrate a critical attitude by his own actions? By his sharp appraisal of students' work? By his knowledge of what each student is contributing? Do the stated purposes facilitate the teacher's critical analysis of pupil achievement?

3. How would students in this case learn the appreciations stated? What would they learn if forced into or commanded to take part against their will? Is it true that appreciations will develop faster if pupils

like what they are doing? Get satisfaction out of work being well done? Can people learn to like to solve problems?

4. Could discovered weaknesses in students be corrected by extra assignments, homework, and guidance by special drills and exercises during other study periods?

5. Did this teacher properly relate the film to the class problem in Section E? Did pupils on the committees know what to look for in the film? Did everyone know why the film was being shown? Do you believe pupils react to and put in more hours of work when a teacher is well organized and knows how to put his materials together for better learning?

6. It is not easy to organize a class group for action on a problem that calls for new responses. Teachers willing to tackle problems with pupils are to be commended. Do you believe some students would be willing to work on such a project after school, that is, if the progress became slow and the deadline were approaching?

7. Do you recognize the fact that the production of the display was the central hub around which all activity revolved? Was the motion picture thus primary or secondary in the stream of activity? But would it not be an important learning experience? Is this not a vastly different process from just looking at a film that happened to be in the school?

8. Did the class committees work on their project like a research team? Is this a good way to develop the ability to work together?

9. Not every problem has to be a large class project. Some problems may take the form of a question that can be completed by a film and a follow-up discussion fifteen minutes long. These are matters of teacher decision, timing, and pacing, as related to the nature of the objectives in view.

10. Refer to section D, Film Title. The film in question was used in direct relation to the pupils' problem (the pupils' purpose). Is it correct to also say that the film was selected to serve the teacher's purposes? Are pupils' problems means for acquisition of desired understandings, abilities, attitudes, and appreciations?

Case Study Number 4

The first three case studies have shown the use of a motion picture in vital relationship to a problem already formulated and accepted by the class. That is, the pupil problem, assignment, or project came first, and the motion picture, books, and other instructional materials such as slides, filmstrip, and textbook illustrations were brought in as sources of information, of directions for procedure, and as sources of vicarious experience.

In Case Study Number 4 we show the same teacher[8] as in Case Study Number 2 in a vastly different design for the utilization of the same film to achieve the same set of objectives. The main point of this case is to show that pupil activities can grow out of the film showing and subsequent discussion and guidance. The teacher in this case may or may not know what actually will be done after the film showing is completed. In this particular instance the teacher actually had planned a series of questions and then finally wished, or hoped, to introduce to her pupils the class project of constructing a school-corridor exhibit about the Panama Canal for Pan-American Day.

The case therefore is a variant of Case Study Number 2. Its statement in brief form tends to sharpen the emphasis on the positioning of the main pupil activity.

PLAN FOR USING THE FILM,
PANAMA CANAL
(Teacher Decisions)

A. CLASS DESCRIPTION

Same as for Case Study Number 2.

B. THE SELECTION PRINCIPLE IN ACTION

Teaching purposes are the same as for Case Study Number 2, and the statements in that case about film quality and its fitness for a specific group of teachers are also applicable to this case.

C. MAIN PROBLEM

There is no main problem before the film is shown.

D. FILM TITLE

Same as for Case Study Number 2.

E. THE READINESS PRINCIPLE IN ACTION
(Elements of the Readiness Plan.)

1. I plan to introduce the film as follows:
"We have been studying the North and South American countries and it certainly would be unwise for us to end our study of this hemisphere without having taken a close look at one of the most important zones in this hemisphere. This zone is the Panama Canal Zone.

The Panama Canal is a good example of cooperation between many countries.

We are going to see a film today which will help us

---

[8] Cora Kibbe Pelletier, Ledyard, Connecticut, Public Schools. By permission.

to understand more about the Panama Canal Zone; the film is called *Panama Canal*."

2. "By means of this motion picture we can take a trip to this locality to observe how the canal operates and to get a better idea of the problem of accomplishing this great engineering feat. Before we set out on our film journey, I suggest that you do three things. I have them written on the chalkboard:

(a) Skim through the pages of your text to find the meanings of the two terms which I have written on the chalkboard
(1) Panama Canal Zone.
(2) Locks.
(b) Find the Panama Canal Zone on the wall map and trace the route of the Canal.
(c) Look at the map in your textbook—trace the route of the Canal—note the land forms on either side of the Canal."

3. "We shall discuss our film journey and our observations and any questions you wish to ask as soon as it is over. Ready? Here we go to this world famous place!"

F. THE CONTROL PRINCIPLE IN ACTION

Same as in Case Study Numbers 1 and 2.

G. THE ACTION PRINCIPLE AT WORK
(Elements in the plan to elicit pupil responses.)

1. I plan to hold a discussion about our film journey emphasizing concepts and abilities listed in my teaching purposes. After this discussion period, I intend to move toward specific projects guiding this work by individuals and groups with work sheets, map work and discussion.

2. Specifically, I will elicit questions from the pupils and will ask the following questions of my own proceeding from simple thought-type questions to the formulation of a project involving the entire class in committee work, reports, research and final construction:

(a) What was the main reason for the building of the Panama Canal?
(b) For what reasons was the Panama Canal built in the Panama area?

Figure 6–9. In Case Study Number 4, the teacher used the film, Panama Canal, *as a "magic carpet" to travel to a distant country for on-the-spot observation. These views of the operation of the Canal indicate how the film would serve as a potentially great springboard, to catapult pupils by their own newly stimulated interests into desirable pupil activity. (Courtesy Coronet Instructional Films)*

(c) What conditions had to be overcome before the Canal could be built?

(d) Could additional information be found to help us better understand how great these difficulties were?

(e) Many people do not know how the locks of the Canal actually work. In what ways may we help them understand their operation? Could we work as a production crew to make an exhibit for Pan American Day for the main corridor to show: the vital location of the locks; the importance of the Canal; and the world-wide cooperation which they foster?

3. Once the class accepts the problem I shall guide pupils in analyzing the work that has to be carried out to complete the project, and shall work along with them in solving problems and helping class leaders direct the work of their respective groups.

H. The EVALUATION Principle at Work

Same as for Case Study Number 1.

ANALYSIS OF CASE STUDY NUMBER 4

Again the reader is urged to review or peruse concurrently with the analysis of the case, the pertinent material provided at the beginning of this chapter, and he should also bear in mind the teacher decisions made in Case Study Number 2.

Ordered Sequence of Responses

1. Note first the generality of the *readiness* plan, an introduction to future activity, not yet known to pupils. At this point, maybe the teacher has doubts about pupil acceptance of the project she hopes to set up. Would the trip idea add a touch of glamour to the film showing? Is it better psychology to suggest *going* instead of *bringing* the Canal to the class?

2. Note next the *action* plan, G, Elements 1, 2. The discussion can be guided by the teacher, but it can be widely diversified because of the unrelated questions of each of the pupils. Could such a discussion be too time consuming? What should be done if pupils do not react to the project suggestion by the teacher?

3. Now, going back to the *action* plan in Case Study Number 2 for contrast. What advantage is there to having a problem first? Is there a more definite relationship of the film showing to what is going on in class? Are both teacher and pupils likely to make more direct observations in the film content? Feel a keener sense of involvement? Can there be a more direct and efficient attack on a problem as soon as the film has been completed? Would the teacher know better what to discuss and could she get at it quickly?

4. Could teachers arrange to set up a larger number of smaller activities, questions, and problems after an introductory film showing?

5. Could teachers arrange to have work sheets for students to fill out after a film in the case where the film was used to present subject matter to be mastered? Should the problem or problems in this case be highly specific, and should the responses be in accordance with the teaching objectives?
6. Could teachers prepare and issue guide sheets prior to film showings that raise a series of questions to be answered later? Could such questions direct the attention of the learner to important items in film content?
7. How should the required responses of pupils either during work on large class problems, or on special guide sheets be related to the teacher's objectives?
8. Check through the learning activities and judge whether or not the objectives of the teacher help her to choose the right activity, emphasize the right points, guide the pupils in their study, observations, and conclusions.

Case Study Number 5

In Chapter 2 several examples of teacher purposes were quoted, and this case study refers directly to the first set, Example 1, formulated by a teacher[9] in connection with a teaching unit about *The Westward Movement.* Refer therefore to that set of purposes now, and check the edited excerpts of the teacher's plans for achieving them. In Case Study Number 5 we are dealing specifically with the *readiness* and *action* principles. These decisions show that no major problem was established before the showing, and this means that despite a listing of specific and varied questions for pupils to discuss, the really important and challenging projects had to be set up after the film.

PLAN FOR USING THE FILM,
PIONEERS OF THE PLAINS[10]

Class Relationships

For an eighth-grade class in Social Studies. The teaching unit was The Westward Movement. The special aspect for consideration was the life, problems and character of the pioneer. (Refer to statement of objectives, Example 1, in Chapter 2.)

Readiness Plans

We join the teacher at the point in her plans where

---

[9] Shirley M. Titus, West Hartford, Connecticut, Public Schools. By permission.
[10] Encyclopaedia Britannica Educational Corp.

she expects to introduce the possibility of a trip to the West with a pioneer family.

1. "Yes, the best way to learn more about the pioneer is to actually join members of a pioneer family in their trek from Illinois to the Great Plains, and we can do this by means of a film. In just a few minutes, Bob will flick the light switch and this will automatically take us back to the year 1870, and then Gary will turn another switch to transfer us from this room to the covered wagon of the Carter family. Remember, this wagon won't have the same comfortable seats as our automobiles, and the trails won't be as smooth as our highways of today. Be prepared for a good jouncing! Bring a pillow!

    Before anyone starts a journey, he usually knows where he's going. Sue, please find Illinois on the map and run your finger from it to the Great Plains region. Thank you. This is the route we'll travel. After reading your special assignment for today, do you have any questions that you think our trip may answer? I've already prepared a trip guide which I think will help us to really see things, let's look it over now and see if you wish to add some items."

2. The trip guide posed the following questions:
    (a) Would you like to live in a sod hut?
    (b) What is a pioneer? Do you think there were pioneers living three thousand years ago? Are there any living now? Will there be any in the future?
    (c) Would you like to be a pioneer? If so, what kind? What preparations would you have to make to become this kind of pioneer?
    (d) Why do you think the Carter family was willing to leave their established home and friends to settle in an unknown region?
    (e) How long do you think the Carter family had been planning their trip westward? Explain.
    (f) During what month did they leave Illinois? Why do you think they chose this time to begin their journey?
    (g) If you had been traveling with the Carters, what would you have eaten, where would you have slept, and what would your chores have been?
    (h) What problems and dangers did the Carter family face?
    (i) Was the Carter family completely self-sufficient or did they have to depend on others once in a while? Do you ever depend on others?
    (j) In what ways was life on the plains different from life in Illinois?
    (k) How do you think Mrs. Carter felt when she saw her new home? Have you ever felt this way? How did she meet her problem?
    (l) Do you think you could build a sod hut? How would you begin?
    (m) Do you think music is an important part of people's lives? Was it important to the Carters?

3. The teacher plans to proceed as follows:

Figure 6–10. In Case Study Number 5 a motion picture is again, as in the previous case study, used as a film journey back into the days when people trekked West. These views indicate how the film, through its realistic enactments of historic events, can open up new problems for class groups and individuals. These views are from the film, Pioneers of the Plains. *See also Figure 2–6 in connection with Chapter 2, Example 1, Statement of Teaching Purposes. (© Encyclopaedia Britannica Films, Inc.)*

"Item (*m*) is especially for Ellen and Jane (introverts) because they have a special talent in music. They can be the music authorities while en route. Take some brief notes if you wish about important observations you want to mention later. Ready? The wagon is about to leave. Get your pillows! Bob and Gary, transfer us to the year 1870 and to the wagon in Illinois."

The Action plans

1. I plan to start my action plans as soon as the film ends by saying, "I am very interested in discovering who among you have made some keen observations while traveling West!"

2. While working on the questions on the trip guide, I plan to encourage my pupils to work individually and in groups on a number of additional activities that will call for the development of the understandings, abilities, attitudes and appreciations that constitute my teaching purposes or teaching unit outcomes. The activities are as follows:
   (*a*) Make tape recordings of songs of the period.
   (*b*) Construct dioramas showing life on the Great Plains or displaying contrasts to life in New England.
   (*c*) Write letters describing some of the emotions the pioneer must have experienced.
   (*d*) Make a model of a sod house for the school library.
   (*e*) Make a pictorial chart arranged chronologically which illustrates pioneers of various kinds in various periods of history.
   (*f*) Make illustrations that define new terms.
   (*g*) Construct salt and flour maps which emphasize topography.
   (*h*) Use reference books in the school library to find answers to research questions raised by pupils.

ANALYSIS OF CASE STUDY NUMBER 5

It should be noted that important questions were introduced in the *readiness* plan and that these same questions (as a trip guide) became the first order of business when the film journey was ended. It should be noted also that after the film showing was over that new projects were to be identified and worked on by individuals and groups.

Ordered Sequence of Responses

1. Refer to the listing of the teacher's purposes, Example 1, stated in Chapter 2, and observe the relationship of the questions and projects to the understandings, abilities, attitudes, and appreciations.

2. Is it not then for the teacher to decide how to develop optimum readiness? Does it not seem quite correct to say that this film served as an introduction to a teaching unit? Could not the problem section after the film have been expanded to involve more media such as films, filmstrips, tapes, maps, and globes? Some used by the teacher, others used by pupils in reports, etc.?

3. Do questions raised during the readiness phase constitute a *main problem* in the same sense as Case Study Numbers 1 and 2? Was any one of the questions in the trip guide broad enough to consume the energies of the entire class? Were the projects in the *action* plan large enough to demand the cooperative work of groups of pupils? Is it correct to say in general that when a larger number of questions is used, everyone works on all of them, and when one large problem is raised everyone works on at least a part of the whole problem, that is, contributing in some way to the final completion? If a large number of separate projects are assigned or formulated by the class then is it a good idea for the class to be split up into groups, each completing and possibly reporting on its separate assignment?

4. Is it often necessary to use audiovisual materials and devices in combination? Additional materials like maps, filmstrips, slides, and tape recordings for additional presentations?

Case Study Number 6

This case study is unconventional in nature. It emphasizes the processes of:

1. Organizing pupils in vastly different ways for specific learning activities. The particular emphasis is upon individualized instruction through specially prepared materials.

2. Selecting audiovisual materials for use by individuals subjected to control by devices and materials.

3. Preparing unique self-teaching materials in the form of mimeographed guide sheets and self-teaching sequences.

4. Guiding the reactions of various groups along desired paths of progress by means of audiovisual materials in conjunction with programmed sequences of question-and-answer sheets, textbook references, and special project work during unscheduled time.

For details of this case we turn to a doctoral dissertation[11] describing a research experiment that pitted two methods for teaching an eighth-grade unit in the social studies against a control group. Pertinent excerpts are selected and arranged in this presentation for the purpose of showing how the design, even though vastly different in operation, follows the five basic principles presented earlier in this chapter, and how technology facilitates the guidance of pupils by unique methods in a regular classroom teaching situation. It should be borne in mind that

[11] George E. Ingham, "Comparison of Two Methods of Self-Instruction in Teaching a Unit in Social Studies" (Ph.D. Dissertation, The University of Connecticut, 1962), pp. 189–512. By permission.

Case Study Number 6 is a part of a controlled instructional experiment and therefore it is not presented as a recommended model to be followed in every detail. In a normal situation, many other materials as valuable adjuncts might be used with pupils in larger groups, with the teacher playing a greater part in face-to-face guidance of pupil responses, at least during a part of the class period. The reader may be interested to know that the self-instructional methods represented in this case study seemed to the researcher to produce as much of the learning measured by the achievement tests as the conventional methods employed in the control groups.

PLAN FOR USING A COMBINATION OF PROGRAMMED LEARNING, INDIVIDUALIZED USE OF FILMSTRIPS, AND TAPE-RECORDED INSTRUCTION

Class Relationships

For an eighth-grade class in Social Studies. The teaching unit was titled *Uncle Sam Enters Manhood.* Eleven specific topics served as focal points around which broadly stated problems and specific questions were listed. The eleven topics[12] were: (1) The United States Engages in 'Dollar' Diplomacy; (2) Causes and Results of Building the Panama Canal; (3) The United States Interferes in the Affairs of Latin America; (4) Industrialism, Nationalism, and Imperialism Begin to Arise in Europe; (5) The Results of Sarajevo; (6) Uncle Sam Walks the Tight Rope, War or Peace; (7) Uncle Sam Goes to War; (8) The Versailles Treaty; (9) The League of Nations; (10) The Flaming Twenties; and (11) Depression Threatens the World.

The Selection Principle in Action

Teaching Purposes. In this instructional design the objectives are stated in a list for the entire teaching unit, and presumably all materials and processes were selected to achieve those objectives. Excerpts from the list showing understandings, abilities, attitudes, and appreciations follow:

4. The United States has passed through an agonizing period of growing up.
   (*a*) One of our first unhappy experiences with foreign countries resulted in the Spanish-American War.
   (*b*) Central and South American nations were angry because of the means by which the United States acquired the land for the Panama Canal.

[12] Ibid., p. 255.

(c) American citizens got their first real *baptism by fire* under comparatively modern practices, during World War I.

(d) The United States antagonized the Allies by failing to join the League of Nations.

(e) The depression starting at the close of the 1920's subjected the United States to a period of heartbreak and soul-searching.

(f) Because, on occasion, the United States seems to act foolishly, the reaction of other nations toward the United States is adverse.

. . . .

8. Extravagance can lead to economic disorder.

(a) The depression which started in the late twenties followed a period of wild spending.

(b) World War I was succeeded by a recession.

(c) The "Great Depression" proved the old saying that "Whatever goes up must come down."

. . . .

1. The ability to judge whether political decisions on the international level are more democratic and liberal or totalitarian and reactionary in nature.

2. The ability to discover causes of world events today.

3. The ability to find the facts underlying the reactions of other nations towards acts of the United States.

4. The attitude of concern for wise and humanitarian international leadership.

5. The attitude of criticalness.

6. The attitude of helpfulness.

7. The attitude of responsibility.

8. The appreciation of democratic action.

9. The appreciation of clear thinking.

10. The appreciation of courageous action.[13]

Selection and General Use of the Self-Instructional Materials.

Twenty filmstrips were selected, and a pupil-response sheet for each filmstrip was prepared. Students used individual filmstrip viewers, inserting the strips themselves and carrying on the viewing and responding activity as directed by the sheets, frame by frame. About ten such viewing devices were in the classroom and groups of pupils took their turns. Four prerecorded tapes were made by the researcher for use by teachers of the experimental groups. For each tape, a pupil response sheet was prepared that called for filling in blanks and carrying on certain map analysis activities as well. In addition, a 295-item programmed learning sequence in the form of a linear-type programmed booklet was prepared, which each pupil was asked to complete. Each pupil received a *Learn-By-Yourself Kit*, so named by the researcher. Two different kinds of teacher activity accompanied the employment of the materials in their experimental use. Some classes of pupils had no direct teaching or counsel at all. In this case the teacher was simply present as

[13] *Ibid.*, pp. 189–191.

an organizer of pupils, devices, and materials, explaining nothing having to do with subject content. In other classes the teacher served as an organizer as just stated, but also held small group conferences for tutorial purposes.

Excerpted Materials

Two of the self-instructional sheets, one for a filmstrip and the other for a tape recording, and some sample items of the programmed learning sequence are reproduced below.

ONE OF TWENTY FILMSTRIP WORKSHEETS FROM THE LEARN-BY-YOURSELF KIT[14]

Name_____   Number Right_____

Social Studies—Grade 8
UNCLE SAM ENTERS MANHOOD
Work Sheet #12

This work sheet is to be used in connection with the filmstrip: *The First World War* (27 frames—color—Eye Gate—1957)

PROBLEM:

As you have learned from your reading, wars are always dreadful and affect not only those whose profession is fighting but often many innocent citizens. Through the centuries man has made war on his fellow man and, although the cause may have seemed to be high-sounding, generally the basic reason has been economic and selfish. World War I was no exception. This was the most terrible and far-reaching war man had known. In it were involved many nations and because of it many people suffered and died. Why was this war fought? Were economic reasons behind it? What new devices for fighting and killing were used in it?

LOOK FOR THESE IMPORTANT POINTS:

1. The underlying reasons for World War I.
2. The nations making up the Allies.
3. The nations making up the Central Powers.
4. The then new methods of war.

DIRECTIONS TO HELP YOU ANSWER QUESTIONS BASED ON THE CONTENT OF THE FILMSTRIP:

Observe each frame of the filmstrip carefully. Examine the illustration in detail and read the caption thoroughly. Draw conclusions from the information offered. Study the problem and note the important points. After viewing each filmstrip frame, write, in the space indicated, the answer which seems best. After you have done this, check yourself for the correct answer which will be found, printed upside-down, folded

[14] Ibid., pp. 316–320.

under, on the right-hand side of the paper. At the top of the front page of your work sheet, write the number of your correct answers. If you were completely correct, you will have 28 right. Discover for yourself why you were wrong when you made incorrect replies. Learn the correct replies.

1. Frame #1—In June of 1914, the Archduke of Austria-Hungary was assassinated in the town of Sarajevo in Serbia. This murder at _____ was the spark which set off World War I.

    1. Sarajevo

2. Frame #2—Austria-Hungary, encouraged by Germany, therefore declared war on _____ .

    2. Serbia

3. Frame #3—Russia was Serbia's ally. Troops were immediately mobilized on the borders of_____ .

    3. Russia

4. Frame #4—France called up her army since, by treaty, she had to fight if _____ did.

    4. Russia

5. Frame #5—Since Germany had urged Austria-Hungary to declare war on Serbia, she immediately declared war on the two allies, _____ and Russia.

    5. France

6. Frame #6—Germany promptly attacked _____ by invading Belgium.

    6. France

7. Frame #7—Because of this invasion, the war spread when Great Britain declared war on _____ .

    7. Germany

8. Frame #8—The Allies now were made up of _____, _____, and _____ and the smaller nations fighting with them.

    8. Britain or England, France, Russia

9. Frame #9—The Central Powers included Turkey and Bulgaria as well as _____ and _____, both of which had been originators of the war.

    9. Germany and Austria-Hungary

10. Frame #10—Italy, originally bound by treaty to Germany, did not fight on her side but joined the group of nations known as the _____ .

    10. Allies

11. Frame #11—The basic reason for the war was economic. Germany had always wanted to get control of the nations in southeastern _____ .

    11. Europe

12. Frames #12, #13—Germany wanted to build a railroad to the Near East so that she could establish new markets for her products in the _____ .

    12. Near East

Fundamentals of Teaching with Audiovisual Technology

Figure 6–11. These eighth-grade students are hard at work on their Learn by Yourself Kit *filmstrip viewers and accompanying work sheets. (Courtesy Board of Education, Westport, Conn., and George E. Ingham)*

13. Frame #14—By means of this railroad, oil and other valuable materials for maintaining an industrial society could be brought back to _____.

14. Frame #15—Germany also wanted to take the Suez Canal from England so that the rich markets of India would be cut off from _____.

15. Frame #16—Germany hoped that, if she were victorious in this war, she might build an empire by obtaining many _____.

16. Frame #17—In the first years of the war, Germany was highly successful and drove the English and French armies back as far as the Marne River in _____.

17. Frames #18, #19, #20—After this, the opposing armies settled down to trench warfare with neither side able to win a decisive _____.

18. Frame #21—Both warring groups of nations, the _____ and the _____, needed to have supplies of food and war materials shipped to them from overseas.

19. Frames #22, #23—The English navy was used to blockade German ports and to sink _____ merchant ships.

20. Frame #24—Germany's reply to this was to use her submarine fleet to sink _____ supplying the Allies.

21. Frame #25—Poison gas, the most terrible weapon of its time, was developed and used during the _____.

13. Germany
14. England
15. colonies
16. France
17. battle or victory
18. Allies and Central Powers
19. German
20. ships or boats
21. war

22. Frame #26—Tanks were first used as weapons of _____ .

23. Frames #27, #28—Appearing for the first time for purposes of war was the _____, primarily used for scouting.

Summarization:

The main problem for this Work Sheet emphasized that all wars have been dreadful and have left their mark on those actively involved as well as on civilians. Generally, war occurs for economic and selfish reasons. World War I was no exception. It involved many nations, it was the most terrible and far-reaching of its time, and had the highest casualty list of any war fought up to the early Twentieth Century. Why was this war fought? Were economic reasons behind it? What new devices for fighting and killing were used in it? Go over your answers to the questions above and on the bottom and/or back of this sheet write a paragraph or two, summarizing the answers to these three questions.

ONE OF THE FOUR TAPE WORK SHEETS FROM THE LEARN-BY-YOURSELF KIT[15]

(Note: The recorded tapes were presentations calling for immediate, constructed answers by pupils.)

Name _____

Social Studies—Grade 8
UNCLE SAM ENTERS MANHOOD
Work Sheet #4

This work sheet is to be used with Tape #4—*The Flaming Twenties.* (7½ IPS-27 minutes)

Problem:

This tape will briefly tell you a little of the story of the 1920's, one of the wildest periods in Uncle Sam's life. You will learn that as one privilege was taken from the American people, another took its place. The new industries that arose and boomed in the early Twenties and their effect on the life of Americans will be described. You will also be given a glimpse into why the 1920's were called "The Flaming Twenties." What changes in their ways of living did American soldiers find when they returned from Europe? What great industries boomed in the early Twenties? Why were the 1920's such a wild period?

Questions Based on the Content of the Tape Recording:

As you listen to the recording, there will be certain directions

---

15 Ibid., pp. 511–512.

Fundamentals of Teaching with Audiovisual Technology

Figure 6–12. This section of a class group is shown listening to special tape-recorded presentations that also called for participation by pupils in constructing responses. The correct answers were given after short pauses in the tape commentary to permit students to check the correctness of their work. Looking at the rear of the tape recorder, the white cord is the power supply cord, and the jack below and to the left of the power plug is the external speaker jack (may be used also as in this case for the aggregate box) to which all the headsets are connected. (Courtesy Board of Education, Westport, Conn., and George E. Ingham)

and questions for you. These will be in reference to this work sheet. Follow the directions as you receive them and write your answers on this work sheet, as the tape tells you. Review what you have written when the tape indicates what your answer should be. Find out for yourself why you were wrong when you answered incorrectly.

1. What was the Amendment, popularly called Prohibition? When was it approved? What were its provisions?

   _____
   _____
   _____

2. Are there bootleggers operating in the United States today? Is liquor still being manufactured illegally?

   _____
   _____
   _____

3. What important right of citizenship was given to women who could qualify? When did this take place?

   _____
   _____
   _____

4. Other than radio, what new industry boomed after the war? What was the effect of this industry on one already in existence?

   _____
   _____
   _____

5. What new advantages were there for the small family and for the householder after the war? How was life improved for the small family and for the householder?

_____

_____

_____

6. What improvement in communications was made in the 1920's? Did this have any effect on entertainment?

_____

_____

_____

7. What was the effect of the 18th Amendment on the American people in the 1920's?

_____

_____

_____

8. What does it mean to declare a moratorium on the payments of debts? Why did Uncle Sam declare a moratorium for foreign nations?

_____

_____

_____

Summarization:

In this tape you have been told a little of the story of the 1920's. You discovered that, as one privilege was taken from the American people, another took its place. New industries that arose and boomed in the early Twenties were described. You also were given a glimpse into why the 1920's were called "The Flaming Twenties." What changes in their ways of living did American soldiers find when they returned from Europe? What great industries boomed in the early Twenties? Why were the 1920's such a wild period? On the bottom or on the back of your work sheet, write a paragraph or two, summarizing the answers to these questions.

SOME SAMPLE ITEMS FROM THE PROGRAMMED BOOKLET OF 132 PAGES ON THE TOPIC THE THREAT TO WORLD PEACE [16]

(Note: The items are shown consecutively here instead of being arranged as in the text originally with item and answer appearing on succeeding pages.)

[16] Ibid., *Items* #108–#115, pp. 414–429; *Item* #144, pp. 428–429; *Item* #295, pp. 496–497.

Figure 6–13. In this picture, pupils are shown as they worked item by item through their programmed booklets. (Courtesy Board of Education, Westport, Conn., and George E. Ingham)

Topic Four
THE THREAT TO WORLD PEACE

Item #108

Imperialism and nationalism are apt to be partners. Nationalism is the doctrine that states that the interests of one's country are more important than international considerations. If the philosophy of a nation's leaders is imperialistic, it will also be _____.

Answer to Item #108

   nationalistic

Item #109

"Militarism" is the glorification of the ideals and attitudes of the professional soldier and the policy of maintaining powerful armed forces for instant use. Aggressive preparedness is

_____ .

Answer to Item #109

   militarism

Item #110

Imperialism, nationalism, and militarism usually go hand in hand. To what policy must a country's leaders subscribe in order to further the cause of imperialism and nationalism?

_____

Answer to Item #110

   militarism

The Teacher Uses Media

Item #111

Militarism needs industrialism. Industrialism is a social and economic organization indicated by machine production, assembly-line techniques, and concentration of workers. What is the basis for militarism? _____

Answer to Item #111

industrialism
   Industrialism is necessary for peacetime activities, too.

Item #112

Can you think of a country in Africa whose leaders are both nationalistic and militaristic and who are showing a tendency to imperialism? _____ What is the country? (As a clue, the country was once ruled by a famous queen.) _____

Answers to Item #112

yes

Egypt
   If you missed on the second part of this, the queen was Cleopatra.

Item #113

If a small boy walks around ready to fight to protect what he considers to be his interests, what is he practicing? _____

Answer to Item #113

militarism
   This is "a chip on the shoulder" attitude.

Item #114

As new, independent nations are created out of former colonies, what charge is frequently made against the West by the Iron Curtain countries in the UN? _____

Answer to Item #114

imperialism

Item #115

Could the charge of imperialism be made against any of the

Iron Curtain countries? Your answer will be your own opinion but should be based on fact. _____

Answer to Item #115

> *As stated previously, your answer is your own opinion. Did you base it on fact?*

Item #144

The balance was bad, though. If nations on either side became involved in war, all nations, because of their treaties, would also go to war. This would destroy the _____.

Answer to Item #144

peace

> *This concludes topic four—"The Threat to World Peace." Go back and review what you have learned before proceeding . . .*

Item #295

It is only fair in a democratic society that all citizens in good standing have the same privileges and responsibilities. In many instances, the vote of _____ has been a deciding factor in an election.

Answer to Item #295

women

> *Congratulations! You have completed topic nine—"New Laws of the Land" and, with it, the requirements of your self-teaching workbook. Read the last section in your activity guide for special instructions for review of the material you have just covered.*

The Readiness Principle in Action

The pupils' *Learn-By-Yourself Kit* was complete with motivational material, and the teacher had introduced the teaching unit before distributing the kit. The pupil was led from general motivational material to specific problems in each guide sheet, and the programmed booklet was also introduced to the pupil in an appealing preface. Each of the work sheets may be scrutinized for readiness-building elements. The reader is certain to find problems and questions at every point throughout the material. Points to look and listen for are stated, and a challenge seems obvious. Motivational material in the preface of the programmed booklet is a good example of the way special readiness material may be prepared and presented to pupils. The quotation follows:

THE PROGRAMMED BOOKLET PREFACE[17]

Preface

As a teenage citizen of the United States, you enjoy certain privileges found only in the democracy in which you live. With these privileges, however, go certain responsibilities—to your family and to your friends, to your church and to your school, to your community and to your nation, and—to yourself.

Are you an active participant in family affairs? Do you help your parents, your brothers and sisters, and your friends? Do you work for the good of your church, your school, your community, and your nation? Can you make good judgments? Do you listen to both sides of the story before forming an opinion? Can you tell good from bad, right from wrong? Are you considered to be a fair and wise leader in your group or are you a good and loyal follower? Both are needed, you know. And what does all this have to do with this "Self-Teaching Workbook?"

As the title implies, this is a guide for your work. "Workbook" means just that—work. If you work on it carefully, you will learn from it. You should be able to arrive at worthwhile conclusions and to form your own opinions, based on fact and not fancy. It will be your responsibility, as an individual student in your class, to do this work by yourself and at your own speed. By so doing, you will be gaining additional experience in the assumption of responsibility as a teenage citizen now and as an adult later. In short, you can expect to be an even better citizen than you are now.

Directions as to procedure to follow are on the next page. Read them carefully and then begin when you understand them completely. Remember—it's your responsibility! You are on your own!

An examination of the guide sheets and programmed text material is certain to reveal a potential for a maximum of response activity for each minute of class time. Problems and questions were clearly stated, and these questions and responses provide not only significant readiness-building material but they also constitute the basic activity that pupils need to engage in to learn in terms of the teacher's objectives. Thus the newer technological devices and processes may be used under the guidance of the basic principles that have operated in the more conventional classroom situations depicted in the other case studies.

It is the teacher's responsibility to make good decisions about materials and devices, and about how best to fit them into an effective instructional design to achieve

ANALYSIS OF CASE STUDY NUMBER 6

[17] Ibid., p. 363.

valid objectives. Case Study Number 6 reveals a teacher at work in a situation where she was assumed by pupils to have prepared a phenomenal array of self-teaching materials, and what remained was to offer them to pupils and expedite their use with little if any face-to-face verbal activity. The following sequence of questions will assist the reader to analyze this case study for the purpose of developing insight into what constitutes effective planning and utilization of audiovisual technology in less conventional patterns.

Ordered Sequence of Responses

1. Name some differences in basic teaching methods between Case Study Number 6 and the other case studies. As to the degree and kind of control by the teacher? Freedom of pupils to make progress? Control and guidance of pupils by written instructions?

2. What should the teacher do about the pupils who finish self-instructional materials first, thus having free time? (See Item 4.)

3. How could motion pictures have been put to work in this case study? In the introductory phase? Used with *readiness and action* guide sheets?

4. Does it appear that pupil activity was geared more to the learning of subject matter? Read the statement of abilities, attitudes, and appreciations again, and ask yourself if other significant problem-solving activities should have supplemented the activity with self-teaching materials in optimum balance? How could work in the library help? Surveys? Interviews?

5. Identify the elements of readiness in the samples of self-teaching sheets. Note the pupil problem focus. Note the directed observation items and the directions for procedure on the first section of the filmstrip Work Sheet #12.

6. Note the required written response blanks and the request for a written summary at the end of the work sheet.

7. What determines (or should determine) the nature of the responses that pupils need to make? Study some of the called-for responses in the filmstrip and tape guide sheets and the responses to the programmed text items and determine the nature of the objectives involved.

8. What similar, though not as formal and prolonged, self-instructional activities could teachers develop for use with a film, a filmstrip, a tape, a chart, or a transparency? Problems and response processes or illustrated guide sheets? Have simple guide sheets and special reference material been prepared by good teachers for many years before the term *programmed instruction* was ever used?

9. Do the excerpts in this case study constitute, if all elements were included, a teaching unit? An instructional system? Do you perceive that several media were employed? Note the two roles of this teacher: the creator of the unique teaching materials, and the manager of the day-to-day situation? Note also the role of motivator and communicator.

More simple to organize, prepare, and operate than the learn-by-yourself package in Case Study Number 6 is a system for using taped instruction and illustrated work sheets as an integral part of teaching in a conventionally organized classroom. A series of pictures will tell the story of the operation, and a set of questions will direct attention to relationships between tape, response sheets, and other class activities.

Case Study Number 7

THE USE OF TEACHER-MADE TAPES[18]

The Class and Teacher

This case study deals with a group of fourth-grade elementary school pupils in the Burr Farms School being taught in this instance by instructional tapes prepared by the teacher. The subject is science, and the specific topic is *Structure of Green Plants*.

Relationship of the Taped Instruction to Teaching Objectives

As in the other case studies it is necessary to take note of the objectives that pupil activity was designed to achieve. The following statements of purpose are based upon a personal interview with the teacher, the content of the prerecorded tape, and personal observation of the activities of the pupils during a visit to their classroom.

UNDERSTANDING THAT:
1. Scientists who study plants are called botanists.
2. Most of the plants in home gardens are green, seed-making plants.
3. The main parts of a plant are the roots, stem, leaves and blossom, and each has its own special job to do.
4. There are three kinds of roots: trunk roots, feeler roots and root hairs. The coarser roots carry the dissolved food picked up by the root hairs up into the plant. Coarser roots also hold the plant upright and firmly in the ground. The food picked up by root hairs is in the form of minerals dissolved in moisture in the soil.
5. Root systems of plants are very complex and when the

---

[18] Annette Fournier, teacher and tape producer, Westport Public Schools, Westport, Conn. By permission.

lengths of all roots in the ground are added together, the total distance may be many feet, even miles.

6. Stems of plants move liquids from one part of the plant to another, they hold plants up toward the sun, and they are able to produce leaves.

7. Without the leaves of plants we and many other animals would go hungry.

8. Leaves are the food making factories of a plant and this whole process is made possible because they are able to make chlorophyll. Leaves take in carbon dioxide from the air and give off oxygen when this food making process is going on. Leaves also have veins that carry food made in the leaves to other parts of the plant, even to the roots.

9. Leaves are made up of cells, some of which act like doors through which leaves breathe. These little breathing cells are called stomata.

10. Plant blossoms or flowers produce seeds from which new plants may grow.

ABILITY TO:

1. Make accurate observations.
2. Keep correct records.
3. Draw conclusions from facts.
4. Solve problems.
5. Find needed information.

ATTITUDE OF:

1. Curiosity.
2. Openmindedness.
3. Objectivity.

APPRECIATION OF:

1. Accuracy.
2. Reliable data.
3. Opinions based on facts.

Relationship of Taped Instruction to the Larger Teaching Design

It is also important to know just how this particular use of technology was related to previous classroom activity. We have already observed the teaching purposes. We need now to note that (1) the taped instruction activity was related to a stream of pupil activity, that is, it was not just superimposed as an end in itself, but rather was tied to other projects and pupils' needs, and to action plans for a particular science period; (2) pupils had been made ready for this activity by planned teacher activity; and that (3) the taped instructional experience would achieve the specified objectives directly, or make a predicted contribution to their accomplishment.

Relation to Pupil Action:
Past and Present

Pupils were at work on a teaching unit, the topic for which was *Plant Life*. Each pupil had started a plant experiment a number of weeks previously. Seeds had sprouted and plants were growing. Some of the plants were being grown in water, for comparison with plants grown in soil; some were kept cool,

others were being grown under an opaque paper cover. These experiments intrigued the youngsters and they discussed each other's observations. The class had made two displays for the bulletin board; one was a labeled diagram of the parts of a flower, and the other identified the parts of a plant. New facts were needed. Pupils were ready for deeper insights as they worked together on their projects.

The instructional tape, requiring approximately twenty minutes, provided a direct presentation by the teacher. The class was divided into two groups for the presentation; one group was assigned to the tape-listening work tables, and the other group was called together by the teacher, who had planned to give each pupil a chance to observe seeds under a magnifying glass. The teacher directed this activity personally and also provided guidance for on-the-spot textbook reference work. When the two groups exchanged places on schedule, the teacher repeated her demonstration and observation session, working closely with the pupils.

The Readiness Plan of the Teacher

The pupils were basically ready for more advanced work on the structure of green plants because of their continuing class activity, but, at the beginning of this session, the teacher, in the opening minutes, explained the nature of the plan of activity for the day. She tied the presentation on tape to her concurrent demonstration and the pupils' observation of seeds. She also explained how the pupils were to study the work-sheet diagram during the listening session. She mentioned the exper-

Figure 6–14. Members of this fourth-grade science class are listening to their teacher's introduction to the multi-group activity for that session. This is how youngsters react to a good readiness plan. Evidence of individual and group activity is everywhere. A work table covered with pots and pans containing individual plant-life experiments is out of the picture at right near the window wall. Only a portion of the class is in the picture. Note the two boxes on the table near the chalkboard. The larger one is labeled Spare Time Arithmetic *and the small one is labeled* Answer Box. *The intrusion of the camera disturbed their basic attention patterns to only a minor degree. (Courtesy Board of Education, Westport, Conn. Photo by C. W. H. Erickson)*

iments now in process and how the tape contained valuable information that would help them to understand better some of their observations and findings.

Contribution to the Teacher's Objectives

In discussing the contribution of the tape to the achievement of teaching objectives the teacher emphasized that the tape and work sheet presented the vital information pupils needed in carrying on their class work. The teacher also believed that her own voice on the tape actually allowed her to be in two places, doing two different teaching jobs at the same time. Another point was that an audio presentation permitted the presentation and development of science concepts by some fourth-graders who were as yet unable to comprehend such material in regular reading references or encyclopedias. The information thus gained through explanation enabled pupils to extend their factual basis for making keener observations and judgments.

The Technological System in Operation

In this case study the first point for observation is that the teacher prepared her own instructional tapes and work sheets and decided how best to relate them to the curriculum. First we present the audio content on the tape in the form of the tape script.[19]

SCIENCE #17—GENERAL STRUCTURE
OF TYPICAL GREEN PLANT

Hello boys and girls. Have you been discovering how many things there are to learn about plants? Well, we've really just begun—there are ever so many fascinating and exciting things still to learn and do.

With so many thousands of plants growing on earth, it is impossible for any one person to know them all. Yet a plant scientist, who is called a *botanist,* can often look at a strange plant and tell what plant family it belongs to. How does this scientist classify a plant he has never seen before?

The answer is structure. The botanist looks at the parts of a plant and how they are put together. He studies the structure of the stem, the leaves, the flower, and the roots, and finds clues in each one. Putting all the clues together, he can often place the plant in the family group to which it belongs.

The first thing he must do is place the plant in one of these two groups:
1. plants that make seeds
2. plants that do not make seeds.
The botanist knows many things about each plant group. Therefore, finding the right group allows him to learn many things about each plant.

Let us assume that our botanist has decided that the plant

[19] Tape script and tape were produced by Annette Fournier, fourth-grade science teacher, Burr Farms Elementary School, Westport, Conn. By permission.

in question is a seed maker. Although there are countless numbers of seed-making plants, there is much information that is true of all of them.

Today, then, let us look at the structure of a typical, green, seed-making plant to see what we can learn about it.

Most of the plants in our gardens at home fall into this category. Some are low and bushy like pansies and others are tall and straight like hollyhocks or delphiniums. They produce flowers in all sizes and colors but all are green, seed-making plants.

Look at Page 1 of your work sheet now. Here you will see a drawing of a typical, green, seed-making plant. Study the drawing as I tell you about it. The main parts of a plant are the roots, stem, leaves, and blossom. Each part has a very special job to do and our work today will be to discover exactly what each section of the plant has to do.

We have said that this is a seed-making plant. Therefore, we know that its life began when a seed was planted. When you plant a seed, you really plant stored-up food, because the seed has within itself, the energy (which means strength or force) for growth. When it is first placed in the soil, the seed takes in water equal to half its weight. As it begins to grow, the seed uses the food that is stored inside it. And the soil helps in the growth of the young seedling by supplying minerals and water.

As the seed grows, the roots develop and spread through the soil bringing food to the hungry plant. But how does the plant get this food from the soil?

Tiny hairs, called *root hairs*, grow from the finest roots when they are beginning to sprout. These root hairs grow into the soil and take in food that has been dissolved in water. They have no holes or openings, so solids cannot enter. But liquid food can pass through the very thin tissue. From the root hair, the food is carried inside the plant.

Root hairs do not grow on the larger, coarser roots, so these roots do not take in food for the plant. It is the job of the bigger roots to carry the food up to the plant after it has been taken in by the root hairs.

In addition to getting food and sending it up into the plant, the roots also hold the plant firmly in the ground and allow it to reach up into the air toward the sun. You probably know that when plants are knocked down and lie along the ground, that they soon die and rot.

It is interesting to note that roots of common garden plants are really quite long and involved. The root system of a single cabbage plant may spread through as much as 200 feet of soil. That of a common tomato plant may be much more. The total length of the root hairs of a winter rye plant may be more than 5,000 miles! Roots then are pretty important parts of a plant and are surely amazing things themselves.

Before we go on to examine the rest of the plant, let's stand up and stretch for a moment. (30 sec.)

Ready? We have learned about the roots of plants and the next important part to consider is the stem. We are quite familiar with stems. We know that if we cut a stem, the flower and leaves above the cut will wither and die. We know that if you put the end of the stem in water, the flower and its leaves that have been removed from the parent plant will not wither so quickly. This is because the stem is able to get water to the leaves and to the flower and keep them supplied with at least some of their needs.

From this we know that one of the uses a plant finds for stems is that of moving liquids from one part of the plant to another. The stem also holds the plant up toward the sun and is able to produce leaves.

Leaves do some of the most important work in the world. Without them you and many other animals would go hungry. Leaves contain a green coloring matter called *chlorophyll*. If there were no chlorophyll, you could not live. No other animals could live either. Scientists are trying to do the work that chlorophyll does by experimenting with chemicals, but so far they have had little success. Only a plant can make the wonderful chemical, chlorophyll. The whole process that uses chlorophyll is so involved and so important that we will not go into it today. For now, it is enough to remember that the leaves make this chemical, chlorophyll.

The most common kinds of leaves are broad and thin, and are arranged along the stems, usually near the tips. They are most commonly the greenest part of a flowering plant. Leaves, like stems and roots, are of many different kinds. Some are juicy and crisp like those of lettuce and others are tough and wiry like pine needles.

Each leaf is made up of millions of cells. We must use a lens or a microscope if we want to examine these cells. The plant breathes through some of these cells that are found on the underside of the leaf. These cells act like doors and are called *stomata*. "Stomata" means little mouths. The doors in the leaves can open and close. When they are open, air can go in and out.

We know that our own bodies take in oxygen from the air and breathe out carbon dioxide. Plants, however, do just the opposite. They take in carbon dioxide and breathe out oxygen.

In addition to the stomata, or little mouths, the leaves also contain veins. These veins transport the food that is made in the leaves, to other parts of the plant.

The last part of our plant is the blossom, or flower. We know that there are ever so many different kinds. They come in all sizes, shapes and colors and some have a very pleasant smell. The biggest job that a flower must do is to produce seed. And of course we know that seeds eventually produce new plants. But how is this done? What structure and organs do flowers contain that allow them to produce new plants? Because this is such an involved topic, we will work on it at another time and really explore the question fully. For now, it is enough to remember that a flower produces seeds which will then produce new plants.

Would you believe that we've only begun our study of

Figure 6-15. The Overall Classroom Activity of Students in Two Working Groups. *One of the groups is at work with the teacher in a demonstration-observation session with seeds. The other group is getting instruction via a tape-recorded presentation with a diagram to illustrate some of the verbal content. (Courtesy Board of Education, Westport, Conn. Photo by C. W. H. Erickson)*

the structure of plants? We still have much to learn about both leaves and flowers. But we did cover a lot of ground today, didn't we?

Many of the things that you have heard today will be used again and again in class when we are performing our plant experiments.

Now I'd like to see what kinds of listeners we were today. On page 2 of your work sheet you will find an outline that lists the various topics that we have discussed today.

When you remove your earphones, fill in as many sections of this outline as you can. Bring it to class tomorrow and we will help one another to complete it. When it is finished you will have a handy reference page to add to your notebook.

You may remove your earphones and begin working on your outline now.

Suggestions for Observing Figure 6-15

1. Did valid teaching purposes constitute the basis for this teacher's selection of this particular medium? What roles did this tape-recorded instruction play in assisting the teacher? (If you are not sure about the answers to these questions refer again to the preceding sections for explanation.)
2. Is this teacher to be admired for her ability to innovate?
3. Do you believe from your observation of the pupils that they were ready to participate in this activity? In other words, do you believe the teacher followed the second basic principle (readiness) described earlier in this chapter?
4. How is the control principle being carried out in this situation? What basic conditions have been met?

Figure 6–16. The Simplified Arrangement of Tape Recorder and Headsets. (Courtesy Board of Education, Westport, Conn. Photo by C. W. H. Erickson)

5. In this operation how are the tape and worksheet related? Can you identify the learning products?
6. How is the *action* principle being applied to the use of this tape?

Suggestions for Observing Figure 6–16

1. Note the convenient pipe-rack arrangement for storing the headphones, with headphones ready for use without loss of time.
2. Note simple headphone channel connecting to the tape recorder-player unit.
3. Does the worktable arrangement provide space for reference books and work sheet?
4. In this situation who would start and adjust the tone and volume controls of the tape player?
5. Note the simple connections for headphones and channel.

Suggestions for Observing Figure 6–17

1. These pupils like this way of learning. They concentrate and work industriously. They listen, follow directions, and respond.
2. How much sustained activity of this kind would youngsters of this age be able to undergo? How might this presentation-response activity be balanced with other significant problem-solving activity? Project work and crafts? Library research and extensive reading?

Page 1 of the work-sheet diagram is visible in Figure 6–18. This particular diagram for study during the tape presentation does not call for written responses by the pupils. Other diagrams in the series do call for such responses. Page 2 of the work sheet calls for students to fill in blanks summarizing the

Figure 6–17. The Pupils at Work. *In this segment of the class, instruction is being given by means of a teacher-recorded tape. The teacher's own voice presents information and guides the students in their reactions, yet the teacher is actually nearby working with the other half of the class in a demonstration and discussion group. (Courtesy Board of Education, Westport, Conn. Photo by C. W. H. Erickson)*

Figure 6–18. These pupils receive guidance from the teacher's commentary on the tape, hence the instruction is personalized. Could this kind of activity be carried on in large groups as well, provided, of course, enough equipment was available? Is the kind of mental and physical activity called for determined by the nature of teaching purposes? Is this kind of taped material easy to duplicate? Could textbook illustrations be effectively utilized as a reference base for taped instruction? (Courtesy Board of Education, Westport, Conn. Photo by C. W. H. Erickson)

parts of a green plant and the roles those parts play in the life of the plant.

ANALYSIS OF CASE STUDY NUMBER 7

We note in this case study that audio content prepared by the teacher could take many forms, such as direct explanations, step-by-step directions for carrying out a kind of performance, or directions for analyzing content of verbal and/or pictorial references, all prepared by the teacher, and perhaps calling for some kind of a pupil answer, either covert (thought), written, or figured. In the light of the foregoing, we urge you to answer the following analytical questions and make the judgments called for.

Ordered Sequence of Responses

1. Based on the excerpts of audio content and the work sheet, which objectives would the taped presentation be likely to accomplish? What other routes to understanding does this case study reveal?
2. Is taped instruction a self-teaching activity? How could it be used for remedial work? Applied to spelling? To map work? To number concepts and computation? To science activities? To English expression? To reading activity?
3. What kind of teacher activity would be needed to get pupils ready for this exercise? How do problems, projects, and extensive reading prepare pupils for action? Could an introductory sheet be prepared for readiness? Could a special introduction be included on the tape? Under what condition would an introductory talk by the teacher suffice?
4. Can response sheets of all kinds serve to get the necessary *action* by students?
5. Can tape-recorded instruction by the teacher serve to multiply the teacher's effort, that is, serve as an extension in time and place of the teacher's personality?
6. Could activity like this be carried on for one part of the class only, as one segment of valid multi-group activity? For example as remedial work? As special work for a group of fast-moving students?
7. Could teachers cooperate by working as a team to produce materials, or could each prepare separate units, according to agreed specifications, then exchange them; for example, prepare and donate one tape and get ten in return?
8. Is the work by the teacher to create such materials worthwhile? Economical because of subsequent repetition? Does such work provide good basis for later revision?

The Teacher Uses Media

We now turn to a case study that focuses on the employment of devices and materials by a number of teachers working as a group called a *teaching team*. While not forsaking for a moment the important and direct relationship between valid teacher purpose, namely, that of *means* and *ends*, we omit the statement of purposes and show only the nature of the devices, materials, and processes in such a highly systematized operation.

We therefore present a series of classroom examples that show various aspects of teacher-pupil-media relationships, especially in a large group of up to ninety pupils. We must point out that teachers may now, because of technology, extend their influence and control in new patterns of action.

EQUIPMENT, MATERIALS AND STUDENT GROUPING IN A TEAM-TEACHING SITUATION[20]

Team-Teaching Situation

The team-teaching situations shown in this case study are in a number of elementary schools where several teams of teachers are engaging in experimental work. The groups shown are taught by a team of five persons. One of these is a *team leader*, three are designated as *cooperating teachers*, and the other as the *teacher aide* with the rating of a secretary. These teaching teams plan their schedules, and work together in preparing materials and deciding on the design for large and small group activities to meet specific teaching objectives. A wide array of technological equipment and material is brought into use singly and in combination, such as taped instruction and work sheets, overhead projectors, motion pictures, filmstrips, displays, devices, television, and others. Thus the total enrollment of the large group is approximately ninety, and these pupils meet in large instructional spaces certain times during the day on a prearranged schedule. After instruction that lends itself to large-group presentation, the class divides into smaller groups of varying sizes for multi-group activity in the same or different classroom spaces.

Statements by Teachers

Several specific examples from language arts and science at the elementary school level will help to portray the nature of the instruction being given by teams of teachers. We now turn to descriptions by the teachers themselves through the courtesy of *Grade Teacher Magazine*. The quotations are as follows:

QUOTATION NO. 1: LARGE-GROUP HANDWRITING

I have been using the overhead almost exclusively to teach my fifth- and sixth-graders how to write. First, and perhaps most important of all, I am assured that my whole group (usually

20 Norwalk Public Schools, Norwalk, Conn.

eighty children) is progressing at the same rate; they are able to see exactly how their writing paper should look, line-for-line.

As for noting individual progress, I can, and often do, leave the machine to give help and offer suggestions; my cooperating teacher often does the same. All this is going on while the rest of the class is continuing with another area of practice.

Frequently during the lesson I call on children whose handwriting presents a special kind of difficulty to give us a sample on the overhead projector. This enables the class and me to analyze it and offer corrective criticism. They love to emulate the teacher![21]

QUOTATION NO. 2: LETTER WRITING

One day I wished to have total group instruction by reviewing parts of a letter and punctuation. Seventy-three children certainly would have a hard time seeing the chalkboard. The chalkboard also had to be used right up to the Language Arts period; therefore, I would waste time writing the letter during my Language Arts period. My teacher's aide made the transparency of the letter before the lesson. When it was time for English, the letter was ready. We reviewed the parts of the letter together, then the children came to the projector and corrected the letter.[22]

QUOTATION NO. 3: INCREASING WORD ANALYSIS SKILLS

Tapes can be used for remedial purposes, to increase skills, for enrichment, follow-up activities, practice, reinforcement of known skills, and review. The tapes have been used in all the grades from second to sixth.

Through the use of tapes, we have touched upon every phonetic and word analysis skill. The tapes have been prepared with the intent to review and to reinforce all skills required in previous grades. Having accomplished these objectives, the child is better prepared to assimilate all new concepts. Therefore, all tapes are prepared in a series in order that the child may use a previously learned skill as a tool in learning his newly taught skill.

The children are given the opportunity to respond orally; for example, sounding out hard and soft consonants, blends, digraphs and long and short vowels. Each child is also supplied with a work sheet on which he responds individually to the tape. The work sheet is carefully prepared to afford the child an opportunity to use the given concepts as a tool while working on his own. This work sheet thus provides not only an opportunity to work with a given concept immediately after it has been presented, but also a clear picture of the child's achievement for that day for evaluation purposes.[23]

---

[21] The original statement was written by Josephine Mears of the Norwalk, Connecticut Public Schools. By permission of *Grade Teacher Magazine*—"Teamwork Produces Audio-Visual Techniques," *Grade Teacher Magazine* (June 1960), 55–58, 60–62, 64–72.

[22] Ibid., p. 57

[23] Ibid., pp. 62, 64.

As part of the Science curriculum in our school, I presented a lesson utilizing the tape recorder. This was done as a review follow-up exercise. To prepare this lesson, a script was written. After it was checked for errors, accuracy and time allotment, it was transferred onto a tape. The pupils were first introduced to the unit; the topic being "Simple Machines."

As part of the introductory work, I had prepared a transparency which helped greatly in the introductory phase. Following the introduction, which incidentally was presented to the total group of approximately 80 pupils, we distributed work sheets which graphically pictured the various simple machines. This was also used in conjunction with the taped lesson. The presentation included a film in addition to lecture, discussion, and tape. For greater interest and understanding, two lessons consisted of demonstrations, these being actual examples of the simple machines. Also as part of these demonstrations, explanations were given by me in a rather detailed manner.

The tape, demonstrations, and use of film made an interesting unit, and the pupils were motivated. Results of tests indicated that the material was understood, not just memorized. The tape and transparency have become a part of the Curriculum Materials Center and are available to all teachers.[24]

The Technological System in Operation

With these descriptions of actual operations by the teachers themselves let us turn to five photographs (Figures 6–19 to 6–23) for a visual presentation of technology at work. Each illustration is accompanied by a series of suggested observations.

This picture shows a Norwalk teaching team in action, illustrating an instance of total group instruction:

Suggestions for Observing Figure 6–19

1. In this setting the cooperating teacher is presenting visualized instruction in arithmetic. The team leader is observing the work of pupils, and the teacher aide at the right is performing clerical duties. Would this situation be likely to utilize unique abilities of teachers in the team?

2. Note the fact that the teacher at the overhead projector is seated. Line-of-sight vision to the bottom of an image on the screen is necessary or the view will be blocked.

3. Are assignment sheets and textbook references being used? Is there evidence that pupils are being asked to respond to directions of the teacher?

4. Is everyone being asked to do the same thing at the same time? Is this likely to be a characteristic of the kind of presentation shown?

5. A science presentation in this room for these pupils would undoubtedly call for diagrams and multiple overlays in color, with notes being taken by pupils. Problem situations could be introduced and noted for creative productivity by individuals and/or smaller groups during subsequent work periods.

[24] Ibid., p. 68. The original statement was written by Daniel Bardos of the Norwalk, Connecticut Public Schools.

Figure 6–19. Total Group Instruction Using the Overhead Projector. (Courtesy Board of Education, Norwalk, Conn.)

6. Would the use of motion pictures, television, filmstrips, slides, and other media be usable in large groups (or larger) than the group shown? *Note the rear-projection screen between the regular screen and the television receiver. Films, filmstrips, or slides may be projected onto this translucent screen from an adjacent workroom.*

7. What planning is necessary by teachers?

8. How would the basic principles of selection, readiness, control of arrangements, action, and evaluation be applied to large-group use of such instructional media as are shown in this panel?

9. What valid pupil performance (ability) is obviously being developed in this picture? In this case what information is being presented? What objectives should be kept in mind by the teachers?

10. What functional practice should be carried out? Related to practical problems? Related to other subjects? What reading reference work?

Suggestions for Observing Figure 6–20

This section of a "total group" has been scheduled for planned activities that either follow a session, such as depicted in Figure 6–19, or precede it. Do you recognize the teacher's aide from Figure 6–19? She is now in charge of the tape-playing operation and has just started to play the taped lesson:

1. Note the tape-listening operation in a booth-type installation for one group of pupils, while, simultaneously, the

Figure 6–20. A Segment of the Total Group Engaging in Planned Activities. (Courtesy Board of Education, Norwalk, Conn.)

rest of the group is working on a textbook exercise. Can such a program of split activity be used for remedial work? For extra instruction for the gifted? Study period? Creative construction?

2. Note the typewriter on the desk. Does this suggest emphasis on preparation of unique teaching materials? Does it also suggest duties for the teacher's aide?
3. Does emphasis seem to be placed on pupil activity? Where does teacher activity show up in this illustration?
4. Could the taped lesson be a short lecture? An explanation of a process? A presentation of a problem for a special assignment? Could a rotation plan be worked out for exchange of a number of activities, so that all pupils would take turns at different activities on a planned schedule?
5. Where does library work fit into this scheduling process? During after-school hours? During specified study hours? Voluntary homework?

Suggestions for Observing Figure 6–21

A small-group section is shown being involved in two different activities simultaneously. A scheduled television program from a nearby station or from the school-system closed-circuit installation is used instructionally for one group while a group of classmates has a face-to-face presentation by the teacher. Notice that the students watching television are wearing headphones.

Suggestions for Observing Figure 6–22

This illustration shows students hard at work on a language arts lesson. Note plug-in jacks for headphones. Also note the overhead projector obviously assigned to that classroom, and answer the following questions:
1. What precautions should be taken for tape-player failure?

Figure 6–21. A Segment of a Total Group Being Instructed by both Television and Teacher. (Courtesy Board of Education, Norwalk, Conn.)

Spare tape player nearby? Spare sets of headphones needed?

2. How should students' work be checked? By teacher's aide? By on-the-spot observation, noting those in need of remedial work?

3. How to provide for fast learners? Library work? Helping teachers help other pupils? Voluntary work on special problems as individuals or in groups?

Suggestions for Observing Figure 6–23

This teaching team is making detailed plans, a crucial aspect of team success:

1. In the team-teaching operation specific decisions must be

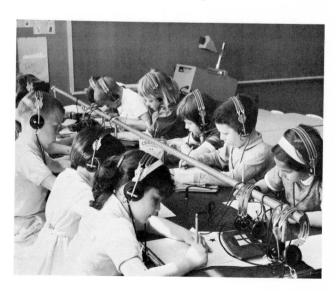

Figure 6–22. Simple Facilities for Taped Instruction as an Integral Part of the Team-teaching Process. (Courtesy Board of Education, Norwalk, Conn.)

The Teacher Uses Media

Figure 6–23. Team Planning. (Courtesy Board of Education, Norwalk, Conn.)

formulated by the group. Identify objectives? Plan activities for total group? For small group sections? Who is to do *what* and *when?*

2. What instructional media need to be used? Film? Television? Textbooks? In what combinations? What materials are already available in the school system and school-building service centers? What materials need to be prepared and by whom? Slides? Tapes? Transparencies? Work sheets?

3. Where do curriculum guides, resource units, programmed sequences fit into team teaching?

This case study presented a series of illustrations and a group of quotations by teachers, all showing or implying the action of a number of teachers working in teams. The reader is now directed to an ordered sequence of questions and observations relative to the instructional technology in this situation.

ANALYSIS OF CASE STUDY NUMBER 8

1. Why do teachers of large groups believe that audio-visual media are important in making presentations? Hold attention? Provide easy-to-understand standard explanations? Make drawings and reading matter visible through enlargement?

2. Why not simply present a 40-minute lecture to pupils?

3. Do teachers that handle both large and small groups seem to need specially prepared transparencies, tapes, and slides for their own situations?

4. Do teachers in these situations count heavily on introductory, explanatory, and response sheets as a part of their teaching method?

5. How are the total-group sections ordinarily supervised?

6. Specifically what presentations in your field can be

Ordered Sequence of Responses

made to large groups without loss of instructional effect? Directions for a specific required action? Present introductory material by film, television, and filmstrip? Give assignments and explanations? Present programmed learning sequences in steps requiring an immediate response?

7. What kinds of operations need to be carried out in small groups?

8. What kind of teacher preparation is needed for multi-group activity within one class?

9. How much of the total diet of pupil *activity* can be of the work sheet, blank-filling, and small-step variety? When should effort be expended on creative production and research by pupils? Do objectives determine this? Can teachers fall into the trap of "teaching the book" in team teaching perhaps more easily than in conventional teaching processes? If so, need this be the case?

Case Study Number 9

This final case study shows the medium of television in use in two widely separated school systems, namely, Anaheim, California, and Dade County, Miami, Florida. Although it has already been pointed out that television may be put to work at a number of different levels, we wish to show its use in schools where its full potentiality for reaching both conventionally organized classroom groups and large, reorganized groups with superior teaching is being utilized. Furthermore, we wish to show the nature of the instruction employed where the television teaching is planned and originated within the school system itself. Therefore in Case Study Number 9 we turn to the published guidebooks and telelesson teaching outlines supplied by the television directors of two school systems.[25]

For the purposes of this observation, excerpts and explanations will, for the large part, be confined to one telelesson in each school system, to show the kinds of teaching processes being carried on by both the studio television teacher and the classroom television teacher, and to reveal some of the many ways that technological media, including television, are being applied. In Anaheim, the subject is science, and the pupils are third-graders in conventional class groups. In Dade County the subject is American history, and the learners are eleventh graders in large groups of 320 or more students meeting in high school auditoriums.

[25] James D. Brier of Anaheim City Schools, California, and Clif Mitchell of the Dade County Board of Public Instruction, Miami, Florida. By permission.

DIRECT TEACHING BY TELEVISION—
PART I:
ANAHEIM

The Actual Situation

The situation[26] in the Anaheim aspect of this case study simply stated is that approximately thirty-two third-grade science pupils in the Anaheim City Schools, Anaheim, California, are being taught not only by their regular teacher in a conventional self-contained classroom every day of the school week, but in addition by a television teacher two days a week on schedule. Their regular face-to-face teacher watches the telelesson with the students, but she has also prepared her pupils for the program and has had the benefit of an Instructional TV Guide and also specific teaching outlines from which quotations will be excerpted a little later. Actually, this third-grade science class in our case study receives direct instruction by television according to the following schedule:[27]

> Social Studies: Monday, Wednesday, Friday at 10:45 A.M.
> Science: Tuesday and Thursday at 10:45 A.M.
> Music: Monday at 1:20 P.M.
> Arithmetic: Wednesday at 1:20 P.M.

Now let us turn to the use of technology, to the teaching acts of the television studio teacher and of the classroom teacher and to the activities of pupils as they make contact with a segment of Unit VII, *Simple Machines,* of the major topic, *Matter and Energy.* The segment is *Lesson 50,* entitled *Wheels.*[28]

Objectives in Elementary Science

In addition to concepts relative to simple machines, wheels in particular, and their operations, the following objectives identified as skills are clearly set forth in the TV guide prepared for teachers:

> Science also provides many opportunities for developing the language art skills of reading, writing, speaking, listening, and research. In addition, these science skills should be developed: formulation of scientific principles and generalizations, accurate observations, problem-solving ability, and the skills of scientific thinking.[29]

With these objectives in mind we turn to the teaching outline[30] to find out what the classroom teacher was asked to do to prepare the class for the telelesson.

---

[26] The Anaheim Plan, Anaheim City School District, Anaheim, Calif.

[27] Anaheim City School District, Instructional Television Project, *TV Schedule—1962–63, Grade 3.*

[28] *Lesson 50, Wheels,* Tuesday, April 23, Science Grade 3, Instructional Television, Anaheim City School District, Anaheim, California, Mimeographed, 1963.

[29] *Instructional TV Guide,* Anaheim City School District, Anaheim, California, Mimeographed, p. 28.

[30] *Lesson 50,* op. cit.

Figure 6–24. This third-grade science teacher is following the telelesson closely, and is pointing for emphasis as the pupils watch. Other media are in evidence as resources. By being well acquainted with this program, this teacher is quick to demonstrate, using some available equipment along with a telecast diagram. (Courtesy Anaheim City Schools District, Anaheim, Calif.)

Classroom Teacher Activity Prior to Telelesson

According to suggestions in the special guide sheets, the teacher conducts a discussion with her pupils centered on specific questions listed in the teacher outline as follows:

What makes a bicycle move? On what part does it move? What makes these parts move? Use a real bicycle in the classroom to answer these questions.[31]

In addition, the teacher distributes some special work sheets for use during the telelesson, and the necessary textbooks are on the pupils' desks. The television set is turned on and tuned just before starting the discussion. The studio clock appears on the screen of the receiver to help the teacher time her discussion and class preparation activities properly. At precisely 10:45 A.M. as scheduled the telelesson teacher at the studio greets the class and assumes control.

The Studio Telelesson Teacher in Action

The studio teacher then uses models, apparatus, and motion picture clips to make a well-prepared, well-timed, appealing,

[31] Ibid., p. 1.

motivating, and challenging presentation that demonstrates the following understandings as presented in the teacher outline for Lesson 50:

Wheels make work easier.
Wheels help us work faster.
Wheels work together to make work easier and/or faster.[32]

The studio teacher stimulates the young students to carry on additional activities and refers to the textbooks the pupils have on their desks. In fact she suggests some specific problems for the regular classroom teacher in her presentation and has already presented such additional activities to the classroom teacher three weeks previous in the teacher outline which in the Anaheim plan is prepared by the studio teacher as one of her basic responsibilities.

Classroom Teacher Activity Following the Telelesson

Immediately following the telelesson, the regular teacher organizes activity on the special problems just suggested. The students proceed to experiment, observe, and draw conclusions, study their textbook and other classroom library references, and view a filmstrip entitled *How Wheels Help Us* as they engage in the following learning experiences. Such activities are referred to as related classroom instruction and are listed in the teaching outline for Lesson 50 as follows:

If possible, use a wagon to show how wheels are useful. Then remove the wheels and try to move the wagon. How would the wagon be of greater value, with wheels or without wheels?

Have a hand egg beater in class. Let the children examine it. How many wheels does it have? Are these wheels different from the wagon wheels? How? What happens when the handle of the egg beater is turned? Have the students observe very carefully and closely as the beater is turned. Do all of the wheels turn at the same rate of speed? Which turns faster, the little wheel or the handle? How is the egg beater used to help us in our work?

Explain to the children that wheels with teeth on them are gears. Find gears on a bicycle. What other machines have gears? Examine pictures from magazines and point out wheels and gears.

Make a very simple model of the wheel and axle or windlass. Use a long-handled broom over the backs of two chairs. Wrap cord around the middle of the broom handle. A weight can be tied to the cord and lifted up as the broom is turned. (The handle of the broom acts as the axle and the brush of the broom would act as the wheel.)

Lead the students to discover that the pencil sharpener and the door knob in the classroom are other illustrations of the wheel and axle.

Have a bicycle in the classroom. The pedals act as the

[32] Ibid.

Figure 6–25. After the telelesson the classroom teachers are assisted by detailed suggestions to promote significant learning activities. In these pictures the teacher is providing additional information by means of a filmstrip. Other classroom activities such as textbook study and pupil demonstrations as shown indicate that the formal viewing of instructional television is not a passive process for youngsters in Anaheim. (Courtesy Anaheim City Schools, Anaheim, Calif.)

The Teacher Uses Media

spokes of the wheel. Examine the gear wheels and the chain used to drive the wheels.[33]

While teachers are encouraged to utilize a wide range of reading materials, the teaching outlines submitted in advance include specific references suggested by the studio teachers. The following were listed for the telelesson in this case study.[34]

Science Far and Near, pp. 250–255
How and Why Wonder Book of Machines: Let's See Why, pp. 117–121
How Do We Know? pp. 74–85
Science is Exploring, pp. 134–135

We now need to examine the basic aspects of the application of television technology and to direct the observation of the reader to the teacher's plans and processes.

1. Is the television presentation (the telelesson) a carefully integrated complex of audiovisual cues, that is, language, models, apparatus, charts, film clips, slides? Are new concepts thus presented to many groups throughout the school district? Directions given for attacking and working on problems?
2. Do regular classroom teachers in this situation carry out the design created by the studio teacher? (Check the classroom teacher's responsibilities at Anaheim by referring to the outline, Responsibilities of the Classroom Teacher under *Television and Videotape* in Chapter 5.)
3. Is the television program or telelesson then treated

---

[33] Ibid., pp. 1–2
[34] Ibid., p. 2

ANALYSIS OF CASE STUDY NUMBER 9: PART I—ANAHEIM

Ordered Sequence of Responses

Figure 6–26. In Grade 5 the Anaheim plan for instructional television calls for the use of television for large groups. Such learning spaces are called resource classrooms. They are well equipped to provide opportunities for the use of other media during sessions following the scheduled telelesson. Such a resource classroom is shown in this illustration with teacher activity in progress. (Courtesy Anaheim City Schools, Anaheim, Calif.)

by the regular classroom teacher as a unique instructional medium, as for example a special kind of motion picture?

4. What is the basis of planning for the telelesson content? Teaching objectives? Name some of them: Understandings? Abilities?

5. Do the follow-up activities suggested by the *studio* teacher and organized and carried on by the *classroom* teacher appear to contribute to the valid objectives stated? Explain, using a specific example.

6. How did the classroom teacher apply the readiness principle in preparing for the telelesson? List the elements in the readiness plan.

7. Is problem solving a characteristic of the related classroom instruction? Where does textbook reading fit into this activity? Where could additional films and filmstrips fit?

8. Is control of physical arrangements by the classroom teacher important?

9. What would you do as a classroom teacher if the television receiver failed just as the telelesson was about to start?

10. Supposing there were no plans for related instructional activity following the telelesson. What then would be the nature of the telelesson plans? How would they have to differ from the described format for Anaheim? Provide for student responses on worksheets during the telelesson? Assume complete control of assignments perhaps at home? Call in written work for grading by trained assistants?

DIRECT TEACHING BY TELEVISION—
PART II:
DADE COUNTY

In the Anaheim aspect of this case study the studio teacher taught a third-grade science telelesson to a large number of classroom groups of conventional size, and the classroom teacher played an important role in preparing the students and in following the telelesson with planned instructional activities. In the Dade County[35] aspect of this case, based on mimeographed reports and teaching outlines, we show a situation where a group of some 320 high school juniors receive instruction by television in American history, in the high school auditorium daily from 1:20 to 1:47.

[35] *Dade County ETV* (*1962–63*), Dade County Board of Public Instruction, Miami, Fla., Mimeographed.

The situation as reported here refers to Lesson #83, on *Political Theories (1800–1828)* described in the ETV Teacher's Guide.[36] In the class of some 320, a team of two teachers and a teacher's aide takes charge. In this instance, the history teacher takes charge of the group and conducts follow-up teaching activity for history telelessons and is assisted by the English teacher on the team. Preceding the history telelesson is the English telelesson from 11:50 to 12:17, and during this daily telecast the English teacher takes charge and is assisted by the history teacher. The teacher's aide takes attendance, sets up equipment, and assists with other clerical work. There is one 23-inch table model television receiver for each group of 50 pupils, and all the sets are turned on with a master switch. A studio clock is shown on the receivers, so the classroom teacher can time his preparatory comments at the opening of the class.

The telelesson lasts for twenty-seven minutes, after which other teaching activities, suggested in the Guide, are carried out with all of the students participating in some way in the assignments.

Purposes and Content of the Telelesson

According to the guide[37] for Lesson #83 the purpose was, "To show the changes occurring in the Republican Party," and the content presented by the studio teacher over WSEC-TV, Channel 17, was as follows:

I. Revolution of 1800

[36] *American History, 11th Grade, ETV Teacher's Guide, Second Semester, 1962–63.* Dade County Board of Public Instruction, Miami, Fla.
[37] Ibid., Lesson Outline, p. 1.

Figure 6–27. This studio teacher in the Dade County Instructional Television program has a wide range of media at her command. Such resources are an essential element in the success of television teaching. Studio teachers work closely with classroom teachers. Together they plan optimum arrangements for pupil participation in learning activities. (Courtesy Dade County Board of Public Instruction, WTHS-TV, Miami, Fla.)

A. Jeffersonian Republicanism
B. Decline and Fall of the Federalists
II. One Party Government (1816–1824)
    A. Republican unity
    B. Split in Republican Party
III. National Republicans
    A. Leaders
    B. Platform
IV. Democratic Republicans
    A. Leaders
    B. Platform

Studio teachers devote full time to their presentations and they make wide use of charts, slides, film clips, and other pictorial and graphic illustrations for effective communication.

Learner Activity in Large Groups

The studio teacher and classroom teachers work together in workshops to improve teaching processes, and they devote a great deal of attention to the planning of learner activity in the classroom portions of the lessons. In this instance, Lesson #83 on *Political Theories (1800–1828)* calls for background readings in the textbooks of twenty-seven pages and participation in one or more of the activities, suggested in the teaching outline as follows:

Suggested Classroom Activities

1. Have students prepare transparencies cartooning the issues of 1800–1828.
2. Prepare a two-column display. In column one put Jefferson's stand on controversial issues. Students list compromises he had to make in column two.
3. Show film "Thomas Jefferson" EBF 20 min. Students preview, summarize.
4. Map work: Louisiana Purchase. Construct a map of the area, identifying key cities, capitals, products (dollar volume), population; compare to nation.
5. Assign student reports on Napoleon and how his rise to power affected our history.
6. Depict Louisiana Purchase by symbols such as "Breadbasket of the United States."[38]

The classroom activities and assignments are an integral part of the television teaching process and the classroom teacher follows up the studio teacher's stimulating presentation by making arrangements with students for participating in the assignments. Student notebook and project work are checked periodically. Under ETV conditions teachers of large groups have but three teaching periods daily, two large and one regular-size class.

ANALYSIS OF CASE STUDY NUMBER 9: PART II—DADE COUNTY

Ordered Sequence of Responses

We now review the situation just presented and ask the reader to examine the process and perceive some crucial relationships.

1. Note that the follow-up activities for the telelesson

[38] Op. cit. p. 2

Figure 6–28. Note the placement of television receivers for this group of some 320 students. Note also evidence of other media. The screen on the auditorium stage is used for presentations following the telelessons. A motion picture projector and an overhead projector are at the front of the room. (Courtesy Dade County Board of Public Instruction, WTHS-TV, Miami, Fla.)

were for one day only. Additional activities were prescribed every day. If the film were ready for projection at the conclusion of the telelesson only seven minutes would remain for a student summary. Note that a group of students would have previewed the film and prepared pertinent summary statements.

2. What planning and checking on the part of large-group television teachers would it require to make sure that one or more activities were accepted by pupils and completed on schedule? How could the teacher's aide help with this work? How to get optimum balance for each pupil? How many of the activities listed do you believe an eleventh grader could complete in a 54-minute study period?

3. Assuming that each day a stimulating visualized presentation were made by the studio teacher about crucial content in eleventh-grade history, would additional activities beyond note taking be necessary? What abilities, attitudes, and appreciations, in addition to understandings, should students develop in a history course? What homework and library work become necessary to achieve these objectives?

4. If the large-group teacher uses a microphone would not students on stage in a role-playing situation also need to use microphones?

5. Would a discussion in a group of 320 pupils be a waste of time? Could you get participants to "talk up"?

6. What student-work exhibit areas are needed for the display of art work, posters, and so on?

7. Could notebook work or completed work sheets based on the studio teacher's presentation and textbook reading be easily checked by the classroom teachers?

8. Can students get lost and lose interest with too many miscellaneous activities to complete? What is the relationship between proper pacing and the established teaching objectives?

Problems and Activities

1. Locate resource catalogs in your teaching field. Identify and list several of each of the following media which could be applied to a course that you might teach:
   (*a*) Motion Pictures
   (*b*) Filmstrips
   (*c*) Audio Programs
   (*d*) Other Media

2. Preview and evaluate several audiovisual presentations (films, filmstrips, videotapes, or slide sets—one of each kind, several of one kind, or a combination of media) appropriate to your teaching field. Respond to the selection criteria on pages 163–167 or use evaluation forms supplied by your instructor.

3. Explain why having *a problem that is important to the students* is an excellent way to develop readiness to use media as sources of information. Give examples of problems introduced before use of media (readiness principle) as well as afterward (action principle).

4. List several active problems that would be meaningful to your students. Examples: Construct a display showing. . . . ; write an article for. . . . ; write and produce a TV program on. . . . ; make a (mural, diorama, slide set, filmstrip, super-8 film) to depict or explain. . . . : make a scrapbook for the library about. . . . ; prepare a self-instructional program for the laboratory on. . . . ; and so on. Specify key behavioral objectives for each problem.

5. Respond to the following statement: "My students don't need busywork like making models and murals and taking pictures to use up their time. There's little enough time now for them to cover the subject matter."

6. Explain how *problem-based* use of media is different from the traditional written or oral report assigned by the teacher.

7. Examine each of the case studies in Chapter 6. Expand into the form of behavioral objectives the teaching purposes or objectives stated in one case study.

8. Prepare a plan for using a specific motion picture (or videotape, sound filmstrip, or sound-slide set) in a class you might teach. Use the case studies as a guide, being

sure to include a meaningful problem-base. Expand your teaching purposes into behavioral objectives.

9. Modify the above plan for use of the same medium *without* a problem-base. (For ideas, refer to Roles of Media in Chapter 1).

10. Respond to the following statement: "Writing behavioral objectives is a bore. I would rather just show a film and then assign students to write reports about it. I don't see how behavioral objectives can help me to evaluate my teaching."

11. Explain how you would prepare students for viewing each of the following films (or explain why you would *not* use the film).
   (*a*) An instructional film of significant content, relevant to student interests and needs, but produced in the early 1950s with fashions, cars, and acting style of that time.
   (*b*) A relevant film, produced in what you consider to be good taste, but including scenes (i.e., human birth, interracial marriage, heroin injection) that some of your students are likely to complain about to conservative parents.
   (*c*) A film that is relevant and technically accurate, but that repeatedly mentions the products or services of the film's commercial sponsor.
   (*d*) A film brought into your classroom by another teacher who says: "I know you're not studying about this now, but the film is in the building and I know you'll want to show it to your class even though you haven't previewed it. My kids *loved* it!"

12. Examine Case Studies Number 6 and 7 in Chapter 6. Did the teacher in each case provide too much information for the students or not enough information? Are these units too highly structured or not structured enough? Do they allow for sufficient student response? Rewrite portions of either of these case studies to reflect the approach or format you might use if you were the teacher/programmer.

Selected References

Audio Cardalog. Box 989, Larchmont, N.Y. 10538, revised periodically. A subscription service which provides standard catalog cards describing and evaluating audio recordings. A *Directory of Record Producers* lists sources.

BROWN, JAMES W., KENNETH NORBERG, and SARA K. SRYGLEY. *Administering Educational Media,* 2nd ed. McGraw-Hill Book Co., 1221 Avenue of the Americas, New York, N.Y. 10020, 1972. Guidelines, recommendations, and case studies of interest to persons responsible for comprehensive or specialized media programs at all levels.

Choosing a Classroom Film (16mm film, 18 min) McGraw-Hill Films, 1221 Avenue of the Americas, New York, N.Y. 10020, 1963. Suggests a process of selectivity which teachers should apply in choosing films. Emphasizes unique advantages of various types of educational films and film techniques.

Educator's Guides to Free Materials. Educators Progress Service, Randolph, Wisc. 53956, six titles, revised periodically. Separate directories list descriptions and sources of available films, filmstrips, tapes, scripts, transparencies, and guidance, science, and social studies materials.

Educator's Purchasing Master. Fisher Publishing Company, Inc., 3 West Princeton Ave., Englewood, Colorado 80110, 2 vols, revised periodically. Includes product information and trade names of instructional materials and equipment and a guide to publishers, producers, manufacturers, and dealers.

EFLA Evaluations. Educational Film Library Association, 17 West 60th St., New York, N.Y. 10023. A subscription service providing cards with complete bibliographical citations plus general and technical ratings, annotations, and suggested uses for each film. Back issues are available in bound form as the *Film Evaluation Guide.*

EPIE Reports. Educational Products Information Exchange Institute, 386 Park Ave. South, New York, N.Y. 10016, issued periodically. A subscription service offering "consumer oriented" listings and evaluations of instructional hardware, software, and systems.

ERICKSON, CARLTON W. H. *Administering Instructional Media Programs.* The Macmillan Company, 866 Third Ave., New York, N.Y. 10022, 1968, 660 pp. A handbook for coordinators and directors of media programs from elementary school through college level.

Film Tactics. (16mm film, 22 min) National Audiovisual Center, Washington, D.C. 20409, 1945. This classic U.S. Navy film humorously and unforgettably illustrates how and how not to use informational and factual films in a classroom setting.

Free and Inexpensive Learning Materials. Division of Surveys and Field Services, George Peabody College for Teachers, Nashville, Tenn. 37203, revised biennially. Lists descriptions and sources of a wide variety of materials in different subject areas.

GARRISON, CECIL. *1001 Ideas for the Classroom Teacher.* McCutchan Publishing Corp., 2526 Grove St., Berkeley, Calif. 94704, 1968, 200 pp. A concise outline of basic media production and utilization techniques. Contains outlines and review tests.

Guides. Serina Press, 70 Kennedy St., Alexandria, Va. 22305, 12 vols, revised periodically. Each guide contains synopses and sources of materials in one of the following categories: educational recordings, government-loan film, free-loan training films, films about famous people, foreign government loan-film, military loan film, films about Negroes, state loan-film, films about drugs and narcotics, films about ecology and pollution, personal guidance films, government loan-filmstrips and tapes.

HENDERSHOT, CARL H. *Programmed Learning, A Bibliography of Programs and Presentation Devices.* Hendershot

Programmed Learning Consultants, 4114 Ridgewood Dr., Bay City, Mich. 48706, 2 volumes, revised periodically. Includes off-the-shelf programs in 55 subject areas. Updated by periodic supplements.

How to Use Classroom Films. (16mm film, 15 min) McGraw-Hill Films, 1221 Avenue of the Americas, New York, N.Y. 10020, 1963. Demonstrates the creative responsibility of the teacher throughout five basic steps in using an instructional film: (1) selecting the film, (2) preparing for its use, (3) developing class readiness, (4) showing the film, and (5) managing follow-up activities.

Instructional Media. (diazo master book) Keuffel & Esser Co., Hoboken, N.J. 07030, 1969. Prepared by Stanley A. Huffman, Jr., this looseleaf collection of line drawings contains masters created mainly to assist media specialists in teaching about media.

JONES, EMILY S. *Manual on Film Evaluation.* Educational Film Library Association, 17 West 60th St., New York, N.Y. 10023, 1967, 32 p. Guidelines for selection and evaluation of films—how to go about it and how to work with a committee or an organization in a program of evaluation. Includes sample forms.

Landers Film Reviews. Bertha Landers, P.O. Box 69760, Los Angeles, Calif. 90069. A subscription service with bibliographic information plus descriptive and evaluative reviews of motion pictures produced by more than 150 different producers. Back issues available.

Learning Directory. Westinghouse Learning Corporation, 100 Park Ave., New York, N.Y. 10017, 7 volumes, revised periodically. Lists more than 200,000 instructional materials in 47 categories for all educational levels.

LEE, THOMAS G., and CHARLES ST. LOUIS. *Administering an Instructional Film Program: A Handbook for the Building Audiovisual Coordinator.* Instructional Media Services, Mona Shores School District, 3429 Henry St., Muskegon, Mich. 49441, 1971, 40 pp. An "in-basket" of facsimile forms, memos, checklists, catalogs, etc., upon which a successful instructional film program operates.

Library of Congress Catalog: Motion Pictures and Filmstrips. Library of Congress, Card Division, Washington, D.C. 20541. Listing by title and subject of all educational motion pictures and filmstrips released in the United States and Canada and catalogued on the Library of Congress printed cards.

National Center for Audio Tapes Catalog. National Center for Audio Tapes, University of Colorado, Stadium Building, Boulder, Colo. 80302, revised periodically. Lists more than 12,000 instructional tapes on deposit at the Center, which may be re-recorded for use in schools.

NICEM Indexes. National Information Center for Educational Media, University of Southern California, University Park, Los Angeles, Calif. 90007, 10 vols, revised periodically. Includes brief descriptions and sources of materials indexed by subject, title and producer/distributor code. Volumes deal with the following topics: 16mm films, 35mm filmstrips, audio tapes, video tapes, recordings, 8mm film cartridges, overhead transparencies, ecology (multimedia), Black history & studies (multimedia), and producer and distributor index.

Resources for Learning (16mm film, 20 min) McGraw-Hill Films, Inc., 1221 Avenue of the Americas, New York, N.Y. 10020, 1968. Shows media being used in three different patterns, or modes, of instruction: presentations by the teacher, independent learning activities by students, and stimulation of interaction between students and teachers.

ROWE, MACK R., et al, *The Message is You.* AECT Publications Sales, 1201 16th St., N.W., Washington, D.C. 20036, 1971, 40 p. Guidelines for effective visual presentations by people who are unfamiliar with the technical aspects of audiovisual media.

RUFSVOLD, MARGARET I., and CAROLYN GUSS, *Guides to Educational Media,* 3rd ed. American Library Association, 50 East Huron St., Chicago, Ill. 60611, 1971, 116 pp. Annotated listings of catalogs, periodicals and professional organizations concerned with technological media.

SCUORZO, HERBERT E. *The Practical Audio-Visual Handbook For Teachers.* The Parker Publishing Co., Inc., 1 Village Sq., West Nyack, N.Y. 10994, 1967, 211 pp. An "audiovisual building coordinator in a book," this folksy publication offers how-to-do-it tips for classroom teachers.

Selecting and Using Ready-made Materials (16mm color film, 17 min) McGraw-Hill Films, Inc., 1221 Avenue of the Americas, New York, N.Y. 10020, 1963. Illustrates how teachers can bring imagination to the task of adapting commercially-produced or "borrowed" instructional materials.

Standards for School Media Programs. American Library Association, 50 E. Huron St., Chicago, Ill. 60611 and National Education Association, 1201 16th St., NW, Washington, D.C. 20036, 1969, 66 pp. Suggested standards for selection and organization of materials, staff, facilities and services of the school media center.

TANZMAN, JACK, and KENNETH J. DUNN. *Using Instructional Media Effectively.* Parker Publishing Co., 1 Village Sq., West Nyack, N.Y. 10994, 1971, 217 pp. Analyzes practical solutions to school media problems, with emphasis on instructional facilities.

Teaching With Instructional Materials (set of 6 filmstrips with tapes, 17 min, each) Oates Learning Materials, 81 Wonder Hills Dr., Athens, Ohio 45701, 1969. Topics include general orientation, filmstrips, sound recording, bulletin boards, flat pictures, and duplicating methods.

U.S. Government Films. National Audiovisual Center, General Services Administration, Washington, D.C. 20409, revised periodically. Subject listing and descriptions of films produced by and for government agencies and available for sale. Inquiries about films for loan may be addressed to the same source.

The object of teaching a child is to enable him to get along without his teacher.

—ELBERT HUBBARD

"Which dinosaur is *Tri-cer-a-tops?* . . . Stop the tape recorder and look at the models now." . . . A boy wearing headphones does as he is instructed—examines four plastic model dinosaurs for a moment—then again presses the "play" button . . . "That's right, *Tri-cer-a-tops* means *three-horned* dinosaur . . . He's the one with *three horns* to fight with, and a *bony collar* to protect his neck . . . Was Triceratops a *meat-eater* or a *plant-eater?* . . . How could you find out? . . . Do animals' *teeth* show what kind of food they eat? . . . Look at Triceratops' *teeth* and see whether you think he ate mostly meat or mostly plants . . . Stop the tape recorder now . . ."

Figure 7–1. "Look at Triceratops' teeth and see whether you think he ate mostly meat or mostly plants. . . ." Study of dinosaur models is guided by a teacher-made cassette tape. Cassette and models are kept together as one unit of a "Prehistoric Life" kit. Other units contain books, fossils, and commercial filmstrips. (Photo by David H. Curl)

Audiovisual tutoring employs an ordinary tape recorder as a programming device to guide and direct the learning activities of an individual student. Self-instruction is rapidly becoming an accepted method of learning, with teachers and administrators discovering that mediated independent study can be fully as effective as much traditional instruction and save time for both students and faculty. Case Studies 6, 7, and 8 in Chapter 6 described varied uses of audio tapes, visual materials, and worksheets to provide a degree of independent learning activity. Two more examples will amplify this approach and show how it can be used with older students in different areas of study.

A modishly dressed teenager studies a vividly colored slide depicting a cross-section of the Earth's crust, briefly holds down the rewind lever on her tape deck to listen again to a missed definition, enters the new term on her work sheet, then advances the projector to the next slide. Instead of sitting passively through a geography lecture, she has her own private tutor.

The familiar aroma of the zoology lab permeates the room, but nothing else is like a traditional science class. Students are up and around the room individually, examining specimens, viewing film loops and displays, then returning to their carrels to confirm or correct their ob-

Audiovisual-Tutorial Instruction

Figure 7–2. An audio-tutorial science lesson. What are some advantages of a self-instructional laboratory? Are there any disadvantages? Is audio-tutorial or audiovisual-tutorial instruction the same thing as programmed instruction? For which subjects and age levels is self-instruction most appropriate? Would this approach be effective for every student? (Photo by James McKittrick, Kalamazoo College)

servations with the instructor's tape-recorded commentary. The instructor isn't up in front demonstrating or lecturing—he's walking about the laboratory—helping one student adjust a microscope—administering a brief quiz to another student who has completed the week's assignment.

Mediated self-instruction (self-instruction through use of media), or audiovisual-tutorial (AVT), can take the form of individually prescribed instruction. AVT can save a lot of time for students and teachers and make learning more interesting, meaningful, and efficient. Students like the audiovisual-tutorial method. Ninety per cent or more say they would choose a well-organized AVT course over the same materials taught by conventional lecture-recitation methods. Students often learn more with AVT—making higher scores on achievement tests, developing more positive attitudes toward subject matter, and mastering up to a third more information in a typical course.

Edgar Dale observed: "A good learning situation is a student at one end of a *dialog* and a teacher at the other." Effective dialog occasionally takes place in a classroom containing thirty students and a teacher, but it occurs more often in seminars or in small group discussions. Effective dialog is the heart of the tutorial ap-

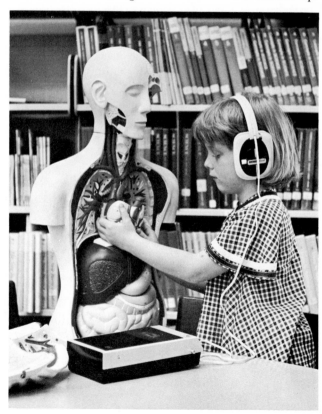

Figure 7–3. This first grader knows "Gus," the take-apart man, like a book, even though a book about him would be quite beyond her reading level. She wanted to find out more about human and animal anatomy, so her teacher made a tape for her while her interest was at its peak. She has learned the names of all "Gus's" internal organs and where each belongs. Next year, the tape cassette will be in the library for the use of other students. (Photo by David H. Curl)

Media for Individualizing Instruction **247**

proach. Obviously, we could solve many problems of individualizing education if we had one teacher for each student. But we do not. Neither can we assume that all students are alike. But we can arrange a one-to-one relationship with *every* student, at least part of the time, by putting the teacher on tape or film.

With AVT, individual learners may be guided through a wide range of experiences in a learning program integrating sight, sound, and tactile examination of the subject matter. Tape-recorded commentary by a master teacher provides the base for the necessary visual elements: printed materials, slides, filmstrips, or motion pictures.

Figure 7–4. Do the terms individually prescribed instruction *and* individualized instruction *have the same meaning as the term* independent study? *Can you tell whether the students in this picture are working on* individualized programs of study? *(Courtesy Chester Electronic Laboratories, Inc.)*

Fundamentals of Teaching with Audiovisual Technology

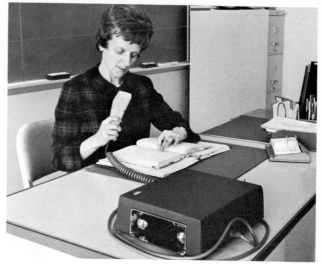

Figure 7–6. Recording graded dictation exercises is a simple expedient which enables this business education teacher to allow for differing ability levels in her shorthand course, yet work closely with individual students who need help. Students enjoy the freedom of self-instruction. In business education recorded materials are especially suitable because they simulate actual office practice situations. Can you think of other applications of audiovisual-tutorial programming in business education? In other subject matter? (Courtesy IBM Corporation)

On the tape, the teacher/narrator (in a personal, conversational tone) directs the learner to various activities in the listening booth or elsewhere in the learning laboratory, questions him, clarifies important data gathered from various sources, directs him to reach conclusions from the data, and confirms or corrects his responses. Each learner, therefore, has the benefit of personal tutoring of the highest quality, identical in content to that received by every other student, but available to him at the most convenient time in his daily schedule, and self-paced at his own most efficient rate of progress.

Some courses of study, such as typing and shorthand, lend themselves easily to the AVT approach, but most subjects require a great deal of program preparation in making the transition from traditional methods. Experienced programmers frequently budget up to 60 hours of preparation time for each hour of laboratory presentation; even more time is required for preparation of complex programs and associated demonstration-and-response materials. Pre-testing is essential at each stage.

The authors of this book devoted some 300 hours to development of the first of a series of programs to teach operation of 16mm motion picture projectors and other audiovisual equipment. The task was first analyzed then broken down into small steps. Each step was sketched onto a file card and captioned, and students were asked to go through the "mock-up" card program. Several trials and revisions eliminated most problems in the program before the final photography and artwork were produced.

Individualized instruction is not necessarily the same thing as *independent study*. Fully individualized self-instructional programs differ in procedure from most

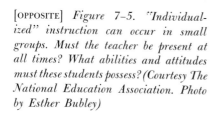

[OPPOSITE] *Figure 7–5. "Individualized" instruction can occur in small groups. Must the teacher be present at all times? What abilities and attitudes must these students possess? (Courtesy The National Education Association. Photo by Esther Bubley)*

ordinary learning experiences. Regardless of the facilities or media used, the following principles apply:

1. Course objectives and required levels of student performance must be clearly stated.
2. Procedures and alternatives for reaching the objectives are specified.
3. The learner sets his own pace.
4. The learner responds actively to the material presented.
5. Confirmation or correction of the learner's responses is immediately available.
6. The learner checks his own progress against explicit standards.
7. The learner decides when he is ready to have his performance evaluated.

Good programs enable most students to reach a higher proficiency level in less time, but *poor programming* may actually increase the number of failures! The most common mistake made by teachers is merely to record a lecture; or worse—to read a textbook onto the tape or photograph an entire page of type. Not only are such materials organized inefficiently for self-instruction, but students quickly become bored or disgusted with being lectured at or read to.

In some courses, students may spend as much as two-thirds of their school day pursuing independent learning experiences in media-equipped study carrels and laboratories. Students' remaining time may be divided between observing large-group presentations by master teachers, and participating with other students and faculty in active small-group reaction seminars and discussion sections. Other courses may rely more heavily on group interaction. Organizational guidelines suggested initially for secondary schools by J. Lloyd Trump and others allow about 40 per cent of the learners' time for guided independent learning activity; 40 per cent for receiving presentations of background information, viewing longer films, and so forth in large groups; and the remaining 20 per cent for interaction with peers and instructors in small groups. In the small groups, students discuss what happened during their independent research activities and clarify what they saw and heard in the large group sessions.

A curriculum emphasizing individualized learning demands that both teachers and learners play new roles. In the traditional presentation method, the teacher himself is the center of attention as well as the primary source of information. The teacher decides how much of the officially prescribed content is to be "covered" during each lesson, often following faithfully the organization and content dictated by the textbook author, regardless

Fundamentals of Teaching with Audiovisual Technology

Figure 7–7. Can large lecture sections be effective? Do you think members of this high school biology class of 100 students are receiving as much information as if there were only the usual 25 or 30 students present? In what ways do you think the overhead projector is adding to this teacher's effectiveness? Should all meetings of this class be as a group of 100? (Photo by George Zimbel, Peekskill, N.Y.)

of its appropriateness. For the traditional teacher, films, filmstrips, transparencies, specimens, charts and the chalkboard may be used occasionally as "aids" to illustrate or emphasize certain points during a lecture or demonstration, or to provide variety. But as "aids," media serve only an incidental role—the teacher's explanation and the students' listening and reading being the principal means of instruction in traditionally organized courses.

Self-directed study requires much more effort and personal discipline on the part of each student. Instead of being passively dependent on tidbits of knowledge tossed out by a teacher, students must search and evaluate, and work actively toward known goals. Teachers

Figure 7–8. Small-group viewing of sound motion pictures is facilitated by the use of pairs of headphones and an aggregate- or jack-box (the box shown in the picture was locally made from a 35mm film can). (Courtesy La Mesa-Spring Valley School District, La Mesa, Calif.)

Media for Individualizing Instruction

Figure 7-9. Both teachers and students have to get used to individually prescribed instruction—new roles and relationships are required. Students build self-confidence because they are trusted to locate their own learning materials and to manage their own time. The bulletin board shown in the picture at upper left instructs students to "Prepare a program of studies, a schedule, and a contract." Then to "Complete your program of studies, follow your schedule of check points, meet all requirements, pass your survey tests." What responsibilities are left for the teacher? (Courtesy The National Education Association. Photos by Joe Di Dio, Esther Bubley and Ben Spiegel; Carrel photo courtesy 3M/Wollensak)

therefore serve no longer as mere purveyors of information, but in the much more challenging and satisfying role of creator and manager of stimulating learning experiences. Each student, instead of being forced into uncritical acceptance of the goals, values, and methods of his teachers, must learn to establish and pursue his own goals at his own optimum rate as far as his abilities and aspirations will carry him. Teachers remain as counselors and, when necessary, authority figures, but relinquish their physical dominance of the learning process, requiring each student to accept more responsibility for his own intellectual and cultural growth.

Students Learn About Themselves— and the Subject

Teachers open the door.
You enter by yourself.
—CHINESE PROVERB

Many teachers are accustomed to thinking of their "subject" as a vast store of facts and problems and of themselves as transmitters of ancient wisdom. They strongly disagree with Oscar Wilde's aphorism: "Nothing that is worth knowing can be taught." However, to survive as adults in tomorrow's world, children need to learn to discipline themselves—to identify and pursue important goals; to discriminate between the essential and the superfluous; between the "must know" and the "nice to know;" to determine their own strengths and weaknesses and to find the best methods of utilizing their own abilities. Too often, only those students who are able to interpret the teacher's wishes and who are willing to conform to the teacher's idiosyncrasies and pet methods can obtain high grades. Creative students may receive low grades regardless of their ability or knowledge of the subject because they refuse to submit to what amounts to forced busywork.

Students learn more by an integrated-experience audiovisual-tutorial approach. Samuel Postlethwait of Purdue University, a pioneer user of AVT methods for teaching science, reported student achievement up as much as the equivalent of one full letter-grade over previous traditional lecture/recitation/laboratory methods of teaching. Under Postlethwait's system, students' attitudes toward the course improved noticeably, vandalism in the laboratory was reduced, and it was found that at least one-third more information could be presented in an equivalent amount of time. [1]

Postlethwait emphasizes in his book, *An Integrated Experience Approach to Learning*, that individuals per-

[1] S. N. Postlethwait, J. Novak, and H. Murray, *An Integrated Experience Approach to Learning*. (Minneapolis: Burgess Publishing Co., 1964), p. 98.

ceive ideas and concepts through different channels. He suggests, "If the goals can be carefully and critically identified, a student arriving at these goals independently along some avenue other than that provided by the teacher should be accorded the same respect as one who has attended carefully to the details of a program outlined by the instructor. A teacher can only provide guidance, facilities and motivation. The student must do the learning." [2] Postlethwait found that students did indeed learn by themselves, not only attaining significantly higher levels of achievement than students taught by traditional lecture/laboratory methods, but mastering a larger amount of material in the same amount of time. Most users of AVT systems report similar success when skillful programming takes human factors into consideration.

Independent learning may take place in an elaborate and expensive electronically-equipped laboratory, or it may occur effectively in a library carrel, at a lab bench, or in one corner of a busy classroom. The method is essential, but the hardware is optional. In such environments students participate actively throughout each lesson. They receive prompt confirmation or correction of every response and may adjust to individual rates of learning by repeating or skipping portions of programs as needed and desired.

In schools where electronic learning laboratories are not a permanent fixture, students may check out from the media center inexpensive cassette tape recorders, cassettes, and visual materials as easily as they can check out books. Listening through headphones, students may use any library carrel or lab table as an independent study station without disturbing others. Or students might even take a tape recorder outdoors. Ecology is brought to life at the University Lake School in Hartland, Wisconsin along an ingenious self-guiding nature trail; students carry cassette tape recorders as they walk. At the same school, students become aware of the fantastic distances within our solar system by pacing off a cassette-guided tour of the planets that has been laid out on the school grounds.

Inexpensive filmstrip and slide viewers complement the cassette tape player perfectly, providing a complete AVT hardware package for less than $100. Almost any school can afford the equipment, but preparing the software, or tutorial program, is the hardest part of getting started with an AVT unit. Few such programs are commercially available, and many teachers would rather prepare their own. But programming takes a lot of time, according to veteran AVT programmers. Careful pretesting of each part of the program is necessary, with frequent revisions.

[2] Ibid., p. 3.

Figure 7–10. Individualization in a conventional classroom. An inexpensive junction box and sets of headphones can allow individuals or ability/interest groups to pursue a different activity while the rest of the students continue regular work. (Courtesy Avedex, Inc.) Library-type study carrels can be arranged to isolate part of a classroom for individualized work. (Courtesy Northern Natural Gas Company)

Media for Individualizing Instruction

Figure 7–11. A three-pound cassette tape recorder provides the guide for a self-discovery nature trail. The tape need not be simply descriptive. It should call for observation and response by the student. What would it be like to listen to Beethoven's Pastoral *symphony while walking in the woods? (Photo by David H. Carl)*

The best plan is to use file cards for outlining, then for detailed planning. Shuffle the cards around until they make sense, then try out the card program with a few students. The students will find the gaps, ambiguities, and inconsistencies in a hurry. Finally, after all the bugs are out of the planning-card sequences, you can do the finished production work with assurance of having a workable program.

Once a good program has been developed and validated, however, it can be reused as long as the material remains up to date. The teacher can be free to meet with groups of students on a seminar basis, to counsel individuals having special needs or unusual difficulties, and to create additional programs.

We *talk* a lot about individualizing instruction, but what can we *really* do about it? We *can* say an instructional system is individualized when:

What Is Individualized Instruction?

- The characteristics of each student play a major role in the selection of objectives, sequence of study, choice of materials and procedures.
- The time spent by each student in a given subject area is determined by his performance rather than by the clock.
- The progress of each student is measured by comparing his performance with his specific objectives, rather than with the performance of other students.

Further, an instructional system is individualized *to the extent that students*:

- Have available, in writing, the objectives toward which they are working.
- Work toward a variety of objectives, at their own pace.
- Use a variety of materials and procedures.
- Move freely around the classroom.
- Talk freely to each other about their work.
- Pursue their objectives individually, with small groups of classmates, or with their teachers.

Also, an instructional system is individualized *to the extent that teachers*:

- Encourage students to have a variety of objectives.
- Allow students to move from place to place, based on what it takes to achieve their objectives.
- Spend more time answering questions of individuals and small groups than lecturing to the entire class.
- Encourage students to help determine the materials they work with and the procedures they follow.[3]

As we have discussed earlier, there are alternative ways to teach and to learn; some people learn better by certain methods than others. The *presentation* method is an efficient way of reaching dozens, hundreds, or even thousands of students at the same time with the same material; and sometimes large group presentations can be very effective. Another method, *individualized learning* activity, can occupy a large part of a student's school day; because, hopefully, the student is doing something interesting, he knows exactly what he is doing and why he is spending the time. A third mode, *interaction* sessions, gives each student a chance to compare notes with other students, to question or challenge teachers, and to become known as a person.

To put it simply, the audiovisual-tutorial method guides students through a wide range of experiences such as reading from reference materials; performing experiments; collecting and analyzing data; manipulating tools, equipment, and materials; watching filmed demonstrations; observing specimens and models, photographs, charts, diagrams; and listening to selected lectures, dialogs, dictation, and musical performances.

AVT is an instructional method in which the learner must provide his attention, his active response, and his own estimate of progress and success (subject of course to confirmation by his teacher). Media are used in AVT for the repetitive chores of presenting information and illustrations, and confirming or correcting responses during each study session. A tape recorder, projector, or

[3] Richard Bumstead, "Individualized Instruction," *Educate*, **2**: **1** (January 1969), 19. Adapted from a checklist prepared by the National Laboratory for the Advancement of Education.

computer, unlike a teacher, will not become tired, bored, cranky, or impatient. When equipment breaks down mechanically, it can be replaced. But teachers cannot be replaced; they should be performing human roles in humane and involved ways instead of trying to compete with the hardware. Perhaps the teacher who *can* be replaced by a tape recorder or a teaching machine *ought* to be!

Individualized instructional methods are here to stay. More reliable hardware is becoming available and teachers are learning how to prepare simple, valid, learning programs to make effective use of the new hardware. The inevitable march of technology toward low-cost computer systems will make audiovisual-tutorial systems practical everywhere and for aspects of nearly every subject. Machines do the mechanical, repetitive presentation of material far more efficiently than teachers can. Students will participate actively in more significant learning experiences in less time. During his own daily efficiency peak, each student will be able to study at his own pace and to review or repeat sequences at will, testing himself until he feels confident that he can meet the desired standard of performance. Teachers, freed from multiple preparations, will have time for painstaking development of excellent instructional programs and for the research needed to organize and update such materials. Extra time will be available, too, for teachers to develop a degree of interpersonal rapport with students which is impossible under most traditional administrative patterns.

One thing is certain. Students can teach themselves fundamental skills and concepts, and they often can do so more efficiently by themselves than they can be taught as a member of a class meeting together with a teacher in a classroom. Perhaps students can teach themselves far more than anyone now realizes, at the same time harvesting rich dividends of discovery and self-confidence.

> Discovery consists of seeing what everybody has seen and thinking what nobody has thought.
> —Albert Szent-Gyorgyi

Awareness, Spontaneity, and Intimacy

In the following case study, which should be compared with and contrasted to Case Studies 6, 7, and 8 in Chapter 6, William Stonebarger[4] describes the adventures of a student who encounters, for the first time, an

[4] C. William Stonebarger, *Finding a Way to be a Human* (unpublished manuscript), 1970. Excerpted and slightly adapted. At the time this material was written, Mr. Stonebarger was Director of Studies at the University Lake School, Hartland, Wis. By permission.

individually oriented science curriculum designed to foster the "new trinity" of awareness, spontaneity, and intimacy:

It's nine A.M. on a Monday morning. A shy little seventh-grade girl appears for the first time in your Center. What happens?

We ask her what she would like to do.

And she says, "I don't know."

Right. Then we say, "Well, Daisy, you have your choice of seven different things. You see over here . . . this is a Science Learning Center and we have divided up the world for you into six different scales. You can choose to learn more about the Universe (stars, planets, space travel), the Biosphere (ecology, pollution, the way things relate to one another on planet earth), Organisms (your own body, structure and function of other animal and plant bodies—and souls too!), The Cell (including how you inherit things from your parents, how life began in the ancient oceans), Atoms and Molecules (what you might know as chemistry), or, lastly, Particles and Waves (stuff like electricity, light, nuclear energy). Now you probably don't know too much about some or any of these right now, and if you would like to try out a short introduction (it takes about 15 minutes for each one) to each of these topics, go ahead. The introduction is generally some kind of film or tape that you can use here in our "learning dome," and it will give you a better idea of what we have to offer you here on that topic. After you find one you would like, tell me and I'll show you how to go on from there."

"You said *seven* things," she says. A sharp kid.

"Right. And the seventh is whatever you want to make it. You needn't study any of the levels of the natural world we have set out for you. If you have some particular idea or beginning of an idea that you want to take off on by yourself (or with one of your friends), that's not only O.K., we encourage it.

"And remember, if you don't have an idea of your own you want to pursue right now, at ANY time in your work on a program flow sheet you can take off in a direction of your own. Just keep in touch with me. We're interested in any ideas you come up with."

Let's assume she looks at the introductions and decides she wants to "study" the universe. What happens then? She chooses the universe; she opts to get involved with the universe (to use the most current jargon). She wants to carry on some meaningful transactions with the stars, although she might not be able to put it that way.

To start her off we would give her a "flow sheet" that would look like this (Figure 7–12):

Starting off on her flow-sheet journey, Daisy would go into the inner space capsule (the "learning dome"—see Figure 7–13) taking with her a cassette tape and a slide tray "Introduction to the Universe." Using some slides purchased from Mount Palomar Observatory along with some others collected from

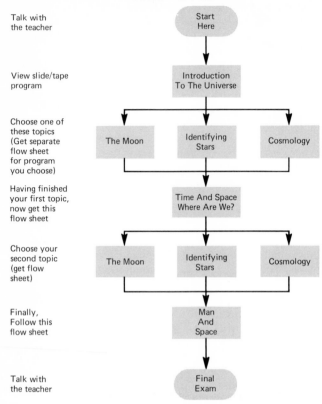

Flow-Sheet
THE UNIVERSE
TRIP ONE

Figure 7–12. (Adapted from Finding a Way to be a Human *by permission of C. William Stonebarger)*

Talk with the teacher — **Start Here**

View slide/tape program — **Introduction To The Universe**

Choose one of these topics (Get separate flow sheet for program you choose) — **The Moon** | **Identifying Stars** | **Cosmology**

Having finished your first topic, now get this flow sheet — **Time And Space Where Are We?**

Choose your second topic (get flow sheet) — **The Moon** | **Identifying Stars** | **Cosmology**

Finally, Follow this flow sheet — **Man And Space**

Talk with the teacher — **Final Exam**

various astronomy books in the library by the use of a single-lens reflex camera, I prepared this "lesson" myself. Here's what the text amounted to. Sorry we can't afford to print all 80 slides in full color (one of the points incidentally in favor of our system from an economic point of view—each student can get involved with whole new visual and audio worlds that would be enormously expensive if they had to be printed in the old textbook technology, one for each student). You will have to imagine how it would come across to you to hear the following script at the same time you are encountering large, realistic images on a big wrap-around screen, fine stereo sound, no distractions in any spatial dimension around you, somehow surrounded instead by warm friendly security. Each * means another slide change.

> * Welcome to Astronomy! Let's begin with a flower. A poet, after reading of Newton's discovery of the Universal Law of Gravitation, wrote: "To pick a flower disturbs the furthest star." Why? (pause) . . . Because everything—all things in this wide universe are connected, one to another, by gravity. Perhaps also by light, by radiation, by ?? (pause) . . . Perhaps by things we don't even know about yet, things that *you* may discover!

We say everything is connected—all things * including you. Especially you. For you alone out of all this beautiful universe are AWARE of it, aware of being a part. You alone, as a part of the universe are yet able to stand aside, to stand back, to stand under—to understand—what is going on! I hope this experience you are now beginning with astronomy will help you to better understand your place and the place of our earth in the grand scheme of things universal.

* Let's start out with a little trip to make sure of our address in space. As we move up and away from our local school, we see that it is a part of a larger natural community, an oak-hickory glacial hilltop woods in * south-western Wisconsin, * United States of America, * Western Hemisphere, * Planet Earth, * which revolves around a star we call our sun, * as one of nine planets in * a solar system with no special name because we haven't as yet found any other such systems; yet we are pretty certain there are some out there.

* Taking the planets one at a time, moving out from the sun, we get * Mercury, * Venus, * Earth plus its moon,

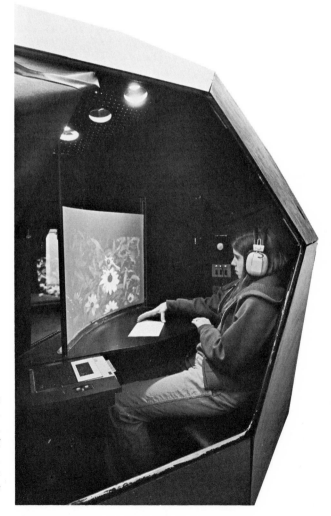

Figure 7–13. For each student in the inner space capsule "nothing exists except for the transactions occurring between the reality of the wrap-around screen and stereo sound and themselves. No one else can see them, even know they are there." (Courtesy University Lake School. Photo by David H. Curl)

* Mars in four views with two moons, * Jupiter with four moons (visible ones—14 in all!), * Saturn with rings, * Uranus and Neptune, * far away Pluto, * a comet—Halley's Comet to be exact. All of these are our near neighbors in space—though not all that near . . . at the speed of present-day space ships, for instance, it will take over nine years to make a round trip to Saturn and over 40 years for a jaunt to Pluto! If we could and we did move out past Pluto's orbit what would we find? . . . (pause) . . . * nothing much, * and more nothing, * and more and more and more nothing. Well, not completely empty space . . . maybe a few atoms of hydrogen now and then, but still pretty dull, empty going. Around you, as a matter of fact, would be so few atoms of anything that it would be a much better vacuum than any ever created on Earth. However, if we did keep going *long* enough (like about 150,000 years at present space ship speeds . . . four-and-a-half years if we could get going at the speed of light), eventually we would come to another star (if we happened to be pointed that way!)

* What's this? Would it have a solar system too? We don't know really. There would be a good chance though. Intelligent life on one of its planets? (pause) . . . Maybe. Why not? (pause) . . . The best estimate I have been able to come across today is that maybe one in ten stars have planets with life. So if we don't find anyone at home around the nearest star we could hop in and go another 150,000 years of travel.

* By naming certain sections of the sky like we name states of the U.S., we navigate in space. This section would be the constellation of the Big Dipper (at the bottom of the slide) and Little Dipper (at the top). Ancient people thought they saw * bears and such like in the sky and gave these constellations their names. We use the same names, although except for fun, we don't put much emphasis on the figures they are supposed to trace out. * How many stars are there to visit? (pause) . . . Here, through a telescope, is a small section of the bright Milky Way band. * Here's another in Orion, * in Sagittarius. Quite a few stars, eh? That white glow is literally millions of individual stars which seem so close together to us at this great distance away that the light begins to blur into glow in many places.

* Here's something called the Crab Nebula, a star that exploded not so very long ago. * The Horsehead Nebula, a huge cloud of dark gas with glowing gas behind it. * A spectacular mass of glowing gas in Orion. * The Lagoon Nebula in Sagittarius. * The Trifid Nebula and * the Veil Nebula in Cygnus, the Swan constellation. All glowing hydrogen gas of fantastic size. Unfortunately you do need a very large telescope to see them this way. All of these slides were taken with the 200-inch Mount Palomar telescope, the largest in the world.

But where ARE all these pretty gas clouds, exploding stars, Big Dippers, and attendant planets, comets, etc.? (pause) . . . * They are all organized into a system called a GALAXY, the Milky Way Galaxy, which would look

Figure 7–14. The planet Jupiter. (Photograph from the Hale Observatories)

Figure 7–15. Milky Way, Sagittarius. (Photograph from the Hale Observatories)

Figure 7–16. "Horsehead" Nebula in Orion. (Photograph from the Hale Observatories)

Figure 7–17. "Crab" Nebula in Taurus. (Photograph from the Hale Observatories)

Figure 7–18. "Lagoon" Nebula in Sagittarius. (Photograph from the Hale Observatories)

Figure 7–19. Galaxy in Andromeda. (Photograph from the Hale Observatories)

Figure 7–20. Great Galaxy in Andromeda. (Photograph from the Hale Observatories)

Figure 7–21. Galaxy in Virgo. (Photograph from the Hale Observatories)

Fundamentals of Teaching with Audiovisual Technology

something like this if we could get outside of it for a look. A disc shape, sort of like a flying saucer. * Here's an end-on view with a diagram of where our own little medium-size star, which we call the sun, would be—out on the edge, moving in a rotation around the central mass of stars. * Another view from the top and from one side. The plus sign marks the position on our sun. (pause) . . . Remember now! All we have seen so far—from black-eyed susan to Horsehead Nebula—is within, a part of, makes up this gigantic Milky Way Galaxy. . . . And what is outside that? (pause) . . .

* Nothing. And more nothing, and still more nothing . . . until a few hundred thousand years from now at the speed of light we come to * another galaxy! This is the great galaxy in Andromeda, our nearest galactic neighbor. This is the one object in the sky that is not a member of the Milky Way Galaxy and that you can see (just barely, if you have very good eyes) with your naked eye. This view, of course, is through a large telescope. Any more of these galaxies around? (pause) . . .

* Sure. Here's a more unusual looking one, like a top. * Another one. * A beauty! * Another * Still another. * Here you are looking at a picture taken through the Mt. Palomar telescope of a tiny section of the sky and every dot you see here is not a simple star but a complete galaxy of stars!! * Here's another view of another section again—all galaxies! As you can see by now, the Milky Way is only one of many . . . BILLIONS of galaxies!!! How many of those stars in those galaxies have planets with schools with intelligent, good-looking vivacious students thinking at this instant of the possibility that *you* exist? (pause) . . . We may never know. And again, we just might!

* Actually, the galaxies themselves are arranged in loose kinds of groups, too, that we don't know much about as yet. Here's how our own local group of galaxies seem to be spread in space. And that's about as much as we know today about our address. Well, except for this guy * a strange one. We call it a quasar but can't yet figure out much about it. It seems to be a single star, but so far away and giving out more radiation than a whole galaxy! What is it? (pause) . . . We don't know. See your daily paper for more news of quasars.

* At this point, let's pause and have you actually write down in your notebook your personal address as I have done here. Put in more units if you can think of them. Stop the tape now long enough to actually do this. (pause) . . .

* With me again? O.K. From here on in you can relax on this particular tape-slide program, and just look, listen, and get the feel of what you are about to get involved with. When I give the signal, set the timing mechanism of the projector for 8-second intervals. The slides will automatically advance as you listen to some music and some thoughts other men at other times and places have had about the universe.

One of my favorite poets, Robert Frost, once called poetry "something that begins in delight and ends in wisdom." I think that holds for science as well. Or we might alter it to say that science begins in WONDER and ends in wisdom. Set the timer now and relax and listen.

(Music is now interspersed between and under and around the quotes that follow)

To see the world in a grain of sand
And a heaven in a wild flower
Hold infinity in the palm of your hand
And eternity in an hour. . . .

—WILLIAM BLAKE[5]

(Music)

Venice, 1610. The SIDEREAL MESSENGER unfolding great and marvellous sights and proposing them to the attention of everyone but especially to philosophers and astronomers, being such as have been observed by Galileo Galilei, a gentleman of Florence, Professor of Mathematics in the University of Padua, with the aid of a TELESCOPE lately invented by him, respecting the moon's surface, an innumerable number of fixed stars, the Milky Way, and Nebulous Stars, but especially respecting four planets which revolve around the planet Jupiter at different distances and in different periodic times, with amazing velocity, and which, after remaining unknown to everyone up to this day, the Author recently discovered, and determined to name the Medician Stars.

—GALILEO GALILEI[6]

(Music)

The most beautiful thing we can experience is the mysterious. It is the source of all true art and science. He to whom this emotion is a stranger, who can no longer pause to wonder and stand rapt in awe, is as good as dead.

—ALBERT EINSTEIN[7]

(Music)

It's lovely to live on a raft. Sometimes at night we'd have the whole river to ourselves for the longest time. We had the sky up there, all speckled with stars, and we used to lay on our backs and look up at them, and discuss whether they was made or only just happened. Jim, he allowed they was made, but I allowed they just happened. I judged it would of took too long to make so many. Jim said the moon could a laid 'em; well, that looked kind of reasonable, so I didn't say nothing against it, because I've seen a frog lay most as many, so of course it could be done. We used to watch the

---

[5] William Blake, "Augeries of Innocence" in *The Portable Blake.* (New York: Viking Press, 1946), p. 150.

[6] Galileo Galilei, *Discoveries and Opinions of Galileo,* trans. by Stillman Drake, (Garden City, N.Y.: Anchor Books, 1957), p. 21.

[7] Albert Einstein, *The World As I See It,* trans. by Alan Harris (New York: Philosophical Library, 1949), p. 8.

Figure 7–22. Filamentary nebula in Cygnus. (Photograph from the Hale Observatories)

stars that fell too, and see them streak down. Jim allowed they'd got spoiled and was hove out of the nest.

—Mark Twain [8]

(Music)

It is not the immensity of space that should command our wonder; but rather the man who measured it.

—Author Unknown

(Music)

Who can number the sand of the sea,
and the drops of rain,
and the days of eternity?
Who can find out the height of heaven
and the breadth of the earth
and the deep, and wisdom?

Ecclesiasticus (Apocrypha) I: 2–3

(Music)

I must confess to a feeling of profound humility in the presence of a universe which transcends us at almost every point. I do not know what I may appear to the world, but to myself I seem to have been only like a boy playing on the seashore, diverting myself in now and then finding a smoother or a prettier shell than ordinary, whilst the great ocean of truth lay all undiscovered before me.

—Isaac Newton[9]

(Music)

He burned down his house for the fire insurance and bought
A telescope with what it came to . . .
The best thing that we're put here for's to see;
The strongest thing that's given us to see with's

[8] Mark Twain, *Huckleberry Finn* (New York: The Pocket Library, 1955), p. 153.
[9] Isaac Newton, *Brewster's Memoirs of Newton,* Vol. II (N.Y.: Johnson Reprint Co., 1965), p. 407.

Figure 7–23. Radio galaxy in Centaurus. (Photograph from the Hale Observatories)

A telescope. Someone in every town
Seems to me owes it to the town to keep one.
In Littleton it may as well be me.

—ROBERT FROST[10]

(Music)

It is colder now,
        there are many stars,
                we are drifting
North by the Great Bear,
           the leaves are falling . . .
I will tell you everything;
The earth is round
         there are springs under orchards,
The loam cuts with a blunt knife,
           beware of
Elms in thunder,
        the lights in the sky are stars—
We think they do not see,
         we think also
The trees do not know nor the leaves of the grasses
hear us . . .
     As for the nights I warn you the nights are dan-
     gerous . . .
It is very cold,
      there are strange stars near Arcturus,
Voices are crying an unknown name in the sky.

—ARCHIBALD MACLEISH[11]

(Music)

In the beginning God created the heaven and the earth. And
the earth was without form, and void; and darkness was upon

[10] Robert Frost, exerpt from "The Star-Splitter," *The Complete Poems of Robert Frost,* (New York: Henry Holt & Co., 1949, pp. 218–219).

[11] Archibald MacLeish, exerpts from "Epistle To Be Left in The Earth," *Collected Poems,* (Boston: Houghton Mifflin Co., 1952), p. 61–62.

the face of the deep. And the spirit of God moved upon the face of the waters. And God said, "Let there be light": and there was light.

—Genesis I: 1–3

Suppose now Daisy comes out of the learning dome and says she has decided she wants to study the Moon. We then give her a flow sheet like this (see Fig. 7–24):

We do have a record-keeping system, again mainly for Daisy's benefit, so that she can both keep track of where she is if she is following a program like THE MOON and to help out her own sense of accomplishment when she can look back to see what she has done. As I write this I realize that a broader way of putting it would be that we want the individual to get a sense of continuity in his own work; to be involved with the present but to make that present richer by continual incorporation of what happened yesterday and anticipation of what will happen tomorrow.

Figure 7–24. (Adapted from Finding a Way to be a Human *by permission of C. William Stonebarger)*

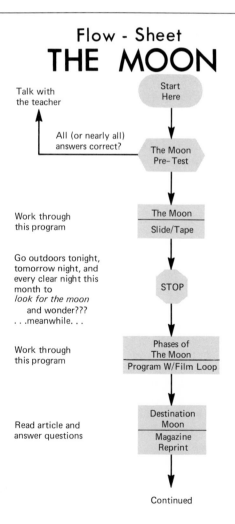

Continued

Read article and answer questions | Trip To The Moon — Magazine Reprint

Listen to this "Idea Generator" tape | What Good Is The Moon? — Tape

What haven't you found out about the moon that you would like to know? What puzzles you about the moon and you and me?

What should we do about the moon?

Take a few quiet minutes now and write down in your science notebook any of your questions, plans, or hypotheses that relate to the moon.

STOP

Your Science Notebook

Special Projects ?

Talk with the teacher before going further.

STOP

The Moon Post–Test

Turn in both test and dialog, to teacher for evaluation

Written Dialog

Talk with teacher

FINISH

Write a short (400–800 words) dialog between HAL, the friendly computer who knows all and Jerry, the suspicious janitor.

Jerry begins: "HAL, you know so much, so will you tell me please why on earth they're spending so much money— — my tax money —— to fly men to the moon?

Finish the dialog

Media in an Open Classroom

Tell children they *may*:
  Reach for the stars
  Try hard things
  Make mistakes
  Admit them
  Correct them
  Try again differently.

—PATRICIA M. PRATT

Commenting finally upon frequently asked questions about discipline and evaluation in a truly individualized program of learning, Stonebarger describes the way learning occurs in the Science Center at the University Lake School:

When a visitor comes into our Science Center, probably no one will even notice him for a while. He will have to make himself known to some individual or small group and then they will respond naturally and realistically to what he has in mind. Each in the center is "doing his own thing," and it is assumed that visitors are doing the same. If their "thing" happens to mesh with or conflict with my "thing," well then we will have to meet and see what happens. But that does not mean that everyone else in the room need be or will be involved at all.

[If it weren't so unusual in academic situations in schools we wouldn't think anything of this, of course. It happens all the time in restaurants, offices, libraries, (not school libraries), studios, shops, department stores!]

At any given time, for instance, four or five students will be individually sequestered in the inner space capsule encountering new worlds of reality from stars to electrons. For each of them, nothing exists except for the transactions occuring between the reality of the wrap-around screen, the stereo sound, and themselves. No one else can see them, even know they are there.

A seventh-grade boy is lying on the carpet with an encyclopedia; he is looking up how to build an electric motor. Another seventh-grade boy is behind the checkout counter putting slides and tapes into order. Two eighth-grade girls are sitting in the easy chair corner talking about their parent troubles. Four or five ninth graders and a teacher are grouped around a table discussing rather heatedly some burning question, such as how polluted the Bark River is or whether science and religion are in conflict or how important IQ is (and what does it mean?).

A tenth-grade girl is helping a seventh-grade girl set up a distillation apparatus at one lab table. At another table three eighth-grade girls, with a Spanish teacher, who just happened to stop in, looking over their shoulders unnoticed, are opening a chicken egg to see a four-day embryo. At the third lab table a very conscientious ninth-grade boy is going through a physics experiment from his program flow sheet with note book and

Figure 7–25. The Science Center described by C. William Stonebarger in the text is an example of an "open" classroom. In this environment formal "classes" are rare—the teacher (foreground) spends most of his time as a counselor and resource person while students pursue learning projects independently in the "inner space capsule" (right), in the laboratory, or elsewhere in the school building or outdoors. (Courtesy University Lake School. Photo by David H. Curl)

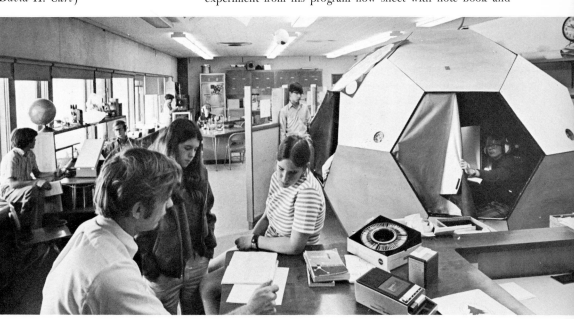

stop watch and meticulous care. Another, sloppy, ninth-grade boy is watching him with admiration and??—, it's hard to tell what he's thinking as a matter of fact, but he is interested.

At the fourth table a couple of new seventh graders and an immature tenth grader are blowing glass and sometimes arguing with one another. Sometimes they argue about glass sticking and sometimes about other students, teachers, or parents. Standing at the door, the Headmaster and I discuss a coming Board meeting, no one else paying the least attention to either of us. In fact no one in the room is paying the least attention to anyone else not directly involved with them at the moment.

Here comes a ninth-grade boy at loose ends wandering from table to table, from group to individual. He makes little progress until he finds the glass-blowing table and settles down there for a while, not really interested in that either. Eventually I may go over to him, interested, not to chew him out nor to give him a moral lecture on the benefit of work, but to make contact—to listen to him. I may or may not make contact this time, but eventually there is a good chance he will come out of his shell and begin moving somewhere he wants to go.

If it is an especially busy period, there might still be lots more going on in this fairly small room. In the darkroom might be a seventh grader showing a couple of ninth graders how to develop pictures. In the back discussion room two eighth graders might be listening to two different "Earth tape-trips" which will take them outside in a few minutes to the parking lot, up the woods path and around to the septic tank—all designed to bring them into contact with new ideas relating to the real earth around them as connected to the magic potions on the chemistry stock shelf.

Out in the woods is another eighth-grade boy—slow witted but terribly keen on nature—watching birds. Another girl is taking temperatures in a variety of habitats as part of a study she designed herself on relating temperature to type of vegetation cover.

A ninth-grade girl is taking the Time Tunnel trail, another tape-trip using a cassette player, that dramatically gets across an evolutionary time line by taking the student over a quarter-mile trail from today backwards to the Big Bang, at one million years per stride.

Two eighth grade girls have snuck out and are smoking in their secret den and happily exchanging notes on their boy friends and parents, impressing each other with dirty words. Learning to grow up.

Three ninth-grade boys, having just started their own company EXIT UNLIMITED (motto: "There's always a way out") are building a secret hide-out in a far corner of the woods and learning, all three of them, for the first time the joys of having close buddies. (Having each been loners for a good many years.)

In a storage room at the bottom of the gym a tenth-grade boy and a ninth-grade boy are tearing down an inboard boat engine together.

Perhaps you can begin to see why I like to think of control here in an ecological metaphor. There IS a great deal of a kind of control, but not a military type centered in the general. Rather it is a fluid kind of participant environmental structure where at least the thrust is toward more and more response control and personal responsibility.

We had very few real "discipline" problems during the first year of our program. And it was not that we simply let chaos reign. We had much less vandalism than ever before (even though we made less attempt to directly control equipment and materials—most everything was available on open shelves— from expensive cameras to final exams). The noise level was lower; very few graffiti on walls, desks, books, equipment; maybe most important of all, not only very little harrassment of each other but on the positive side more good feeling, good respectful feeling between each other (including the teachers). As one boy said in his evaluation, "I learned that teachers aren't pigs."

Of course you can't have it both ways, as I'm afraid I once thought you could. If you want to raise a bumper crop of corn, you'd better not expect it to grow from a climax pond or prairie. The classroom instruments of evaluation are mostly based on the bumper crop of corn goal, and students trusted to do their own thing will not necessarily produce corn. A few will, but many won't.

Unfortunately we are all pretty much hypnotized by num-bers—by objective tests to which you can assign a number at the end. A boy trusted and encouraged to get really involved on his own level of interest and drive and depth in Biology, let's say, will not necessarily score high on standardized tests after a year of intense involvement. He might, but then again he might not. The standardized tests have the handicap that they are just that—standardized—not individualized. He may have been fascinated by trees, for instance, and spent an entire year studying, being with, getting to know some of the trees around him. Now it's true that in his study, especially if he talks about it to others who know something about Biology, he will almost certainly learn a good deal about things like cells, maybe photosynthesis, birds, how to use keys, insect life cycles, galls, evolution, and ecological principles. Still he may end up grossly ignorant of the function of the pancreas in digestion, and his ignorance about such "important" matters will count heavily against him on Biology Achievement Examinations.

Here, for instance, is the way a ninth-grade girl put it. She had given herself an F for the term, but the teacher thought she had been pretty involved at times in her own personal experiences with nature. So he asked her to reconsider her grade and this is her reconsideration:

My "experiences with nature" have been many, but none have been exactly new or different. I love to walk *anywhere*—through fields, on golf courses, roads, woods, and near lakes, etc. etc. because it's neat to see all the leaves, flowers, and animals which make up my environment. I consider all these "working parts of nature," because they work together to keep each other alive and also serve as a "check" on one another. That's what's dangerous about man. Instead of being a working part, he almost always tends to use his environment to make life easier and more pleasant for *himself*—upsetting the other parts—like a machine . . . when one part doesn't work the way it's supposed to, the machine as a whole can't function properly. Man pollutes, cuts up trees, clears areas for building, etc. which all kill other working parts. I hope I'm making sense. . . .

I love watching fish and other things in the water. Down at our section of the lake shore the water is very deep and there are a lot of frogs and bass and minnows around when the water is still. I like to watch them just wriggle around. You probably don't think this is a neat experience, but it really is.

I also like to glance along the shore all around the lake and look at patterns . . . of colors, shapes, sound . . . of trees, houses, waves, clouds.

I don't see how this can raise my grade to a D, can you? Experiences are hard to describe—what I've written here bores me . . . but when I think of what I saw, felt, smelled—it seemed really exciting and neat. . . .

Next year I think I should have 3 science classes a week to get my Biology credit, and three times (labs) a week to work on my project (or special interest). I think after two weeks I should write a progress report (short) for each or maybe just the class work one, stating what I've done and what I get out of it.

What do *you* say? Is Becky finding a way to be a human? Does she deserve F? D? A? No grade at all? Is her biggest gap in awareness, in not knowing the function of the pancreas in digestion, [or] in not respecting her own experience enough? Or in being too dominated by past conceptions of what "education" is about?[12]

[12] C. William Stonebarger, op. cit.

Figure 7–27. Teachers find that students who are trusted to work independently toward their own goals generally prove to be worthy of trust. What may happen to the work habits and attitudes of students who are required to conform at all times to group norms and adult authority? (Courtesy of EDL/McGraw-Hill, Huntington, New York)

Not every teacher will agree with Stonebarger that students can be trusted to find their own way. Many still believe that it should be left largely to experienced adults to decide what young people should "study" and how "learning" should be measured. The time may come, however, and perhaps in the not-too-distant future, when teachers no longer wield their present authority based on a system of standardized achievement tests and paper qualifications. Instead of invoking rigid discipline, teachers may lead by a moral authority granted to them by students and based upon mutual confidence and respect.

Media will play a major role in educational change. Wise and creative use of media can increase real learning and improve retention of material that is meaningful. Media can make more efficient use of the valuable and limited time of teachers and students alike. Furthermore, economies of time and resources realized through employment of self-instructional systems and the necessary

Figure 7–28. Some teachers complain that administrators measure teacher competency by the quietness of the classroom. Other teachers and administrators declare that noise is "the sound of learning." As a teacher, how can you ensure that most of the noise in your classroom or laboratory is creative confusion instead of disruption? (Courtesy Westinghouse Learning Corporation)

Media for Individualizing Instruction

Figure 7-29. An instructional system is individualized to the extent that teachers spend more time working with individual students and small groups than lecturing to the entire class. How can media technology make possible this distribution of teacher time? (Courtesy Westinghouse Learning Corporation)

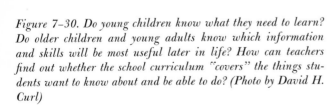

Figure 7-30. Do young children know what they need to learn? Do older children and young adults know which information and skills will be most useful later in life? How can teachers find out whether the school curriculum "covers" the things students want to know about and be able to do? (Photo by David H. Curl)

administrative streamlining, if wisely used, will result not, as some fear, in generations of conditioned button-pushers, but in a nation of more liberally educated and self-directing citizens. Goethe summed up the case for individualized education nearly two centuries ago when he wrote: "If you treat an individual as he is, he will stay as he is, but if you treat him as if he were what he ought to be and could be, he will become what he ought to be and could be."

Problems and Activities

1. React to the following statement by Edgar Dale: "A key task of the teacher is to prove to students day by day that they are much smarter than they think they are."[13]

2. Compare or contrast THE UNIVERSE and THE MOON program excerpts from Chapter 7 with Case Studies 6 and 7 in Chapter 6. Explain the fundamental differences in structure and apparent differences in the teachers' underlying philosophies.

3. Examine Stonebarger's THE UNIVERSE and THE MOON program excerpts in Chapter 7. Where are the *behavioral objectives*? What is the *problem base*? As you ponder these questions, remember that the utilization principles given in Chapter 6 are based primarily upon teacher-directed use of media. Re-examine the Roles of Media in Chapter 1, then explain whether you think Stonebarger's programs fit in. Would you use programs like Stonebarger's or would you structure them more like Case Study 6 or 7?

4. Prepare a sample audiovisual-tutorial unit in your subject area. Describe the conditions under which this program will be used by students. Show how the material and method relate to instructional objectives.

5. Explain the difference between *independent study* and *individualized instruction*.

6. Do young children know what they need to learn? Do older children and young adults know which information and skills will be most useful later in life? How can teachers find out whether the school curriculum "covers" the things students want to know about and be able to do? Describe how you, as a teacher, can discover what your students' goals or purposes are and how you can work with them to establish behavioral objectives that will be meaningful both to them and to you.

7. Respond to Charles Silberman's criticism of the Individually Prescribed Instruction (IPI) approach: ". . . IPI's

---

[13] Edgar Dale, "In Conclusion," *The News Letter* **XXXVI:8** (May 1971), 2.

version of individualization does not permit the individual student to define his own goals and attempt to reach them; it permits him only to reach someone else's goals at his own rate of speed." [14]

8. React to the following statement by Lee Cronbach: The lesson, as Cronbach suggests in distinguishing between *education* and *training*, is merely "a vehicle by and through which one develops values, self-confidence, abilities to reason, analyze, and learn. . . . one can forget the lesson itself, and indeed must, when it is rendered obsolete." [15]

9. Some teachers complain that school administrators judge teacher competency by the quietness of the classroom. Other teachers and administrators declare that noise is "the sound of learning." Explain how, as a teacher, you can ensure that most of the noise in your classroom or laboratory is *creative confusion* instead of *disruptive disorder*.

Selected References

Audio-Tutorial System, The, 2nd ed. (16mm film, 25 min) Purdue University Film Library, West Lafayette, Ind. 47906, 1968. Demonstrates how an audio-tutorial approach works at the college level. Emphasizes the freedom and responsibilities of the students and the unique relationship between students and instructor.

ESBENSEN, THORWALD. *Working With Individualized Instruction.* Fearon Publishers/Lear Siegler, Inc., 6 Davis Dr., Belmont, Calif. 94002, 1968, 122 pp. The story of a school system that decided to give its students a better education without outside support. Gives examples of how teachers in Duluth, Minnesota public schools developed a workable system for individualizing instruction.

HOWES, VIRGIL M. *Individualization of Instruction.* The Macmillan Company, 866 Third Ave., New York, N.Y. 10022, 1970, 243 pp. A collection of readings intended to answer questions about how to implement individualized instruction.

Individualized Instruction (kit including six 35mm filmstrips with tapes, case studies, and administrator's manual) Association for Educational Communications and Technology, 1201 16th St., NW, Washington, D.C. 20036, 1970. Shows examples of individualized instruction projects from all areas of the U.S.; from different kinds of school districts; from elementary and secondary schools. Offers specific advice to planners and implementers of individualized instructional systems.

LEWIS, JAMES Jr., *Administering the Individualized Instruction Program.* Parker Publishing Co., Inc., 1 Village Sq., West Nyack, N.Y. 10994, 1971, 238 pp. A guide for organizing and developing independent study units. Facilities

[14] Silberman, Charles E., *Crisis in the Classroom,* (New York: Vintage Books, 1971), p. 199.

[15] Ibid, p. 202.

and resources are discussed and examples are given of independent study units in various formats.

POSTLETHWAIT, S. N., J. NOVAK, and H. T. MURRAY, *The Audio-Tutorial Approach to Learning*, 2nd ed. Burgess Publishing Company, 246 South Sixth St., Minneapolis, Minn. 55415, 1969, 149 pp. Describes the audio-tutorial concept employed at Purdue University for the teaching of botany and other basic sciences. Suggests methods for solving some technical and administrative problems in developing and operating a self-instructional learning laboratory.

WEISGERBER, ROBERT A. (ed), *Developmental Efforts in Individualized Learning*. F. E. Peacock Publishers, Inc., 401 West Irving Park Rd., Itasca, Ill. 60143, 1971, 360 pp. Examples of large-scale individualized learning programs, packaged learning units, and current developments in the field at local-school and college levels.

———— (ed), *Perspectives in Individualized Learning*. F. E. Peacock Publishers, Inc., 401 West Irving Park Rd., Itasca, Ill. 60143, 1971, 360 pp. Readings on theoretical aspects of individualized learning and analysis of specific educational components.

8
Producing Audiovisual Media

The pieces of the educational revolution are lying around *unassembled.*

—JOHN W. GARDNER

START WITH WHAT YOU HAVE

Most of the audiovisual ideas presented in this book may be adapted or adopted without your becoming either a mechanic or an artist. Some of them are so commonplace that much of the necessary equipment may already be found in your own school building or media center. Most schools have a thermographic copy machine; if not in the audiovisual center or teachers' workroom, then probably in the business office. If so, all you need is the proper film and you are ready to make transparencies for overhead projection. You may be surprised to learn how easy it is to make simple, super 8 instructional motion pictures, although 35mm slides may be quicker to produce and less costly for presenting most visual concepts that do not require motion. Either you or your school may already own a good 35mm single-lens reflex camera, or one can be purchased. Even simple, inexpensive cameras can be used to make good photographs. The techniques are easy to learn.

Photography—a Tool for Visual Literacy

In the hands of a child a simple camera can open up a new world of things to see, to feel, and to express. In the hands of a teacher the camera can be a tool for producing visuals for instruction and for recording memorable events, classroom projects, and interesting activities.

Cameras

Anyone can take good outdoor pictures on sunny or hazy days or indoor pictures with flash. The most inexpensive cameras have a single shutter speed, a constant lens opening, and a fixed-focus lens. This type of camera takes fairly sharp pictures of subjects from about five feet away to as far as you can see. Slightly more expensive cameras have "fast" f/3.5 or f/2.8 lenses and automatic exposure meters that allow natural looking pictures to be taken indoors (even without flash) in average, well-lighted classrooms, or outdoors on overcast days or in shade. Extreme close-up photographs can be made with most cameras by attaching some kind of close-up device

or supplementary lens. Single-lens reflex cameras are especially good for close-up photography because most models focus quite close without attachments and their built-in viewfinding and focusing systems tend to be quite accurate.

    The most usual lighting for taking outdoor pictures is in direct sunlight, with the subject facing toward the sun. This is called *frontlighting*. But suppose you want to use *sidelighting* or *backlighting* for a dramatic effect, or simply to keep your subjects from squinting because of the bright sunlight. In such cases, a piece of white cardboard or aluminum foil can be used to reflect some light into the shadows. The soft lighting from a hazy

Outdoor Lighting

Figure 8–2. People of all ages love to take pictures. While photography may not necessarily be the way to "turn on" every student, teachers who are able to introduce their students to photography will likely be rewarded by seeing channels of communication open between students and between students and themselves. Besides discovering an excellent tool for documenting school activities and reporting on projects, some students may develop heightened perception and awareness of the surrounding world and be encouraged to pursue photography as a life-long hobby or vocation. (Photo by David H. Curl)

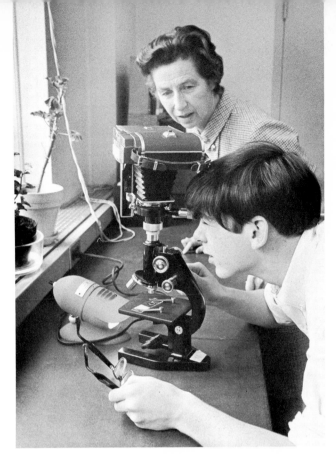

Figure 8–3. As part of his research project, this young scientist photographs a microscope slide with a Polaroid camera. How much should the teacher tell him about what to photograph? How do you suppose the student has learned how to set up the experiment and operate the equipment? (Courtesy The National Education Association. Photo by Esther Bubley)

or slightly overcast sky is ideal for pictures of people. All but the very cheapest cameras can take pictures under these conditions.

Fill-in Flash   Would you believe there are times when you might take a picture with a flashcube or flashbulb outdoors, even in bright sunlight? Flash can sometimes be used effectively to brighten shadows on the faces of subjects who are facing away from the sun. Without fill-in flash, the subjects' faces might be too dark; facing them toward the sun might cause them to grimace or squint.

Figure 8–4. Inexpensive close-up lenses are available to fit over the regular lens of nearly every camera. Single-lens reflex cameras require no special calculations when using a close-up lens, beyond extra care in focusing; most other cameras demand precise measurement of camera-to-subject distance and field size when copying artwork and photographing small subjects such as flowers, postcards, or stamps. (Courtesy Eastman Kodak Company)

◄ **DO** For bright, sparkling pictures, keep the lens clean by wiping it with a soft, lintless cloth.

A dirty lens will make **DON'T** ►
your pictures look hazy.

◄ **DO** Hold the camera steady and gently squeeze the shutter release. It pays off in sharp pictures.

Jiggling the camera as **DON'T** ►
you snap the shutter blurs the entire picture.

◄ **DO** Hold the camera level and the horizon will be level in your picture.

If your camera isn't level **DON'T** ►
when you snap the shutter, your subject will look as if it's sliding downhill.

◄ **DO** For sharp pictures, focus accurately. With simple cameras, check the manual to see how close you can get to your subject.

If you don't focus correctly, or if you get too **DON'T** ►
close with a simple camera, your subject will be blurred.

◄ **DO** Get the whole picture—don't obstruct the lens.

A finger, part of the **DON'T** ►
camera case, or strap in front of the lens causes dark areas in your pictures.

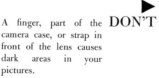

Indoor Flash   You will want to capture many indoor events in flash pictures. Just be certain your subject stays within the flash distance range recommended in the camera instruction booklet. For most simple cameras, this range is from about four to about nine feet, although adjustable cameras may be set for a greater range.

Some flash pictures are too dark because the subject is too far from the flash. This happens if you try to include too large an area and back out of the recommended flash distance range. On the other hand, getting the camera and flash too close to the principal subject may cause the foreground to appear washed out and overexposed, as well as possibly being out of focus.

Action Pictures   When taking action pictures with a simple camera, you should bear in mind that fast-moving objects may be blurred in the picture. Most simple cameras have fixed, preset shutter speeds of about 1/60 of a second, which will not stop fast action. But a moving subject will appear sharper when the direction of its motion is *toward* or *away from* the camera, instead of at a right-angle to the camera. Another way to stop fast action is by panning. Just follow the subject with your camera, keeping it centered in the viewfinder, then snap the picture as you pan. Panning blurs the background, giving an impression of motion.

Camera Holding   Not only the subject has to be motionless; your camera has to be steady, too, unless you are panning. An unsteady hand may spoil a picture of a subject as steady as a statue. For sharper pictures, hold your camera steady and gently squeeze the shutter release without moving your wrist or arm. Brace the camera against your face, even if you wear glasses, and hold your elbows against your body.

Be careful not to include your finger in the picture, nor any part of the camera case or strap. Check the instruction booklet for the best way to hold the camera so your fingers do not block the lens or cover the light-gathering cell of the exposure meter.

Keep your camera clean inside and out. Blow dust and film chips from inside the camera and remove dust from the lens with a clean, camel's hair brush. Remove fingerprints and smudges from the lens with lens-cleaning tissue and a drop or two of lens-cleaning fluid.

Composition   Good composition means keeping your pictures simple. Move in as close as you can to the main part of the subject and do not allow distracting elements such as lamp posts, telephone wires, and unwanted subjects to invade the image. Sometimes, however, including a tree branch or a person in the foreground will add interest and a feeling of depth to a scenic or landscape picture and fill otherwise wasted space. You should center your

[OPPOSITE] *Figure 8–5. Some hints for better pictures. Are there other DO'S and DON'TS that can affect the quality of your photographs? (Courtesy Eastman Kodak Company)*

Figure 8–6. The Ektagraphic Visual-maker *is a fixed-focus copy stand for use with an* Instamatic *camera. Limited to two formats, approximately* 8 × 8 *inches and* 3 × 3 *inches, the* Visual-maker *is nonetheless handy to have around the school media center because anyone can make good slides with it. Light to take the picture is supplied by a flashcube. (Courtesy Eastman Kodak Company)*

eye in the camera viewfinder, but because all viewfinders are not accurate, especially at close distances, you should experiment to find out whether your camera suffers consistently from parallax and cuts off heads or other parts of the picture. The preceding and other hints for taking good pictures are summarized below:

Hints for Better Pictures

1. Solve problems of exposure and focus before posing your subjects. People expect you to take the picture right away, once they are in position. If they have to wait long, children can be expected to make funny faces and to start clowning around.

2. Compose subjects, people or objects, carefully in the viewfinder. Try to visualize the final picture at this stage so that you won't have trees growing out of peoples' heads or have the horizon slanting because you accidentally tilted the camera.

3. Fill the frame. Move in as close as you can without cutting off important parts of the scene. But remember, the closer you get the more accurate the focus has to be and the more careful you must be with many cameras to avoid parallax.

4. Keep the background simple. Eliminate unnecessary things in the picture. The blue sky is often an excellent background, but be sure there is adequate contrast between subject and background. Try not to pose dark against dark or light against light, except for special effects.

5. Compose the picture to give emphasis to the most

important subjects so the viewer will know where to look first.

6. People in informal situations should appear to be busy. Ask them to pose as if they were doing something, or catch them unaware.

7. When possible, avoid having subjects partly in bright sunlight and partly in the shade. In bright sunlight, especially at mid-day, the shadows may be too dark. Turn people so their faces are well lighted, use fill-in flash, or, if your lens will allow, take the picture entirely in the shade.

8. Hold the camera level and steady by bracing it against your body. Squeeze the shutter release gently to avoid moving the camera.

Finally, after you have received your prints or slides back from the processer (or have done your own developing and printing!), examine your pictures critically, arranging the *best* pictures in the right sequence to tell your story.

Producing Motion Pictures and Videotapes

Lengthy sound motion pictures generally are expensive to produce and are best left to the professionals. However, an enterprising teacher or student with a super 8 or 16mm camera may shoot a short film of an important demonstration, process, or activity for only a few dollars. And if a magnetic-recording motion picture projector is available, or if the school owns a synchronizing system

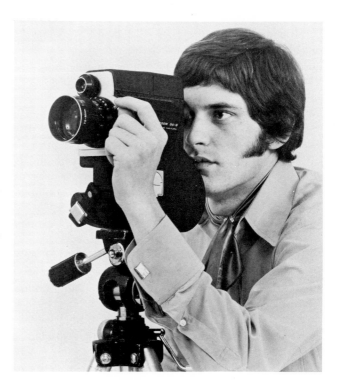

Figure 8–7. Students and teachers can produce excellent short single-concept or simple-concept films with super 8 cameras, some models of which provide such professional features as variable shutter and powered rewind for optical effects, long-run film capacity for documentary shooting, and provision for sound synchronization. Are professional features necessary? Can effective films be made with an inexpensive camera? Besides the camera, what other equipment is needed for classroom filmmaking projects? (Courtesy Bell & Howell Company)

Producing Audiovisual Media

Figure 8–8. Single-*concept, or simple-concept movies are not hard to make with modern equipment, provided that careful planning is done before filming begins. Is this demonstration being filmed from an* objective, *or* subjective *camera angle? Why is the camera position important? (Courtesy Eastman Kodak Company)*

for super 8 motion picture camera and cassette tape recorder, a sound track may be added that will preserve and standardize significant instructional commentary. Portable television cameras and videotape recorders allow production of certain types of synchronized sound "films" with great convenience and with the advantage that tapes can be erased and used again. Teachers should remember that a 20-minute motion picture or videotape, as desirable as it may be for certain purposes, may not serve as effectively as a short how-to-do-it film segment, or *single-concept* film. Causes of local river erosion or the method for planing the edge of a board are examples of subjects that might be effectively analyzed in an easy-to-make two- or three-minute film sequence. Both educational and commercial television programming has revealed beyond doubt the value of short film sequences or film "clips" to show pertinent action.

Teachers and students who are going to produce their own film or television sequences need to jot down in advance just what needs to be shown. They should be liberal with close-up shots to provide necessary details. When the person who does the planning is not to do the actual shooting, it is especially important that everyone understand and agree upon the content and treatment of the production. Planning cards and/or a shooting script are the best known ways to achieve such concensus. For those who are interested we now discuss a number of vital aspects of the film and television production process.

PREPLANNING

Never try to do any ambitious form of instructional media production without a script. Skipping this crucial planning phase will almost certainly result in spending

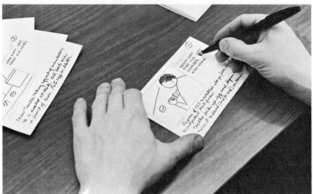

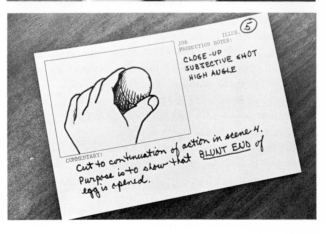

Figure 8–9. Planning or "storyboard" cards are a big help in organizing an audiovisual presentation. Cards may contain a sketch of each slide or scene, brief production notes, and narration ideas. Arrange the cards in appropriate order and use this sequence as a "shooting script." (Courtesy Eastman Kodak Company)

more time later in shooting overlooked scenes and in patching and refitting shots (or reshooting the entire show) than you would have spent had you planned properly at the outset. Perhaps the most convenient scripting aid is a set of planning-board cards. A panel with plastic pockets to hold the cards is ideal, but thumb tacks and a bulletin board will do.

The secret of good planning is to put each fact or idea on a separate blank index card, using as few words as possible, and then to arrange the cards in the most effective order. After content and sequence have been agreed upon by everyone concerned, simple sketches can show the visual elements on each card, as well as captions and titles. The planning-board cards may then serve directly as a working script for the artist and photographer, whether the actual production is done by media center professionals, by students, or by the teacher himself. The planning board, also called a "storyboard," is the best method, both to avoid overlooking subject matter and to obtain approval from all concerned before shooting any film. Show the planning-board sketches to students for their reactions. If your ideas are not yet clear or not explicit enough, students will let you know. Revision is much easier at the planning stage than it is after the photography and artwork have been completed. If desired, a final two- or three-column shooting script may be prepared when the planning is complete. Many teachers cut short this final script stage, however, and shoot directly from the planning-board card sequence.

Creative camera work requires skill and experience, and the process is too complex to deal with fully in these pages. However, a few fundamental practices and suggestions are stated here to help teachers begin their own productions or help them guide students in special filming and television projects. Here, then, are some helpful hints:

BASIC MOTION PICTURE AND TELEVISION TECHNIQUES

1. Establish the locale for action by beginning with a *Long Shot* (abbreviated LS in the script). A long shot usually covers the entire principal subject and some significant surroundings and background.
2. Much of the film action often will be shown in *Medium Shots* (MS) which include the most significant portion of the subject.
3. *Close-up Shots* (CU) focus attention on small details of the subject or provide "cut-ins" or "cut-aways" for smoother continuity. (Some very short films may consist almost entirely of close-ups).
4. When a scene has to be interrupted and then resumed, do one of the following: (*a*) take a cut-away shot of another related subject or portion of the action, or (*b*) move the camera to a considerably different angle. Do not resume action from the same angle and distance once the action has been stopped.
5. When action continues from one shot to another, do one of the following to ensure smooth continuity: (*a*) match the action from shot to shot by *overlapping* the action (for motion pictures—not television). Have the camera running before the action starts, then leave it running for two or three seconds after the action is completed for each shot—the overlaps are trimmed out during editing, or (*b*) have your actor

Figure 8–10. Don't shoot every scene from the same distance. Establish the location of the main subject with a Long Shot (abbreviated LS), move in for a Medium Shot (MS), and show important detail with a Close-up (CU). If many close-ups are involved, it's a good idea to re-establish the scene occasionally with another LS or MS. (Courtesy Eastman Kodak Company)

Producing Audiovisual Media

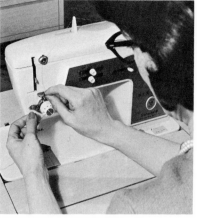

Figure 8–11. To avoid confusing the viewer, most how-to-do-it demonstrations should be photographed from a subjective *camera angle—the way the process is seen by the person doing it.* An over-the-shoulder shot allows a smooth transition from an objective establishing shot to a series of subjective close-ups of the main action. (Courtesy Eastman Kodak Company)

freeze the action while you change camera position (for example, reach for a telephone, then wait with hand on receiver before picking it up in the next shot).

6. Whenever possible, place the camera on a sturdy tripod, whether shooting indoors or out. Hand-held cameras usually result in jumpy projected images.

7. Use camera movement effects (pan, tilt, zoom) sparingly. There is a tendency to overuse these effects for novelty when there is insufficient action. Pans, tilts, and zooms are nearly always jerky and distracting when done with amateur equipment.

8. When shooting how-to-do-it demonstrations, place the camera in *subjective* position (over the shoulder of the demonstrator) so that hand positions will be as seen by the person actually performing the task.

9. When a subject is in continuous motion from one shot or scene to the next, maintain consistent *screen direction* (for example, a person shown walking left to right should still be moving left to right in subsequent scenes unless he is shown changing his direction).

10. Compress time (as in eliminating waiting time between stages of an experiment) by inserting brief *cut-away shots* of the subject or other related objects. Unimportant action can be eliminated in the same way by showing the first step, then a cut-away, and finally the last step.

11. When it is necessary to film indoors under artificial light, a "movie light" clamped to the camera may give adequate illumination, but better results can be obtained by using two or more lights as follows: (*a*) *key light*—placed fairly high and to one side—provides the main source and direction of light and creates the dominant shadows; (*b*) *fill light*—placed near the camera to reduce dark shadows on the

Figure 8–12. Being members of a real "movie production crew" makes kids feel very important. But movies cost money. Where do funds come from to pay for film and processing? Should the school own a camera, tripod, lights, and editing equipment? Besides the instructional value of the film they make, what value might there be to students who follow through as a team to complete a motion picture production? (Reprinted by permission of Technicolor, Inc.)

subject—should be one-half to one-fourth as bright as the fill; (*c*) *accent light*—placed high and out of camera range behind the subject or to one side—adds highlights and creates a feeling of roundness and depth; and (*d*) *background light*—placed behind the subject, hidden from the camera—removes shadows from the background and makes the subject stand out.

12. When your film has been returned from processing, edit it carefully to conform to the original script. If you shot motion picture film, throw away all bad

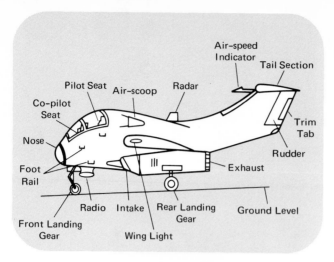

OVERCROWDED

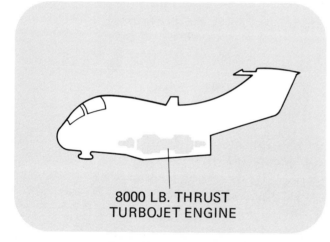

8000 LB. THRUST
TURBOJET ENGINE

SIMPLIFIED

IF YOU CAN READ 2 x 2"
SLIDES WITHOUT A MAG-
NIFIER, PEOPLE IN REAR
SEATS CAN PROBABLY
READ THEM ON THE
SCREEN

Figure 8–13. Keep visuals simple and legible. If you have to include a lot of detail, prepare a series of illustrations, each showing part of the subject, instead of trying to crowd all of the information onto a single slide, transparency, or chart. ([ABOVE] Courtesy of Eastman Kodak Company)

footage (incorrect exposure, out-of-focus, jerky camera handling, or poor action), and splice together the good scenes in proper order. If you thought to shoot a few extra cut-away shots at various stages of the action, such shots may improve the continuity if inserted between scenes where any rough transitions may occur. Videotape, however, is not usually spliced; it is edited electronically by re-recording selected portions on a second videotape recorder in the same manner as audio recording. If you do not have access to equipment with electronic editing capability it will be necessary to shoot and record scenes in exact sequence.

Fundamentals of Teaching with Audiovisual Technology

Artwork for Films, Filmstrips, Slides, and Television

Instructional slides, filmstrips, and motion pictures often contain information that is more easily photographed by copying a series of intermediate drawings or "flats," all made to the same size and format, than by shooting the actual subjects directly onto the final film. Many visuals contain too much material to be grasped readily. When words and figures and tabular data must appear on the screen, such data should be reduced to the simplest essentials, and only one idea should appear on the screen at a time. Complex lists or outlines are more effective when revealed one item at a time, building to a climax. Because of the relatively low resolving power of the medium, visuals for use on television must be especially clear and bold.

If a considerable amount of tabular data and reading matter must be presented, it is better to reproduce the material in printed handout form so that students can study it at their leisure and file it for future reference. Students are likely to be overwhelmed or even repulsed, rather than impressed, by large amounts of data. Also, viewers tend to read ahead of the presenter; while they are reading from the screen, they cannot be listening to what is being said.

LETTERING STANDARDS

Establishing a lettering-size standard will help to eliminate the perennial problem of too much data. Most producers standardize on a small "flat" or card for all master artwork. A popular size is 10 × 12 inches, because construction paper comes cut to this size, making an ideal background, and flats of this size may be kept in a standard filing cabinet. On a 10×12-inch flat, the

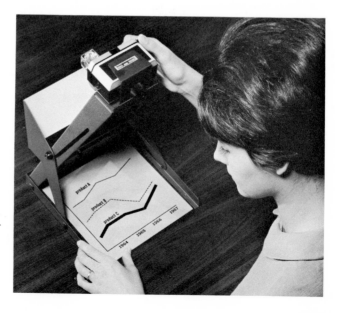

Figure 8–14. Simple charts with a neat, professional appearance can be made in minutes with colored paper, charting tapes, and adhesive transfer letters. If made to an appropriate format, such charts may be photographed as color slides or movie titles. (Courtesy Eastman Kodak Company)

projected area for 35mm slides is about 5¾ × 8½ inches, allowing a wide margin for framing in the camera viewfinder. The absolute minimum size for typewritten material for this size field would be 12-point letters, corresponding to upper case letters of pica type.

For viewing at normal classroom distances of up to six times the width of the projected picture, a more readable minimum letter size would be 24-point type. A "point"—approximately 1/72 of an inch—is the printer's basic unit of measurement. Twelve points equal one

Figure 8–15. Adhesive transfer lettering is very effective for titling slide, filmstrip, movie, and TV artwork. Since letter spacing must be done by eye, it is best to draw a rough pencil layout to scale on tracing paper to use as a guide. Cut-out figures, collages, photographic enlargements, and projection traced drawings all make excellent title backgrounds. (Courtesy Eastman Kodak Company)

Figure 8–16. Three dimensional letters lend a professional touch to titles. Some types have sticky backs that will adhere to glass or to actual objects for special visual effects. Line up these letters with a ruler or T-square. (Courtesy Eastman Kodak Company)

Figure 8–17. Colored chalks or pastel pencils can be used on a dark surface to make dramatic title slides with an informal appearance. Black construction paper works well. Colored chalk is O.K., too, on a freshly washed chalkboard, but don't take the picture with flash or with other lights too near the camera because reflected glare may obscure the lettering. (Courtesy Eastman Kodak Company)

pica, or about 1/6 of an inch. Twenty-four point letters are available in some typewriter types (primer or bulletin), in adhesive transfer letters, and in templates used with draftsmen's lettering pens. Use of 36-point or larger type adds variety and legibility to headings, as do three-dimensional cut-outs and movie title letters.

If an ordinary typewriter must be used, the size of the working area should be reduced proportionally to about $3 \times 4\frac{1}{2}$ inches. This is about the size of photographic prints that photofinishers call "jumbo" in black and white and "3X" or "3R" in color. When this smaller working area is used, caption material prepared on a typewriter with ordinary pica type, double spaced, will be quite legible when projected. Photo enlargements in the standard 8×10-inch size are excellent when masked to the $5\frac{3}{4} \times 8\frac{1}{2}$-inch format and captioned with large type.

Captions may be typewritten on white or colored paper (yellow construction paper is good). Be sure to use a

Figure 8–18.

This is "Primer" typewriter type.

This is 24-point type. Lettering should be at least this large for visuals made within a 6 x 9 inch picture area, such as overhead project-ion transparencies or slide "flats."

This is 36-point type.
This is 48-point type.

Figure 8–19.

Ordinary typewriter type is too small to be used effectively for overhead transparencies. If a regular typewriter must be used to produce artwork to be photographed, work within an area no larger than 3 X 4½ inches and double-space between lines.

new black ribbon. Keep the type clean and strike the keys firmly and uniformly in order to make even, black letters. If you are not using a carbon ribbon, a second typing over the first will strengthen the impression, but retype each line before advancing the carriage, or double images may result. Edit and condense caption and title copy as much as possible. Be brief. An outline should contain no more than four or five lines consisting of three to five words each. If more commentary is needed, record the additional material on tape or include it in supplementary readings.

Registration

Some system should be used to simplify the use of overlays and to eliminate refocusing and reframing of the camera when each flat is photographed. Most producers of slides and filmstrips use a pin registration system; motion picture and filmstrip producers use an animation punch and pegs. However, an economical homemade registration system can be worked out by using a notebook punch to perforate the material in uniform style, and by placing each flat on simple metal or wooden pegs for photographing.

Format

Except when a square-format camera is being used, or when vertical pictures are being copied from books and magazines, artwork for slides should be kept to a horizontal format whenever possible. Square screens are not always available for projection, and the trend toward low-ceilinged classrooms frequently means either that part of the information from vertically-oriented slides spills over at the top or bottom of the screen or that the projected image must be made smaller, at the sacrifice of legibility, to allow vertical slides to fit the screen.

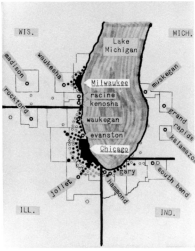

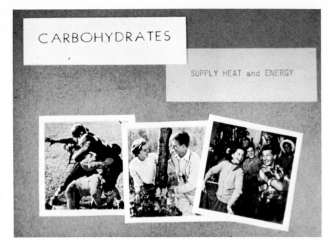

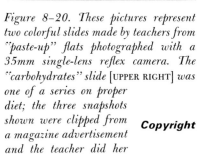

Figure 8–20. These pictures represent two colorful slides made by teachers from "paste-up" flats photographed with a 35mm single-lens reflex camera. The "carbohydrates" slide [UPPER RIGHT] *was one of a series on proper diet; the three snapshots shown were clipped from a magazine advertisement and the teacher did her own lettering. (Courtesy Louise M. Haire and Eastman Kodak Company). The map slide* [ABOVE] *was one of a series showing urban development of a geographic area. The artwork was prepared by the teacher using colored paper, markers, opaque tapes and dry-transfer symbols. The labels were prepared on a primer-size typewriter. (Courtesy Ross Stephens, The University of Connecticut)*

Copyright

Another reason for making all artwork horizontal and for allowing generous margins is so that your artwork may be converted later for filmstrip, television, or motion picture use if desired. The proportion of width to height is not the same for all media. Television systems, particularly, tend to cut off material near the edges of the picture.

Teachers frequently ask whether it is legal to copy pictures and diagrams from books and magazines to make slides and transparencies for projection without permission of the copyright holder. The best answer is that such copying, while not strictly "legal" according to present statutes, is often done by teachers who are producing slides solely for their own instructional use. Selling or renting such copies, charging admission when they are shown, or duplicating materials in quantity instead of purchasing them would be abuse of the teacher's "fair use" privilege, thus unquestionably constituting a violation of copyright laws. The correct procedure is to obtain specific written permission from the publisher of the materials which you intend to reproduce.

Copying with a Single-lens Reflex Camera

As mentioned before, the 35mm single-lens reflex is an ideal camera for teachers to own and use, although it will represent an investment of more than a hundred dollars; perhaps even several hundred dollars. The advantages of the single-lens reflex (SLR), of course, from the teacher's point of view, are its convenience and relative accuracy for close-ups and copy work as well as its versatility for general photography.

Excellent slides can be made with a relatively inexpensive model SLR camera with no accessories whatever, except possibly a supplementary close-up lens. Shooting can be done outdoors, with the camera hand held, using daylight-type color film and the exposure

Figure 8–21. When slides are to be made frequently from artwork and copied from various sources, a rigid copy stand should be built or purchased. Two photoflood-type lights placed at 45 degrees from the copy surface provide adequate illumination (be sure to check the data sheet that comes packed with the film for exposure and filter data). (Courtesy Eastman Kodak Company)

settings recommended by the film manufacturer for outdoor pictures. Accessories including a tripod, additional lenses, an exposure meter, light balancing filters, lighting equipment, and a copy stand may be added later as the photographer's skill improves and his needs increase.

Besides the conventional 35mm- and certain 126-format cameras, special *half-frame*, single-lens reflex cameras are available for teachers who wish to specialize in the production of filmstrips. These cameras use regular 35mm film, but they make exposures half the size of the standard 35mm format, corresponding to the frame size of 35mm filmstrips. Flats produced from photographic enlargements or artwork, as described earlier in this chapter, could easily be photographed either with a half-frame camera to make a filmstrip or a standard 35mm-format camera for slides. Users of half-frame cameras are cautioned, however, that *all* artwork must be *horizontal* and oriented when photographed so that the finished filmstrip will project properly (see Figure 8-22). Photographers ordinarily should *not* attempt to shoot filmstrips "live" with a half-frame camera because all exposures must then be perfect with no chance for editing.

A vertical copy stand supports the camera rigidly and level but allows it to be raised and lowered easily to focus on pictures and objects ranging in size from postage

SHOOTING ON A COPY STAND

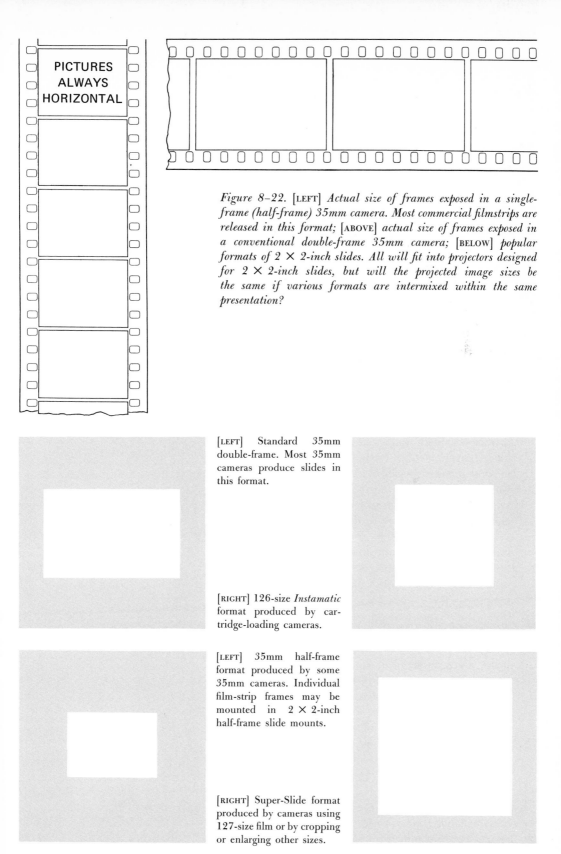

Figure 8–22. [LEFT] *Actual size of frames exposed in a single-frame (half-frame) 35mm camera. Most commercial filmstrips are released in this format;* [ABOVE] *actual size of frames exposed in a conventional double-frame 35mm camera;* [BELOW] *popular formats of 2 × 2-inch slides. All will fit into projectors designed for 2 × 2-inch slides, but will the projected image sizes be the same if various formats are intermixed within the same presentation?*

[LEFT] Standard 35mm double-frame. Most 35mm cameras produce slides in this format.

[RIGHT] 126-size *Instamatic* format produced by cartridge-loading cameras.

[LEFT] 35mm half-frame format produced by some 35mm cameras. Individual film-strip frames may be mounted in 2 × 2-inch half-frame slide mounts.

[RIGHT] Super-Slide format produced by cameras using 127-size film or by cropping or enlarging other sizes.

stamps to small posters. If a pair of photoflood-type or professional 3200°K lamps are positioned permanently at a 45-degree angle to the copyboard surface, exposure tests can be made and then standardized camera settings may be relied upon without constant need for redetermining exposure. If you know how to load and operate the camera, the following procedures should result in slides (or a filmstrip) of excellent quality:

1. Place the material to be copied on the copyboard directly beneath the camera lens. Books and magazines may be held flat by the use of binder clamps to hold the pages together and by placing thinner books underneath to level the surface. Glass is not usually recommended because of the possibility of reflections. Even so-called "non-glare" glass often is unsatisfactory because it tends to reduce contrast.

2. Center, crop, and focus the picture in the camera viewfinder. Attach a supplementary lens if necessary to bring the image into focus, adjusting both camera height and focus as required.

3. If shutter speed and lens opening have not already been standardized, determine these settings from an exposure meter. If a meter is built into the camera, it is usually best to make readings from a neutral gray test card placed on the copyboard; such cards may be obtained from a camera store. When a separate exposure meter must be used, the incident-type is recommended because it will not be affected by variations in background tone or by reflections.

4. Determine the film speed (ASA rating) of the film and consider this figure in determining exposure. If daylight-type color film is being used instead of indoor-type film, be sure to cover the lens with the blue, light-balancing filter recommended by the film manufacturer, and adjust the ASA setting accordingly.

5. Shoot the picture, releasing the shutter with a cable release if one is available. If in doubt about the correctness of exposure settings, or if the material being photographed is unusually light or dark, it may pay to "bracket" exposures by shooting one picture exactly at the settings determined, and then, leaving the shutter speed as it was, take another picture with the lens opened up 1/2 or one whole stop (toward the *lower* numbers that is, 4 instead of 5.6) and another picture with the lens stopped down 1/2 or one whole stop (toward *higher* numbers; that is, 8 instead of 5.6).

6. Send the roll of film to the manufacturer or to another reliable laboratory for processing. *Indoor-type color film* is recommended for *all* slide and filmstrip

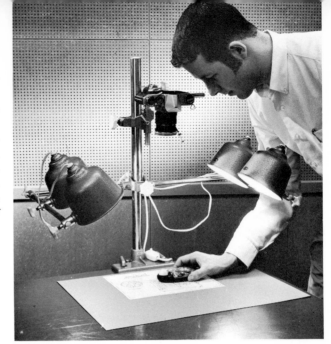

Figure 8–23. This copy stand holds a 35mm single-lens reflex camera steady, while allowing it to be moved up and down for framing and focusing upon artwork of various sizes. Note that the lights are adjusted to approximately 45° from the table surface. The photographer is determining evenness of illumination and exposure settings required by reading the light with an incident-type exposure meter placed over the material to be copied. (Courtesy The University of Connecticut)

copy work, including the copying of black-and-white originals, because upon return from processing the slides are already mounted and ready for projection. Unless a learning activity is involved, the money saved by processing and mounting your own slides seldom compensates for the time expended. If you have shot a filmstrip, place a bold DO NOT MOUNT label around the film magazine and notify the laboratory not to cut apart and mount the individual frames.

Transparencies for Overhead Projection

The overhead projector is one of the most versatile tools available for effective visual presentation. It is easy to operate, and materials are easily prepared for use on it. The overhead projector may be used in the same manner as a chalkboard, simply by writing or drawing on a piece of clear acetate placed over the glass stage. Cleared X-ray film is excellent for this purpose; it will accept india ink and many types of colored marking pens, as well as wax china-marking pencils. Acetate rolls are available for most overhead projectors, but the rolls tend to be awkward to handle and messy to clean. Most experienced teachers prefer the flexibility of a file of separate transparencies. The big advantage of the overhead transparency over the conventional chalkboard, of course, is that materials can be prepared in advance and used repeatedly, so there is no need to take valuable class time for writing.

THE THERMOCOPY PROCESS

There are several simple methods for making quality transparencies for the overhead projector. Perhaps the most popular, because of its speed, is the thermocopy

Producing Audiovisual Media

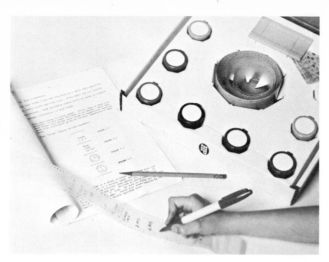

Figure 8–24. Students and teachers can make their own filmstrips without photography, using a special 35mm sprocketed film available from audiovisual dealers. Well-sharpened colored pencils or fine-tipped markers can be used to draw or write stories, arithmetic problems, spelling words, etc. directly onto the film's frosted surface. (Photos courtesy Bro-Dart, Inc. Filmstrip excerpt [OPPOSITE] courtesy Campus School, Western Michigan University)

[BELOW] Figure 8–25. In these pictures a teacher is shown preparing a transparency of his own drawings by means of a thermographic copier. He may use this transparency as illustrated in the second picture to lay over students' drawings to detect variations from the specifications of the assignment, or he may mount the transparency in the usual way for projection. (Courtesy 3M Company)

process. Transparency film for use in this process can be used in a standard thermographic office copying machine to produce an "instant" transparency from a master prepared on ordinary bond paper. The major limitation is that the original transparency master must be reproducible—that is, composed of black lines containing carbon. Soft pencil, black india ink, certain special, reproducible black ballpoint pens, typewriting (with a good ribbon), mimeographing, and black printer's ink are all suitable. Black transfer letters give a neat, professional appearance to the transparency, but after placing them on the master sheet, the letters should be covered with a single strip of transparent "magic mending" tape to keep them from coming off in the heat of the copy machine. An electric typewriter with large sans-serif primer or bulletin type is a faster way of producing written copy. If the typewriter is not electric, type over each letter two or three times to make it blacker. Ordinary typewriter type is too small for most uses of the overhead projector. If a typewriter must be used, use pica or larger type, all capital letters, and double space between the lines; but don't plan to use such a transparency with a large audience.

Lines and figures may be drawn with a ruler and a soft (No. 1) lead pencil. Avoid small lettering, close spacing, and fine detail because the lines may tend to bleed together and become hard to read on the screen.

With a set of draftsman's transparent plastic templates it is easy to draw charts, graphs, and flow diagrams. Graph paper with colored lines makes an excellent transparency master sheet; it provides a layout guide that will ensure neat squares or rectangles and will help with lettering and spacing. The colored grid lines ordinarily will not reproduce on the final transparency.

Adding Color

Color is easily added to transparencies produced by the thermocopy process. The films most commonly available will accept the ink from certain types of marking pens. These pens produce brilliantly colored lines, which make beautiful graphs or can serve to emphasize key words. Colored, adhesive-backed films may be cut to shape and used for coloring large or small areas. If color is wanted just for variety, transparency films are available that reproduce the original black lines as colored lines, or which show black lines against solid-color backgrounds. Negative films also are available that appear dramatically on the screen as colored letters against a dark background.

When material is printed in colored ink and is not reproducible by the thermographic copying process, an intermediate paper copy can be made on an office-type electrostatic copier. Usually, the intermediate will make

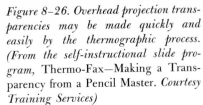

Figure 8–26. Overhead projection transparencies may be made quickly and easily by the thermographic process. (From the self-instructional slide program, Thermo-Fax—Making a Transparency from a Pencil Master. *Courtesy Training Services)*

Make dense, black lines with a No. 1 (soft) lead pencil on plain white paper...Use a ruler or template and lettering guide, or draw freehand...The lines will reproduce better if you retrace them more than once. DON'T INCLUDE TOO MUCH...(See next slide)...

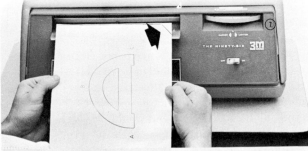

Place one sheet of transparency film ON TOP of the master (hold materials vertically)... Cut-off corner of film must be at UPPER RIGHT

Insert film and master together into top slot...Remove both from bottom slot...

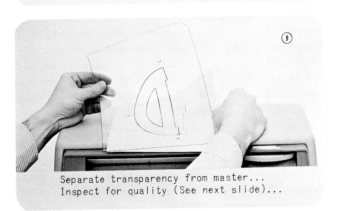

Separate transparency from master... Inspect for quality (See next slide)...

Fundamentals of Teaching with Audiovisual Technology

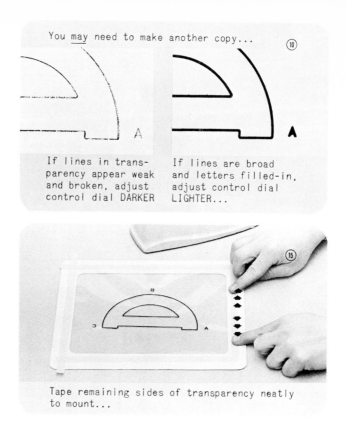

You may need to make another copy... ⑩

If lines in trans-
parency appear weak
and broken, adjust
control dial DARKER

If lines are broad
and letters filled-in,
adjust control dial
LIGHTER...

Tape remaining sides of transparency neatly
to mount...

a satisfactory transparency when reproduced again on film
by the thermocopy process. Special films and adjustments
make it possible to make transparencies directly on various kinds of office copiers, but most users prefer the
thermocopy system because it is readily available, extremely fast, and completely dry.

**TRANSPARENCIES FROM
THE SPIRIT DUPLICATOR**

The familiar spirit duplicator is a useful partner to
the overhead projector. When you want to give a copy
of a handout to each student and then have an identical
transparency for projection, you can use a commercial
thermal spirit master, or simply run a sheet of heavy-
gauge acetate through the duplicator at the beginning
of the run, while the master is printing dark, then proceed
to run off as many paper copies as you need. The process
works best when you hand-feed the acetate into the
duplicator, then hand-crank the cylinder slowly and
evenly at a high roller-pressure setting. Cleared X-ray
film works well in this way. Covering the printed side
of the finished transparency with a second sheet of clear
film will keep the image from smearing. Sometimes,
acetate that has a matte or frosted surface will take a
sharper image. If this is used, the frosted side should
be made transparent by coating it after it is printed with

Figure 8–27. Most schools have fluid duplicators for teachers and students to use. How many kinds of special-purpose master sets can you name that are available for use on fluid duplicators? Can you make fluid duplicator masters on a thermocopy machine? Can overhead projection transparencies be produced on a fluid duplicator? How do you create a multi-color printed diagram or poster on this versatile machine? (Courtesy A. B. Dick Co.)

an even coat of clear plastic spray. Special spirit-master sets may be purchased that will reproduce anything that can be prepared by the thermocopy process. Some of these special masters are transparent so that the master itself becomes a projection transparency after the paper copies have been run.

Many teachers try to cram too much information into a single transparency. The lettering standards described earlier for slide artwork apply equally to overhead transparencies. Quarter-inch (or 24-point) letters are about the smallest that will allow good readability from an overhead transparency at average viewing distances. And transparencies, like most other visuals, should be prepared in a horizontal format whenever possible for convenience in projection.

In showing transparencies, the audience sometimes should be kept in suspense. If the whole transparency is shown at once, viewers tend to read ahead and miss much of what the teacher is saying. The line-at-a-time ("revelation") technique is helpful. Use a sheet of typing paper or light colored construction paper to cover all of the transparency except the part to be shown at the moment; the paper will be sufficiently transparent for you to see the covered portion, but the class will not be able to see it. Some teachers like to hinge strips of cardboard cut from a manila file folder to the transparency; they write key words on the strip to indicate the material that will show on the screen when each strip is lifted.

Legibility

[OPPOSITE] *Figure 8–29. The versatility of the overhead projector is based upon the various ways in which transparencies can be prepared. (A) Simple masks can be hinged on either side to cover portions of the transparency; (B) overlays can be prepared to build upon an idea; (C and center) the transparency can be written or drawn upon with a marker or special pencil; or (D) a simple sliding mask will allow progressive disclosure of one line at a time.*

Figure 8–28. A primer-size typewriter is ideal for quick lettering of diazo and thermographic transparency masters. A diazo master is being prepared here, the tracing paper master sheet having been placed into the typewriter with carbon paper facing the back of the master to increase opacity of the letters. Thermographic masters may be typed on ordinary bond paper, but typing over each line a second time will improve the reproduction. For best results with either process, the type should be clean and the ribbon new and black. (Courtesy Tecnifax Corporation)

Figure 8–30. Opaqued masters are necessary for the diazo (ammonia-developing) process. Areas which are to appear in color on the finished transparency must either be opaque cut-outs or inked-in with opaque india ink on a base of high-quality tracing paper or clear acetate. Opaque charting tapes may also be used. (Courtesy Tecnifax Corporation)

Overlays

Complex transparencies call for the overlay process. Each part of a diagram or chart is made into a separate transparency with a clear film base, but all are hinged with tape to the same mount. If all overlays are hinged on the same side, like a book, then they must always be used in the same sequence. When overlays are hinged on opposite sides of the mount, however, they may be projected singly or in any order.

Beautiful colored overlays can be made by the diazo (ammonia-developing) process. But this process takes more time than thermographic copying, and it requires special equipment that is less likely to be available in the school. Masters for the diazo process must be prepared on *translucent* vellum or tracing paper or on transparent film. All lines or areas which are to show in color must then be made absolutely *opaque* by use of black india ink, opaque tape, transfer letters, or cutouts from heavy paper or aluminum foil (a black-line thermographic transparency makes a good diazo master). Colored diazo film is then exposed to strong light, each color of film through the appropriate master. After the films have all been developed in ammonia vapor they are hinged and mounted for use. If the services of a well-equipped local media production center are available, the technicians there can probably help you to make diazo transparencies.

PICTURE LIFTS

Another type of overhead transparency is the "picture lift." Lifts are made by transfering the ink directly from a printed page onto a sheet of transparent adhesive plastic. Pictures can be transferred either by a cold process, using transparent plastic material with an adhesive backing which is rubbed down firmly and evenly over the picture, or by the use of laminating film applied in a laminating machine or dry-mounting press. In all cases the illustration must have been printed on clay-coated paper (rubbing a moistened finger in the margin of the page is a test for clay coating—if some white residue appears on your finger the picture will lift). After laminating the surface either by the hot or cold process, the picture is soaked for a few minutes in a lukewarm solution of mild detergent until the paper can easily be peeled away from the back. All the clay must be rinsed away before drying the picture. Brightness of the colors is improved by giving the picture side of the transparency a smooth, even coating of clear plastic spray.

Although we have been discussing so far in this chapter media that are primarily visual, all of these visual media—films, filmstrips, slides, transparencies—may take on the added dimension of sound when prepared for classroom demonstration or self-instructional use. We now turn our attention to the *audio* in *audio*visual.

Sound Recording and Synchronization

The tape recorder is a useful tool for preserving and presenting lectures and discussions, and for improving communication skills. Everyone knows, or thinks he knows, how to use a tape recorder (some specific helps are offered in Chapter 9). Tapes of classroom discussions or committee reports that are good enough to be transcribed by a secretary are easy to make, but skill and planning are needed to make tapes that can be re-recorded or played back for instructional purposes. All tape recorders have basically similar parts and functions and are easy to operate (see Chapter 9). Whether a tape recorder produces high quality sound or unintelligible noise depends largely upon how it is used.

MICROPHONE TECHNIQUE

Proper microphone placement is the most important factor. If the microphone is too far away from the person speaking, the result will be excessive reverberation (echo), and extraneous noise will be picked up from inside and outside the room. Human hearing is selective—the brain screens out most of the background noise and concentrates on what is wanted—but a microphone records everything indiscriminately. Most low-priced microphones that are supplied with tape recorders are omnidirectional; that is, they pick up sound (and noise) more or less equally from all sides. The remedy for unwanted noise is to keep the microphone within about 6 to 12 inches of the speaker's mouth, whenever possible. In speaking, good technique applies equally to public address systems and to recording. Talking slightly to the side of the microphone instead of directly into it may reduce "breathiness" and popping or hissing sounds. And keep the volume level constant, by moving back a little bit from the microphone when talking louder. Wind noise may be reduced in recordings made outdoors by slipping a heavy woolen sock or mitten over the microphone.

When recording a conference or a panel discussion, make sure that the microphone can pick up all voices equally; ordinarily the microphone should be about the same distance from each participant. If one person speaks much more softly than the others, place the microphone closer to him, and adjust the volume level accordingly.

Recording Group Discussion

If the microphone is to be placed on a table, be sure to put a pad such as a folded sweater or towel under it to insulate it from vibrations from the tape-recorder motor and other sources. Ask participants not to shuffle papers, drum fingers or pencils on the table, open and close notebooks and purses, cough, or whisper to one another while the recording is being made. Avoid handling the microphone, and do not pass it around the table from person to person without first shutting off the recorder or turning the volume down. When taping a speech, or a demonstration in which the speaker has to move around, use a "lavaliere" microphone that fastens around the neck with a cord or hook, or one that clips on the lapel or breast pocket. This will leave the speaker's hands free and will keep the recording volume the same no matter how much he moves around.

The script for a slide set, film, or instructional tape should be typewritten double or triple spaced on heavy paper that will not crinkle noisily when handled. The narrator should practice reading the script aloud until it flows smoothly. Recording should be done with the microphone on a stand or soft pad and with the script

Recording Narration

Figure 8–31. This teacher has improvised a recording studio in her classroom by using folding partitions made from acoustical ceiling tile cemented to a plywood backing. Hard plaster walls and extensive window areas in large rooms tend to create too much echo, and intelligibility of the recording is affected. Blankets and carpeting can also be used to "deaden" a room acoustically. (Courtesy Board of Education, Norwalk, Conn.)

lying on the table. If the microphone cord is long enough and you have someone to help you, try to put the tape recorder in another room or behind a partition, so as to minimize pickup of mechanical noises. For most instructional purposes, the ideal sound recording studio is a small room isolated from extraneous noise, which has an acoustical tile ceiling, drapes on one or more walls, and a carpeted floor. Ordinary rooms have hard surfaces that reflect sound and create echos and, thus, are often too "live." To improvise an effective studio, partition off a corner of an office or classroom with drapes (or even blankets) and put a soft rug on the floor.

EDITING TAPES

One advantage of tape is that it is easy to edit. When a mistake is made, simply stop, rewind, and replay the tape up to the end of the previous sentence; push the "record" button and re-record right over the mistake. No one will ever detect the correction if it is done carefully.

With reel-to-reel tapes, careful cutting and splicing will eliminate any unwanted pauses, words, coughs, or extraneous noises. Splicing is not difficult. Mechanical splicers may be used, but a pair of sharp scissors and a roll of special splicing tape will suffice. Use only audio splicing tape. Ordinary cellophane tape should not be used for

Figure 8–32. Recording tape is easy to splice, but be sure to use special splicing tape only, not ordinary office-type tape: (1) overlap ends of the tape to be spliced and cut diagonally; (2) align both ends with shiny side up; (3) affix splicing tape; burnish with fingernail; (4) trim splice, cutting slightly into recording tape.

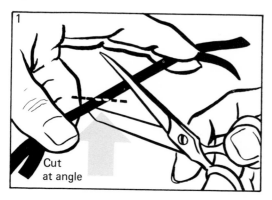

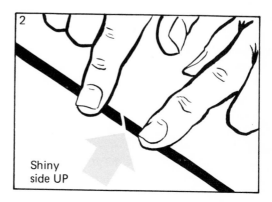

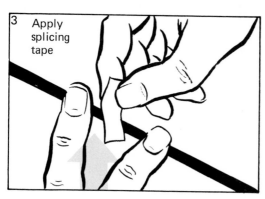

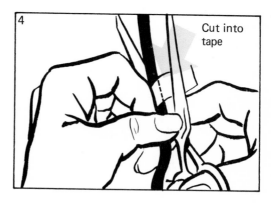

splicing; the adhesive will bleed and may gum up the recorder heads and cause layers of tape to stick together on the reel, or it may dry out and cause the splice to come apart.

To keep the splice from being noticeable on playback, cut the recording tape diagonally and butt the cut ends together. Join the ends with splicing tape applied to the back (shiny side) of the recording tape. When the splice is finished, cut slightly into both edges of the tape to be sure no adhesive oozes out to stick to other layers of tape on the reel. After editing, it is a good idea to splice two or three feet of audio leader at the beginning of the tape.

On professional recorders, reels can be worked back and forth manually to locate a single syllable or an unwanted noise that is to be deleted. The place to be cut is marked with a red wax pencil as the tape passes over the playback head. Editing can be done almost as precisely on any tape recorder, with practice, patience, and careful listening. Mark the tape on the back (shiny) side with a red wax pencil; double check by playing back again past the mark to be sure the mark is where the cut should be. Editing is much more conveniently done, of course, on three-head professional tape recorders and on machines having a cueing knob or pause control.

Tape Cassettes

Because of their small size and foolproof handling, tape cassettes are by far the most convenient for use in self-instructional learning programs. But cassette tapes are not intended to be cut and spliced. Narration should first be recorded on a standard reel-to-reel machine (or transferred from cassette to reel), then edited as necessary, and finally transferred to the cassette by re-recording or "dubbing" from a conventional recorder to a cassette recorder. This service is provided by many media centers.

Re-Recording and Mixing

Valuable original tapes should always be stored safely away from danger of loss or accidental erasure, and used only as masters for subsequent re-recording.

Virtually every tape recorder provides a "line" or "auxiliary" input receptable (jack) for recording from sources other than a microphone, as well as a "monitor", "external amplifier," or "speaker/headphone" output jack for playing tapes into another tape recorder or public address system. Tapes can be duplicated merely by connecting the *output* of the machine playing the tape to the proper *input* of the machine being used for re-recording. Of course you must obtain a "patch cord" with appropriate plugs (or adapters) to fit into both machines. Unfortunately, audio connectors are not standardized, so it is helpful to have various cords and adapters available to use with different recorders.

Electronic editing is possible with the two tape-

Figure 8–33. Duplicating a tape is an important process for some teachers to carry out. These pictures show front and rear views of a pair of tape recorders of the easy-to-operate classroom type linked together by appropriate connecting cords. The connector cord for copying links the player instrument to the recording instrument. Note that the output from the preamplifier of the master tape player on the right, bottom picture is connected to the recording input of the recording instrument. The rest of the process is simply to operate both machines paying particular attention to the problem of starting at the desirable playing and recording volume settings. (Courtesy The University of Connecticut)

recorder set-up described. To do this, you simply stop the *recording* unit with the pause or "instant stop lever," holding it down while the *playback* unit plays on through the unwanted portion, then releasing the pause control whenever you want to re-commence recording. Because the tape is not cut when edited electronically, there is no danger of destroying other material that may have been recorded on adjacent tracks. But because it is very difficult to locate single words and sounds, this process is usually reserved for removing commercial announcements from between musical selections, shortening lengthy pauses, and re-arranging the sequence of various recorded selections.

A disc recording may be transferred or "dubbed" onto tape in a manner similar to duplicating a tape. A special patch cord with metal-jawed "alligator" clips may be attached directly to the speaker terminals of a phonograph, radio, or TV receiver which does not provide an appropriate output jack. In any of the re-recording processes described, the recording volume is adjusted for the proper level by observing the VU meter or indicator light on the machine doing the recording. This of course is the same procedure used when recording with a micro-

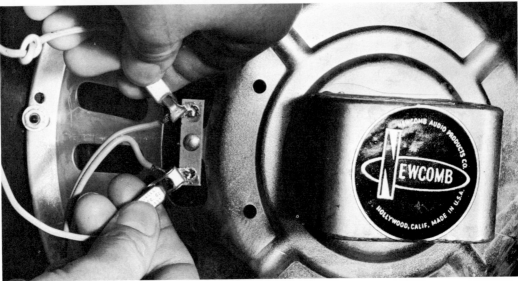

phone, but in some cases the volume of the *playback* record player or tape recorder may have to be adjusted also to avoid overload distortion from too much volume, or excessive background noise or hiss, if the volume is set too low.

Some tape recorders allow simultaneous combining or mixing of sound from a microphone and other source such as another tape recorder or a record player. When using such a machine it is necessary only to connect up the sources as we have described and experiment with the level settings and the timing until the desired effect is obtained. An inexpensive little box with knobs and jacks, called a *mixer*, is a useful recording accessory because it makes it very easy to combine two or more

Figure 8–34. These pictures show how, with appropriate connecting cords, a phonograph record may be transferred, or "dubbed" onto tape. In the first picture the connecting cord is plugged into the record player audio output jack and then into the tape recorder input. The rest of the process is straightforward operation of both instruments. The second picture, a close-up view, shows the use of "alligator" clips for fastening one end of a connecting cord to the two terminals of the speaker on a record player, radio, or TV set not equipped with an output jack. The other end of the cord goes to the tape recorder input. (Courtesy The University of Connecticut)

Figure 8–35. The arrangement of in-struments in these pictures is similar to that shown in Figure 8–34, except for the addition of a microphone and a mixer for microphone and record player. Identify these units and trace the mixing process by noting the connecting cords from record player and microphone to the mixer inputs and then on to the single tape-recorder input.

Types of Tapes

Observe in the top picture: (1) the rear, input view of the tape recorder, and (2) the rear, input view of the mixer. In the bottom picture the front view of each component is shown with all con-nections complete. In this view trace once again the mixing and connecting process. (Courtesy The University of Connecticut)

audio channels for special effects. Of course the easiest way to obtain background music on a narrated tape is simply to have a record playing nearby while recording the narration into the microphone. When you want the music louder, simply hold the microphone closer to the speaker of the record player. Although the sound quality will not be as pleasing to the critical ear, and there is always the problem of picking up unwanted noises through the microphone, this simple mixing method will be satisfactory for many applications.

The cheapest ordinary recording tape is coated onto an acetate base .0015 inch (1½ mils) thick. Acetate tape may be identified by holding the full reel up to a strong light and looking through it broadside; it will appear translucent, whereas the denser polyester-base tapes are opaque. Another way to identify acetate is to try to break the tape. Acetate tape will snap in two easily, without stretching. Mylar or polyester-base tape is much more resistant to breaking and aging and is therefore preferred for repeated use and long storage, but it is more expensive initially.

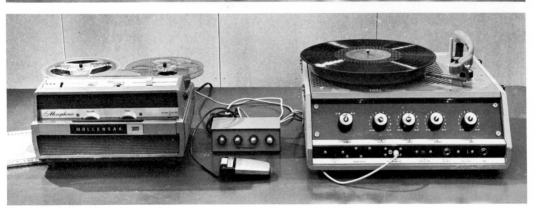

Reel tape is available in various lengths for different recording times. A standard tape reel is seven inches in diameter. The seven-inch reel contains 1200 feet of standard-play tape, 1800 feet of thin long-play tape, 2400 feet of thinner double-play tape, or 3600 feet of extra thin triple-play tape. Most users prefer the 1½-mil polyester tape for valuable master recordings and for tapes that are to be used by students. The very thin tapes are useful for long, uninterrupted recording sessions, but they may tend to stretch and twist with repeated handling. The chart in Figure 8–36 gives the playing times for various lengths of tape at various speeds. The C-30 and C-60 cassettes are generally preferred to longer playing cassettes for the same reasons as the thicker reel tapes. Although the cassette itself will protect the tape from handling damage, the thinner tapes occasionally tend to twist or jam inside the cassette.

Although some cassette tape recorders reproduce sound surprisingly well at the slow standard cassette speed of 1⅞ ips (inches per second), professionals often make original recordings on reel-to-reel tape recorders at a speed of 7½ ips, which represents 30 minutes on each side of a standard 1200-foot reel of tape, and gives a wider tonal range on good equipment than 3¾ or 1⅞ ips speeds. However, the difference in quality may not be noticeable when recording narration, a lecture, or classroom discussion. In such cases, if extra recording time is needed, a slower speed may be used to avoid changing reels. Remember that, other factors being equal, the faster the tape speed, the higher is the fidelity of the recording. High-quality music recording for commercial purposes is generally done at 15 ips.

Recording Speed

Most portable tape recorders owned by schools will record and play back two separate recordings that go

Full-Track, Dual-Track, and Stereo

TAPE LENGTH & TIME (Recording Both Directions)							
Recording Speed	150 Ft.	300 Ft.	600 Ft.	900 Ft.	1200 Ft.	1800 Ft.	2400 Ft.	3600 Ft.
1⅞ I.P.S.	30 min.	1 Hr.	2 Hrs.	3 Hrs.	4 Hrs.	6 Hrs.	8 Hrs.	12 Hrs.
3¾ I.P.S	15 min.	30 min.	1 Hr.	1½ Hrs.	2 Hrs.	3 Hrs.	4 Hrs.	6 Hrs.
7½ I.P.S.	7½ min.	15 min.	30 min.	45 min.	1 Hr.	1½ Hrs.	2 Hrs.	3 Hrs.

TAPE CASSETTES (1 7/8 I.P.S.)		
	One Direction	Both Directions
C–30	15 min.	30 min.
C–60	30 min.	60 min.
C–90	45 min.	1½ Hrs.
C–120	1 Hr.	2 Hrs.

Figure 8–36. Recording and playing times for various lengths of tape at different speeds. NOTE: The digital counter on your recorder does not count footage; it counts revolutions of the supply reel and is only an approximate reference.

in opposite directions on the same tape, each utilizing a track half the width of the tape along its entire length. Recordings made in this way are called "dual-track" or "half-track." They can be edited only by selective re-recording; cutting and splicing one track would destroy the other. A dual-track recording cannot be played back on a professional recorder (such as used in radio stations) that is equipped with full-track heads that span the entire width of the tape. Stereo recorders compound the problem by adding two more tracks, making a total of four tracks to consider. For flexibility, a good procedure is to record original master tapes on a monaural (not stereo) machine in one direction only, using 1½-mil polyester tape at 7½ ips speed. Then if you want to edit the tape you may do so easily; if you want to play it back on a different type of tape recorder or release it for playback by a radio or television station, the tape may be used without re-recording.

Figure 8–37. Tape recorder head configurations: (A) Full-track monophonic—the type of tape recorder used primarily in broadcasting stations and professional recording studios—the recording goes across the full width of the tape and in one direction only. (B) Dual-track (half-track) monophonic—the type of recorder most common in schools—on these machines it is possible to make two separate recordings on each reel of tape; the first track is recorded on the upper half of the tape, the second track on the lower half. To record or play back the second track, simply take the full reel from the take-up spindle on the recorder, turn the reel over, place it on the supply spindle, and re-thread the machine. (C) Four-track stereo—the most popular format for home music recording—the first and third tracks are recorded simultaneously on the first run through the recorder, and the second and fourth tracks are recorded simultaneously on the reverse run. Recording two parallel tracks simultaneously is the principle behind stereophonic sound. How is it possible to edit dual-track or four-track stereo tapes?

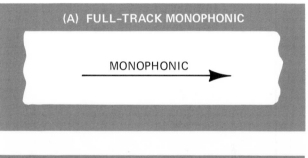

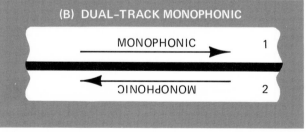

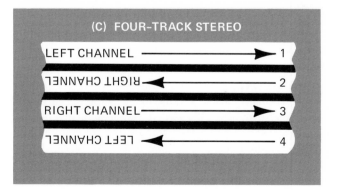

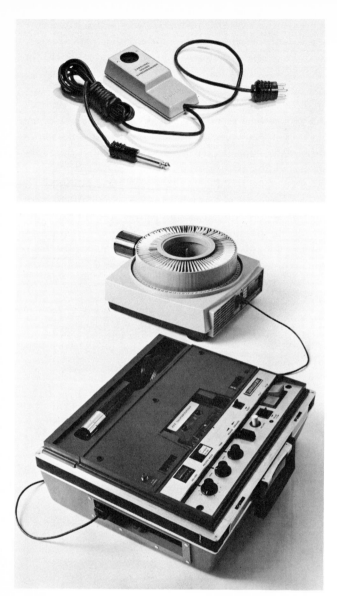

Figure 8–38. Although practice and careful planning are required, synchronized slide/tape programs can be prepared and played back using either of the two types of equipment shown. The top photo shows a synchronizer which, when connected between channel two of a stereo tape recorder and the remote control socket of a slide projector, allows slide-change signals to be recorded and played back with the same equipment. (Courtesy Eastman Kodak Company). The cassette tape recorder shown in the second photo contains a built-in synchronizer and needs only to be connected to a projector remote control socket and power outlet to record or play back synchronizing pulses. (Courtesy 3M/Wollensak). Very smooth transitions may be obtained by adding a second slide projector and a dissolve control unit which fades from one projector to the other by varying the power to the projection lamps.

The smooth, dramatic presentation in which taped narration and music are synchronized with slides or a filmstrip is a job for an experienced audiovisual technician. Excellent combination units and electronic devices that connect a tape recorder with a slide or filmstrip projector are available, but without proper equipment, the process of synchronization is difficult for the inexperienced, especially when a program is being set up for someone else to use. The worst problem is that once the show gets "out of sync" the amateur operator may become flustered and not be able to get the picture and sound back together again. Needless to say, this creates a disaster from the point of view of the audience. In

SYNCHRONIZED SOUND

addition, the need for making and testing several connections and level settings increases the usual probability for error when a nontechnical person attempts the process. Even commercially produced sound filmstrips occasionally become bewilderingly out of synchronization.

Cueing

When recorded sound is to accompany slides or a filmstrip, whether electronically synchronized or not, the best procedure is to prepare a script with small reproductions or brief descriptions of each visual, or the frame number, adjacent to the appropriate commentary, marking each slide or frame change cue prominently at the correct spot in the script. Even if synchronizing equipment is going to be used, someone should be following along with the script during the showing to correct the synchronizer if necessary. Projectionists who are unfamiliar with the content of the presentation will find a cued script especially helpful. Of course, explicit directions will be given for the guidance of the student when tape and visuals are to be integrated into a self-instructional program.

Producing Sound Movies

The locally produced sound motion picture is perhaps the ultimate in low-budget production. However, special equipment is required, and attempts to synchronize an ordinary tape recorder with a motion picture projector should be made only for experimental purposes. If close timing is required, the variations in motor speed will be highly frustrating, to say the least.

Projectors that record and play back magnetic sound are available in both 16mm and in super 8. Before narration or music is recorded, the film must be sent to a commercial laboratory to have a thin magnetic oxide strip applied along one edge. The magnetic projector

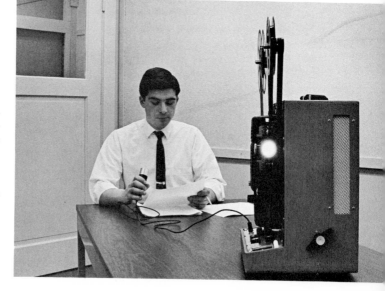

Figure 8–39. A few motion picture projectors have provision for recording sound directly onto a thin magnetic stripe applied to the film. Certain motion picture cameras and projectors may be run in synchronization with a separate tape recorder. "Wild" sound, recorded sound that is not synchronized with the projector, is often satisfactory for background music, general narration, etc., when precise timing is not required. (Courtesy Eastman Kodak Company)

Producing Audiovisual Media

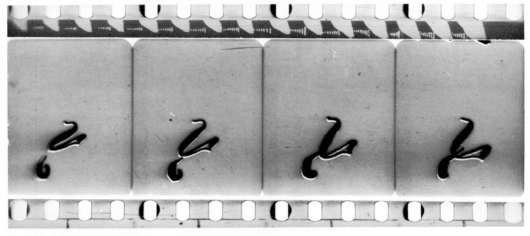

Figure 8–40. Animation without a camera. Some intriguing short motion pictures have been made by drawing or etching directly onto the film. Pioneered by Canadian film-maker Norman McLaren, this process requires planning, concentration, and manual dexterity, but it can even be done on 16mm film (35mm film is shown here). Blank, clear, or opaque film "leader" stock often can be obtained from film libraries, processing laboratories, and military surplus sources. Note that the sound track is etched or drawn along the edge of the film where it will be "seen" by the photoelectric cell in the projector's sound system—on 16mm film this will be the edge without sprocket holes. Examine a commercial sound film for the exact alignment of sound track and picture frames. (From Dots and Loops *and* Rythmetic, *courtesy National Film Board of Canada)*

simply incorporates a built-in tape recorder, and the cautions and practices that apply are the same as for any tape recorder in regard to acoustics, microphone placement, and avoidance of extraneous noise. The projector motor itself is the worst noisemaker, so many film makers set up the projector in an adjoining room or corridor, projecting the picture through a glass door or partition onto the wall of the quiet room where the narrator sits with his microphone. The narrator thus can watch the film as he reads the script. Practice will get the timing right; a second person can help by touching the narrator's shoulder to give the cue to begin each new scene.

The magnetic sound projector can be a great boon when foreign language or literacy problems exist. Educational films with standard optical sound tracks can be

Figure 8–41. These girls are planning their own television program which will be acted out by members of their class and recorded on videotape. How can the teacher manage to spend this time away from the group? What might the other students be doing? (Courtesy The National Education Association. Photo by Esther Bubley)

modified by having a magnetic strip applied over or alongside the existing sound track, and then recording the translated or modified narration.

Synchronization

"Lip sync" is the term film makers use to describe the technique of photographing people so their lip movements match the words coming from the sound track. This process requires expensive professional recording equipment to obtain high quality and will be outside the scope of all but the most fortunate schools and educational media centers. Videotape may be a better answer than film for documenting important dialogue such as live demonstrations, role playing sessions, and student performances and presentations.

Videotape

When videotape is first introduced into the school program, many students and teachers have difficulty getting used to being "on camera." A good way to overcome any reluctance or stage fright is simply to allow people to practice with the equipment. Recording and observing themselves privately will soon build enough confidence to master the medium, or at least will help those who do poorly to recognize their shortcomings in time to bow out gracefully in favor of other media.

PREPLANNING

Good televised and filmed demonstrations require much more effort to produce than ordinary lectures. This means planning, rehearsal, timing, and hours of preparation. It means using properly prepared visuals and audio effects in an intimately visual medium. It means considering the camera when making every move, so that nothing is obscured, and ensuring that visuals and props are close enough to the camera to be easily seen when they are needed. It takes practice to put on a good televised or filmed presentation. It also requires smooth organization and plenty of skill. Anyone with poise can stand up and lecture to a camera, but students expect, and deserve, something better. They are used to viewing

Figure 8–42. Students are surprisingly creative and imaginative. They are stimulated by viewing network-quality television and professionally produced motion pictures. Should students be encouraged to express some of their own ideas on tape and film? By what standards should the quality of student productions be judged? (Courtesy The National Education Association. Photo by Esther Bubley)

slick commercial television. In-school presentations seldom need to be polished to network quality, but they are being judged by similar standards—so make them as good as you can.

Not every teacher will use all the media described in this chapter; many will be limited by lack of time, funds, and equipment, to reliance upon more traditional forms of presentation. We encourage all teachers, however, to explore all possibilities available for becoming a *more effective and more efficient communicator.*

Problems and Activities

1. React to the following statement: "Photography can help people see themselves and things around them in new ways. Observing his world through the camera's eye can help an individual sharpen his perception, develop a greater sense of identity, and relate with more awareness to his environment."

2. Using a simple camera and black-and-white film, shoot at least one roll or cartridge including the subjects listed (you may use a more versatile camera, of course, if you know how to determine proper exposure):
   (*a*) My Neighborhood
   (*b*) My Home
   (*c*) My School
   (*d*) My Family
   (*e*) My Best Friend
   (*f*) My Most Prized Possession
   (*g*) My Favorite Place
   (*h*) Myself
   Develop the film and make prints as directed by your

instructor, or have the pictures processed by a commercial photo finisher.

3. Using a format specified by your instructor, prepare a series of original "flats" for a filmstrip, slide, movie, or TV production; use photographs, artwork, or mounted illustrations. Add title lettering by any appropriate process. Shoot a slide from this flat using a Visualmaker or 35mm camera on a copy stand.

4. Plan, shoot, and organize a sequence of at least 10 2×2-inch color slides. Make your pictures tell a story, whether they are in sequence as a "how-to-do-it" or related to a common theme, such as a photo essay. Include some indoor pictures with either natural light (window or room light) or flash, and some outdoor pictures. Your sequence should include closeups whenever appropriate and possible with your equipment. Include at least one title slide. Prepare a narrative script or content outline and description of how the slides are to be used. Storyboard cards will probably be very helpful in preplanning before you take the pictures.

5. Make a hand-drawn overhead transparency using either colored pencils on frosted acetate or suitable inks or markers on clear plastic film.

6. Prepare an original black-line reproducible master, using soft pencil or india ink on plain white paper. From this master, make a transparency for overhead projection using a thermographic copier and infrared transparency film. Add color with marking pen, adhesive color sheet, or transparent colored tape.

7. Prepare a set of at least three original diazo-reproducible masters consisting of opaque images on translucent vellum. From these masters make a diazo overhead transparency including base plus at least two different colored overlays.

8. Make a "picture lift" transparency using either a dry mounting press or cold adhesive laminating film.

9. Plan a multi-colored instructional hand-out or poster, prepare a master, and run off several copies. Use the spirit duplicating process with at least three different colors of carbons on the master sheet.

10. Use a thermographic copier and thermal spirit duplicating master to produce an overhead transparency and several copies of an instructional handout.

11. Demonstrate or explain why the content of transparencies and slides should be planned to fit into a horizontal format whenever possible.

12. Prepare a storyboard sequence for a short single-concept

or simple-concept motion picture. If equipment is available, shoot and edit the film and add a sound track.

13. If you are teaching now, set up an audio (or video) tape recorder unobtrusively in your classroom and record an entire class period. Later, either in private or with your instructor, evaluate your recorded performance: Was your speech clear, pleasant, devoid of mannerisms? Did you dominate the discussion or were you able to stimulate student participation? Did the tape help you to detect some needs of students that you were not aware of before?

14. Copy a portion of a record (or a radio or TV program soundtrack) onto tape without using a microphone. Add some of your own narration, explanation, or study questions to the recorded excerpt. Try mixing voice recording with a background of music or sound effects.

Selected References

Art-Work Size Standards for Projected Visuals, Kodak Pamphlet No. S–12. Motion Picture and Education Markets Division, Eastman Kodak Co., Rochester, N.Y. 14650, 1968, 8 pp. It is both convenient and economical if artists producing originals from which projected visuals are made can adopt certain size standards. This pamphlet offers recommendations and provides a 3×4-inch template for photo prints or typewritten copy.

Audiovisual Planning Equipment. Kodak Pamphlet No. S–11. Motion Picture and Education Markets Division, Eastman Kodak Co., Rochester, N.Y. 14650, 1969, 8 pp. Gives specifications and suggested applications for three time-, money-, and work-saving devices; a planning board, planning cards and a slide-sequence illuminator made from readily available, inexpensive materials.

Audiovisual Production Techniques Series (30 titles, super-8 film loops, 3–4 min each) McGraw-Hill Films, 1221 Avenue of the Americas, New York, N.Y. 10020, 1966–69. Each short film demonstrates in detail one of the processes involved in the production of basic audiovisual materials.

Basic Art Techniques for Slide Production (2×2-inch slides with tape, 14 min) Eastman Kodak Co., Rochester, N.Y. 14650, 1970. Outlines basic steps in the preparation of various forms of artwork for photographing into slides.

BRUMMITT, W. B., R. W. BURNETT, and H. S. ZIM. *Photography.* Golden Press, 850 Third Ave., New York, N.Y., 10022, 1964, 160 pp. Simple but comprehensive manual on basic photography.

CRAIG, WALT. *Learning Photography.* Grid, Inc., 4145 N. High St., Columbus, Ohio 43214, 1970, 58 pp. A slim programmed book which takes the student who wants to advance beyond the simple camera, step-by-step through the confusing world of f/stops, shutter speeds, and focal lengths.

Creating Instructional Materials (16mm film, 18 min) McGraw-Hill Films, Inc., 1221 Avenue of the Americas, New York, N.Y. 10020, 1963. Stresses that the creation of instructional materials in the classroom contributes significantly to the student's learning experiences.

Duplicating by the Spirit Method (16mm film, 14 min) BFA Educational Media, 2211 Michigan Ave., Santa Monica, Calif. 90404, 1961. Demonstrates methods for preparing single and multicolored masters and the operation and care of spirit duplicating equipment. Surveys commonly used duplicating equipment, such as photocopy machines, office-type offset presses, mimeograph; and points out specific advantages of the spirit duplicator.

Effective Lecture Slides. Kodak Pamphlet No. S–22, Motion Picture and Education Markets Division, Eastman Kodak Co., Rochester, N.Y. 14650, 1969, 8 pp. Compares examples of slides which are good in design and legibility with those which are visually poor because of overcrowded content, lettering too small, or because the producer wrongly assumed that legibility on a printed page assures legibility on the screen.

ESPICH, JAMES E., and BILL WILLIAMS. *Developing Programmed Instructional Materials.* Fearon Publishers/Lear Siegler, Inc., 6 Davis Dr., Belmont, Calif. 94002, 1967, 138 pp. Although intended primarily for industry, this little book is one of the most clearly written guides available for the beginning programmer.

GASKILL, ARTHUR L., and DAVID A. ENGLANDER. *How to Shoot a Movie Story*. Morgan & Morgan, Inc., 25 Main St., Hastings-On-Hudson, N.Y. 10706, 1959, 135 pp. Concise treatment of visual continuity as applied to motion picture production.

Handbooks for Teachers, series of 11 titles. Visual Instruction Bureau, University of Texas, Drawer W., University Station, Austin, Texas 78712, revised periodically. Booklets on various production and utilization topics include helpful hints and instructions, illustrations, and lists of sources.

How to Make a Movie Without a Camera (16mm film, 5 min) Rainy Day Films, 18 Avenue 23, Venice, Calif. 90291, 1971. Examples of simple and colorful images produced by drawing, painting, and scratching directly onto motion picture film.

Index to Kodak Technical Information, Kodak Pamphlet No. L–5. Professional, Commercial, and Industrial Markets Division, Eastman Kodak Co., Rochester, N.Y. 14650, revised annually. Lists alphabetically by both subject and by code number hundreds of currently available Kodak publications relating to photography and graphic presentation.

In-Service and Pre-Service Instructional Materials (10 kits including filmstrips, tapes, transparencies and guides). Scott Education Division, Holyoke, Mass. 01040, 1968. Each kit is a self-contained course of instruction in a specific area. Designed for workshops, institutes and in-service training.

KEMP, JERROLD E. *Planning and Producing Audiovisual Materials*, 2nd ed. Science Research Associates, Inc., 259 East Erie Street, Chicago, Ill. 60611, 1968, 252 pp. Comprehensive basic reference to techniques for preparing picture series, slide sets, filmstrips, transparencies, graphics, sound recordings, motion pictures, and television materials.

Glossary, bibliography and source lists for equipment, supplies and services.

Kodak Art Work Template, Kodak Pamphlet No. S–25. Motion Picture and Education Markets Division, Eastman Kodak Co., Rochester, N.Y. 14650, 1966, 8 pp. plus 2 templates. Templates based upon an approximately 6×9-inch picture area show projected areas for single-frame filmstrips, 16mm motion pictures and 35mm slides and give recommended letter heights and line widths for various viewing distances.

Kodak Projection Calculator & Seating Guide. Kodak Publication No. S–16. Motion Picture and Education Markets Division, Eastman Kodak Co., Rochester, N.Y. 14650, 1969, 6 pp. Consists of a table of seating capacities for rooms of various shapes and sizes and a three-part dial calculator interrelating the four key factors of image/screen size, frame size of transparency mask or projector gate, projector distance, and lens focal length.

Let's Make a Film (16mm film, 13 min) Van Nostrand Reinhold Film Library, 450 West 33rd St., New York, N.Y. 10001, 1971. A middle-grades film-making class produces some creative short films using various techniques of live action and animation.

LIDSTONE, JOHN, and DON McINTOSH. *Children as Film Makers*. Van Nostrand Reinhold Co., 450 West 33rd St., New York, N.Y. 10001, 1970, 111 pp. Explains basics of camera operation, editing, splicing, animation, titling, and projection. Suggests ways to guide children in planning and structuring of their films.

MARKLE, SUSAN MEYER. *Good Frames and Bad*, 2nd ed. John Wiley & Sons, Inc., 605 Third Ave., New York, N.Y. 10016, 1969, 308 pp. A short course in programming techniques, with examples of various program formats and types of frames.

MERCER, JOHN. *An Introduction to Cinematography*, Rev. ed., Stipes Publishing Co., 10–12 Chester St., Champaign, Ill. 61820, 1971, 181 pp. Basic facts and technical exercises in motion picture production.

MILLER, THOMAS H., and W. B. BRUMMITT. *This is Photography*. Doubleday & Co., 501 Franklin Ave., Garden City, N.Y. 11530, 1959, 260 pp. An easy-to-follow basic textbook on photography; includes student assignments.

Mimeographing Techniques (16mm film, 16 min) BFA Educational Media, 2211 Michigan Ave., Santa Monica, Calif. 90404, 1958. Demonstrates the process of typing a stencil, making corrections, handlettering with a mimeoscope, and operating an electric mimeograph machine. Discusses purposes and advantages of different duplicating processes.

MINOR, ED, and HARVEY R. FRYE. *Techniques for Producing Visual Instructional Media*. McGraw-Hill Book Co., 1221 Avenue of the Americas, New York, N.Y. 10020, 1970, 305 pp. Comprehensive guide for producers of all types of visual media. Describes and illustrates familiar and practical graphic processes and newer, more complex production techniques. Extensive annotated bibliography and listing of sources for materials and equipment.

Movies and Slides Without a Camera. Kodak Publication No. S–47. Motion Picture and Education Markets Division, Eastman Kodak Co., Rochester, N.Y. 14650, 1971, 8 pp. Describes how to obtain and clear motion picture film and how to create visual effects and sound tracks directly on the film.

Movies With a Purpose. Motion Picture and Education Markets Division., Eastman Kodak Co., Rochester, N.Y. 14650, 1968, 28 pp. Clear and simple introduction to the planning, shooting, and editing of short instructional or informational motion pictures. Emphasizes the importance of logical sequence of action, visual interest, and continuity in films produced on a low budget.

PETZOLD, PAUL. *All-in-One Movie Book.* American Photographic Book Publishing Co., 915 Broadway, New York, N.Y. 10010, 1969, 222 pp. As the title suggests, a handbook of basic movie-making knowledge.

PINCUS, EDWARD. *Guide to Filmmaking.* New American Library, Inc., 1301 Avenue of the Americas, New York, N.Y. 10019, 1969, 256 pp. A comprehensive paperback text covering much technical knowledge needed by the serious filmmaker.

PIPE, PETER. *Practical Programming.* Holt, Rinehart and Winston, Inc., 383 Madison Ave, New York, N.Y. 10017, 1966, 70 pp. This slim volume introduces the reader to the characteristics and preparation of programmed instruction.

Planning and Producing Visual Aids, Kodak Pamphlet No. S–13. Motion Picture and Education Markets Division, Eastman Kodak Co., Rochester, N.Y. 14650, 1969, 16 pp. Describes a "team approach" to the planning and production of audiovisual materials. Offers suggestions on scripting and titling, and describes some simple, but effective photographic techniques used by Kodak's Audiovisual Service.

Producing Slides and Filmstrips, Kodak Publication No. S–8. Motion Picture and Education Markets Division, Eastman Kodak Co., Rochester, N.Y. 14650, 1968, 56 pp. Intended to help the small-scale producer of audiovisual presentations prepare professional quality slide sets and filmstrips with ordinary equipment. Emphasizes the use of the planning board and basic photographic and titling techniques.

Projecting Ideas on the Overhead Projector (16mm film, 17 min) University of Iowa, Audiovisual Center, Iowa City, Iowa 52240, 1960. Shows a variety of uses of the overhead projector with various types of materials.

Projecting Ideas, II: Diazo Transparency Production (16mm film, 11 min) Audiovisual Center, University of Iowa, Iowa City, Iowa 52240, 1964. Demonstrates exposure and development of diazo film and procedure for preparing a transparency.

Projecting Ideas, III: Direct Transparency Production (16mm film, 5 min) Audiovisual Center, University of Iowa, Iowa City, Iowa 52240, 1964. Introduces various techniques and materials for producing hand-drawn transparencies.

Research in Educational Media (overhead transparency set) Audiovisual Center, University of Iowa, Iowa City, Iowa

52240, 1968. Includes such subjects as the importance of size in pictures, display captions, color, type size for overhead transparencies, etc.

RHODE, ROBERT B., and FLOYD H. McCALL. *Introduction to Photography*, 2nd ed. The Macmillan Company, 866 Third Ave., New York, N.Y. 10022, 1971, 264 pp. A comprehensive photography text that goes fairly deeply into the technical aspects.

Self-Instructional Audiovisual Equipment Operation Series (20 titles, 2×2-inch captioned slide sets) Training Services, 8885 West F Ave., Kalamazoo, Mich. 49009, 1965–72. Step-by-step instructions for operating equipment including Seal dry mounting press, WRICO lettering guides, and Thermo-Fax transparency maker.

Simple Camera, The (set of 12 filmstrips or 500 slides, with guides) Eastman Kodak Co., Rochester, N.Y. 14650, 1965. Intended for teachers who know relatively little about photography. Covers basic photographic theory and good picture-taking practices. Each lesson is described in a manual that presents objectives, materials, activities, and assignments for students.

Slides With a Purpose. Motion Picture and Education Markets Division, Eastman Kodak Co., Rochester, N.Y. 14650, 1970, 28 pp. Clear and simple introduction to the planning, shooting, and presentation of instructional slide sequences.

SMALLMAN, KIRK. *Creative Film-Making.* The Macmillan Company, 866 Third Ave., New York, N.Y. 10022, 1969, 245 pp. Concise introduction to the fundamentals of film-making and how they can be employed for personal cinematic expression at little expense.

SUID, MURRAY. *Painting with the Sun.* CSCS, Inc., 60 Commercial Wharf, Boston, Mass. 02110, 1970, 52 pp. A first book of photography for young children, stimulating seeing and providing basic fundamentals through interesting picture assignments.

WARSHAW, MICHAEL and MIMI. *How to Make a Movie Without a Camera.* Rainy Day Films, 18 Avenue 23, Venice, Calif. 90291, 1971, 49 pp. Just about everything you need to know to get your class started on a low-budget, camera-less movie making project. Intended to be used with the demonstration film of the same title.

Young Art, The: Children Make Their Own Films (16mm film, 16 min) Van Nostrand Reinhold Film Library, 450 West 33rd St., New York, N.Y. 10001, 1971. Students of different ages, from early elementary to high school, produce excellent short, animated films during a film-making workshop.

Your Programs from Kodak. Publication No. AT–1. Eastman Kodak Co., Dept. 841, Rochester, N.Y. 14650, revised annually. Describes motion pictures, slide series, and print sets available on loan to teachers and groups. Most materials deal with various aspects of photography.

Anything that *can* go wrong, *will!*

—MURPHY'S LAW

Some remarkable things are happening to the classroom environment in this technologically advanced age, all of which concern the teacher. The symbol of technological change is the *pushbutton*. In some sophisticated classrooms, multi-media presentation classrooms, hidden projectors project on command through rear-projection screens built into walls; the shape of rooms can be altered by moving partitions to new locations, screens can be lowered and raised, and room lighting control systems can be operated, all by pushing buttons or throwing switches. In such classrooms and auditoriums the teacher now has to decide where to stand so as to be near the switches, for instance so that lights may be dimmed during the introduction of a film; then again, when the film is over, so that lights may be brought back gradually to full brightness without eye discomfort. Some classrooms that have been designed for media presentations feature lecterns that pin the teacher down in front of a control panel, and thus the teacher enters a new era of planning where timing, scripting, and programming become crucial.

But some communities have not yet appropriated sufficient money to install enough electrical outlets to permit the use of just one overhead projector in each classroom, to say nothing of installing the sophisticated multi-media presentation room described above. So probably for several years, many teachers will have to continue to use the array of modern media within rather conventional classroom conditions.

Your Responsibility as a Teacher

The teacher is ultimately responsible for the selection and guidance of learning activities. Rather than hide behind the lame excuse, "I dare not deviate from the course of study," the imaginative teacher, the one who finds unique and creative ways to lead students toward achieving valid objectives, is the teacher who earns the respect of students and their parents. Not only that but he also is the teacher who is considered for the new

Figure 9–1. This professor operates several electronically controlled projectors that show their images through a large, rear-projection screen to classes of 300 or more students seated in a large auditorium. Because technicians load, adjust, and maintain the hardware, the instructor himself need not be concerned with the mechanical aspects of equipment operation, but he does have to be a master showman and expert in preparing meaningful audiovisual presentations. Note in the group of pictures the close-up view of the control panel. When these buttons are pushed, films, slides, filmstrips, and television images are projected as needed. Switches to control lights in the auditorium and a volume control for sound level are also located on the instructor's lectern panel. (Courtesy University of Miami, Coral Gables, Fla.)

Fundamentals of Teaching with Audiovisual Technology

Figure 9–2. Should teachers (or students) have to carry heavy equipment up and down stairs and around the building? Many schools make arrangements for screens to be mounted permanently in each classroom and for frequently used equipment to be left set up at each teaching station or stored nearby. What kinds of audiovisual equipment would you use often enough to justify having it permanently assigned to your classroom? (Courtesy The National Education Association. Photo by Joe Di Dio)

supervisory position; the one who receives praise and recognition at community affairs and professional meetings.

Teachers need to keep up to date on new developments in their field and also know which materials and devices are being made available locally for classroom use. The operation and use of all kinds of available projectors, tape recorders, transparency makers, mounting and laminating presses, duplicating machines, and copy cameras should be familiar skills to every teacher. There is no better way to prepare for new methods of the future than by steady growth in the skillful use of tools and methods that are available today. Teachers should accept responsibility for keeping abreast and alert, staying open-minded, and making an effort to try anything and everything available which might provide a better environment for learning.

Teachers may be called upon to actually operate audiovisual equipment in classroom presentation situations, to supervise student operators assigned for this purpose, or to teach their own students how to use simple equipment routinely as they have opportunity to use audiovisual media independently in learning carrels, resource centers, and in the classroom.

Figure 9–3. Teachers are responsible for learning every technique and trying every method available which might provide a better environment for learning. College courses and in-service workshops introduce teachers to audiovisual technology. (Photo by David H. Curl)

Operating Audiovisual Equipment

In this chapter we discuss the operation of basic equipment only. Rather than examining all kinds of hardware, we describe operational principles and procedures in general, supplemented by helpful checklists and illustrations. Most college and university teacher education programs require some laboratory practice with audiovisual equipment before student teaching or before certification. Unfortunately, not enough time is generally available for mastery of the needed skills and besides, prospective teachers often learn to operate one brand of equipment and then find unfamiliar brands in their schools. Teachers who have mastered equipment operation skills to the point of self-confidence, however, seldom find great difficulty in making the transition from one make of equipment to another. When unfamiliar equipment is delivered to the classroom, or when malfunctions occur, it is the timid and unprepared who have trouble. The experienced teacher always takes steps to find out what kinds of teaching tools are available in the school and then arranges for practice sessions with this equipment to gain confidence and efficiency in setting it up and operating it.

In many teacher preparation programs, prospective teachers learn to operate audiovisual equipment by a process of self-instruction. This procedure offers several advantages: Instruction is consistent, while allowing for individual differences in aptitude; equipment inventories can be limited to one item of each type; scheduling conflicts are all but eliminated—students can arrange their own hours; because practice is self-paced and private, no student need feel "forced" into a humiliating mechanical confrontation before others; fewer instructors are needed, and they can use their time for solving problems and working with individuals who need special help.

In a typical self-instructional laboratory, each individual booth or carrel contains one item of equipment or one process to be learned. In each carrel a carefully programmed slide series (or audio tape or display and workbook) breaks down each task into demonstration-practice segments of optimum size and complexity. Film loops may be integrated into some programs to give an overview of an entire process or to demonstrate concepts involving motion. Students ordinarily are free to start any program and to work with each program and the appropriate equipment and materials in any sequence, matching their own actions to those shown in the program, then testing themselves on the correctness of each step as they proceed (see Fig. 3–9).

Individual controls allow students to skip, reverse, and repeat portions of the program as needed and desired. The emphasis should be on confidence with equipment

Figure 9–4. Familiarization with AV equipment. A student teacher sits down in a self-instructional carrel with a formidable-looking 16mm motion picture projector; less than an hour later she is operating it with confidence and is ready to move on to a different type of equipment. Is it better to practice equipment operation by one's self, or with other students? When groups of students work together on equipment, does one person tend to get most of the experience while others watch? (Photo by David H. Curl)

and processes, rather than on strict perfection of the skills themselves. Most prospective teachers learn well in self-instructional labs. They are so motivated by desire to make a good showing in methods classes and student teaching that they often learn the skills sufficiently for transfer just by completing the programs, providing they are allowed to determine their own practice schedules and to set their own pace without close supervision. Perhaps readers of this book will have access to independent learning opportunities. Competence and confidence result from frequent practice.

In the following pages we outline the major steps in operating basic types of audiovisual equipment, concluding with several tips for "good showmanship" when using projected media. Additional practice will be required, preferably in a self-instructional laboratory. We do not offer complete instructions in this chapter—only basic familiarization with each type of equipment. More direct help will be available from your instructor and from the publications and audiovisual materials listed among the references at the end of the chapter.

Filmstrip and Slide Projection

Beginning teachers will be almost certain to find filmstrip or combination filmstrip and 2×2-inch slide projectors available in their schools. Some schools, however, are purchasing automatic projectors that show only 2×2-inch slides. In the combination projector there is usually a basic projector body with two additional interchangeable units; the filmstrip unit and the slide carrier or changer. These projectors are extremely easy to operate, but, nevertheless, teachers must be prepared through practice to handle this mechanical job without clumsiness.

Figure 9–5. Should students be depended on to operate audiovisual equipment, even in large-group situations? How can students gain the necessary skills? Can students be trusted with costly equipment? Would you allow a student to take home a projector or tape recorder? (Courtesy Eastman Kodak Company)

There are many brands and models of projectors, but only a few are shown in the accompanying illustrations. A given school system may, of course, have several different types of projectors available, hence beginning teachers will need to complete their operational practice on the job, with a few sessions in the audiovisual equipment operation laboratory serving as an introduction. This discussion will therefore present some of the critical procedures in preparation for laboratory sessions, for self-study of the projector, and for its actual classroom use. Obtain an actual slide/filmstrip projector upon which you can practice the following operations:

FILMSTRIP PROJECTION

1. Lift the projector out of its case, plug the power cord into a wall outlet or a heavy-duty extension cord, and point the projector at the screen. If it is a separate accessory, make sure that the filmstrip unit is inserted properly, turn on the light and blower switches, and then do these three things:
   (*a*) Focus the field of light by turning the lens one way or the other until the edges of the light field are sharp.
   (*b*) Center the projected light field on the screen.
   (*c*) Make sure that the field of light is even and bright. If there are dark or bright areas, or if there are dark streaks present, report it and ask that service technicians make the needed adjustments, immediately or later.
2. Take the filmstrip out of its container. If it is a single-frame filmstrip each frame is smaller than the picture area in a 2×2-inch slide; precisely, the dimensions are 17mm by 23mm according to ASA standards. Grasp the beginning of the filmstrip and

unroll the strip to reveal the title or focus frame right side up (readable). Now rotate the title (and the whole filmstrip of course) clockwise to the 6 o'clock position as you face the screen, and insert it into the filmstrip slot. So as not to buckle the leading part of the strip, push the film gently through to the teeth of the sprocket. Engage the film cautiously, making sure sprocket teeth are seated in the film perforations, and advance the filmstrip until the focus or title frame is reached. Locate the framing lever or knob and move it one way or the other until one complete picture frame only is projected on the screen.

3. If the filmstrip is of the long-picture type (double frame, 23mm by 34mm according to the ASA standards), and if your projector accepts this format, remove the single-frame mask from the filmstrip unit, thus adjusting the aperture size to project the larger picture area. Now find out if the pictures run vertically or horizontally. If the latter, rotate the front portion of the projector 90 degrees, after inserting the filmstrip. Insert properly as in Step 2. Double-frame filmstrips advance in two turns of the knob instead of one as for single-frame strips.

Figure 9–6. Automatic, remote control slide projectors simplify the use of visuals in group presentations as well as independent study. Did you know there are eight ways to insert a slide into the projector tray, only one of which will result in right-side-up and right-way-round projection of the image on the screen? Can you tell how a slide should be placed into the tray by examining the slide? (Courtesy Eastman Kodak Company)

4. Focus sharply by turning the lens. Test the focus by going past the sharpest point, then return through "dead-center" focus in the opposite direction. Now return to the sharpest possible image. This exploration of focus gives a chance to see how sharp the focus can be.

5. Move the projector and its stand or cart backward or forward to obtain the optimum size of the projected picture image.

2 × 2-INCH SLIDE PROJECTION

1. Set up the projector on its stand and proceed as with the filmstrip operation, except as follows: Prepare the projector to receive slides by removing the filmstrip unit and inserting the slide carrier or tray as needed.

2. There are *eight* ways to insert a slide into the projector or slide tray; only *one* way is correct: Select a slide and hold it up to the light, so that it can be read directly. The emulsion (dull) side of the film (usually the printed side of the slide mount) should face *toward the screen*. Now rotate the slide clockwise to an upside-down position. Insert the slide into the carrier or tray and advance it into projection position.

3. Focus, using the same procedure as for filmstrips.

4. Move the projector toward or away from the screen until the optimum size of picture image is obtained. If available, a "zoom" lens or projection lenses of different focal lengths (longer focal length for a smaller image, shorter focal length for a larger image) may be interchanged to vary picture size without moving the projector.

5. Sometimes, vertically oriented slides give trouble. Unless the projection screen is square and mounted so that the bottom is at least four feet above the floor, shadows of viewers' heads may appear at the bottom of the image, or the top of the image may spill over beyond the top of the screen. The solution, of course, is to move the projector closer to the screen or obtain either a longer focal length lens or a larger screen.

6. Some slide changers are of the so-called semi-automatic type, some ejecting and stacking slides; and there are many manual and automatic projectors on the market that employ a variety of slide magazines or trays holding large numbers of slides. Each of these projectors has unique, although similar operating features that may include remote-control slide advance and reverse, remote focusing (or even automatic focusing), automatic interval timer, filmstrip adapter, tachistoscope attachment, or other varia-

tions. Teachers should find out which of these special types of slide projectors are available and be sure not to be confused by differences between makes.

Although producers are releasing many timely new filmstrips with accompanying sound tracks, schools do not always have projectors available that synchronize the record or tape cassette sound with the filmstrip frame changes. But these sound filmstrips can be shown with a regular filmstrip projector and conventional phonograph or tape player. The best way to insure synchronization between sound and picture is to follow a cued script, when one is available. Otherwise it will be necessary to determine precisely how the opening music and narration fit among the beginning frames and to determine also the kind of "beep" or other signal that calls for change to the next frame. Once this information is known the presentation can be started in proper synchronization, and kept "in sync" so long as some cues are not missed. If a mix-up does occur, and the content is unfamiliar,

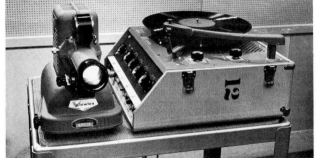

Figure 9–7. Sound filmstrips may be accompanied either by disc or taped sound tracks. Some schools are equipped with special combination projectors in which disc or tape cassette playback units are built into the projector. If equipment of this type is not available, sound film-strips can be presented manually simply by setting up projector and audio play-back unit side-by-side. Frames must be kept in synchronization by listening for recorded "beep" tones, preferably while following the narration on a copy of the script. (Courtesy Viewlex, Inc. and The University of Connecticut)

Operating Audiovisual Equipment

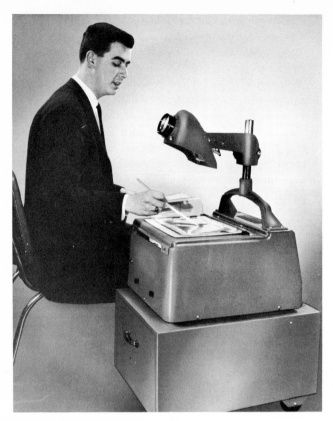

Figure 9–8. A low stand permits the overhead projector to be used from a comfortable, seated position, affording an unobstructed view of the screen from all parts of the classroom if the bottom of the screen is at least four feet above the floor. Do you know how to make focusing, elevation, and image-size adjustments with the different brands of overhead projectors available in your school? (Courtesy Tecnifax Corporation)

there is little to do except repeat portions of the program in an attempt to match picture and sound, or to go back to the beginning and start again.

Overhead Projection

There are several kinds of overhead transparency projectors now available; some are portable, lightweight models and others, intended mainly for auditorium use, are large and bulky to handle, although desirably rugged in construction. All the larger projectors should be placed on their own mobile stands and wheeled from room to room or assigned permanently to those teachers who use them frequently. The overhead normally should be placed on a low stand (16 inches is a good height), so the teacher can use it conveniently while seated. Some overheads have unique features such as automatic lamp switch, automatic fan shut-off, polarizing motion attachments, or adapters for showing $3\frac{1}{4} \times 4$-inch lantern slides, but all types may be operated easily and successfully with practice. Obtain an overhead projector and proceed as follows:

1. Place the projector at the front of the room and center it with the projection screen. Make sure the head of the projector is in proper position. In studying these steps, refer to Figure 9–8 through 9–11.

Figure 9–9. When using an overhead projector, if the screen is placed high enough so that everyone in the class can see the entire image, the projected image is likely to be distorted by keystoning. This problem can be avoided only by ensuring that the projector lens is at a 90° angle to the surface of the screen. If the screen is mounted so the top can be tilted toward the projector, keystoning can be corrected.

2. Plug the power cord into a wall outlet or heavy-duty extension cord, then turn on the lamp switch. (This switch also usually turns on the cooling fan.)
3. Now tilt the machine by the knobs or screws provided to position the field of light on the screen. Some projectors do not have elevating legs; instead they provide a tilting head. The main idea here is to tilt either the machine itself or the movable part of the machine, as the case may be. The head is tilted either by moving the entire head on its mounting bar, or by turning a knob at the rear of the head to move an interior mirror. Move the projector closer or farther away to adjust the size of the image on the screen.
4. Focus the edge of the projected light field by raising

Figure 9–10. How was keystone distortion eliminated in this projection situation? Notice the way in which the screen is suspended from the ceiling and mounted so the angle can be adjusted. (Courtesy Board of Education, Greenwich, Conn.)

Operating Audiovisual Equipment

or lowering the projection head (the part holding objective lenses and mirrors).

5. Place a transparency on the projection stage face up as you face the stage of the projector, check the sharpness of the focus, and adjust the size of the projected image.

6. Make sure that the transparency frame is properly positioned on the projection stage in a fixed place; otherwise the projected image will not be properly located on the screen. If the projector is tilted, then adjust the horizontal and vertical mounting frame guides. If transparency guides are lacking, tape two strips of cardboard to the top of the projector as shown in Figure 9–11. The cardboard guides will position each transparency correctly on the projection stage and consequently the image will be straight and level on the screen.

7. Adjust the positioning of horizontal and vertical frame guides on the projector to accept both vertically and horizontally oriented transparencies. A vertical transparency demands a square screen, and one that is mounted higher on the wall, for the bottom of a projected vertical picture is lower than that of a horizontal projection. Therefore in many situations a horizontally oriented transparency is best. Sometimes a compromise may have to be made as to how much of a vertical transparency needs to be sacrificed at the top so that students can read material at the bottom.

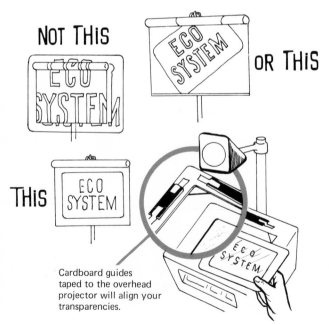

Cardboard guides taped to the overhead projector will align your transparencies.

Figure 9–11. Set up the projector in advance and have it the right distance from the screen so the image fits the screen and is straight and level. Cardboard guides can be taped to the stage of an overhead projector not provided with locating pins or stops.

Fundamentals of Teaching with Audiovisual Technology

Opaque Projection   The old, familiar opaque projector that projects an image by light reflected internally has been improved gradually over the years. Nevertheless, these projectors are still bulky and large, rather noisy, and require a fairly dark room because of their relatively low light output. Despite its limitations, however, the opaque is the fastest way of getting an image of something up to about 10 × 10-inches on the screen. Unless a transparency maker or 35mm slide-copy camera is available, it may be the only way of projecting illustrations from books, postcards, small specimens, students' papers, and so on. The opaque still finds use in schools that provide slide and transparency production equipment, however, primarily because of its convenience for projection tracing—enlarging of maps, diagrams, and other pictures by tracing around the projected image onto the chalkboard or poster paper. Obtain an opaque projector and proceed as follows:

1. Position the projector approximately 12 feet from the screen. Plug the projector cord into a wall outlet or heavy-duty extension cord.
2. Darken the room; otherwise projected images will not be of optimum brightness.
3. Turn the lamp switch on.
4. Insert a picture or a white paper into the left side of the projector and turn the roll-feeder crank until the image is positioned on the screen. Focus the picture by turning the knob that moves the lens back and forth. Materials may also be placed in the projector by lowering the projection platen. When this is done, the brightness of the light may cause extreme discomfort to pupils sitting in back of or to the side of the projector. *Therefore, turn the lamp off before lowering the platen.*
5. Raise the front of the projector by loosening the holding devices and then guide the projector upward until the picture is centered on the screen.
6. Increase or decrease the size of the projected image as needed, by moving the projector farther away from or closer to the screen.
7. Make sure the projector does not block your students' view!
8. Insert materials while you are standing or sitting to the rear of the projector, facing the screen. In every case the material, for example, a picture, should be placed into the projector so that the *bottom of the picture is toward the screen.*
9. To improve the overall focus when projecting a book, cover the book with a piece of plate glass; otherwise the center of a book may not be in the same focus as the outside edges of the pages.
10. When viewing one or more thick objects, such as

crystals, the objects may have to be focused in planes, that is, one level at a time. A few trials will have to be made to discover which focus adjustment is best.

11. Locate the pointer on your projector. It is usually operated by turning a knob or moving a lever back and forth.

The Tape Recorder

Cassette tape recorders are simple to operate and once teachers familiarize themselves with the nature of a basic tape recorder they can operate almost any of the regular reel-to-reel type classroom models after a few minutes of study and practice. All such machines have similar controls even though they are located in different places and operated somewhat differently on various models. A teacher (or a student) must carry out a definite pattern of operations to record, and another set of operations to play a prerecorded tape or to play back what has just been recorded. Let us look at the two processes separately and treat the processes in general so that they may be applied to almost any one of the many models of classroom-type tape recorders. Have an actual tape recorder at hand while you practice the generalized recording and playback procedures described below:

TO RECORD

1. Plug in the power cord and turn on the machine.
2. Set the speed selector switch to the desired speed (faster speeds are better for music, slower speeds for tape economy).
3. Thread the tape into the head slot, past the capstan, past the automatic shut-off pin, if there is one, and attach it to the empty take-up reel. (If using a cassette, merely place it over the spindles with the open edge toward you and press it down until it "clicks.")
4. Plug the microphone directly into the input jack of the recorder, or into the microphone mixer if musical background is to be added.
5. Test the microphone by speaking into it and at the same time observe the level indicator (a flashing light or a VU meter), adjusting the level by turning the volume control. Good voice recording generally demands a short distance from mouth to microphone—try six to 12 inches. (Note: some tape recorders must be operating in *record* mode to make this test (see step 6).
6. Depress the recording lock and depress the *record* key or button to start the machine, adjust the volume control to the predetermined setting, and begin the recording.

Figure 9–12. *Nearly all tape recorders have similar functions, although the controls may be different—some machines have push-buttons, while others use knobs or levers. While cassette recorders are more compact, their controls operate like reel-to-reel machines. (Photo by David H. Curl)*

7. After completing the recording, turn the volume level to zero and then depress the *stop* key.
8. Disconnect the microphone from the input jack.
9. Rewind the tape.

TO PLAY BACK

1. Turn on the machine.
2. Thread the tape or insert the cassette as for recording.
3. Be sure the tape is compatible if not recorded on the same machine (some stereo tapes will not play back satisfactorily on monaural machines and vice versa).
4. Determine the speed in inches per second at which the tape was recorded. Set the speed selector at the same speed.
5. Depress the *play* key and turn up the volume to the optimum level, whether listening through the speaker or through headphones. (Headphones are plugged into the extension speaker jack.)
6. Depress the *stop* key when finished listening.
7. Rewind the tape onto its original reel.

By looking at the preceding list of tape recording and playback operations it is obvious that teachers need to know the location and function of each of the following connections and controls: (find them on the tape recorder you are using) the *on-and-off* switch, *feed* spindle, *take-up* spindle, *record* key, *play* key, *stop* key, *rewind* control, *fast forward* control, *automatic shut-off* pin, *volume* control, *tone* control, *speed selector* switch, *input* jack(s), and

Figure 9–13. The Bell & Howell Model 552 Autoload is one of the new semi-automatic motion picture projectors which eliminate tedious hand-threading of the film. While some models of self-threading projectors are more difficult to manually thread and unthread when it is desired to show only a portion of a film, they save time and often prevent film damage when used by less experienced operators. The simple steps to thread this projector are shown in Figure 9–14. (Courtesy Bell & Howell Company)

output jack(s). This list may seem like a long one to remember, but most elementary school students can learn to identify and use these basic tape-recorder controls. A demonstration or examination of the instruction manual or self-instructional program, plus a little practice are all that is needed for anyone to be reasonably self-sufficient and confident with tape recorders. Be sure to see the specific teaching practices for audio recordings listed in Chapter 5 and the descriptions of tape recording techniques and special adaptations of audio equipment in Chapter 8.

Motion Picture Projection

Some motion picture projectors encountered by teachers will be old and relatively complex; others will be new types that are much easier to operate. Some machines require the film to be threaded carefully over several sprockets, rollers, and guides. Others are almost unbelievably simple, the film merely being inserted into a slot. But since it probably will be many years before all the manually threaded projectors are out of circulation (some people prefer them), teachers should prepare themselves to operate all types. Despite their formidable appearance, motion picture projectors of all types are easy to operate. Enough courage and skill to operate even the most complex models can be gained in less than an hour of learning time, but a lot more practice time is needed, of course, to develop speed and unhesitating confidence. One needs to use a process often to gain dexterity and frequent use of equipment is the solution to this problem. Use films often in the classroom, and if you feel your skills getting rusty, stop by and practice on a preview projector at the instructional media center. Ask that a threading diagram and a reel of practice film be kept available for teachers to use.

Each stage in the operation of a motion picture projector will be described separately in this chapter, concluding with a master checklist for your reference. Remember, however, that you can hardly be expected to master the operation of a complex machine by reading about it in this, or any other book. The following paragraphs are intended as introductory background for intensive, guided, hands-on experience with the types of projectors available for your use. As you work through the various steps described, study the illustrations to identify in several models some of the features and control mechanisms common to all motion picture projectors.

SETTING UP
THE PROJECTOR

1. Place the projector on its stand or cart at the rear of the classroom and point the front of the projector toward the screen in such a way that an imaginary line from the front of the projector to the screen would be perpendicular to it. Some screens are in corners; others are at the center of a room or a little to the right or left of the center. (Note: If *rear screen projection* is used, the projector will have to be at the front of the room, behind the screen, or at the side, projecting the image to a mirror first and then through the screen.)

2. Remove the cover (if the projector is encased when picked up or delivered), and proceed to move the feed and take-up arms into their proper positions, or insert them in their receptacles as required. Then make sure that if there are any drive belts, they are around the pulleys and in their grooves properly.

3. Plug the power cord into a wall outlet or a heavy-duty extension cord, then turn on the motor switch. Next, turn on the lamp switch and then the amplifier switch (but make sure volume has been turned down), to check that motor, lamp, and amplifier are ready for projection. While carrying out other procedures turn off the lamp and motor but leave the amplifier switch on.

4. If the loudspeaker is in a separate case, place it on a table at the front of the room, the projector at the rear of the room. Many projectors have loudspeaker systems built into the projector case for convenient sound distribution in normal size classrooms. External speaker output jacks are available on these projectors for connecting to separate loud-

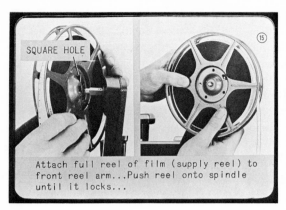

(15)

SQUARE HOLE

Attach full reel of film (supply reel) to front reel arm...Push reel onto spindle until it locks...

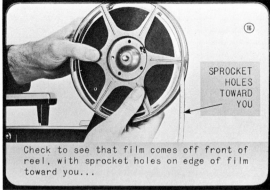

(16)

SPROCKET HOLES TOWARD YOU

Check to see that film comes off front of reel, with sprocket holes on edge of film toward you...

(17)

Attach empty take-up reel to rear reel arm. (Be sure it locks onto spindle)...

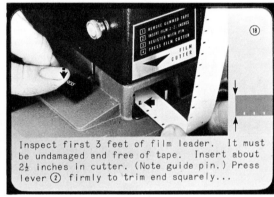

(18)

Inspect first 3 feet of film leader. It must be undamaged and free of tape. Insert about 2½ inches in cutter. (Note guide pin.) Press lever ② firmly to trim end squarely...

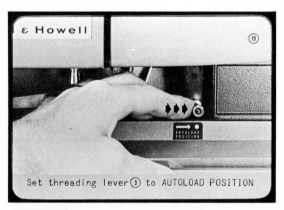

(19)

Set threading lever③ to AUTOLOAD POSITION

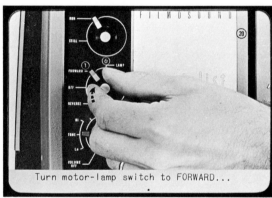

(20)

Turn motor-lamp switch to FORWARD...

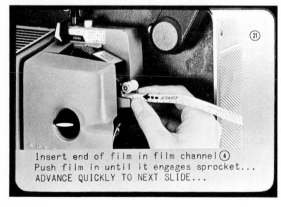

(21)

Insert end of film in film channel④ Push film in until it engages sprocket... ADVANCE QUICKLY TO NEXT SLIDE...

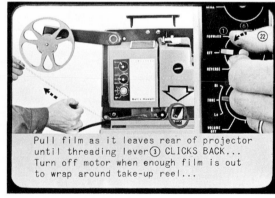

(22)

Pull film as it leaves rear of projector until threading lever③ CLICKS BACK... Turn off motor when enough film is out to wrap around take-up reel...

Place film around snubber roller ⑤
(See diagram on projector)...

Secure end of film leader in slot in
take-up reel...

Figure 9–14. These ten frames from a self-instructional slide program on operating the Bell & Howell 552 Autoload projector depict the simple threading process. Are the reels attached in the same manner as for manual-threading models? Why is it essential to trim the end of the film leader? Do you know what happens if the threading lever (Frame 19) is not pushed forward before threading? What happens if this lever is not released (Frame 22) by pulling on the film after it has been threaded? (From Bell & Howell 552 Autoload Motion Picture Projector, *courtesy Training Services)*

speakers located at the front of classrooms and auditoriums, or other large instructional spaces. There is little doubt that front-of-room locations for loudspeakers are ideal, but convenience must also be considered. For many purposes the rear-of-room method of distributing sound is satisfactory. Connect the loudspeaker cable to the speaker case, if it is separate, and then connect it to the projector sound-output jack.

5. By now, the amplifier has been on for a few minutes and is warmed up, so you can turn up the volume control and listen for the speaker "hiss"—the characteristic sound a speaker makes when amplifier volume is turned up. If the speaker emits no noise whatever at a high-volume setting, check to see if the exciter lamp is on and if the cable connections are tight and inserted properly. Projectors with "instant on" transistorized amplifiers may have to be running to test the sound system.

6. Select a take-up reel of the proper size and check to see that it is not bent. Then push it onto the take-up arm spindle. Make sure it goes on as far as is necessary to be locked in place securely. If the projector has a clutch on the take-up arm, check to see that it is in position to drive the reel in the take-up direction (clockwise).

7. Now turn on the motor and lamp switches again and center the projected light field on the screen. Focus on the edges of the light field, and check to see that the field of light is even. If there are streaks in it, serious enough to warrant it, report it after the showing. After having ascertained that all is in readiness, turn off the lamp and motor switches. A common error made by operators is to thread the film first, and then start the showing without the picture being in focus and properly centered on the screen. Usually, before the needed adjustments can

be made, the title and even the opening footage and sound will have passed.

8. Set tone control knob on *medium* to *medium high* for more intelligible sound. Adjust it later during operation if necessary.

The second stage in conventional classroom motion picture projector operation is the threading process. This is important not only because of its bearing on the smoothness of the presentation, but also because this is precisely the point where, through carelessness, irreparable damage may be done to the film itself. Of course damaged film footage can be replaced through purchasing channels, but this takes weeks and sometimes months. The really serious result of such action is the inconvenience and disappointment caused other teachers who had counted on and contracted for the use of the same film at later dates. Hence every teacher should take all necessary precautions during this stage of projector operation to fulfill the obligation of being extremely considerate of colleagues in their own and other schools. In the illustrations a number of threading diagrams are shown so you can examine the ways in which they differ. The following general suggestions will facilitate such study, will speed the learning process in the laboratory or classroom, will help prevent film damage, and will raise the level of showmanship in the handling of film-viewing activities by pupils. The operations in the second stage follow. Refer to Figures 9–15, 9–16, 9–17, 9–18, and 9–19.

1. Be sure that the film is ready to thread by noting that (*a*) the head of the film is at the beginning with title of film and/or the title leader readable, by unwinding three or four feet of film; (*b*) the square spindle hole in the reel is on the side of the reel away from the operator when the loose end of the film is pulled off the top of the reel to the right; and (*c*) the sprocket holes in the film are on the edge of the film nearest the operator when the film is in threading position.
2. Now push the reel, with the film being pulled off the top of the reel to the right, onto the spindle of the feed arm. Rotate the reel a little to the right or left until the edges of the square hole on the reel fit the edges of the spindle. Make sure the reel is pushed onto the spindle and securely locked in place.
3. Then draw off four or five feet of film from the reel and let it hang down in front of the projector (the reel should rotate in a clockwise direction). Open the sprocket shoes in preparation for threading. Now

THREADING THE MOTION PICTURE PROJECTOR

A

C

FILM LOOP
(ABOUT TWO FINGERS WIDE)

FILM MUST FEED
FROM FRONT OF REEL

IMPORTANT
FILM MUST BE SNUG
AROUND SOUND DRUM
OR SOUND WILL BE
"MUSHY"

FILM TAKE-UP MUST
BE FROM BOTTOM

AUTOMATIC
LOWER
LOOP
RESTORER

B

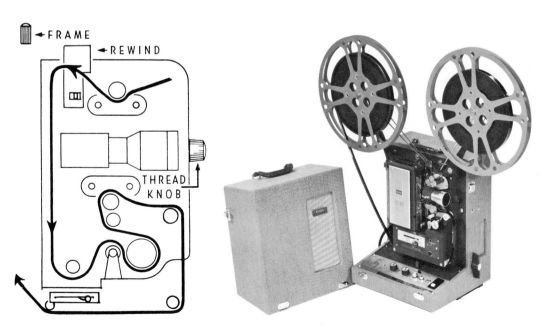

FRAME

REWIND

THREAD
KNOB

Figure 9–17 (A and B) The Graflex Insta-Load 16 projector is threaded something like a tape recorder—the film being laid into a series of slots instead of being threaded onto sprockets. (C and D) Graflex Series 800 and 900 projectors retain two manually threaded sprockets, but the film is merely placed into a slot to be threaded over the sound drum. (Courtesy Graflex Division, Singer Education and Training Products)

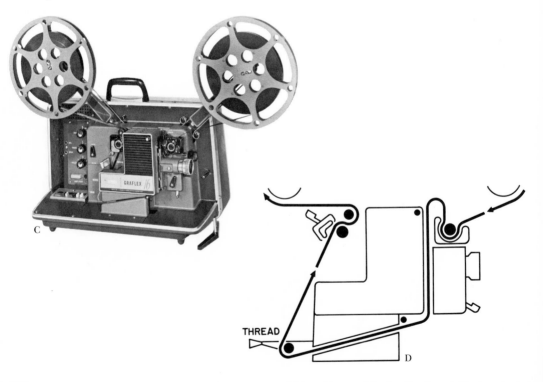

A

B

C

THREAD

D

Figure 9–18. The Viewlex 1600 motion picture projector may be threaded manually or semi-automatically, with an optional "self-threader" accessory. (Courtesy Viewlex, Inc.)

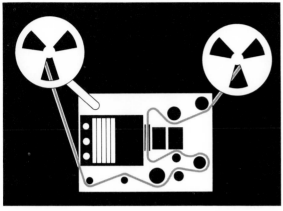

[BELOW] *Figure 9–19. This Kalart-Victor Series 75 motion picture projector differs from other popular makes in that the feed, or supply, reel is at the left and the take-up reel is at the right. Note, however, that the film comes off the top of the supply reel, toward the right, as usual, and that both reels rotate in the customary clockwise direction. The speaker is built into the case cover and must be detached from the projector. (Courtesy Kalart Victor Corporation)*

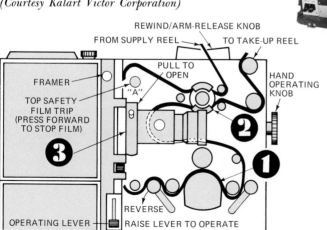

REWIND/ARM-RELEASE KNOB

FROM SUPPLY REEL   TO TAKE-UP REEL

PULL TO
OPEN

FRAMER

"A"

HAND
OPERATING
KNOB

TOP SAFETY
FILM TRIP
(PRESS FORWARD
TO STOP FILM)

2

3

1

OPERATING LEVER

REVERSE
RAISE LEVER TO OPERATE

Operating Audiovisual Equipment

grasp the film near the front of the projector and begin threading, closing the first sprocket shoe after making sure that the sprocket teeth are fitted into the perforations in the film. Be critical at this point. Look sharply, and then gently move the film back and forth to feel that it is properly engaged. (Note: Self-threading projectors call for an entirely different procedure. See Figure 9–14.)

4. Insert or lay the film in the channel behind the lens. Press the film gently just above and below the film gate simultaneously to see that it is deeply seated in the groove.

5. Close the lens, but make sure that when the film gate closes, the pressure plate fits perfectly flat over the film. This is another crucial check point that is essential in preventing film damage. A visual test must be made here as fingers will not be able to reach in and feel this plate.

6. Now complete threading around the remaining sprockets and sound drum, forming loops as recommended in the threading diagrams. The film must fit tightly around the sound drum, and this is another crucial check point as loose film here will result in garbled sound.

7. Now insert the tip of the film past the rim of the take-up reel with one hand and grasp the inserted tip with the other, pushing it then into the slot in the reel hub. Next rotate the reel clockwise two or three turns until the slack is taken up and the end of the film cannot be pulled out of the slot.

8. If the projector is so equipped, turn the knob that advances the film in the projector mechanism by hand. This manual test of the threading should be carried out if possible as a safeguard against film damage. If the film loops remain correct, if the take-up reel does take up the film, and the film remains tight around the sound drum, the projector is ready to be started. (*Note* If your projector does not have a manual control, start the projector for a few seconds to check loops and the sound drum. If time permits, the focus can be checked, after which the projector can be reversed to the desired frame.) The projector is now ready to start.

SHOWING THE FILM

1. When there is time to set up and thread the projector before the viewing group arrives, the film is started merely by turning on the motor and lamp switches. After a proper amplifier warm-up period, focus the picture sharply, check the sound, then stop the projector, and reverse the film to the desired starting point, perhaps the first pictorial frame instead of the

title. Then the projector is ready for action at the flick of a switch.

2. When the projector has no reverse switch, the action in Step 1 is not easy to carry out, therefore proceed as follows: (a) Turn on the lamp and motor, after amplifier warm up, and (b) be ready for immediate action with right and left hands. With the right hand adjust the focus finely, and, simultaneously, with the left hand turn up the sound. Make adjustments in tone and volume as soon as the presentation is under way.

3. As the showing progresses, listen for unusual noises. If you suspect the film is being damaged, pinch the film very lightly between your thumb and forefinger at a point between the projector and the point where the film goes onto the take-up reel to feel if the sprocket holes are being damaged by the sprockets or pull-down claws. As the film passes between your thumb and finger, roughness may be felt if the perforations are being torn or enlarged. This is a worthwhile test to make intermittently as it allows the discovery of damage in time to prevent an entire film from being ruined.

4. When the projected image is out of frame on the screen, that is, when a narrow strip of an adjoining frame is noticeable, turn the framing screw one way or the other until the strip disappears.

5. If the projector is so equipped, the film may be stopped to examine a single frame. In this case, a perforated fire screen drops down to prevent that particular frame from burning up because of the cessation of film motion. Of course, the resulting still picture will not be as bright. Be ready to refocus the picture, and then to refocus again as soon as forward motion is resumed. When some projectors are stopped, the shutter may stop in such a way that the picture does not show, in which case the manual test knob will have to be turned to let the light through to the screen.

6. As the film nears its end, be ready to turn the lamp switch off before the end title leaves the screen; the volume switch is then also turned down to prevent noise from emanating from the loudspeaker. The motor switch may then be turned off or the film may be allowed to run through onto the take-up reel, depending on the plans of the teacher. A teacher may call for lights to be turned on, and then may wish to start discussion or other activity at once, planning to run the balance of the film footage onto the take-up reel, or to disengage it and rewind it a little later.

7. If it is desired to re-examine a film sequence immediately, and the projector is equipped with a reversing feature, the projector may be stopped and reversed to the desired spot, then stopped, restarted, and rerun. Turn down the sound volume while the film is running backward.

8. If the film should break, stop the projector as soon as possible and rethread it. Run off a few feet of film. Pick up the broken end from the take-up reel and slip the portion coming from the projector under it for about a foot, and then hold the sections together and rotate the reel three or four turns to bind the loose ends of film together firmly. Run off a little more film if needed. Make sure that the film will not slip out of the take-up reel when the projector is restarted. Now continue the showing. If possible, mark the spot where the break occurred with a strip of paper. For a temporary film repair a piece of masking tape may be used, but do not use ordinary transparent tape since it may be overlooked by film inspectors. Never use pins, clips, or staples to repair a broken film.

9. If the film loop is lost, that is, when pictures slide by in a rapid fluttering action on the screen, you may, if the projector is so equipped, reset the loop by a special loop-setting lever while the projector is running. In other cases the projector must be stopped, the loop readjusted by rethreading, and then the projector started up to resume the showing.

10. As soon as you start the projector make sure that the take-up reel is winding up the film properly. Also check the clutch position and belts, and if necessary use your finger to put extra pressure on the action of the take-up reel. Report faulty operation at once to the media center.

The last stage of classroom operation of a motion picture projector is rewinding and packing. Each school or school system will probably have an established policy about this phase of operation. In some cases teachers may have permission to leave the projector just as it was at the end of the showing, knowing that the equipment will be picked up after class. In other cases the teachers may be asked to cooperate by rewinding the film, packing up the projector in its case, and returning it in person or by messenger to the media center within agreed time limits.

REWINDING AND PACKING

1. The main job to be done in rewinding is simply to wind the film from the take-up reel back onto

the feed reel the way it came off during projection. It is easy to do this, yet mistakes are made when confusion arises, when belts are to be twisted, shifted, or removed from pulleys, and when film reels are to be shifted from rear to front spindles, depending on which projector is being used. Therefore, find out what the specific process is for your projector, or do not rewind the film at all. Fortunately, newer projector models use easier, more foolproof procedures.

2. Find out what the rewinding policy is at your school. Some film libraries do not want films to be rewound, so follow instructions to minimize inconvenience for others.

3. Take precautions to prevent injury to hands and fingers during the rewinding process. If it is desirable to slow down the speed of moving reels, press the palm of your hand against the side of the feed reel near the rim and exert a little pressure. Keep fingers pointing outward and away from the spokes of the reel. Put pressure only on the reel from which the film is being drawn. Let the reel that is winding up the film run under full power so that the film will wind up snugly.

4. Fasten down the end of the rewound film with a small piece of masking tape and double over the end of the tape to make a tab for easier removal.

5. Now ask a student to help you by winding up the cords. Clean dirt from cords with a paper towel, if handy, or even use a piece of waste-paper. Put cords in their proper places in the case.

6. Remove or fold up the reel arms, if asked to do so, lock the projector case cover in place, and prepare to return the projector or have it picked up, as called for by established procedure.

MASTER CHECKLIST FOR FILM PROJECTIONISTS

Review the following master checklist summarizing the steps already described in detail by way of introduction to the discussion of "good showmanship" which follows. Refer also to specific teaching practices in Chapter 5.

Before Class Begins

1. Place projector toward rear of room on firm stand or movable cart, approximately 42 inches high.

2. Position screen for best visibility. Arrange a center aisle between screen and projector, or raise screen high enough so that persons in rear of room can see over heads of those in front.

3. If speaker is detachable, place it on table near screen or in a front corner of room.

4. Connect power and speaker cables.

5. Place cables and extension cords where they will

Operating Audiovisual Equipment

not be stepped on or tripped over. Tape cables to floor if they must cross aisles or doorways.

6. Turn on projector lamp; roughly pre-focus edges of light beam, then adjust the elevation and projector-to-screen distance to fill screen. Turn off lamp.
7. Turn on amplifier and turn up volume control. A steady hum indicates proper operation (most newer projectors must be running to make this test). Turn down volume control setting.
8. Clean film gate on projector with brush or soft cloth.
9. Thread film carefully, following instructions supplied by projector manufacturer.
10. Test film by running first few feet with projector lamp on; correct focus and framing, and adjust sound volume and tone.
11. Reverse film to beginning titles, or rethread if projector does not reverse.
12. Double-check all control settings.

[OPPOSITE] *Figure 9–20. The best viewing area lies generally within a triangular area no more than 45° on each side of the projection axis. Ordinarily, no viewers should be seated closer to the screen than two picture-widths, nor farther away from the screen than about six picture-widths.*

During Showing

1. Switch motor on first, then turn on lamp after all leader has passed film gate.
2. Stay with projector, adjusting focus, framing, volume, and tone as needed. Be alert for unusual noises or roughness in film; be ready to stop if necessary.
3. Fade down sound volume and turn off lamp at the end of film showing.

After Class Is Over

1. Rewind film (if specified).
2. Pack up and return equipment and film to media center.

Hints for Good Showmanship

With all types of projected media, you owe it to your audience to show them an image that is big and bright and free from distortion. Apply the following hints:

SEATING AREA

Each person in the audience requires about six square feet of space within the "good" seating area. An accepted rule of thumb is that no one should be seated closer to the screen than two picture-widths, nor farther away from the screen than about six picture-widths. Another rule, when a matte-surfaced or lenticular screen is used, is that the best seats are within a triangular area no more than 45 degrees on either side of the projection axis, as shown in Figure 9–20; viewers sitting at greater angles from the screen than 45 degrees may find the distortion unacceptable. When a beaded screen must be used, the useful angle of view may be cut in half, because on some beaded surfaces the projected image falls off rapidly in brightness as viewers move toward the sides of the room.

SCREENS   *Matte screens* have a nonglossy, white surface that diffuses light evenly in all directions, in most cases reflecting about 85 per cent of the light from the projector, regardless of the angle from which the picture is viewed. Matte screens are standard for use with high-wattage overhead projectors and in wide, shallow rooms, in which viewers may be seated at extreme angles. Their smooth surface makes them most suitable when fine detail appears in the material to be projected and when viewers must sit close to the screen. A wall or piece of building-board painted flat white will serve as a makeshift matte screen, as will a white vinyl window shade of the proper size.

Beaded screens work like reflective highway signs. Thousands of tiny glass beads imbedded in the surface reflect all the light that strikes the screen directly back in the direction from which the light came. As a result, viewers seated near the projector beam see a very bright image, but the brilliance falls off rapidly to the sides. At an angle of about 22 degrees from the projection axis the brightness is about equal to a matte screen; at the sides of the room the image may be unacceptably dim. Beaded screens are ideal for long, narrow rooms with good light control.

Lenticular screens may be identified by their distinctive pattern of ribs, squares, or diamond-shaped areas; also, many lenticular surfaces have a silvery metallic appear-

ance. Because of the shape of the reflecting surfaces embossed into the screen fabric, these screens reflect nearly all the light from the projector, concentrating it into the normal viewing angle. Lenticular screens are especially suitable where a wide viewing angle is required and where there may be a considerable amount of ambient light.

All screen surfaces require shielding from extraneous light if the projected image is to show good contrast and rich tone. When severe light problems exist, placing the screen in a corner of the room nearest the windows and facing away from the windows may improve the image some, as will a shadow box built around the screen. When possible, a higher wattage projection lamp, Xenon arc, or other high brightness light source will brighten the picture.

Severe Lighting Problems

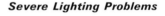

Figure 9–22. Projected images are very bright at close distances, so a small screen can be used satisfactorily even in a brightly lighted room if the surface is shielded from direct light. The inside of the case cover of this super 8 projector makes a suitable screen for individual or small-group viewing. (Courtesy Eastman Kodak Company)

Figure 9–23. Are there times when it would be desirable to project visuals without darkening the room? A curved, aluminized screen is one solution; but as with all screens, the surface should be turned away from windows as much as possible or shaded from the brightest sources of extraneous light if the projected image is to show the best color fidelity and shadow detail. (Courtesy Eastman Kodak Company)

Curved, aluminized screens make it possible to show an adequately bright picture under conditions in which the image projected onto any other type of reflective screen would be almost completely washed out by extraneous light. These screens are rigidly mounted however, somewhat expensive, and available only in relatively small sizes. Despite these limitations, curved aluminized screens are useful for permanent installation in small, brightly lighted rooms.

Rear projection may be an excellent solution when films, filmstrips, and slides must be shown under high ambient light conditions as in exhibits and displays and in some classrooms. Because the projector must be *behind* the translucent screen, however, enough space must be available there, and the projected image must be reversed with a mirror. Dark-surfaced rear-projection screens reflect very little ambient light, so images on these screens will appear brilliant if stray light is kept from the back side of the screen. The same seating and viewing angle rules apply alike to rear projection and conventional projection, except that as long as the projected material is legible, audiences tend psychologically to accept a smaller image from a rear projection screen as readily as they would accept an image of the same size from a TV set. If image details are large enough, the 6W (six picture widths) rule for the farthest row of seats may be stretched, as it often is for television viewing, up to 12W.

Keystone Effect

Roll-down screens are convenient, but if an overhead projector is to be used the screen should be mounted away from the wall so that it can be tilted to eliminate the annoying keystone effect that occurs when the projector is lower than the center of the screen (*see* Figures

Figure 9–24. A small rear-projection screen is ideal for "walk-by" displays and for self-instruction in lab or shop areas. For display use, some automatic slide projectors can be set to the desired time cycle and will continuously repeat a tray full of slides unattended. Rear-projection screens will tolerate a high level of room light so long as none of this light is allowed to fall on the back side of the screen. (Courtesy Hudson Photographic Industries, Inc.)

9–9 and 9–10). A popular practice is to install two screens—a conventional wall screen for motion pictures and slides and a tilted, matte screen set up high in a corner, usually at stage right, for use with the overhead projector. There is a tendency to place the screen too low; this is a problem especially with portable tripod screens. A keystone eliminator bar is a handy accessory for this type of screen. The device allows the top of the screen to be tilted forward when used with the overhead and with other projectors when placed near the front of the room. Vertically oriented or square-format slides and transparencies require a square screen and a rather high ceiling if everyone is to see the bottom of the picture. Test out screen visibility by sitting down in the back row of seats, and imagine that the tallest person in the class is seated directly in front of you.

PROJECTOR STANDS

There are many different kinds of projector stands. Some are collapsible for carrying; some have large wheels for rolling up and down stairs; most kinds offer a choice of heights. The top of a seated adult's head is roughly 52 inches from the floor, so to project from the rear of the classroom you need a tall stand. The common 42-inch high rolling cart is satisfactory, however, if viewers are small children or if the projector beam is aimed between, rather than above the heads of the audience. For overhead projection with the teacher seated, stands 16 to 24 inches high are recommended, and for situations in which the projector is placed in the center aisle, as for opaque projectors, stands or carts 26 to 34 inches high are useful.

Unfortunately, many fixed-seat auditoriums have been built with no provision for projectors. Long-legged portable stands are a lifesaver in these anachronistic rooms, their legs fitting down between the seats, supporting a level projector platform wherever needed.

PROJECTION LENSES　　To get an image of the right size to neatly fill the screen you may need a projection lens of a focal length different from the lens which normally comes with the projector. If the picture should be larger and you cannot move the projector farther from the screen, use a shorter focal length lens for the same effect. Likewise, for a smaller picture, when it is inconvenient for the projector to be moved closer to the screen, try a longer focal length lens. The exact focal length needed may be determined from calculators distributed by manufacturers, from consulting tables such as Figure 9–26, or simply by experimenting. It pays to have available a variety of extra lenses or an adjustable-focal-length "zoom" lens to fit projectors you use frequently.

When more than one projector is being used during a multi-media presentation, all images should be about the same size (unless special effects are being sought), and projection is easier if all equipment is the same distance from the screen. Both results can be attained by using lenses of appropriate focal lengths. For example, at about 30 feet the pictures projected by a 16mm motion picture projector with a 2-inch lens, a single-frame film-strip projector with a 5-inch lens, and a 35mm slide projector with a 7-inch lens will all fit a standard 70 by 70-inch screen.

Special lenses are available for special purposes. In very large auditoriums where projectors are placed in a booth or on a platform to the rear, above the heads of the audience, extra-long focal length lenses reduce the image size to fit the screen. Short-focal-length or "wide angle" lenses project a relatively large image at very short projector-to-screen distances, such as in enclosed rear-

Figure 9–25. Accessory lenses allow image size to be varied without changing the distance from projector to screen. What is the relationship between lens focal length *and* projector-to-screen distance? *(See tables in Figure 9–26.) What is a* zoom *lens? (Courtesy Eastman Kodak Company)*

SUPER 8 MOTION PICTURES AND FILM LOOPS
SCREEN WIDTH

Lens Focal Length	30"	40"	50"	60"	70"	84"	8'	9'	10'	12'	14'	16'	18'
¾"	8'	11'	14'	17'	20'	23'	27'	31'	34'	41'	48'	54'	60'
1"	11'	15'	18'	22'	26'	31'	36'	40'	45'	54'	63'	72'	81'
1½"	17'	22'	28'	34'	41'	47'	54'	60'	68'	84'	95'		

2 × 2-inch DOUBLE FRAME 35MM SLIDES
SQUARE SCREEN SIZE

(ZOOM / STANDARD LENS)

Lens Focal Length	30"	40"	50"	60"	70"	84"	8'	9'	10'	12'	14'	16'	18'
3"	5'	7'	9'	11'	13'	16'	18'	20'	22'	27'	31'	36'	40'
4"	7'	10'	12'	15'	17'	21'	24'	27'	30'	36'	42'	48'	54'
5"	9'	12'	16'	19'	22'	26'	30'	34'	37'	45'	52'	60'	67'
6"	11'	14'	17'	22'	26'	30'	35'	39'	44'	53'	60'	69'	78'
7"	12'	17'	22'	26'	31'	37'	42'	47'	52'	63'	73'	84'	94'
9"	16'	22'	26'	32'	39'	45'	51'	58'	65'	78'	85'	103'	115'

35MM FILMSTRIPS
SCREEN WIDTH

(STANDARD LENS)

Lens Focal Length	40"	50"	60"	70"	84"	8'	9'	10'	12'	14'	16'	18'
1½"	6'	7'	8'	10'	12'	14'	15'	18'	20'	23'	27'	30'
2"	7'	9'	11'	13'	16'	18'	20'	22'	27'	31'	35'	40'
3"	11'	14'	17'	19'	23'	27'	30'	33'	40'	47'	53'	60'
4"	15'	19'	22'	26'	31'	36'	40'	44'	53'	62'	71'	80'
5"	19'	23'	28'	32'	39'	44'	50'	56'	67'	73'	89'	100'
7"	27'	32'	39'	46'	53'	62'	70'	80'	92'	109'	125'	140'

16MM MOTION PICTURES
SCREEN WIDTH

(ZOOM / STANDARD LENS)

Lens Focal Length	30"	40"	50"	60"	70"	84"	8'	9'	10'	12'	14'	16'	18'
1"	7'	9'	11'	13'	15'	18'	21'	24'	26'	32'	37'	42'	47'
1½"	10'	13'	17'	20'	23'	28'	32'	36'	40'	48'	56'	64'	72'
2"	13'	18'	22'	26'	31'	37'	42'	47'	53'	63'	74'	84'	95'
2½"	16'	22'	27'	33'	38'	46'	53'	59'	66'	79'	92'	105'	119'
3"	20'	26'	33'	40'	46'	55'	63'	71'	79'	95'	110'	126'	142'
3½"	23'	31'	38'	46'	54'	64'	74'	83'	92'	110'	128'	147'	165'
4"	26'	35'	44'	53'	61'	73'	84'	95'	105'	122'	147'	169'	190'

10 × 10-inch OVERHEAD TRANSPARENCIES

14" Focal Length Lens	60"	70"	84"	8'	9'	10'	12'	14'	16'	18'
Square Screen Size	60"	70"	84"	8'	9'	10'	12'	14'	16'	18'
Distance Lens To Screen	7'	8'	10'	11'	12'	14'	17'	20'	22'	25'

projection systems where mirrors often are used to condense the length of the projector beam.

POINTERS

An electric pointer is valuable when details must be pointed out on the screen during a showing. Most pointers are battery operated and have a lens that focuses a bright image of the lamp filament on the screen. The best ones have a special bulb in which the glowing filament is shaped like an arrow.

Multi-Media and Multi-Image Presentations

There might be several reasons for using more than one medium in a single presentation. Various media probably appeal in different ways through different senses; sometimes an impressive performance is desired for publicity purposes or to kick off a new team-taught unit; or perhaps certain borrowed materials must be used only in the various forms in which they are available. Whatever the reasons for their use, multi-media presentations should be carefully planned to fit in with definite objectives and arranged and rehearsed so that the mechanical aspects of projection do not detract from the total effect by calling attention to the equipment.

Simple devices are available which connect a tape recorder and an automatic slide projector to provide synchronized slide changes along with narration, questions, or musical background. More sophisticated electronic control units operate two or more automatic slide projectors, a stereo tape recorder, and perhaps a motion picture projector or other equipment for impressive, fully synchronized, smoothly dissolving presentations.

Sometimes all of this equipment is placed on a single stand or movable cart for conventional projection, but now some classrooms and auditoriums are being con-

[OPPOSITE] *Figure 9–26. These screen-size tables are included to provide opportunity to study the relationship of lens focal length to image size. Distance figures are rounded off to the nearest foot; image size is approximated in these tables by the size of screen recommended.*

Figure 9–27. For special purpose multi-media presentations, miniaturized digital programmers enable motion picture, filmstrip, and slide projectors to operate together, separately, or in any combination, with synchronized sound from a tape recorder. Depending on the type of programmer used, projector-operating pulses are recorded either magnetically or on perforated paper tape. (Courtesy Arion Corporation)

Operating Audiovisual Equipment

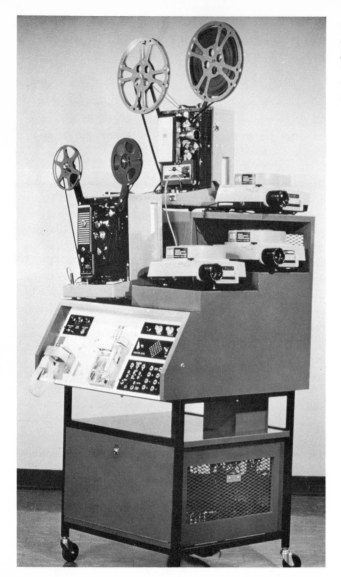

Figure 9-28. Punched paper tape programs this five-projector multi-media projection center. For what purposes could such an installation be justified in a school? Who would prepare programs (software) for its use? (Courtesy Eastman Kodak Company)

structed either with a permanent multi-media projection booth at the rear so machinery can be placed out of sight and hearing, or with a large, translucent rear-projection surface at the front of the room, allowing space for projectors and equipment in an adjoining area behind the screen. Controls for projectors, sound, and room lights in these semi-automated classrooms often are centralized for convenience in a console built into the instructor's lectern.

Although some research has questioned the value of multi-media and multi-image projection for the reason that viewers have been found to perceive only a single channel of information at one time, there appear to be some very valid uses for these techniques. Of course, each teacher must weigh the potential instructional benefits against the time, cost, and complications of arranging such presentations. Some of the following possibilities may suggest applications to help decide whether a multimedia/multi-image presentation is justified.

1. To hold an overview or "long shot" on one screen while showing a series of detailed close-ups on another screen, such as stages of a laboratory procedure or a building-orientation tour.

2. To allow side-by-side comparison of two or more images, such as works of art, "before and after" views of an experimental subject, or schematic drawings compared with the actual object.

3. For "visual outlining" or "visual paragraphing"— holding a title or classification heading on one screen while adding subheadings or a series of examples elsewhere.

4. To supply data or ask questions about a picture while it is being held on one screen, such as in a testing situation.

5. To provide a "sensory saturation" effect, such as simultaneously projecting several related or contrasting still or motion picture views on subjects such as "pollution," "overpopulation," or "traffic congestion." For such purposes, the *total impression* is far more important than information perceived from any single image. In such presentations, which may be extremely fast moving, *the medium*, as McLuhan has said, *is the message!*

All the processes, rules, and hints offered in this chapter regarding equipment operation and good showmanship will apply in varying degree to every presentation you make, ranging from a single overhead transparency to an entire battery of mixed media. Practice and rehearse until you are confident of your ability to

Figure 9–29. What is the advantage of being able to project two different images side-by-side at the front of the classroom? Rear projection is being used here—the projectors are behind the two translucent screens, out of sight and hearing of the students, the instructor changing slides by pressing buttons on his lectern. Notice that room lights are on, yet the images are bright on the screen. Is this a characteristic of rear projection? (Courtesy School of Architecture, Rensselaer Polytechnic Institute)

"bring it off." But one final word of warning: never lose sight of the *purpose* (objectives) of any media presentation, no matter how glamorous the media may seem and how much fun it may be to prepare the materials and push the buttons.

Teachers must be ready to make use of innovative developments as they evolve, and they must be ready to make highly creative professional decisions about media. Such decisions need to involve every available educational and motivational resource, because it is in school that this and succeeding generations will begin the process of identifying and solving the problems that they are certain to face tomorrow. Audiovisual technology is certain to play many vital roles in the future of education.

Problems and Activities

1. Inventory all the types of audiovisual equipment available for your use. Make up your own checklist or use a form provided by your instructor.

2. Operate proficiently at least one make or brand of each type of AV equipment available. Work through self-instructional laboratory programs, if available, or obtain the equipment and follow the generalized instructions in Chapter 9.

3. Demonstrate your skill by operating AV equipment in actual class situations or in videotaped micro-teaching sessions. Reinforce your skill by teaching someone else to operate the equipment.

4. List the audiovisual equipment that you would like to have permanently assigned to your own classroom, laboratory, or media center. Write this up in the form of a request to your principal or department chairman, giving justification for each item. Provide specifications, brand names, and prices if possible.

5. Plan an audiovisual-tutorial laboratory. Design carrels or learning spaces; provide storage and working areas and a conference area. Allow for efficient movement of students and effective supervision by the teacher, aide, or media specialist in charge.

6. Draw a plan or make a model of your present classroom (or an "ideal" classroom). Include seating arrangements, if possible, for both presentational and participative modes of instruction. Indicate windows and light control facilities, electrical outlets, lights, and switches, chalkboard and display areas, storage, placement of screens and projectors and other hardware. Determine screen size and lens focal lengths needed.

7. Demonstrate or explain what you would do if a motion

picture film broke just before or during a showing. Show how to repair film properly if a tape- or cement-type splicer is available.

8. Given several 2 × 2-inch slides in various kinds of mounts, insert each of them into a slide tray or manual projector so they will all be projected right side up and right way around on the screen. State a rule for correctly inserting slides and filmstrips into the projector.

9. Demonstrate or describe two ways to eliminate "keystoning" of the image of an overhead transparency on the screen.

10. Prepare and present a multi-media, multi-image show to a class or a community group. Specify audience and objectives (it might be simply information, entertainment, or esthetic satisfaction, or you might be concerned with formation of opinions or change of attitudes.)

Selected References

Audio-Visual Equipment Directory. National Audio-Visual Association, Inc., 3150 Spring St., Fairfax, Va. 22030, revised annually. This directory is a master reference to nearly all types and makes of AV equipment and accessories. The appendices include many useful charts and tables.

Audiovisual Equipment Operation Series (27 titles, super 8 film loops, 3–4 min. each) McGraw-Hill Films, 1221 Avenue of the Americas, New York, N.Y. 10020, 1965–69. Each short film demonstrates operation of a type of projector. Additional titles deal with splicing and projection practices.

Audiovisual Literature Packet, Code No. U-915. Dept. 454, Eastman Kodak Co., Rochester, N.Y. 14650. A convenient "instant library" containing about 30 Kodak publications on materials, equipment, techniques for filmstrip, slide, and motion picture planning, production and presentation.

Audiovisual Projection, Kodak Pamphlet No. S-3. Motion Picture and Education Markets Division, Eastman Kodak Co., Rochester, N.Y. 14650, 1969, 20 pp. A compact reference for planning room facilities, seating plans, screen, speaker, and projector location, picture size, projector lamp and lens requirements, and other technical details which must be considered in putting on excellent audiovisual presentations.

Audio-Visual Trade Directory. National Audio-Visual Association, Inc., 3150 Spring St., Fairfax, Va. 22030, revised annually. Listing dealers and manufacturers in the U.S. and Canada who are members of NAVA, this booklet indicates by a code the exact types of sales, service, film distribution, and equipment rental available from each dealer, with addresses and telephone numbers for quick reference.

BROWN, JAMES W., and RICHARD B. LEWIS. (eds.) *A-V Instructional Materials Manual: A Self-Instructional Guide to A-V Laboratory Experience,* 3rd ed. McGraw-Hill Book Co., 1221 Avenue of the Americas, New York, N.Y. 10020, 1969, 256 pp. Intended to supplement the Brown, Lewis, and Harcleroad textbook, this manual provides a series of exercises through which individuals may teach themselves many of the basic skills of AV production and utilization.

DAVIDSON, RAYMOND L. *Audiovisual Machines.* International Textbook Co., Scranton, Penna. 18515, 1969. Describes how to operate audiovisual equipment. Emphasizes how to determine when equipment is working properly and how to make minor adjustments and repairs.

EBOCH, SIDNEY C. *Operating Audio-Visual Equipment.* Science Research Associates, Inc., 259 East Erie St., Chicago, Ill. 60611, 1968, 76 pp. Step-by-step checklists and diagrams for operating basic types of AV equipment.

Facts About Film (16 mm film, 13 min) International Film Bureau Inc., 332 South Michigan Ave., Chicago, Ill. 60604, 1963. Basic information about the physical nature of film stock, types of film, preventive care and maintenance and repair of motion picture films, and causes of film damage.

Facts About Projection, 2nd ed. (16 mm film, 13 min) International Film Bureau, Inc., 332 South Michigan Ave., Chicago, Ill. 60604, 1963. States that constant maintenance of projection equipment is necessary. Demonstrates methods for improving projection technique, including methods for smoothly beginning and ending the showing.

ISAACS, DAN LEE, and ROBERT GLEN GEORGE. *Instructional Media: Selection and Utilization.* Kendall/Hunt Publishing Co., 131 South Locust St., Dubuque, Iowa 52001, 1971, 97 pp. Concise guide to media, with emphasis on audiovisual equipment. Includes self-test questions.

OATES, STANTON C. *Audio Visual Equipment Self-Instruction Manual.* William C. Brown Book Co., 135 Locust St., Dubuque, Iowa 52001, 1966, 155 pp. Step-by-step checklists and diagrams for operating basic types of AV equipment.

PULA, FRED J. *Application and Operation of Audiovisual Equipment in Education.* John Wiley & Sons, Inc., 605 Third Ave., New York, N.Y. 10016, 1968, 360 pp. Comprehensive overview of characteristics, principles, and techniques for operating audiovisual equipment.

Self-Instructional Audiovisual Equipment Operation Series (20 titles, 2 × 2-inch captioned slide sets) Training Services, 8885 West F Ave., Kalamazoo, Mich. 49009, 1965–72. Step-by-step instructions for operating equipment including various types and models of projectors and tape recorders.

Wide Screen/Multiple-Screen Presentations, Kodak Pamphlet No. S–28. Motion Picture and Education Markets Division, Eastman Kodak Co., Rochester, N.Y. 14650, 1969, 16 pp. Discusses applications and various formats for widescreen and multiple-screen presentations and shows how to produce visuals and employ one or more slide projectors to achieve dramatic special effects.

WYMAN, RAYMOND. *Mediaware: Selection, Operation and Maintenance.* William C. Brown Co., 135 South Locust St., Dubuque, Iowa 52001, 1969, 188 pp. Includes techniques of operating AV equipment, plus background information on how it works, characteristics for selecting equipment, and procedures for maintenance.

INDEX

Big Dipper, 262
Biosphere, 259
Blake, William, 266
Bock, Barbara, 95
Books and printed matter, 81–85
Boring and Drilling Tools (film case study in media utilization), 171–78
  action principle, 174
  analysis of, 174–78
  class description, 171
  control principle, 173–74
  evaluation principle, 174
  film title, 173
  main problem, 172
  readiness principle, 173
  selection principle, 171–72
Branching, 154
Break in a film, 356
Brueckner, Leo J., 163
"Bucket" theory, 6–7
Bulletin boards and exhibits, 100–102
Bumstead, Richard, 57
Burton, William H., 48, 163

C

Cable release, 302
Cameras, producing audiovisual media and, 281–87
  action pictures, 285
  composition, 285–86
  fill-in flash, 283
  handling of cameras, 285
  hints for better picture taking, 286–87
  indoor flash, 285
  outdoor lighting, 282–83
Cameras, television, 288
Capstan (tape recorder), 344
Captions, 297–98
Carbon ribbon, 298
Cartoons, 97
Case studies in media utilization, 171–239
  Anaheim television use, 230–35
  Boring and Drilling Tools (film), 171–78
  Dade County television use, 235–39
  Mathematician and the River (film),
  Panama Canal (film), 178–83
  Panama Canal (film), 190–94
  Pioneer of the Plains (film), 194–98
  "Simple Machines" (teaching unit), 222–29
  Structure of Green Plants (taped), 212–21
  Uncle Sam Enters Manhood (teaching unit), 198–212
Cassette tape recorders, 288, 314, 318
  operating, 344–46

Cell, 259
Centering on copy stand, 302
Chalkboards and chartpads, 103–106
  as "aids," 251
Characteristics of learners, 165–66
Characteristics of teaching purposes, 50–58
  examples of, 52–58
Chartpads and chalkboards, 103–106
  as "aids," 251
Charts, 97–100, 251
Checklists for film projectionists, 357–58
Chidsey, Jay, 127–29
Choice, 60
Choosing an appropriate film, 124
Close-up photography, 281–82, 290
Cognitive objectives, 48–58
  characteristics of teaching purposes and, 50–52
  three examples of, 53–58
Comenius, John, 82
Communication, systematic, 70–73
Communication, teaching as, 7–12
Competence and confidence, developing, with audiovisual equipment, 334–35
Composition of pictures, 285–86
Compressing time, 292
Computer-based instruction, 154–58
Computers, 3, 154–58
Concepts, communication of, 8–9
  film and, 41–42
Confidence and competence, developing, with audiovisual equipment, 334–35
Confirmation, 37–38, 40
Consequence, learning process and, 37–38
  film and, 40
Constellations, 262
Construction, system-development and, 74–76
Contradiction, 37–38, 40
Control principle of media utilization, 169
  in film studies cases, 173–74, 181, 187, 192
Copernican theory of solar system, 4–5
Copy stand, shooting on, 300–303
Copying with single-lens reflex camera (35mm), 299–303
Copyrights, 299
Counselors, 68
Crab Nebula, 262
Criteria of selection principle of media utilization, 166–67
Criterion performance, 59, 61
Cronbach, Lee J., 36–38, 41
Cropping, 302
Cueing, synchronization and, 321

Motion pictures [*cont.*]
　relationship to seven aspects of
　　learning of, 38–42
　specific teaching practices with,
　　124–27
Motivation, film and, 125
Mt. Palomar Observatory, 262, 265
"Movie light," 292
Multi-media and multi-image
　　presentations, 365–68
Multi-sensory materials, 12
Mylar tape, 317

N

Narration, recording, 312–13
Neptune, 262
New educational media, 12
News broadcasts, television, 124
Newton, Sir Isaac, 260, 267
Non-adaptive behavior, 38
Non-graded schools, 10
Nonprojected visual media, 81–115
　books and printed materials, 81–85
　bulletin boards and exhibits,
　　100–102
　chalkboards and chartpads, 103–106
　field trips, 87–89
　flannelboards, 106–107
　graphic symbols, 97–100
　models and mock-ups, 89–93
　real things, 86–87
　simulation and games, 93–96
　study prints, 107–112
Note-taking, films and, 125

O

Objectives, instructional, 47–62, 67
　behavioral, 59–62
　cognitive, 59–62
Ohio River Flatboat (study print),
　　110–12
Omni-directional microphones, 311
Opaque projection, 145–46
　operation of, 343–44
Open classrooms, media in, 270–77
Operating audiovisual equipment,
　　331–70
　developing competence and
　　confidence, 334–35
　filmstrip and slide projection,
　　335–40
　hints for good showmanship, 358–65
　motion picture projection, 346–58
　multi-media and multi-image
　　presentations, 365–68
　overhead projection, 340–44
　tape recorder, 344–46
　teacher responsibilities, 331–33
Organisms, 259

Orion, 262
Outdoor lighting, 282–83
Output jacks (tape recorder), 346
Overlapping the action, 290
Overhead transparencies, 143–44,
　　303–311
　as "aids," 251
　operating, 340–44
　picture lifts, 310–11
　spirit duplicator process of, 307–310
　thermocopy process of, 303–307
Overlays, 310
Overview, 367

P

Packing a film projector, 356–57
Pan, 292
Panama Canal (film case study in
　　media utilization), 178–83
　action principle, 181
　analysis of, 182–83
　class description, 178
　control principle, 181
　film title, 180
　main problem, 179
　readiness principle, 180–81
　selection principle, 178–79
Panama Canal (film case study in
　　media utilization), 190–94
　action principle, 192–93
　analysis of, 193–94
　class description, 191
　control principle, 192
　evaluation principle, 193
　film title, 191
　main problem, 191
　readiness principle, 191–92
　selection principle, 191
Panning, 285, 292
Parallax, 286
Particles and waves, 259
Patch cords, 314, 315
Pause control, 314
Personal characteristics, learning process
　　and, 37
　film and, 39
Pestalozzi, Johann, 82
Photography, producing audiovisual
　　media and, 281–87
　action pictures, 285
　cameras, 281–82
　composition, 285–86
　fill-in flash, 283
　handling cameras, 285
　hints for better pictures, 286–87
　indoor flash, 285
　outdoor lighting, 282–83
Physical climate of the classroom,
　　television and, 137
Physical limitations, overcoming, 27–29

Readiness principle of media utilization
[*cont.*]
in film case studies, 173, 180–81,
186–87, 191–92, 194–97
in taped case studies, 214–15
in teaching-unit case studies,
214–15
Reading pacers, 143
Realia, 19, 86–87
Rear screen projection, 347, 361
Record key (tape recorder), 345
Recording, sound, synchronization and,
311–24
editing tape, 313–19
microphone technique, 311–13
preplanning, 323–24
for Super 8 cameras, 287–88
synchronized sound, 320–23
Recording speed, 318
Recording with a tape recorder,
344–45
Reel tape, 318
Reel-to-reel, 313–14
Regional Enrichment Center, 40
Registration, 298
Reinforcement principle in film, 121
Relevance principle of film, 122
Relevancy, 6–7
Remedial tools, providing, 33–35
Repeating a film, 126
Re-recording and mixing, 314–17
Resources, 67
Response, guiding student, 24–26
Responsibilities of a teacher in
operating audiovisual equipment,
331–33
Reverberation, 311
Reviewing a film, 126
Rewind control (tape recorder), 345
Rewinding a film, 356–57
Roles played by audiovisual technology,
15–35
extending human experience, 16–19
guiding student response, 24–26
overcoming physical limitations,
27–29
providing diagnostic and remedial
tools, 33–35
providing meaningful information,
19–22
stimulating interest, 22–23
stimulating problem solving, 30–32

S

Sagittarius, 262
Sarnoff, Robert W., 154
Saturn, 262
Science Center (University Lake
School), 270–74

Screen direction, 292
Screens, projection, 359–62
Scripts, shooting, 288–90
Seating area, media use and, 358–59
Selection principle of media utilization,
163–68
characteristics of learners and,
165–66
criteria of, 166–67
in film case studies, 171–72,
178–79, 183–84, 191
sources of media, 167–68
in taped case studies, 212–13
in teaching-unit case studies,
199–201
Self-instruction
audiovisual laboratories, 334–35
audiovisual tutorial instruction and,
246–53
Sensory saturation, 367
Setting up a motion picture projector,
347–50
Severe lighting problems, media use
and, 360–61
Sex and Family Living (instructional
kit), 77
Shooting on a copy stand, 300–303
Shooting script, 288–90
Shorthand, audiovisual tutorial
instruction and, 249
Showing a film, 354–56
Showmanship, hints for good,
358–65
keystone effect, 361–62
pointer, 365
projection lens, 363–65
projector stands, 362–63
screens, 359–60
seating area, 358
severe lighting problems, 360–61
Shutter speeds, 281, 285
copying and, 302
Sidelighting, 282
"Simple Machines" (teaching-unit team
teaching case study in media
utilization), 222–29
analysis of, 228–29
equipment materials and student
grouping in, 222–24
technological system in operation,
224–28
Simulation and games, 93–96
computers and, 156–58
Single-lens reflex cameras (35mm),
281–82
copying with, 299–303
Situation, learning process and, 36–37
film and, 39
Sixteen millimeter camera (16mm),
287
Sixteen millimeter film (16mm), 124